BAKING

BAKING

BREADS MUFFINS CAKES PIES TARTS COOKIES AND BARS

Over 400 step-by-step recipes with over 1,500 photographs

M A R T H A   D A Y

HERMES HOUSE

This edition is published by Hermes House, an imprint of Anness Publishing Ltd,
Hermes House, 88–89 Blackfriars Road, London SE1 8HA; tel. 020 7401 2077; fax 020 7633 9499

www.hermeshouse.com; www.annesspublishing.com

If you like the images in this book and would like to investigate using them for publishing, promotions or advertising,
please visit our website www.practicalpictures.com for more information.

A CIP catalogue record for this book is available from the British Library

Publisher: Joanna Lorenz
Project Editor: Felicity Forster
Text: Carole Clements
Designer: Sheila Volpe
Photography, Styling: Amanda Heywood
Food Styling: Elizabeth Wolf-Cohen, Carla Capalbo,
steps by Cara Hobday, Teresa Goldfinch, Nicola Fowler
Additional Recipes: Carla Capalbo and Laura Washburn,
Frances Cleary, Norma MacMillan
Illustrations: Anna Koska
Index: Dawn Butcher
Editorial Reader: Marion Wilson
Production Controller: Ben Worley

ETHICAL TRADING POLICY

Because of our ongoing ecological investment programme, you, as our customer, can have the pleasure and reassurance
of knowing that a tree is being cultivated on your behalf to naturally replace the materials used to make the book you are
holding. For further information about this scheme, go to www.annesspublishing.com/trees

PUBLISHER'S NOTE

Although the advice and information in this book are believed to be accurate and true at the time of going to press,
neither the authors nor the publisher can accept any legal responsibility or liability for any errors or omissions that may be
made nor for any inaccuracies nor for any harm or injury that comes about from following instructions or advice in this book.

Previously published as: *Complete Baking*

NOTES
Bracketed terms are intended for American readers.
For all recipes, quantities are given in both metric and imperial measures and, where appropriate, in
standard cups and spoons. Follow one set, but not a mixture, because they are not interchangeable.
Standard spoon and cup measures are level. 1 tsp = 5ml, 1 tbsp = 15ml, 1 cup = 250ml/8fl oz.
Australian standard tablespoons are 20ml. Australian readers should use 3 tsp in place of 1 tbsp for
measuring small quantities of gelatine, flour, salt, etc.
American pints are 16fl oz/2 cups. American readers should use 20fl oz/2.5 cups in place of
1 pint when measuring liquids.
Medium (US large) eggs are used unless otherwise stated.

CONTENTS

INTRODUCTION

Nothing equals the satisfaction of home baking. No commercial cake mix or shop-bought biscuit can match one that is made from the best fresh ingredients with all the added enjoyment that baking at home provides – the enticing aromas that fill the house and stimulate appetites, the delicious straight-from-the-oven flavour, as well as the pride of having created such wonderful goodies yourself.

This book is filled with familiar favourites as well as many other lesser known recipes. Explore the wealth of biscuits, buns, tea breads, yeast breads, pies, tarts, and cakes within these pages. Even if you are a novice baker, the easy-to-follow and clear step-by-step photographs will help you achieve good results. For the more experienced home baker, this book will provide some new recipes to add to your repertoire.

Baking is an exact science and needs to be approached in an ordered way. First read through the recipe from beginning to end. Set out all the required ingredients before you begin. Medium eggs are assumed unless specified otherwise, and they should be at room temperature for best results. Sift the flour after you have measured it, and incorporate other dry ingredients as specified in the individual recipes. If you sift the flour from a fair height, it will have more chance to aerate and lighten.

When a recipe calls for folding one ingredient into another, it should be done in a way that incorporates as much air as possible into the mixture. Use either a large metal spoon or a long rubber or plastic scraper. Gently plunge the spoon or scraper deep into the centre of the mixture and, scooping up a large amount of the mixture, fold it over. Turn the bowl slightly so each scoop folds over another part of the mixture.

No two ovens are alike. Buy a reliable oven thermometer and test the temperature of your oven. When possible bake in the centre of the oven where the heat is more likely to be constant. If using a fan-assisted oven, follow the manufacturer's guidelines for baking. Good quality baking tins can improve your results, as they conduct heat more efficiently.

Practice, patience and enthusiasm are the keys to confident and successful baking. The recipes that follow will inspire you to start sifting flour, breaking eggs and stirring up all sorts of delectable homemade treats – all guaranteed to bring great satisfaction to both the baker and those lucky enough to enjoy the results.

INGREDIENTS, EQUIPMENT & TECHNIQUES

KEEPING YOUR KITCHEN STOCKED
WITH THE RIGHT INGREDIENTS
AND EQUIPMENT, AS WELL AS
MASTERING THESE BASIC
TECHNIQUES, WILL ENSURE
BAKING SUCCESS EVERY TIME.

BAKING INGREDIENTS

This guide highlights a few of the most essential items that every baker should keep in their store cupboard and fridge.

BUTTER AND MARGARINE

Butter gives the best flavour for baking and should be used whenever possible, especially when there is a high fat content, as in shortbread.

Butter needs to be at room temperature before being used. It is usually either melted or diced before being worked into the other ingredients to make a batter. This is then beaten by hand or in an electric mixer. For some bread recipes, the butter is kneaded into the dough after the initial rising, since larger quantities of butter can inhibit the action of the yeast.

For a low-fat alternative to butter, try polyunsaturated margarine instead. Low-fat spreads are ideal for spreading on breads and tea breads, but are unfortunately not suitable for baking because they have a high water content.

EGGS

Eggs are a staple ingredient in most baking recipes. They should be stored and used at room temperature, so if you keep them in the fridge, remove the number you want at least 30 minutes before making a recipe.

Above: Properly fed hens lay the best and tastiest eggs.

Above: There are many different types of flour, each with different properties, so make sure you select the one that is best for your recipe.

FLOURS

Mass-produced, highly refined flours are fine for most baking purposes, but for the very best results choose organic stone-ground flours because they will add flavour as well as texture to your baking.

Strong flour

Made from hard wheat which contains a high proportion of gluten, this flour is the one to use for bread-making.

Soft flour

This flour, sometimes called sponge flour, contains less gluten than plain flour and is ideal for light cakes and biscuits.

Wholemeal flour

Because this flour contains the complete wheat kernel, it gives a coarser texture and a good wholesome flavour to bread.

Rye flour

This dark-coloured flour has a low gluten content and gives a dense loaf with a good flavour. It is best mixed with strong wheat flour to give a lighter loaf.

SWEETENERS

Sugars

Most baking recipes call for sugar. Granulated sugar is the best sweetener to use for the creaming method because the crystals dissolve easily and quickly when creamed with the fat. Granulated sugar can also be used for rubbed-in mixtures and when the sugar is heated with the fat or liquid until it dissolves.

Demerara sugar can be used when the sugar is dissolved over heat before being added to the dry ingredients. Soft light and dark brown sugars are used when a richer flavour and colour are called for.

Raw sugar is unrefined sugar which is uncoloured and pure – it also has more flavour than refined sugars, and contains some minerals.

Fruit juice

Concentrated fruit juices are very useful for baking. They have no added sweeteners or preservatives and can be diluted as required. Use them in their concentrated form for baking or for sweetening fillings.

Pear and apple spread

This is a very concentrated fruit juice spread with no added sugar. It has a

Above: Fruits add natural sweetness to baked goods.

sweet-sour taste and can be used as a spread or blended with fruit juice and added to baking recipes as a sweetener.

Dried fruits
These are a traditional addition to cakes and tea breads and there is a very wide range available, including more unusual varieties such as peach, pineapple, banana, mango and pawpaw. The natural sugars add sweetness to baked goods and keep them moist, making it possible to use less fat.

Chop and add dried fruits to breads by hand rather than putting them in an electric mixer or food processor, as the blades will blend the fruit and spoil the appearance and flavour of the loaf.

Honey
Good honey has a strong flavour so you can use less of it than the equivalent amount of sugar. It also contains traces of minerals and vitamins.

Malt extract
This is a sugary by-product of barley. It has a strong flavour and is good to use in bread, cakes and tea breads as it adds a moistness of its own.

Molasses
This is the residue left after the first stage of refining sugar cane. It has a strong, smoky and slightly bitter taste which gives a good flavour to cakes and bakes. Black treacle can often be used as a substitute for molasses.

MILK
Tea breads, sweet breads and cakes are often made with milk, whereas savoury loaves tend to be made using water. Breads made with milk are softer both in the crumb and the crust than those using water.

There are many low-fat alternatives to milk: skimmed milk and semi-skimmed milk have a much lower fat content than milk, and they don't taste as rich as whole milk.

HERBS AND SPICES
Chopped fresh herbs add a great deal of interest to baking. They add flavour to breads, scones and soda breads. In the absence of fresh herbs, dried herbs can be used; less is needed but the flavour is generally not as good.

Spices can add either strong or subtle flavours depending on the amount and variety used. The most commonly used sweet spices for baking are cinnamon, nutmeg, cloves and ginger, and the savoury spices are cumin, fennel, caraway and anise. Mace, pepper and coriander seeds can be used for both sweet and savoury bakes. Spices can be added with the flour or kneaded in with other ingredients.

SALT
Many baking recipes add salt at the beginning, stirring or sifting it into the flour. Salt is one of the few essential ingredients in bread-making, both for flavour and for the effect it has on the yeast and dough.

Above: Check that your store-cupboard supplies are kept fresh and plentiful, and stock up on the ingredients you use most often.

Baking Equipment

Baking sheet
Choose a large, heavy baking sheet that will not warp at high temperatures.

Cake boards
Silver cake boards are perfect for presenting finished cakes. They come in a variety of shapes and sizes, in circles, squares and rectangles.

Cake tester
A simple implement that, when inserted into a cooked cake, will come out clean if the cake is ready.

Cook's knife
This has a heavy, wide blade and is ideal for chopping.

Deep round cake tin
A deep tin is useful for baking fruit cakes.

Electric whisk
Perfect for whisking egg whites and incorporating air into light mixtures.

Honey twirl
For spooning honey without making a mess!

Icing smoother
This will give a wonderfully uniform finish to fondant-covered cakes.

Juicer
Used for squeezing the juice from citrus fruits.

Loaf tin
Available in various sizes and used for making loaf-shaped breads and tea breads.

Measuring jug
Absolutely essential for measuring any kind of liquid accurately.

Measuring spoons
Standard measuring spoons are essential for measuring small quantities.

Mixing bowls
A set of different-sized mixing bowls is essential in any kitchen for whisking and mixing.

Non-stick baking paper
For lining tins and baking sheets to ensure that cakes, meringues and biscuits do not stick.

Nylon sieve
Suitable for most baking purposes, and particularly for sieving foods that react adversely with metal.

Palette knives
These are used for loosening pies, tarts and breads from baking sheets and for smoothing icing over cakes.

Pastry brush
Useful for brushing excess flour from pastry and brushing glazes over pastries, breads and tarts.

Pastry cutters
A variety of shapes and sizes of cutter is useful when stamping out pastry, biscuit and scone doughs.

Plastic chopping board
Use this as a smooth, flat surface for cutting or rolling ingredients.

Plastic scrapers
These can be used to create all sorts of "combing" patterns in butter icing.

Rectangular cake tin
For making tray cakes and other bakes served cut into slices.

Ring mould
Perfect for making angel cakes and other ring-shaped cakes.

Rolling pin
Use a heavy rolling pin for rolling out dough, marzipan and fondant.

Sable paint brushes
These are expensive, but are well worth the extra cost when painting fine details on to cakes.

Serrated knives
Sharp knives are essential for cutting fruit and vegetables, and those with a serrated edge will allow you to cut cakes without them breaking into pieces.

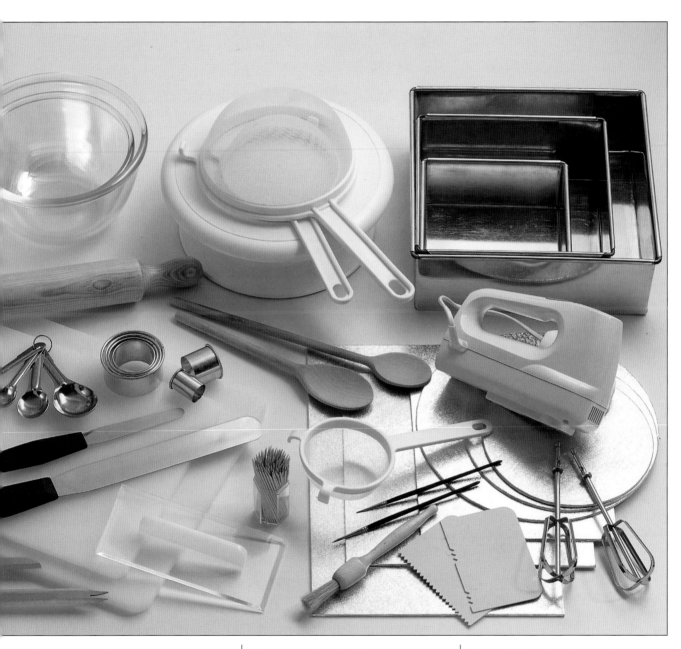

Square cake tin
Used for making square cakes or cakes served cut into smaller squares.

Vegetable knife
A useful knife for preparing fruit and vegetables for your bakes.

Weighing scales
These are essential for accuracy when weighing ingredients for baking.

Wooden cocktail sticks
These can be used to make designs on cakes, or to support pieces of cake to make a particular shape. Always remove them before serving.

Wooden spoons
Essential for mixing ingredients for baking and for creaming mixtures. These are available in a wide variety of sizes.

Above: To be able to bake efficiently and with pleasure, you need good equipment. That is not to say that you should invest in an extensive and expensive collection of tins, tools and gadgets, but a basic range is essential. In addition, buy the best equipment you can afford, adding more as your budget allows. Well-made equipment lasts and is a sound investment; inexpensive tins are likely to dent or break.

BAKING TECHNIQUES

Baking your own muffins and breads is easy and satisfying, even if you're a beginner. Just follow the recipes and the tips, hints, and step-by-step techniques and you'll get perfect results every time.

1 ▲ For liquids measured in jugs: Use a glass or clear plastic measuring jug. Put the jug on a flat surface and pour in the liquid. Bend down and check that the liquid is exactly level with the marking on the jug, as specified in the recipe.

2 ▲ For measuring dry ingredients in a spoon: Fill the spoon with the ingredient. Level the surface even with the rim of the spoon, using the straight edge of a knife.

3 ▲ For liquids measured in spoons: Pour the liquid into the measuring spoon, to the brim, and then pour it into the mixing bowl.

4 ▲ For measuring flour in a cup or spoon: Scoop the flour from the canister in the measuring cup or spoon. Hold it over the canister and level the surface.

5 ▲ For measuring butter: Cut with a sharp knife and weigh, or cut off the specified amount following the markings on the wrapping paper.

6 ▲ For rectangular and square cake tins: Fold the paper and crease it with your fingernail to fit snugly into the corners of the tin. Then press the bottom paper lining into place.

7 ▲ To line muffin tins: Use paper cases of the required size. Or grease and flour the tins.

MAKING SCONES

Scone dough may be rolled out and cut into shapes for baking in the oven or cooking on a griddle. To ensure light, well risen scones, do not handle the dough too much and do not roll it out too thinly.

Drop scones are made from a batter that has the consistency of thick cream. The batter is dropped in spoonfuls on to a hot griddle or frying pan.

1 Sift the dry ingredients into a bowl (flour, baking powder with or without bicarbonate of soda, salt, sugar, ground spices, etc).

2 ▲ Add the fat (butter, margarine, vegetable fat, etc). With a pastry blender or two knives used scissor-fashion, cut the fat into the dry ingredients until the mixture resembles fine crumbs, or rub in the fat with your fingertips.

3 ▲ Add the liquid ingredients (milk, cream, buttermilk, eggs). Stir with a fork until the dry ingredients are thoroughly moistened and will come together in a ball of fairly soft dough in the centre of the bowl.

Date Oven Scones
Sift 8 oz (225 g) self-raising flour with a pinch of salt and rub in 2 oz (55 g) butter. Add 2 oz (55 g) chopped dates. Mix to a soft dough with ¼ pint (150 ml) milk. Roll out and cut 2 in (5 cm) rounds. Glaze with egg or milk. Bake at 450°F/230°C/Gas 8 for 8–10 minutes or until risen and golden brown. *Makes about 12.*

4 ▲ Turn the dough on to a lightly floured surface. Knead it very lightly, folding and pressing, to mix evenly – about 30 seconds. Roll or pat out the dough to ¾ in (2 cm) thickness.

6 ▲ **For griddle scones:** If using a well-seasoned cast iron griddle, there is no need to grease it. Heat it slowly and evenly. Put scone triangles or rounds on the hot griddle and cook for 4–5 minutes on each side or until golden brown and cooked through.

5 ▲ **For oven-baked scones:** With a floured, sharp-edged cutter, cut out rounds or other shapes. Or cut diamond shapes or triangles with a floured knife. Arrange on an ungreased baking sheet, not touching. Brush the tops with beaten egg, milk or cream if the recipe specifies. Bake until risen and golden brown.

Cutting tips
● Be sure the cutter or knife is sharp so that the edges of the scone shapes are not compressed; this would inhibit rising.
● Cut the shapes close together so that you won't have to reroll the dough more than once.
● If necessary, a short, sturdy drinking glass can be pressed into service as a cutter. Flour the rim well and do not press too hard.

MAKING TEABREADS AND MUFFINS

These sorts of bread are very quick and easy to make. The raising agent reacts quickly with moisture and heat to make the breads and muffins rise, without the need for a rising (or proving) period before baking.

The raising agent is usually bicarbonate of soda or baking powder, which is a mixture of bicarbonate of soda and an acid salt such as cream of tartar. Many recipes use self-raising flour which conveniently includes a raising agent. Remember that the raising agent will start to work as soon as it comes into contact with liquid, so don't mix the dry and liquid ingredients until just before you are ready to fill the tin or tins and bake.

1 ▲ For muffins: Combine the dry ingredients in a bowl. It is a good idea to sift the flour with the raising agent, salt and any spices to mix them evenly. Add the liquid ingredients and stir just until the dry ingredients are moistened; the mixture will not be smooth. Do not overmix attempting to remove all the lumps. If you do, the muffins will be tough and will have air holes in them.

2 ▲ Divide the mixture evenly among the greased muffin tins or deep bun tins lined with paper cases, filling them about two-thirds full. Bake until golden brown and a wooden skewer inserted in the centre comes out clean. To prevent soggy bottoms, remove the muffins immediately from the tins to a wire rack. Cool, and serve warm or at room temperature.

Crunchy Muesli Muffins
Make the mixture from 5 oz (145 g) plain flour, 2½ teaspoons baking powder, 2 tablespoons caster sugar, 8 fl oz (240 ml) milk, 2 oz (55 g) melted butter or corn oil, and 1 egg, adding 7 oz (200 g) toasted oat cereal with raisins to the dry ingredients. Pour into muffin tins or deep bun tins. Bake in a 200°C/400°F/Gas 6 oven for 20 minutes or until golden brown. *Makes 10.*

3 ▲ For fruit and/or nut teabreads: Method 1: Stir together all the liquid ingredients. Add the dry ingredients and beat just until smoothly blended. Method 2: Beat the butter with the sugar until the mixture is light and fluffy. Beat in the eggs followed by the other liquid ingredients. Stir in the dry ingredients. Pour the mixture into a prepared tin (typically a loaf tin). Bake until a wooden skewer inserted in the centre comes out clean. If the bread is browning too quickly, cover the top with foil.

4 ▲ Cool in the tin for 5 minutes, then turn out on to a wire rack to cool completely. A lengthways crack on the surface is characteristic of teabreads. For easier slicing, wrap the bread in greaseproof paper and overwrap in foil, then store overnight at room temperature.

MAKING SIMPLE MERINGUE

There are two types of this egg white and sugar foam: a soft meringue used as an insulating topping for pies and baked Alaska and a firm meringue that can be shaped into containers for luscious fillings.

Take care when separating the egg whites and yolks because even the smallest trace of yolk will prevent the whites from being whisked to their maximum volume. All equipment must be scrupulously clean and free of grease.

Meringue Nests
Make a firm meringue using 2 egg whites and 4 oz (115 g) caster sugar. Scoop large spoonfuls of meringue on to a baking sheet lined with baking parchment. Slightly hollow out the centre of each with the back of the spoon, to make a nest shape. Alternatively, put the meringue into a piping bag fitted with a ½ in (1.5 cm) plain nozzle and pipe the nest shapes. Sprinkle lightly with a little extra sugar. Dry in a 200°F/100°C/Gas low oven for 3–4 hours or until crisp and firm but not brown. Leave to cool. To serve, fill with sweetened whipped cream and fresh fruit. *Makes 4–6.*

1 ▲ Put the egg whites in a large, scrupulously clean and grease-free bowl. With a whisk or electric mixer, whisk the whites until they are foamy. If not using a copper bowl, add a pinch of cream of tartar.

3 ▲ For a soft meringue: Sprinkle the sugar over the whites, whisking constantly. Continue whisking for about 1 minute or until the meringue is glossy and holds stiff peaks when you lift the whisk or beaters. The meringue is now ready to be spread on a pie filling or used for baked Alaska.

Sweetened whipped cream
This is used as a topping and filling for many hot and cold desserts. Whip ½ pint (300 ml) chilled whipping or double cream until it starts to thicken. Add 2 tablespoons sifted icing sugar and continue whipping until the cream holds a soft peak on the beaters. If liked, the cream may be flavoured with ½ teaspoon vanilla or almond essence or 2 teaspoons brandy or liqueur, added with the sugar.

2 ▲ Continue whisking until the whites hold soft peaks when you lift the whisk or beaters (the tips of the peaks will flop over).

4 ▲ For a firm meringue: Add a little of the sugar (about 1½ teaspoons for each egg white). Continue whisking until the meringue is glossy and will hold stiff peaks.

5 ▲ Add the remaining sugar to the bowl, with any flavouring the recipe specifies. With a rubber spatula, fold the sugar into the meringue as lightly as possible by cutting down with the spatula to the bottom of the bowl and then turning the mixture over. The meringue is now ready to be shaped into containers or gâteau layers.

Making Shortcrust Pastry

A meltingly short, crumbly pastry sets off any filling to perfection, whether sweet or savoury. The pastry dough can be made with half butter or margarine and half white vegetable fat or with all one kind of fat.

For a 9 in (23 cm) pastry case

8 oz (225 g) plain flour
¼ teaspoon salt
4 oz (115 g) fat, chilled and diced
3–4 tablespoons iced water

1 ▲ Sift the flour and salt into a bowl. Add the fat. Rub it into the flour with your fingertips until the mixture is crumb-like.

2 ▲ Sprinkle 3 tablespoons water over the mixture. With a fork, toss gently to mix and moisten it.

Pastry making tips
- It helps if the fat is cold and firm, particularly if making the dough in a food processor. Cold fat has less chance of warming and softening too much when it is being rubbed into the flour, resulting in an oily pastry. Use block margarine rather than the soft tub-type.
- When rubbing the fat into the flour, if it begins to soften and feel oily, put the bowl in the refrigerator to chill for 20–30 minutes. Then continue making the dough.
- Liquids used should be ice-cold so that they will not soften or melt the fat.
- Take care when adding the water: start with the smaller amount (added all at once, not in a dribble), and add more only if the mixture will not come together into a dough. Too much water will result in tough pastry.
- When gathering the mixture together into a ball of dough, handle it as little as possible: overworked pastry will be tough.
- To avoid shrinkage, refrigerate the pastry dough before rolling out and baking. This 'resting time' will allow any elasticity developed during mixing to relax.

4 ▲ Press the dough into a ball. If it is too dry to form a dough, add the remaining water.

7 ▲ **To make pastry in a food processor:** Combine the flour, salt and cubed fat in the work bowl. Process, turning the machine on and off, just until the mixture is crumbly. Add the iced water and process again briefly – just until the dough starts to pull away from the sides of the bowl. It should still look crumbly. Remove the dough from the processor and gather it into a ball. Wrap and refrigerate.

5 ▲ Wrap the ball of dough with cling film or greaseproof paper and refrigerate it for at least 30 minutes.

Shortcrust pastry variations
- For *Nut Shortcrust:* Add 1 oz (30 g) finely chopped walnuts or pecan nuts to the flour mixture.
- For *Rich Shortcrust:* Use 8 oz (225 g) flour and 6 oz (170 g) fat (preferably all butter), plus 1 tablespoon caster sugar if making a sweet pie. Bind with 1 egg yolk and 2–3 tablespoons water.
- For a *Two-crust Pie,* increase the proportions for these pastries by 50%, thus the amounts needed for basic shortcrust pastry are: 12 oz (340 g) flour, ½ teaspoon salt, 6 oz (170 g) fat, 5–6 tablespoons water. For Nut Shortcrust, as above with 2 oz (55 g) nuts. For Rich Shortcrust, as above but using 9 oz (260 g) fat, 4–5 tablespoons water and 1 egg yolk.

MAKING FRENCH FLAN PASTRY

The pastry for tarts, flans and quiches is made with butter or margarine, giving a rich and crumbly result. The more fat used, the richer the pastry will be – almost like a biscuit dough – and the harder to roll out. If you have difficulty rolling it, you can press it into the tin instead, or roll it out between sheets of cling film. Flan pastry, like shortcrust, can be made by hand or in a food processor. Tips for making, handling and using shortcrust pastry apply equally to French flan pastry.

FOR A 9 IN (23 CM) FLAN CASE
7 oz (200 g) plain flour
½ teaspoon salt
4 oz (115 g) butter or margarine, chilled
1 egg yolk
¼ teaspoon lemon juice
2–3 tablespoons iced water

1 ▲ Sift the flour and salt into a bowl. Add the butter or margarine. Rub into the flour until the mixture resembles fine crumbs.

2 ▲ In a small bowl, mix the egg yolk, lemon juice and 2 tablespoons water. Add to the flour mixture. With a fork, toss gently to mix and moisten.

3 ▲ Press the dough into a rough ball. If it is too dry to come together, add the remaining water. Turn on to the work surface or a pastry board.

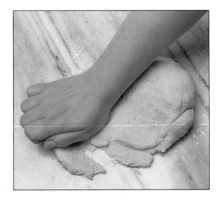

4 ▲ With the heel of your hand, push small portions of dough away from you, smearing them on the surface.

Flan pastry variations
- For *Sweet Flan Pastry:* Reduce the amount of salt to ¼ teaspoon; add 1 tablespoon caster sugar with the flour.
- For *Rich Flan Pastry:* Use 7 oz (200 g) flour, ½ teaspoon salt, 5 oz (145 g) butter, 2 egg yolks, and 1–2 tablespoons water.
- For *Rich Sweet Flan Pastry:* Make rich flan pastry, adding 3 tablespoons caster sugar with the flour and, if liked, ½ teaspoon vanilla essence with the egg yolks.

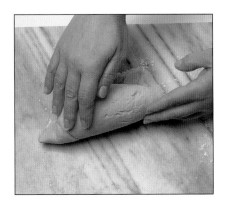

5 ▲ Continue mixing the dough in this way until it feels pliable and can be peeled easily off the surface.

6 ▲ Press the dough into a smooth ball. Wrap in cling film and chill for at least 30 minutes.

ROLLING OUT AND LINING A TIN

A neat pastry case that doesn't distort or shrink in baking is the desired result. The key to success is handling the dough gently. Use the method here for lining a round pie or tart tin that is about 2 in (5 cm) deep.

Remove the chilled dough from the refrigerator and allow it to soften slightly at room temperature. Unwrap and put it on a lightly floured surface. Flatten the dough into a neat, round disc. Lightly flour the rolling pin.

Rolling out and lining tips
- Reflour the surface and rolling pin if the dough starts to stick.
- Should the dough tear, patch with a piece of moistened dough.
- When rolling out and lining the pie or tart tin, do not stretch the dough. It will only shrink back during baking, spoiling the shape of the pastry case.
- Once or twice during rolling out, gently push in the edges of the dough with your cupped palms, to keep the circular shape.
- A pastry scraper will help lift the dough from the work surface, to wrap it around the rolling pin.
- Tins made from heat-resistant glass or dull-finish metal such as heavyweight aluminium will give a crisp crust.
- When finishing the edge, be sure to hook the dough over the rim all the way round or to press the dough firmly to the rim. This will prevent the dough pulling away should it start to shrink.
- If covering a pie dish, roll the dough to a round or oval 2 in (5 cm) larger than the dish. Cut a 1 in (2.5 cm) strip from the outside and lay this on the moistened rim of the dish. Brush the strip with water and lay the sheet of dough on top. Press edges to seal, then trim even with the rim. Knock up the edge with a knife.

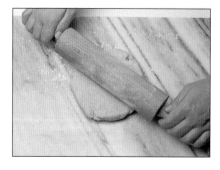

1 ▲ Using even pressure, start rolling out the dough, working from the centre to the edge each time and easing the pressure slightly as you reach the edge.

2 ▲ Lift up the dough and give it a quarter turn from time to time during the rolling. This will prevent the dough sticking to the surface, and will help keep the thickness even.

3 ▲ Continue rolling out until the dough circle is about 2 in (5 cm) larger all round than the tin. The dough will be about ⅛ in (3 mm) thick.

4 ▲ Set the rolling pin on the dough, near one side of the circle. Fold the outside edge of dough over the pin, then roll the pin over the dough to wrap the dough round it. Do this gently and loosely.

5 ▲ Hold the pin over the tin and gently unroll the dough so it drapes into the tin, centring it as much as possible.

6 ▲ With your fingertips, lift and ease the dough into the tin, gently pressing it over the bottom and up the side. Turn excess dough over the rim and trim it with a knife or scissors, depending on the edge to be made.

LINING A FLAN TIN OR RING

A flan tin is shallow, with no rim. Its straight sides (smooth or fluted) give a tart or flan the traditional shape. The most useful tins have removable bases, making it very easy to turn out a tart. Flan rings are straight-sided metal rings that are set on a baking sheet.

In addition to flan tins and rings, there are porcelain quiche dishes and small, individual tartlet tins, both plain and fluted.

Pecan Nut Tartlets
Line six 4 in (10 cm) tartlet tins with flan pastry. Place 1 oz (30 g) pecan nut halves in each. In a bowl, beat 3 eggs to mix. Add 1 oz (30 g) melted butter, 10 oz (300 g) golden syrup and ½ teaspoon vanilla essence. Sift together 4 oz (115 g) caster sugar and 1 tablespoon plain flour. Add to the egg mixture and stir until evenly blended. Fill the tartlet cases and leave until the nuts rise to the surface. Bake in a 350°F/180°C/Gas 4 oven for 35–40 minutes or until a knife inserted near the centre comes out clean. Cool in the tins for 15 minutes, then turn on to a wire rack.

1 ▲ Remove the chilled dough from the refrigerator and let it soften slightly at room temperature. Roll out to a circle about 2 in (5 cm) larger all round than the tin or ring. It will be about ⅛ in (3 mm) thick.

3 ▲ With your fingertips, ease the dough into the tin or ring, gently pressing it smoothly over the bottom, without stretching it.

5 ▲ Roll the rolling pin over the top of the tin or ring to cut off excess dough. Smooth the cut edge and press it against the side of the tin or ring, if necessary, to keep it in place.

2 ▲ Roll up the dough round the rolling pin, then unroll it over the tin or ring, draping it gently.

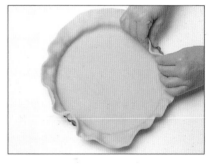

4 ▲ Fold the overhanging dough down inside the tin or ring, to thicken the side of the pastry case. Smooth and press the side of the case against the side of the tin or ring.

6 ▲ **For tartlet tins:** Arrange them close together and unroll the dough over them, draping it loosely. Roll the rolling pin over the top to cut off excess pastry. Press into the bottom and sides of the tins.

FINISHING THE EDGE

1 ▲ For a forked edge: Trim the dough even with the rim and press it flat. Firmly and evenly press the prongs of a fork all round the edge. If the fork sticks, dip it in flour.

2 ▲ For a crimped edge: Trim the dough to leave an overhang of about ½ in (1.5 cm) all round. Fold the extra dough under. Put the knuckle or tip of the index finger of one of your hands inside the edge, pointing directly out. With the thumb and index finger of your other hand, pinch the dough edge around your index finger into a 'V' shape. Continue all round the edge.

3 ▲ For a ruffled edge: Trim the dough to leave an overhang of about ½ in (1.5 cm) all round. Fold the extra dough under. Hold the thumb and index finger of one of your hands about 1 in (2.5 cm) apart, inside the edge, pointing directly out. With the index finger of your other hand, gently pull the dough between them, to the end of the rim. Continue all the way round the edge.

Apple and Cherry Crumble Pie
Mix together 12 oz (340 g) peeled, cored and sliced Granny Smith apples, 10 oz (300 g) stoned cherries and 4 oz (115 g) soft light brown sugar. Put into a 9 in (23 cm) pastry case. For the topping, combine 4 oz (115 g) plain flour, 4 oz (115 g) soft light brown sugar and 1 teaspoon ground cinnamon. Rub in 3 oz (85 g) butter until the mixture resembles coarse crumbs. Sprinkle over the fruit. Bake in a 375°F/190°C/Gas 5 oven for about 45 minutes or until golden. *Serves 6.*

4 ▲ For a cutout edge: Trim the dough even with the rim and press it flat on the rim. With a small pastry cutter, cut out decorative shapes from the dough trimmings. Moisten the edge of the pastry case and press the cutouts in place, overlapping them slightly if you like.

5 ▲ For a ribbon edge: Trim the dough even with the rim and press it flat on the rim. Cut long strips about ¾ in (2 cm) wide from the dough trimmings. Moisten the edge and press one end of a strip on to it. Twist the strip gently and press it on to the edge again. Continue all the way round the edge.

Baking Blind

Baked custard and cream fillings can make pastry soggy, so the cases for these flans and tarts are often given an initial baking before the filling is added and the final baking is done. Such pre-baking is referred to as baking 'blind'. The technique is also used for pastry cases that are to be filled with an uncooked or precooked mixture.

The purpose of using weights is to prevent the bottom of the pastry case from rising too much and becoming distorted, thus keeping its neat shape.

Fresh Strawberry Flan
Make the case using sweet flan pastry or rich sweet flan pastry. Bake it blind fully, then cool. Beat 14 oz (400 g) full-fat soft cheese with 1 ¾ oz (50 g) caster sugar, 1 egg yolk and 4 tablespoons whipping cream until smooth. Fold in 1 stiffly whisked egg white. Pour into the case and spread evenly. Bake at 350°F/180°C/Gas 4 for 15–20 minutes or until the filling is softly set; it will set further as it cools. When cool, arrange halved strawberries on top in concentric circles. Melt 5oz (145 g) redcurrant jelly and brush over the berries to glaze them. Leave the flan to cool before serving. *Serves 6.*

1 ▲ Set the pie or flan tin, or flan ring, on a sheet of greaseproof paper or foil. Draw or mark around its base. Cut out a circle about 3 in (7.5 cm) larger all round than the drawn or marked one.

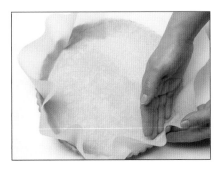

3 ▲ Lay the circle of greaseproof paper or foil in the pastry case and press it smoothly over the bottom and up the side.

5 ▲ **For partially baked pastry:** Bake the case in a 400°F/200°C/Gas 6 oven for 15–20 minutes or until it is slightly dry and set. Remove the paper or foil and beans. The pastry is now ready to be filled and baked further.

2 ▲ Roll out the pastry dough and use to line the tin or ring set on a baking sheet. Prick the bottom of the pastry case all over with a fork.

4 ▲ Put enough dried beans or baking beans in the case to cover the bottom thickly.

6 ▲ **For fully baked pastry:** After baking for 15 minutes, remove the paper or foil and beans. Prick the bottom again with a fork. Return to the oven and bake for 5–10 minutes or until golden brown. Cool completely before adding the filling.

MAKING A TWO-CRUST PIE

Two succulent pastry layers enveloping a sweet filling – what could be nicer? Use the same method for making small pies, such as mince pices.

American-style Apple Pie
Combine 2 lb (900 g) peeled, cored and thinly sliced Granny Smith apples, 1 tablespoon plain flour, 3½ oz (100 g) caster sugar and ¾ teaspoon mixed spice. Toss to coat the fruit evenly with the sugar and flour. Use to fill the two-crust pie. Bake in a 375°F/190°C/ Gas 5 oven for about 45 minutes or until the pastry is golden brown and the fruit is tender (test with a skewer through a slit in the top crust). Cool on a rack.

1 ▲ Roll out half of the pastry dough on a floured surface and line a pie tin that is about 2 in (5 cm) deep. Trim the dough even with the rim.

3 ▲ Roll out a second piece of dough to a circle that is about 1 in (2.5 cm) larger all round than the tin. Roll it up around the rolling pin and unroll over the pie. Press the edges together.

2 ▲ Put in the filling. Brush the edge of the pastry case evenly with water to moisten it.

4 ▲ Trim the edge of the lid to leave a ½ in (1.5 cm) overhang. Cut slits or a design in the centre. These will act as steam vents during baking.

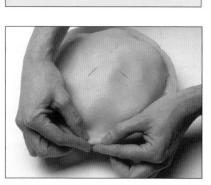

5 ▲ Fold the overhang of the lid under the edge of the case. Press the two together gently and evenly to seal. Finish the edge as wished.

6 ▲ Brush the top of the pie with milk or cream for a shiny finish. Or brush with 1 egg yolk mixed with 1 teaspoon water for a glazed golden brown finish. Or brush with water and then sprinkle with caster sugar or cinnamon and sugar for a sugary crust.

7 ▲ If you like, cut out decorative shapes from the dough trimmings, rolled out as thinly as possible. Moisten the cutouts with a little water and press them on to the top. Glaze the decorations before baking.

MAKING A LATTICE TOP

A woven pastry lattice is a very attractive finish for a pie. Prepare shortcrust for a two-crust pie.

Roll out half of the pastry dough and line the pie tin. Trim the dough to leave a ½ in (1.5 cm) overhang all round. Put in the filling. Roll out the second piece of dough into a circle that is about 2 in (5 cm) larger all round than the pie tin.

Apricot Lattice Pie
Toss together 2¼ lb (1 kg) peeled, stoned and thinly sliced apricots, 2 tablespoons plain flour and 3½ oz (100 g) sugar. Fill the pastry case and make a lattice top. Glaze with milk and bake in a 375°F/190°C/Gas 5 oven for about 45 minutes or until the pastry is golden and the filling is bubbling. Cool on a wire rack.

1 ▲ With the help of a ruler, cut neat straight strips of dough that are about ½ in (1.5 cm) wide, using a knife or fluted pastry wheel.

2 ▲ For a square woven lattice: Lay half of the strips across the pie filling, keeping them neatly parallel and spacing them evenly.

3 ▲ Fold back every other strip from the centre. Lay another strip across the centre, on the flat strips, at right angles to them. Lay the folded strips flat again.

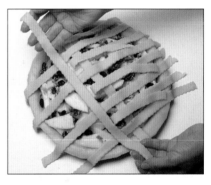

4 ▲ Now fold back those strips that were not folded the first time. Lay another strip across those that are flat now, spacing this new strip evenly from the centre strip.

5 ▲ Continue folding the strips in this way until half of the lattice is completed. Repeat on the other half of the pie.

6 ▲ Trim the ends of the strips even with the rim of the pie tin. Moisten the edge of the pastry case and press the strips gently to it to seal. Finish the edge.

7 ▲ For a diamond lattice: Weave as above, laying the intersecting strips diagonally instead of at right angles. Or lay half the strips over the filling and the remaining strips on top.

MAKING A BISCUIT CASE

A biscuit case is one of the simplest bases to make, and the variations in flavouring are almost endless. Crumbs from any dry biscuit can be used, both sweet and savoury. You can also use breadcrumbs and cake crumbs. Most biscuit cases are sweet, to hold sweet fillings, but there are also unsweetened biscuit cases for savoury cheesecakes.

MAKES AN 8–9 IN (20–23 CM) CASE

8 oz (225 g) biscuits (see below), crushed

4 oz (115 g) butter, melted

3–4 tablespoons caster sugar (optional)

Biscuit case flavourings
- Use digestive biscuits. Sweeten with sugar to taste, if liked. Add 1 teaspoon ground cinnamon or ginger or mixed spice or ½ teaspoon grated nutmeg.
- Use digestive biscuits and sweeten with sugar to taste, if liked. Add 1 teaspoon grated lemon zest or 2 teaspoons grated orange zest.
- Use 7 oz (200 g) digestive biscuits and 1½ oz (45 g) ground or finely chopped nuts (almonds, hazelnuts, pecan nuts or walnuts).
- Use ginger nuts, shortbread, almond butter biscuits, amaretti biscuits or crisp almond macaroons. No sugar is needed.
- Use water biscuits or other cheese biscuits, without adding sugar, for a savoury filling.

Crushing the biscuits
To make fine crumbs, break the biscuits into small pieces. Put them, a small batch at a time, in a heavy plastic bag and roll over them with a rolling pin. Or grind them finely in a blender or food processor.

1 ▲ Combine the biscuits, melted butter and sugar, plus other flavourings, if using. Stir well to mix.

2 ▲ Turn the biscuit mixture into a buttered 8 in (20 cm) springform cake tin or 9 in (23 cm) tart tin. Spread it over the bottom and up the side.

3 ▲ With the back of a large spoon or your fingers, press the biscuit mixture firmly against the tin, to pack the crumbs into a solid crust.

4 ▲ According to the recipe, refrigerate the case to set it, usually at least 1 hour. Or bake the case in a 350°F/180°C/Gas 4 oven for 8–10 minutes; cool before filling.

Easy Chocolate Tart
Prepare the biscuit case using ginger biscuits and pressing it into a 9 in (23 cm) tin. Bake and cool. Melt 6 oz (170 g) plain chocolate with 4 tablespoons milk; cool. Whip ¾ pint (450 ml) double or whipping cream until thick. Fold into the cooled chocolate. Spread evenly in the case. Cover and refrigerate until firm. Just before serving, garnish with chocolate curls or grated chocolate. *Serves 6.*

MAKING CHOUX PASTRY

Unlike other pastries, where the fat is rubbed into the flour, with choux pastry the butter is melted with water and then the flour is added, followed by eggs. The result is more of a paste than a pastry. It is easy to make, but care must be taken in measuring the ingredients.

FOR 18 PROFITEROLES OR 12 ECLAIRS

| 4 oz (115 g) butter, cut into small pieces |
| 8 fl oz (240 ml) water |
| 2 teaspoons caster sugar (optional) |
| ¼ teaspoon salt |
| 5 oz (145 g) plain flour |
| 4 eggs, beaten to mix |

Shaping choux pastry
- For *large puffs:* Use two large spoons dipped in water. Drop the paste in 2–2½ in (5–6 cm) wide blobs on the paper-lined baking sheet, leaving 1½ in (4 cm) between each. Neaten the blobs as much as possible. Alternatively, for well-shaped puffs, pipe the paste using a piping bag fitted with a ¾ in (2 cm) plain nozzle.
- For *profiteroles:* Use two small spoons or a piping bag fitted with a ½ in (1.5 cm) nozzle and shape 1 in (2.5 cm) blobs.
- For *éclairs:* Use a piping bag fitted with a ¾ in (2 cm) nozzle. Pipe strips 4–5 in (10–12 cm) long.
- For *a ring:* draw a 12 in (30 cm) circle on the paper. Spoon the paste in large blobs on the circle to make a ring. Or pipe two rings round the circle and a third on top.

Baking times for choux pastry
Bake large puffs and éclairs 30–35 minutes, profiteroles 20–25 minutes, rings 40–45 minutes.

1 ▲ Combine the butter, water, sugar, if using, and salt in a large heavy-based saucepan. Bring to the boil over moderately high heat, stirring occasionally.

3 ▲ Return the pan to moderate heat and cook, stirring, until the mixture will form a ball, pulling away from the side of the pan. This will take about 1 minute. Remove from the heat again and allow to cool for 3–5 minutes.

5 ▲ While still warm, shape large choux puffs, éclairs, profiteroles or large rings on a baking sheet lined with baking parchment.

2 ▲ As soon as the mixture is boiling, remove the pan from the heat. Add the flour all at once and beat vigorously with a wooden spoon to mix the flour into the liquid.

4 ▲ Add a little of the beaten egg and beat well with the spoon or an electric mixer to incorporate. Add a little more egg and beat in well. Continue beating in the eggs until the mixture becomes a smooth, shiny paste thick enough to hold its shape.

6 ▲ Glaze with 1 egg beaten with 1 teaspoon cold water. Put into a 425°F/220°C/Gas 7 oven, then reduce the heat to 400°F/200°C/Gas 6. Bake until puffed and golden brown.

MAKING CAKES BY THE CREAMING METHOD

The Victoria sandwich, with its tender crumb and rich, moist flavour, is always popular. It is delicious enough to be served plain, with just a dusting of sugar, or it can be filled and iced.

To make cakes by the creaming method, the fat and sugar are 'creamed' – or beaten – together before the eggs and dry ingredients are added. The fat (usually butter or margarine) should be soft enough to be beaten, so if necessary remove it from the refrigerator and leave it at room temperature for at least 30 minutes. For best results, the eggs should be at room temperature.

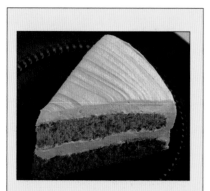

Mocha Victoria Sponge
Make the mixture using 6 oz (170 g) each butter or margarine, caster sugar and self-raising flour and 3 eggs. Divide between two bowls. To one add 1 tablespoon strong black coffee; to the other add 1 tablespoon cocoa powder mixed to a paste with 1–2 tablespoons boiling water. Place alternate spoonfuls of each flavour, side by side, in 2 greased and bottom-lined 7 in (18 cm) round sandwich tins. Lightly smooth the top. Bake at 350°F/180°C/Gas 4 for 25–30 minutes. Turn out on to a wire rack and leave to cool. Sandwich the cakes together with coffee buttercream. Cover the top, or top and sides, with buttercream.

1 ▲ Sift the flour with the salt, raising agent(s) and any other dry ingredients, such as spices or cocoa powder. Set aside.

3 ▲ Add the sugar to the creamed fat gradually. With the mixer at medium-high speed, beat it into the fat until the mixture is pale and very fluffy. The sugar should be completely incorporated. This will take 4–5 minutes. During this process, air will be beaten into the mixture, which will help the cake to rise.

5 ▲ Add the dry ingredients to the mixture, beating at low speed just until smoothly combined. Or fold in with a large metal spoon.

2 ▲ Put the fat in a large, deep bowl and beat with an electric mixer at medium speed, or a wooden spoon, until the texture is soft and pliable.

4 ▲ Add the eggs or egg yolks, one at a time, beating well after each addition (about 45 seconds). Scrape the bowl often so all the ingredients are evenly combined. When adding the eggs, the mixture may begin to curdle, especially if the eggs are cold. If this happens, add 1 tablespoon of the measured flour.

6 ▲ If the recipe calls for any liquid, add it in small portions alternately with portions of the dry ingredients.

7 ▲ If the recipe specifies, whisk egg whites separately until frothy, add sugar and continue whisking until stiff peaks form. Fold into the mixture.

8 ▲ Pour the mixture into a cake tin or tins, prepared according to the recipe, and bake as specified.

9 ▲ To test creamed-method cakes, insert a metal skewer or wooden cocktail stick into the centre; it should come out clean.

MAKING AMERICAN FROSTING

This fluffy white frosting has an attractive gloss and a texture like meringue. It is a delicious filling and icing for sanwich cakes.

MAKES ENOUGH TO FILL AND ICE A 9 IN (23 CM) SANDWICH CAKE

10 oz (300 g) sugar

¼ teaspoon cream of tartar

2 egg whites

4 tablespoons cold water

1 tablespoon liquid glucose

2 teaspoons vanilla essence

1 ▲ Combine the sugar, cream of tartar, egg whites, water and glucose in a large heatproof bowl or the top of a double saucepan. Stir just to mix.

2 ▲ Set the bowl over a saucepan of boiling water. The base of the bowl should not touch the water.

Frosting variations

For *Orange Frosting:* Use orange juice instead of water and add 1 teaspoon grated orange zest. Reduce the vanilla to ½ teaspoon.

For *Lemon Frosting:* Use 2 tablespoons each lemon juice and water and add ½ teaspoon grated lemon zest. Reduce the vanilla to ½ teaspoon.

3 ▲ Beat with a hand-held electric mixer at high speed for about 7 minutes or until the frosting is thick and white and will form stiff peaks.

4 ▲ Remove from the heat. Add the vanilla and continue beating for about 3 minutes or until the frosting has cooled slightly. Use immediately.

Making Cakes by the All-in-one Method

Many cakes are made by an easy all-in-one method where all the ingredients are combined in a bowl and beaten thoroughly. The mixture can also be made in a food processor, but take care not to over-process. A refinement on the all-in-one method is to separate the eggs and make the mixture with the yolks. The whites are whisked separately and then folded in.

1 ▲ Sift the dry ingredients (flour, salt, raising agent, spices and so on) into a bowl.

2 ▲ Add the liquid ingredients (eggs, melted or soft fat, milk, fruit juices and so on) and beat until smooth, with an electric mixer for speed. Pour into the prepared tins and bake as specified in the recipe.

Making Simple Buttercream

Quick to make and easy to spread, buttercream is ideal for all kinds of cakes, from simple ones to gâteaux. The basic buttercream can be varied with many other flavours, and it can be tinted with food colouring, too.

MAKES ENOUGH TO COVER THE TOP AND SIDE OF A 7–8 IN (17–20 CM) CAKE

4 oz (115 g) butter, preferably unsalted, at room temperature

8 oz (225 g) icing sugar, sifted

1 teaspoon vanilla essence

about 2 teaspoons milk

1 ▲ Put the butter in a deep mixing bowl and beat it with an electric mixer at medium speed, or a wooden spoon, until it is soft and pliable.

2 ▲ Gradually add the icing sugar and beat at medium-high speed. Continue beating until the mixture is pale and fluffy.

3 ▲ Add the vanilla essence and 1 tablespoon milk. Beat until smooth and of a spreading consistency. If it is too thick, beat in more milk. If too thin, beat in more sugar.

Buttercream variations
- For *Orange or Lemon Buttercream*, grate the zest from 1 small orange or ½ lemon; squeeze the juice. Beat in the zest with the sugar; use the juice instead of the vanilla and milk.
- For *Chocolate Buttercream*, add 4 tablespoons cocoa powder, beating it in with the sugar. Increase the milk to 3–4 tablespoons.
- For *Mocha Buttercream*: Warm the milk and dissolve 1 teaspoon instant coffee powder in it; cool and use to make chocolate buttercream, adding more milk if needed.
- For *Coffee Buttercream*, warm the milk and dissolve 1 tablespoon of instant coffee powder in it; cool before adding to the buttercream.

MAKING CAKES BY THE MELTING METHOD

Cakes made by the melting method are wonderfully moist and keep quite well. Ingredients such as sugar, syrup (treacle, honey, golden syrup) and fat are warmed together until melted and smoothly combined before being added to the dry ingredients.

Fruit Cake

Sift 8 oz (225 g) self-raising flour, a pinch of salt and 1 teaspoon mixed spice. Melt together 4 oz (115 g) butter or margarine, 4 oz (115 g) soft light brown sugar, ¼ pint (150 ml) water and the grated zest and juice of 1 orange. When smooth, add 4 oz (115 g) each sultanas, currants and raisins and simmer gently for about 10 minutes, stirring occasionally. Cool. Add the fruit mixture to the dry ingredients. Add 2 oz (55 g) each chopped glacé cherries and chopped mixed peel, 1 tablespoon orange marmalade and 2 beaten eggs. Mix thoroughly. Pour into a greased and lined 8 in (20 cm) round cake tin. Bake at 325°F/170°C/Gas 3 for 1½ hours or until firm and golden; a skewer inserted in the centre should come out clean. Cool in the tin for 30 minutes before turning out on to a wire rack.

1 ▲ Sift the dry ingredients (such as flour, raising agent, salt, ground spices) into a large bowl.

3 ▲ If recipe instructs, warm fruit in the syrup mixture. Remove from the heat and leave to cool slightly (if too hot, it will not combine well with dry ingredients).

5 ▲ If called for in the recipe, stir in fruit and/or nuts (if these have not been warmed in the syrup). Turn the cake mixture into a lined tin and bake according to the recipe.

2 ▲ Put the sugar and/or syrup and fat in a saucepan with any other ingredients specified in the recipe. Warm over a low heat, stirring occasionally, until the fat has melted and sugar dissolved. The mixture should not boil.

4 ▲ Make a well in the centre of the dry ingredients and pour in the cooled melted mixture. Add beaten eggs and any other liquid ingredients (milk, water, etc) and beat to a smooth, thick batter.

Maturing for flavour
Melting-method cakes taste best if they are allowed to 'mature' before serving. After the cake has cooled completely, wrap it in greaseproof paper and then overwrap in foil. Keep it in a cool place for 1–2 days before cutting into slices.

MAKING A CLASSIC WHISKED SPONGE

The classic whisked sponge contains no fat and no raising agents – just eggs, sugar and flour. The light, airy texture of the finished cake depends on the large quantity of air beaten into the mixture.

Sometimes the eggs are separated for a whisked sponge and sometimes the cake is enriched with butter. American angel food cake uses egg whites only.

A whisked sponge can be simply dusted with icing or caster sugar, filled with sweetened whipped cream, a fruit jam or fresh fruit, or used to make a Swiss roll.

If you use a table-top electric mixer to beat the eggs and sugar, or if using separated eggs, there is no need to set the bowl over a pan of simmering water.

Whisked Sponge
Make the mixture using 4 whole eggs, 5 oz (145 g) caster sugar and 4 oz (115 g) plain flour. Pour into a greased, bottom-lined and floured 9 in (23 cm) round cake tin. Bake in a 350°F/180°C/Gas 4 oven for 25–30 minutes. Cool in the tin for 10 minutes, then turn out on to a wire rack and cool completely. Before serving, peel off the lining paper. Dust the top lightly with sifted icing sugar.

1 ▲ In a heatproof bowl, combine the eggs (at room temperature) and sugar. Set the bowl over a saucepan of simmering water; the base of the bowl should not touch the water.

3 ▲ Lift out the beaters; the mixture on the beaters should trail back on to the surface of the remaining mixture in the bowl to make a ribbon that holds it shape.

5 ▲ Sift the flour and fold it into the mixture, cutting in to the bottom of the bowl with a rubber spatula or large metal spoon and turning the mixture over, working gently yet thoroughly to retain the volume of the whisked egg and sugar mixture.

2 ▲ Beat with a hand-held electric mixer at medium-high speed, or a rotary beater or whisk, until the mixture is very thick and pale – about 10 minutes.

4 ▲ Remove the bowl from over the pan of water and continue beating for 2–3 minutes or until the mixture is cool.

6 ▲ Pour the mixture into the prepared tin or tins and bake as directed in the recipe. To test a whisked sponge, press the centre lightly with your fingertip: the cake should spring back.

MAKING A SWISS ROLL

A rolled sponge reveals an attractive spiral of filling when it is sliced. The filling could be sweetened whipped cream, ice cream, fruit jam or buttercream.

The whisked sponge mixture can be made using whole or separated eggs, as preferred.

Line the tin with greaseproof paper or baking parchment, grease the paper and dust with flour.

Chocolate Ice Cream Roll

Make the sponge mixture using 4 eggs, separated, 4 oz (115 g) caster sugar and 4 oz (115 g) plain flour sifted with 3 tablespoons cocoa powder. Pour into a prepared 15 × 10 in (37.5 × 25 cm) Swiss roll tin. Bake in a 375°F/190°C/Gas 5 oven for about 15 minutes. Turn out, roll up and cool. When cold, unroll the cake and spread with 1 pint (600 ml) softened vanilla or chocolate ice cream. Roll up the cake again, wrap in foil and freeze until firm. About 30 minutes be-fore serving, transfer the cake to the refrigerator. Sprinkle with caster or icing sugar before serving. If you like, serve with warm bittersweet chocolate sauce. *Serves 8*.

1 ▲ Pour the mixture into the prepared tin and spread it evenly into the corners with a palette knife. Bake as specified in the recipe.

3 ▲ Carefully peel off the lining paper from the cake. If necessary, trim off any crisp edges from the side of the cake.

5 ▲ Remove the towel and unroll the cake. Lift off the paper. Spread the chosen filling over the cake.

2 ▲ Spread a tea towel flat and lay a sheet of baking parchment on top. Sprinkle the paper evenly, as specified, with caster or icing sugar, cocoa or a sugar and spice mixture. Invert the cake on to the paper.

4 ▲ Carefully roll up the cake, with the paper inside, starting from a short side. Wrap the towel round the cake roll and leave to cool on a wire rack.

6 ▲ Roll up the cake again, using the paper to help move it forward. Sprinkle with sugar or ice the cake, as the recipe specifies.

PREPARING CAKE TINS

Instructions vary from recipe to recipe for preparing cake tins. Some are simply greased, some are greased and floured, some are lined with baking parchment or greased greaseproof paper. The preparation required depends on the type of cake mixture and the length of the baking time. Proper preparation aids turning out.

Flavourful coatings

Some cake recipes specify that the greased tin be coated with sugar, cocoa powder or ground nuts. Follow the method for flouring.

1 ▲ **To grease a tin:** Use butter, margarine, or a mild or flavourless oil. If using butter or margarine, hold a small piece in a paper towel (or use your fingers), and rub it all over the bottom and up the side of the tin to make a thin, even coating. If using oil, brush it on with a pastry brush.

2 ▲ **To flour a tin:** Put a small scoopful of flour in the centre of the greased tin. Tip and rotate the tin so that the flour spreads and coats all over the bottom and up the side. Turn the tin over and shake out excess flour, tapping the base of the tin to dislodge any pockets of flour.

3 ▲ **To line the bottom of a tin:** Set the tin on the sheet of paper and draw round the base. Cut out this circle, square or rectangle, cutting just inside the drawn line. Press the paper smoothly on to the bottom of the tin.

4 ▲ **To line the sides of a tin** (for rich mixtures and fruit cakes): Cut a strip of paper long enough to wrap round the outside of the tin and overlap by 1½ in (4 cm). The strip should be wide enough to extend 1 in (2.5 cm) above the rim of the tin.

5 ▲ Fold the strip lengthways at the 1 in (2.5 cm) point and crease firmly. With scissors, snip at regular intervals along the 1 in (2.5 cm) fold, from the edge to the crease. Line the side of the tin, with the snipped part of the strip on the bottom.

6 ▲ For square and rectangular cake tins, fold the paper and crease it with your fingernail to fit snugly into the corners of the tin. Then press the bottom paper lining into place.

7 ▲ If the recipe specifies, grease the paper before you put it in the tin. If the tin is to be floured, do this after the paper is in place.

8 ▲ **To line bun and muffin tins:** Use paper liners of the required size. Or grease and flour the tins.

9 ▲ **To line a Swiss roll tin:** Cut a rectangle of paper 2 in (5 cm) larger all round than the tin. Grease the bottom of the tin lightly to prevent the paper from slipping.

10 ▲ Lay the paper evenly in the tin. With a table knife, press the paper into the angle all round the bottom of the tin, creasing the paper firmly but not cutting it.

11 ▲ With scissors, snip the paper in the corners, from top to bottom, so it will fit neatly into them. Grease the paper according to recipe instructions, unless using baking parchment.

USING SEPARATED EGGS FOR A WHISKED SPONGE

This version of whisked sponge is easier to make than the classic one that uses whole eggs, but the results are no less light and delicious. There is no need to set the bowl over a pan of simmering water for whisking, although if you are using a balloon whisk rather than an electric mixer or rotary beater you may want to do so to speed up the thickening of the egg yolk and sugar mixture and to increase its volume. Bowls and beaters used with egg whites must be scrupulously clean.

1 ▲ Separate the eggs, taking care that there is no trace of yolk with the whites. Put the yolks and whites in separate large bowls.

2 ▲ Add most of the sugar to the yolks. With a hand-held or table-top electric mixer, whisk at medium-high speed until the mixture is very thick and pale. Lift out the beaters: the mixture on the beaters should trail back on to the surface of the remaining mixture in the bowl to make a ribbon that holds its shape.

3 ▲ Whisk the egg whites until they form soft peaks (if not using a copper bowl, add a pinch of cream of tartar once the whites are frothy). Add the remaining sugar and continue whisking until the whites will form stiff peaks.

4 ▲ With a rubber spatula, fold the sifted flour into the egg yolk mixture, then fold in the whisked egg whites. Fold gently but thoroughly. Pour the mixture into the prepared tin and bake as instructed.

A Genoese sponge
This whisked sponge, made with whole or separated eggs, is more rich and trickier to make, as melted butter is folded in just before pouring into the tin.

Making Yeast Dough

Making bread is a very enjoyable and satisfying culinary experience – with no other preparation do you have such 'hands-on' contact. And from the kneading through to the shaping of the risen (or proven) dough, you are working with a living organism, yeast, not a chemical raising agent. You can use either fresh yeast or dried yeast, which is available in an easy-blend variety too.

Everyday White Bread
Sift 1½ lb (700 g) strong plain flour into a large bowl with 1½ teaspoons salt and 1 tablespoon caster sugar. Stir in 2 teaspoons easy-blend dried yeast. Make a well in the centre and add ¾ pint (450 ml) mixed warm water and milk and 1 oz (30 g) melted and cooled butter. Mix to a soft dough, adding more flour or liquid if necessary, then knead until smooth and elastic. Leave to rise until doubled in bulk. Knock back the dough to deflate. Divide it in half and shape each piece into a loaf, tucking the ends under. Put in 2 greased 8½ × 4½ in (21 × 11 cm) loaf tins. Leave in a warm place to rise for 30–45 minutes. Glaze the tops of the loaves with 1 egg beaten with 1 tablespoon milk. Bake in a 450°F/230°C/Gas 8 oven for 30–35 minutes. *Makes 2 loaves.*

1 ▲ If using ordinary dried yeast, put it in a small bowl, add some of the warm liquid (105–110°F/40–43°C) called for in the recipe and whisk with a fork until dissolved. Add a little sugar if the recipe specifies.

3 ▲ Using your fingers or a spoon, gradually draw the flour into the liquids. Mix until all the flour is incorporated and the dough pulls away from the sides of the bowl. If the dough feels too soft and wet, work in a little more flour. If it doesn't come together, add a little more liquid.

5 ▲ Shape the dough into a ball. Put it in a lightly greased bowl and turn the dough to grease all over. Cover the bowl with a towel or cling film. Set it aside in a warm, draught-free place (about 80°F/27°C).

2 ▲ Sift the flour into a large warm bowl (with other dry ingredients such as salt). Make a well in the centre and add the yeast mixture plus any other liquid ingredients.

4 ▲ Turn the dough on to a lightly floured surface. Fold the dough over on to itself towards you and then press it down away from you with the heels of your hands. Rotate the dough slightly and fold and press it again. Knead until the dough looks satiny and feels elastic, about 10 minutes.

6 ▲ Leave to rise until about doubled in bulk, 1–1½ hours. To test if it is sufficiently risen, press a finger about 1 in (2.5 cm) into the dough and withdraw it quickly; the indentation should remain.

7 ▲ Gently punch the centre of the dough with your fist to deflate it and fold the edges to the centre. Turn the dough on to a lightly floured surface and knead it again for 2–3 minutes. If instructed, shape the dough into a ball again and rise a second time.

8 ▲ Shape the dough into loaves, rolls or other shapes as instructed. Put into prepared tins or on to baking sheets. Cover and leave to rise in a warm place for ¾–1 hour. If the recipe instructs, glaze the loaves or rolls.

9 ▲ Bake in the centre of a heated oven until well risen and golden brown. To test, tip the loaf out of the tin and tap the base with your knuckle. If it sounds hollow, like a drum, it is fully cooked. Immediately transfer to a wire rack for cooling.

SHAPING ROLLS

A basket of freshly baked bread rolls, in decorative shapes, is a delightful accompaniment for soups or salads. After shaping, arrange the rolls on a baking sheet, leaving space around each roll for spreading, and leave to rise for 30 minutes before baking.

Working with yeast

Easy-blend (or fast-action) is the most readily available dried yeast. Unlike ordinary dried yeast, there is no need to mix it with liquid. Just combine it with the flour and other dry ingredients and then add the warm liquids.

If using fresh yeast, allow ½ oz (15 g) to each 1 tablespoon dried. Crumble it into a small bowl, add warm liquid and mash with a fork until blended.

If you are in any doubt about the freshness of ordinary dried or fresh yeast, set the mixture aside in a warm place; after 10 minutes or so it should be foamy. If it isn't, discard it.

1 ▲ For Parker House rolls: Roll out the risen dough to ¼ in (5 mm) thickness and cut out 2½–3 in (6–7 cm) rounds using a floured cutter. Brush the rounds with melted butter. Fold them in half, slightly off-centre so the top overlaps the bottom. Press the folded edge firmly. Arrange the rolls on a greased baking sheet.

2 ▲ For crescent rolls: Roll out the risen dough to a large round ¼ in (5 mm) thick. Brush with melted butter. With a sharp knife, cut into wedges that are 2½–3 in (6–7 cm) at their wide end. Roll up each wedge, from the wide end. Set the rolls on a greased baking sheet, placing the points underneath.

3 ◄ For bowknot rolls: Divide the risen dough into pieces. Roll each with your palms on a lightly floured surface to make ropes that are about ½ in (1.5 cm) thick. Divide the ropes into 9 in (27 cm) lengths. Tie each rope loosely into a knot, tucking the ends under. Arrange the rolls on a greased baking sheet.

MAKING PIZZA DOUGH

The range of toppings for a pizza is virtually limitless. Although you can buy pizza bases, it's very easy to make your own at home, and takes much less time than you would expect.

MAKES A 14 in (35 cm) PIZZA BASE

2 teaspoons dried yeast

6fl oz (180 ml) warm water

11½ oz (315 g) strong plain flour

1 teaspoon salt

1½ tablespoons olive oil

Tomato and Mozzarella Pizza
Spread ½ pint (300 ml) tomato-garlic sauce over the pizza base, not quite to the edges. Scatter 4oz (115 g) grated mozzarella cheese evenly over the sauce (plus thinly sliced pepperoni or salami if you like). Sprinkle over freshly grated Parmesan cheese and then add a drizzle of olive oil. Bake in a 475°F/240°C/Gas 9 oven for 15–20 minutes.

Food processor pizza dough
Combine the flour, salt, yeast mixture and olive oil in the processor container. Process briefly, then add the rest of the warm water. Work until the dough begins to form a ball. Process 3–4 minutes to knead the dough, then knead it by hand for 2–3 minutes.

1 ▲ Put the yeast in a small bowl, add 4 tablespoons of the water and soak for 1 minute. Whisk lightly with a fork until dissolved.

3 ▲ Using your fingers, gradually draw the flour into the liquids. Continue mixing until all the flour is incorporated and the dough will just hold together.

5 ▲ Cover the bowl with cling film. Set aside in a warm place to rise about 1 hour until doubled in bulk. Turn the dough on to the lightly floured surface again. Gently knock back to deflate it, then knead lightly until smooth.

2 ▲ Sift the flour and salt into a large warm bowl. Make a well in the centre and add the yeast mixture, olive oil and remaining warm water.

4 ▲ Turn the dough on to a lightly floured surface. Knead it until it is smooth and silky, about 5 minutes. Shape the dough into a ball. Put it in an oiled bowl and rotate to coat the surface evenly with oil.

6 ▲ Roll out the dough into a round or square about ¼ in (5 mm) thick. Transfer it to a lightly oiled metal pizza tin or baking sheet. Add the topping as specified in the recipe. Bake until the pizza crust is puffy and well browned. Serve hot.

MAKING FOCACCIA AND BREAD STICKS

Italian flatbreads, such as focaccia, and bread sticks can be topped with herbs and seeds for tasty accompaniments or starters. Personalize them with combinations of your favourite ingredients for unusual snacks, or split and fill flatbreads with ham or cheese for an Italian-style sandwich.

This basic dough can be used for other recipes, such as pizza. The dough may be frozen before it is baked, and thawed before filling.

1 ▲ **For focaccia:** Warm a mixing bowl by swirling some hot water in it. Drain. Place the yeast in the bowl, and pour on the warm water. Stir in the sugar, mix with a fork, and allow to stand until the yeast has dissolved and starts to foam, 5–10 minutes.

Working with yeast
Easy-blend (or fast-action) is the most readily available dried yeast. Unlike ordinary dried yeast, there is no need to mix it with liquid. Just combine it with the flour and other dry ingredients and then add the warm liquids.

If using fresh yeast, allow ½ oz (15 g) to each 1 tablespoon dried. Crumble it into a small bowl, add warm liquid and mash with a fork until blended.

If you are in any doubt about the freshness of ordinary dried or fresh yeast, set the mixture aside in a warm place; after 10 minutes or so it should be foamy.

2 ▲ Use a wooden spoon to mix in the salt and about one-third of the flour. Mix in another third of the flour, stirring with the spoon until the dough forms a mass and begins to pull away from the sides of the bowl.

3 ▲ Sprinkle some of the remaining flour onto a smooth work surface. Remove the dough from the bowl and begin to knead it, working in the remaining flour a little at a time. Knead for 8–10 minutes. By the end the dough should be elastic and smooth. Form it into a ball.

4 Lightly oil a mixing bowl. Place the dough in the bowl. Stretch a damp dish towel or clear film across the top of the bowl, and leave it to stand in a warm place until the dough has doubled in volume, about 40–50 minutes or more, depending on the type of yeast used. To test whether the dough has risen enough, poke two fingers into the dough. If the indentations remain, the dough is ready to use.

5 ▲ Punch the dough down with your fist to release the air. Knead for 1–2 minutes.

6 ▲ Brush a tin with oil. Press the dough into the tin with your fingers to a layer 2 cm/1 inch thick. Cover and leave to rise for 30 minutes. Preheat the oven. Make indentations all over the focaccia with your fingers. Brush with oil, add filling and bake until pale golden brown.

7 ▲ **For bread sticks:** There's no need for the first rising. Divide dough into walnut-size pieces and roll out on a floured surface with your hands, into thin sausage shapes. Transfer to a greased baking tray, cover and leave in a warm place for 10–15 minutes. Bake until crisp.

BISCUITS & BARS

KEEP THE BISCUIT TIN FILLED WITH THIS WONDERFUL ARRAY OF BISCUITS AND BARS – SOME SOFT AND CHEWY, SOME CRUNCHY AND NUTTY, SOME RICH AND SINFUL, AND SOME PLAIN AND WHOLESOME. ALL ARE IRRESISTIBLE.

Farmhouse Biscuits

Makes 18

4 oz (115 g) butter or margarine, at room temperature

3¹/₂ oz (100 g) light brown sugar

2¹/₂ oz (70 g) crunchy peanut butter

1 egg

2 oz (55 g) plain flour

¹/₂ tsp baking powder

¹/₂ tsp ground cinnamon

¹/₈ tsp salt

6 oz (170 g) muesli

2 oz (55 g) raisins

2 oz (55 g) chopped walnuts

1 Preheat a 350°F/180°C/Gas 4 oven. Grease a baking sheet.

2 With an electric mixer, cream the butter or margarine and sugar until light and fluffy. Beat in the peanut butter. Beat in the egg.

3 ▲ Sift the flour, baking powder, cinnamon and salt over the peanut butter mixture and stir to blend. Stir in the muesli, raisins and walnuts. Taste the mixture to see if it needs more sugar, as muesli varies.

4 ▲ Drop rounded tablespoonfuls of the mixture onto the prepared baking sheet about 1 in (2.5 cm) apart. Press gently with the back of a spoon to spread each mound into a circle.

5 Bake until lightly coloured, about 15 minutes. With a metal spatula, transfer to a rack to cool. Store in an airtight container.

Crunchy Oatmeal Biscuits

MAKES 14

6 oz (170 g) butter or margarine, at room temperature

6 oz (170 g) caster sugar

1 egg yolk

6 oz (170 g) plain flour

1 tsp bicarbonate of soda

¹/₂ tsp salt

2 oz (55 g) rolled oats

2 oz (55 g) small crunchy nugget cereal

1 ▲ With an electric mixer, cream the butter or margarine and sugar together until light and fluffy. Mix in the egg yolk.

2 Sift over the flour, bicarbonate of soda and salt, then stir into the butter mixture. Add the oats and cereal and stir to blend. Refrigerate for at least 20 minutes.

3 Preheat a 375°F/190°C/Gas 5 oven. Grease a baking sheet.

4 ▲ Roll the mixture into balls. Place them on the sheet and flatten with the bottom of a floured glass.

5 Bake until golden, 10–12 minutes. With a metal spatula, transfer to a rack to cool completely. Store in an airtight container.

~ VARIATION ~

For Nutty Oatmeal Biscuits, substitute an equal quantity of chopped walnuts or pecans for the cereal, and prepare as described.

Farmhouse Biscuits (top), Crunchy Oatmeal Biscuits

Oaty Coconut Biscuits

MAKES 48

6 oz (170 g) quick-cooking oats

3 oz (85 g) desiccated coconut

8 oz (225 g) butter or margarine, at room temperature

4 oz (115 g) caster sugar + 2 tbsp

2 oz (55 g) dark brown sugar

2 eggs

4 tbsp milk

1½ tsp vanilla essence

4 oz (115 g) plain flour

½ tsp bicarbonate of soda

½ tsp salt

1 tsp ground cinnamon

1 Preheat a 400°F/200°C/Gas 6 oven. Lightly grease 2 baking sheets.

2 ▲ Spread the oats and coconut on an ungreased baking sheet. Bake until golden brown, 8–10 minutes, stirring occasionally.

3 With an electric mixer, cream the butter or margarine and both sugars until light and fluffy. Beat in the eggs, 1 at a time, then the milk and vanilla. Sift over the dry ingredients and fold in. Stir in the oats and coconut.

4 ▼ Drop spoonfuls of the mixture 1–2 in (2.5–5 cm) apart on the prepared sheets and flatten with the bottom of a greased glass dipped in sugar. Bake until golden, 8–10 minutes. Transfer to a rack to cool.

Crunchy Jumbles

MAKES 36

4 oz (115 g) butter or margarine, at room temperature

8 oz (225 g) caster sugar

1 egg

1 tsp vanilla essence

5 oz (140 g) plain flour

½ tsp bicarbonate of soda

⅛ tsp salt

2 oz (55 g) crisped rice cereal

6 oz (170 g) chocolate chips

~ VARIATION ~

For even crunchier biscuits, add 2 oz (55 g) walnuts, coarsely chopped, with the cereal and chocolate chips.

1 Preheat a 350°F/180°C/Gas 4 oven. Lightly grease 2 baking sheets.

2 ▲ With an electric mixer, cream the butter or margarine and sugar until light and fluffy. Beat in the egg and vanilla. Sift over the flour, bicarbonate of soda and salt and fold in carefully.

3 ▼ Add the cereal and chocolate chips. Stir to mix thoroughly.

4 Drop spoonfuls of the mixture 1–2 in (2.5–5 cm) apart on the sheets. Bake until golden, 10–12 minutes. Transfer to a rack to cool.

Oaty Coconut Biscuits (top), Crunchy Jumbles

Ginger Biscuits

MAKES 36

8 oz (225 g) caster sugar
3¹/₂ oz (100 g) light brown sugar
4 oz (115 g) butter, at room temperature
4 oz (115 g) margarine, at room temperature
1 egg
3 fl oz (85 ml) black treacle
9 oz (250 g) plain flour
2 tsp ground ginger
¹/₂ tsp grated nutmeg
1 tsp ground cinnamon
2 tsp bicarbonate of soda
¹/₂ tsp salt

1 Preheat a 325°F/170°C/Gas 3 oven. Line 2–3 baking sheets with greaseproof paper and grease lightly.

2 ▲ With an electric mixer, cream half of the caster sugar, the brown sugar, butter and margarine until light and fluffy. Add the egg and continue beating to blend well. Add the treacle.

3 ▲ Sift the flour, spices and bicarbonate of soda 3 times, then stir into the butter mixture. Refrigerate for 30 minutes.

4 ▲ Place the remaining sugar in a shallow dish. Roll tablespoonfuls of the biscuit mixture into balls, then roll the balls in the sugar to coat.

5 Place the balls 2 in (5 cm) apart on the prepared sheets and flatten slightly. Bake until golden around the edges but soft in the middle, 12–15 minutes. Let stand for 5 minutes before transferring to a rack to cool.

~ VARIATION ~

To make Gingerbread Men, increase the amount of flour by 1 oz (30 g). Roll out the mixture and cut out shapes with a special cutter. Decorate with icing, if wished.

Orange Biscuits

MAKES 30

4 oz (115 g) butter, at room temperature
7 oz (200 g) sugar
2 egg yolks
1 tablespoon fresh orange juice
grated rind of 1 large orange
7 oz (200 g) plain flour
1 tablespoon cornflour
1/2 teaspoon salt
1 teaspoon baking powder

1 ▲ With an electric mixer, cream the butter and sugar until light and fluffy. Add the yolks, orange juice and rind, and continue beating to blend. Set aside.

2 In another bowl, sift together the flour, cornflour, salt and baking powder. Add to the butter mixture and stir until it forms a dough.

3 ▲ Wrap the dough in greaseproof paper and refrigerate for 2 hours.

4 Preheat the oven to 375°F/190°C/ Gas 5. Grease 2 baking sheets.

5 ▲ Roll spoonfuls of the dough into balls and place 1–2 in (2.5–5 cm) apart on the prepared sheets.

6 ▼ Press down with a fork to flatten. Bake until golden brown, 8–10 minutes. With a metal palette knife transfer to a rack to cool.

Cinnamon-Coated Cookies

MAKES 30

4 oz (115 g) butter, at room temperature
12 oz (350 g) caster sugar
1 tsp vanilla essence
2 eggs
2 fl oz (65 ml) milk
14 oz (400 g) plain flour
1 tsp bicarbonate of soda
2 oz (55 g) finely chopped walnuts
FOR THE COATING
5 tbsp sugar
2 tbsp ground cinnamon

1 Preheat a 375°F/190°C/Gas 5 oven. Grease 2 baking sheets.

2 With an electric mixer, cream the butter until light. Add the sugar and vanilla and continue mixing until fluffy. Beat in the eggs, then the milk.

3 ▲ Sift the flour and bicarbonate of soda over the butter mixture and stir to blend. Stir in the nuts. Refrigerate for 15 minutes.

4 ▲ For the coating, mix the sugar and cinnamon. Roll tablespoonfuls of the mixture into walnut-size balls. Roll the balls in the sugar mixture. You may need to work in batches.

5 Place 2 in (5 cm) apart on the prepared sheets and flatten slightly. Bake until golden, about 10 minutes. Transfer to a rack to cool.

Chewy Chocolate Biscuits

MAKES 18

4 egg whites
10 oz (285 g) icing sugar
4 oz (115 g) cocoa powder
2 tbsp plain flour
1 tsp instant coffee
1 tbsp water
4 oz (115 g) finely chopped walnuts

1 Preheat a 350°F/180°C/Gas 4 oven. Line 2 baking sheets with greaseproof paper and grease the paper.

~ VARIATION ~

If wished, add 3 oz (85 g) chocolate chips to the mixture with the nuts.

2 With an electric mixer, beat the egg whites until frothy.

3 ▼ Sift the sugar, cocoa, flour and coffee into the whites. Add the water and continue beating on low speed to blend, then on high for a few minutes until the mixture thickens. With a rubber spatula, fold in the walnuts.

4 ▲ Place generous spoonfuls of the mixture 1 in (2.5 cm) apart on the prepared sheets. Bake until firm and cracked on top but soft on the inside, 12–15 minutes. With a metal spatula, transfer to a rack to cool.

Cinnamon-Coated Cookies (top), Chewy Chocolate Biscuits

Chocolate Pretzels

MAKES 28

5 oz (140 g) plain flour
1/8 teaspoon salt
3/4 oz (25 g) unsweetened cocoa powder
4 oz (115 g) butter, at room temperature
4 1/2 oz (125 g) sugar
1 egg
1 egg white, lightly beaten, for glazing
sugar crystals, for sprinkling

1 Sift together the flour, salt and cocoa powder. Set aside. Grease 2 baking sheets.

2 ▲ With an electric mixer, cream the butter until light. Add the sugar and continue beating until light and fluffy. Beat in the egg. Add the dry ingredients and stir to blend. Gather the dough into a ball, wrap in clear film, and refrigerate for 1 hour or freeze for 30 minutes.

3 ▲ Roll the dough into 28 small balls. Refrigerate the balls until needed. Preheat the oven to 375°F/ 190°C/Gas 5.

4 ▲ Roll each ball into a rope about 10 in (25 cm) long. With each rope, form a loop with the two ends facing you. Twist the ends and fold back on to the circle, pressing in to make a pretzel shape. Place on the sheets.

5 ▲ Brush the pretzels with the egg white. Sprinkle sugar crystals over the tops and bake until firm, 10–12 minutes. Transfer to a rack to cool.

Cream Cheese Spirals

MAKES 32

8 oz (225 g) butter, at room temperature

8 oz (225 g) cream cheese

2 tsp caster sugar

8 oz (225 g) plain flour

1 egg white beaten with 1 tbsp water, for glazing

caster sugar, for sprinkling

FOR THE FILLING

4 oz (115 g) finely chopped walnuts

4 oz (115 g) light brown sugar

1 tsp ground cinnamon

1 With an electric mixer, cream the butter, cream cheese and sugar until soft. Sift over the flour and mix until combined. Gather into a ball and divide in half. Flatten each half, wrap in greaseproof paper and refrigerate for at least 30 minutes.

2 Meanwhile, make the filling. Mix together the chopped walnuts, the brown sugar and the cinnamon and set aside.

3 Preheat a 375°F/190°C/Gas 5 oven. Grease 2 baking sheets.

4 ▲ Working with one half of the mixture at a time, roll out thinly into a circle about 11 in (28 cm) in diameter. Trim the edges with a knife, using a dinner plate as a guide.

5 ▼ Brush the surface with the egg white glaze and then sprinkle evenly with half the filling.

6 Cut the circle into quarters, and each quarter into 4 sections, to form 16 triangles.

7 ▲ Starting from the base of the triangles, roll up to form spirals.

8 Place on the sheets and brush with the remaining glaze. Sprinkle with caster sugar. Bake until golden, 15–20 minutes. Cool on a rack.

Vanilla Crescents

MAKES 36

6 oz (175 g) unblanched almonds

4 oz (115 g) plain flour

pinch of salt

8 oz (225 g) unsalted butter

4 oz (115 g) granulated sugar

1 teaspoon vanilla essence

icing sugar for dusting

1 Grind the almonds with a few tablespoons of the flour in a food processor, blender or nut grinder.

2 Sift the remaining flour with the salt into a bowl. Set aside.

3 With an electric mixer, cream together the butter and sugar until light and fluffy.

4 ▼ Add the almonds, vanilla essence and the flour mixture. Stir to mix well. Gather the dough into a ball, wrap in greaseproof paper, and chill for at least 30 minutes.

5 Preheat the oven to 325°F/170°C/ Gas 3. Lightly grease two baking sheets.

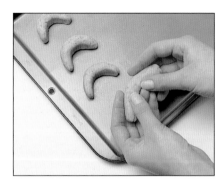

6 ▲ Break off walnut-size pieces of dough and roll into small cylinders about $1/2$ in (1 cm) in diameter. Bend into small crescents and place on the prepared baking sheets.

7 Bake for about 20 minutes until dry but not brown. Transfer to a wire rack to cool only slightly. Set the rack over a baking sheet and dust with an even layer of icing sugar. Leave to cool completely.

Walnut Crescents

MAKES 72

4 oz (115 g) walnuts

8 oz (225 g) unsalted butter

4 oz (115 g) granulated sugar

$1/2$ teaspoon vanilla extract

8 oz (225 g) flour

$1/4$ teaspoon salt

confectioners' sugar for dusting

1 Preheat the oven to 350°F/ 180°C/Gas 4.

2 Grind the walnuts in a food processor, blender or nut grinder until they are almost a paste. Transfer to a bowl.

3 Add the butter to the walnuts and mix with a wooden spoon until blended. Add the granulated sugar and vanilla and stir to blend.

4 ▼ Sift the flour and salt into the walnut mixture. Work into a dough.

5 Shape the dough into small cylinders about $1^{1}/2$ in (4 cm) long. Bend into crescents and place evenly spaced on an ungreased baking sheet.

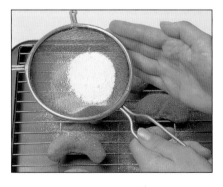

6 ▲ Bake until lightly browned, about 15 minutes. Transfer to a rack to cool only slightly. Set the rack over a baking sheet and dust lightly with confectioners' sugar.

Vanilla Crescents (top), Walnut Crescents

Pecan Puffs

MAKES 24

4 oz (115 g) unsalted butter

2 tablespoons granulated sugar

pinch of salt

1 teaspoon vanilla essence

4 oz (115 g) pecans

4 oz (115 g) plain flour, sifted

icing sugar for dusting

1 Preheat the oven to 300°F/150°C/ Gas 2. Grease two baking sheets.

2 ▲ Cream the butter and sugar until light and fluffy. Stir in the salt and vanilla essence.

3 Grind the nuts in a food processor, blender or nut grinder. Stir several times to prevent nuts becoming oily. If necessary, grind in batches.

4 ▲ Push the ground nuts through a sieve set over a bowl to aerate them. Pieces too large to go through the sieve can be ground again.

5 ▲ Stir the nuts and flour into the butter mixture to make a firm, springy dough.

6 Roll the dough into marble-size balls between the palms of your hands. Place on the prepared baking sheets and bake for 45 minutes.

7 ▲ While the puffs are still hot, roll them in icing sugar. Leave to cool completely, then roll once more in icing sugar.

Pecan Tassies

MAKES 24

4 oz (115 g) cream cheese
4 oz (115 g) butter
4 oz (115 g) plain flour
FOR THE FILLING
2 eggs
4 oz (115 g) dark brown sugar
1 teaspoon vanilla essence
pinch of salt
2 tablespoons butter, melted
4 oz (115 g) pecans

1 Place a baking sheet in the oven and preheat to 350°F/180°C/Gas 4. Grease 24 mini-muffin tins.

2 Chop the cream cheese and butter into cubes. Put them in a mixing bowl. Sift over half the flour and mix. Add the remaining flour and continue mixing to form a dough.

3 ▲ Roll out the dough thinly. With a floured fluted pastry cutter, stamp out 24 2½ in/7 cm rounds. Line the tins with the rounds and chill.

~ **VARIATION** ~

To make Jam Tassies, fill the cream cheese pastry shells with raspberry or blackberry jam, or other fruit jams. Bake as described.

4 To make the filling, lightly whisk the eggs in a bowl. Gradually whisk in the brown sugar, and add the vanilla essence, salt and butter. Set aside until required.

5 ▼ Reserve 24 undamaged pecan halves and chop the rest coarsely with a sharp knife.

6 ▲ Place a spoonful of chopped nuts in each muffin tin and cover with the filling. Set a pecan half on the top of each.

7 Bake on the hot baking sheet for about 20 minutes, until puffed and set. Transfer to a wire rack to cool. Serve at room temperature.

Lady Fingers

MAKES 18

3¹/₂ oz (90 g) plain flour

pinch of salt

4 eggs, separated

4 oz (115 g) granulated sugar

¹/₂ teaspoon vanilla essence

icing sugar for sprinkling

1 Preheat the oven to 300°F/150°C/ Gas 2. Grease 2 baking sheets, then coat lightly with flour, and shake off the excess.

2 Sift the flour and salt together twice in a bowl.

> ~ COOK'S TIP ~
>
> To make the biscuits all the same length, mark parallel lines 4 in (10 cm) apart on the greased baking sheets.

3 With an electric mixer beat the egg yolks with half of the sugar until thick enough to leave a ribbon trail when the beaters are lifted.

4 ▲ In another bowl, beat the egg whites until stiff. Beat in the remaining sugar until glossy.

5 Sift the flour over the yolks and spoon a large dollop of egg whites over the flour. Carefully fold in with a large metal spoon, adding the vanilla essence. Gently fold in the remaining whites.

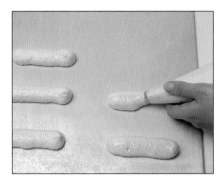

6 ▲ Spoon the mixture into a piping bag fitted with a large plain nozzle. Pipe 4 in (10 cm) long lines on the prepared baking sheets about 1 in (2.5 cm) apart. Sift over a layer of icing sugar. Turn the sheet upside down to dislodge any excess sugar.

7 Bake for about 20 minutes until crusty on the outside but soft in the centre. Cool slightly on the baking sheets before transferring to a wire rack to cool completely.

Walnut Cookies

MAKES 60

4 oz (115 g) butter or margarine

6 oz (175 g) caster sugar

4 oz (115 g) plain flour

2 teaspoons vanilla essence

4 oz (115 g) walnuts, finely chopped

> ~ VARIATION ~
>
> To make Almond Cookies, use an equal amount of finely chopped unblanched almonds instead of walnuts. Replace half the vanilla with ¹/₂ teaspoon almond essence.

1 Preheat the oven to 300°F/150°C/ Gas 2. Grease 2 baking sheets.

2 ▲ With an electric mixer, cream the butter or margarine until soft. Add 2 oz (50 g) of the sugar and continue beating until light and fluffy. Stir in the flour, vanilla essence and walnuts.

3 Drop teaspoonfuls of the batter 1–2 in (2.5–5 cm) apart on the prepared baking sheets and flatten slightly. Bake for about 25 minutes.

4 ▼ Transfer to a wire rack set over a baking sheet and sprinkle with the remaining sugar.

Lady Fingers (top), Walnut Cookies

Italian Almond Biscotti

MAKES 48

7 oz (200 g) whole unblanched almonds
7¹/₂ oz (215 g) plain flour
3¹/₂ oz (100 g) sugar
¹/₈ teaspoon salt
¹/₈ teaspoon saffron powder
¹/₂ teaspoon bicarbonate of soda
2 eggs
1 egg white, lightly beaten

~ COOK'S TIP ~

Serve biscotti after a meal, for dunking in glasses of sweet white wine, such as an Italian *Vin Santo* or a French *Muscat de Beaumes-de-Venise*.

1 Preheat a 375°F/190°C/Gas 5 oven. Grease and flour 2 baking sheets.

2 ▲ Spread the almonds in a baking tray and bake until lightly browned, about 15 minutes. When cool, grind 2 oz (55 g) of the almonds in a food processor, blender, or coffee grinder until pulverized. Coarsely chop the remaining almonds in 2 or 3 pieces each. Set aside.

3 ▲ Combine the flour, sugar, salt, saffron, bicarbonate of soda and ground almonds in a bowl and mix to blend. Make a well in the centre and add the eggs. Stir to form a rough dough. Transfer to a floured surface and knead until well blended. Knead in the chopped almonds.

4 ▲ Divide the dough into 3 equal parts. Roll into logs about 1 in (2.5 cm) in diameter. Place on one of the prepared sheets, brush with the egg white and bake for 20 minutes. Remove from the oven.

5 ▲ With a very sharp knife, cut into each log at an angle making ¹/₂ in (1 cm) slices. Return the slices on the baking sheets to a 275°F/140°C/ Gas 1 oven and bake for 25 minutes more. Transfer to a rack to cool.

Christmas Cookies

_____ butter, at room

_____ sugar

_____

_____

_____ NAL)

coloured icing and small decorations

1 Preheat a 350°F/180°C/Gas 4 oven.

2 ▲ With an electric mixer, cream the butter until soft. Add the sugar gradually and continue beating until light and fluffy.

3 ▲ Using a wooden spoon, slowly mix in the whole egg and the egg yolk. Add the vanilla, lemon rind and salt. Stir to mix well.

4 Add the flour and stir until blended. Gather the mixture into a ball, wrap in greaseproof paper, and refrigerate for at least 30 minutes.

5 ▼ On a floured surface, roll out the mixture about ⅛ in (3 mm) thick.

6 ▲ Stamp out shapes or rounds with biscuit cutters.

7 Bake until lightly coloured, about 8 minutes. Transfer to a rack and let cool completely before icing and decorating, if wished.

Toasted Oat Meringues

MAKES 12

2 oz (55 g) rolled oats
2 egg whites
1/8 tsp salt
1 1/2 tsp cornflour
6 oz (170 g) caster sugar

1 Preheat a 275°F/140°C/Gas 1 oven. Spread the oats on a baking sheet and toast in the oven until golden, about 10 minutes. Lower the heat to 250°F/130°C/Gas 1/2. Grease and flour a baking sheet.

~ **VARIATION** ~

Add 1/2 teaspoon ground cinnamon with the oats, and fold in gently.

2 ▼ With an electric mixer, beat the egg whites and salt until they start to form soft peaks.

3 Sift over the cornflour and continue beating until the whites hold stiff peaks. Add half the sugar and whisk until glossy.

4 ▲ Add the r_____ ____ fold in, then fol___ _ oats.

5 Gently spoon the mixture onto the prepared sheet and bake for 2 hours.

6 When done, turn off the oven. Lift the meringues from the sheet, turn over, and set in another place on the sheet to prevent sticking. Leave in the oven as it cools down.

Meringues

MAKES 24

4 egg whites
1/8 tsp salt
10 oz (285 g) caster sugar
1/2 tsp vanilla or almond essence (optional)
8 fl oz (250 ml) whipped cream (optional)

1 Preheat a 225°F/110°C/Gas 1/4 oven. Grease and flour 2 large baking sheets.

2 With an electric mixer, beat the egg whites and salt in a very clean metal bowl on low speed. When they start to form soft peaks, add half the sugar and continue beating until the mixture holds stiff peaks.

3 ▲ With a large metal spoon, fold in the remaining sugar and vanilla or almond essence, if using.

4 ▼ Pipe the meringue mixture or gently spoon it on the prepared sheet.

5 Bake for 2 hours. Turn off the oven. Loosen the meringues, invert, and set in another place on the sheets to prevent sticking. Leave in the oven as it cools. Serve sandwiched with whipped cream, if wished.

Toasted Oat Meringues (top), Meringues

coloured or demerara sugar, for
sprinkling

2 ▲ With an electric mixer, cream
the butter or margarine, caster sugar
and vanilla together until the mixture
is light and fluffy. Add the egg and
beat to mix well.

refrigerate at least 30 minutes, or
overnight.

4 ▲ Preheat a 350°F/180°C/Gas 4
oven. Roll out the dough on a lightly
floured surface to ⅛ in (3 mm)
thickness. Cut into rounds or other
shapes with biscuit cutters.

5 ▲ Transfer the biscuits to
ungreased baking trays. Sprinkle each
one with coloured or demerara sugar.

6 Bake until golden brown, for about
10–12 minutes. With a slotted spatula,
transfer the biscuits to a wire rack and
let cool.

Chocolate Chip Nut Biscuits

MAKES 36

4 oz (115 g) plain flour
1 tsp baking powder
¼ tsp salt
3 oz (85 g) butter or margarine, at room temperature
4 oz (115 g) caster sugar
1¾ oz (50 g) light brown sugar
1 egg
1 tsp vanilla essence
4½ oz (130 g) chocolate chips
2 oz (55 g) hazelnuts, chopped

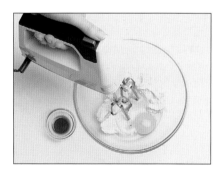

1 ▲ Preheat a 350°F/180°C/Gas 4 oven. Grease 2–3 baking trays.

2 Sift the flour, baking powder and salt into a small bowl. Set aside.

3 ▲ With an electric mixer, cream the butter or margarine and sugars together. Beat in the egg and vanilla.

4 Add the flour mixture and beat well with the mixer on low speed.

5 ▼ Stir in the chocolate chips and half of the hazelnuts using a wooden spoon.

6 Drop teaspoonfuls of the mixture onto the prepared baking trays, to form ¾ in (2 cm) mounds. Space the biscuits 1–2 in (2–5 cm) apart.

7 ▲ Flatten each biscuit lightly with a wet fork. Sprinkle the remaining hazelnuts on top of the biscuits and press lightly into the surface.

8 Bake until golden brown, about 10–12 minutes. With a slotted spatula, transfer the biscuits to a wire rack and let cool.

paper and grease the paper.

2 ▼ Melt the chocolate in the top of a double boiler, or in a heatproof bowl set over a pan of hot water.

slightly. Brush each ball with a little water and sift over a thin layer of icing sugar. Bake until just firm, about 20–25 minutes. With a metal spatula, transfer to a rack to cool.

4 ▲ In a mixing bowl, whisk the egg whites until they form soft peaks. Fold in the sugar, vanilla and almond essence, ground almonds and cooled melted chocolate. Refrigerate for 15 minutes.

~ VARIATION ~

For Chocolate Pine Nut Macaroons, spread 3 oz (85 g) pine nuts in a shallow dish. Press the chocolate macaroon balls into the nuts to cover one side and bake as described, nut-side up.

Coconut Macaroons

MAKES 24

1½ oz (45 g) plain flour

⅛ tsp salt

8 oz (225 g) desiccated coconut

5½ fl oz (170 ml) sweetened condensed milk

1 tsp vanilla essence

1 Preheat a 350°F/180°C/Gas 4 oven. Grease 2 baking sheets.

2 Sift the flour and salt into a bowl. Stir in the coconut.

3 ▲ Pour in the milk. Add the vanilla and stir from the centre to make a very thick mixture.

4 ▼ Drop heaped tablespoonfuls of mixture 1 in (2.5 cm) apart on the sheets. Bake until golden brown, about 20 minutes. Cool on a rack.

Chocolate Macaroons (top), Coconut Macaroons

processor, blender or nut grinder. If necessary, grind in batches.

2 Preheat the oven to 425°F/220°C/ Gas 7. Grease 2 baking sheets.

using a metal spoon. With an electric mixer, cream them together until light and fluffy.

5 ▲ Working in small batches, drop tablespoonfuls of the mixture 3 in (7.5 cm) apart on one of the prepared sheets. With the back of a spoon, spread out into thin, almost transparent circles about 6 cm (2½ in) in diameter. Sprinkle each circle with some of the slivered almonds.

6 Bake until the outer edges have browned slightly, about 4 minutes.

7 ▲ Remove from the oven. With a metal spatula, quickly drape the biscuits over a rolling pin to form a curved shape. Transfer to a rack when firm. If the biscuits harden too quickly to shape, reheat briefly. Repeat the baking and shaping process until the mixture is used up. Store in an airtight container.

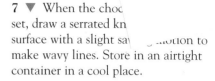
Florentines

MAKES 36

1¹/₂ oz (45 g) butter
4 fl oz (125 ml) whipping cream
4¹/₂ oz (125 g) sugar
4¹/₂ oz (125 g) flaked almonds
2 oz (55 g) orange or mixed peel, finely chopped
1¹/₂ oz (45 g) glacé cherries, chopped
2¹/₂ oz (70 g) plain flour, sifted
8 oz (225 g) plain chocolate
1 teaspoon vegetable oil

1 Preheat the oven to 350°F/180°C/ Gas 4. Grease 2 baking sheets.

2 ▲ Melt the butter, cream and sugar together and slowly bring to the boil. Take off the heat and stir in the almonds, orange or mixed peel, cherries and flour until blended.

3 Drop teaspoonfuls of the batter 1–2 in (2.5–5 cm) apart on the prepared sheets and flatten with a fork.

4 Bake until the cookies brown at the edges, about 10 minutes. Remove from the oven and correct the shape by quickly pushing in any thin uneven edges with a knife or a round biscuit cutter. Work fast or they will cool and harden while still on the sheets. If necessary, return to the oven for a few moments to soften. While still hot, use a metal palette knife to transfer the florentines to a clean, flat surface.

5 Melt the chocolate in the top of a double boiler or in a heatproof bowl set over a pan of hot water. Add the oil and stir to blend.

6 ▲ With a metal palette knife, spread the smooth underside of the cooled florentines with a thin coating of the melted chocolate.

7 ▼ When the choc... set, draw a serrated kn... surface with a slight sa... ...otion to make wavy lines. Store in an airtight container in a cool place.

2 With a sharp knife, chop the almonds as fine as possible. Alternatively, use a food processor, blender, or coffee grinder to chop the nuts very fine.

4 Drop teaspoonfuls $2^{1}/_{2}$ in (6 cm) apart on the prepared sheets. Bake until golden, about 5 minutes. Cool on the baking sheets briefly, just until the wafers are stiff enough to remove.

transfer to a rack to cool completely.

Oatmeal Lace Rounds

MAKES 36

$5^{1}/_{2}$ oz (150 g) butter or margarine
$4^{1}/_{2}$ oz (125 g) quick-cooking porridge oats
$5^{3}/_{4}$ oz (165 g) dark brown sugar
$5^{1}/_{4}$ oz (150 g) caster sugar
$1^{1}/_{2}$ oz (45 g) plain flour
$^{1}/_{4}$ teaspoon salt
1 egg, lightly beaten
1 teaspoon vanilla essence
$2^{1}/_{2}$ oz (70 g) pecans or walnuts, finely chopped

1 Preheat the oven to 350°F/180°C/ Gas 4. Grease 2 baking sheets.

2 Melt the butter in a saucepan over low heat. Set aside.

3 In a mixing bowl, combine the oats, brown sugar, caster sugar, flour and salt.

4 ▲ Make a well in the centre and add the butter or margarine, egg and vanilla.

5 ▼ Mix until blended, then stir in the chopped nuts.

6 Drop rounded teaspoonfuls of the mixture about 2 in (5 cm) apart on the prepared sheets. Bake until lightly browned on the edges and bubbling, 5–8 minutes. Let cool on the sheet for 2 minutes, then transfer to a rack to cool completely.

Nut Lace Wafers (top), Oatmeal Lace Rounds

1 Place the blanched almonds and 3 tablespoons of the flour in a food processor, blender or coffee grinder and process until finely ground. Set aside.

equal parts. Working with one section at a time, roll out to a thickness of ¹/₈ in (3 mm) on a lightly floured surface. With a 2¹/₂ in (6 cm) fluted pastry cutter, stamp out circles. Gather the scraps, roll out and stamp out more circles. Repeat with the remaining sections.

6 ▲ Whisk the egg white with the salt until just frothy. Chop the flaked almonds. Brush only the biscuit rings with the egg white, then sprinkle over the almonds. Bake until very lightly browned, 12–15 minutes. Let cool for a few minutes on the sheets before transferring to a rack.

7 ▲ In a saucepan, melt the jam with the lemon juice until it comes to a simmer. Brush the jam over the biscuit circles and sandwich together with the rings. Store in an airtight container with sheets of greaseproof paper between the layers.

Brandysnaps

MAKES 18

2 oz (55 g) butter, at room temperature
5 oz (140 g) caster sugar
1 rounded tbsp golden syrup
1½ oz (45 g) plain flour
½ tsp ground ginger
FOR THE FILLING
8 fl oz (250 ml) whipping cream
2 tbsp brandy

1 With an electric mixer, cream together the butter and sugar until light and fluffy, then beat in the golden syrup. Sift over the flour and ginger and mix together.

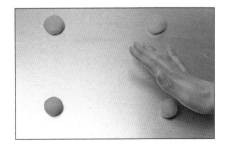

2 ▲ Transfer the mixture to a work surface and knead until smooth. Cover and refrigerate for 30 minutes.

3 Preheat a 375°F/190°C/Gas 5 oven. Grease a baking sheet.

4 ▲ Working in batches of 4, form the mixture into walnut-size balls. Place far apart on the sheet and flatten slightly. Bake until golden and bubbling, about 10 minutes.

5 ▼ Remove from the oven and let cool a few moments. Working quickly, slide a metal spatula under each one, turn over, and wrap around the handle of a wooden spoon (have 4 spoons ready). If they firm up too quickly, reheat for a few seconds to soften. When firm, slide the snaps off and place on a rack to cool.

6 ▲ When all the brandy snaps are cool, prepare the filling. Whip the cream and brandy until soft peaks form. Fill a piping bag with the brandy cream. Pipe into each end of the brandy snaps just before serving.

½ tsp ground cardamom

½ tsp ground cinnamon

½ tsp grated nutmeg

½ tsp ground ginger

½ tsp ground allspice

½ tsp salt

½ tsp freshly ground black pepper

8 oz (225 g) butter or margarine, at room
temperature

3½ oz (100 g) light brown sugar

½ tsp vanilla essence

1 tsp finely grated lemon rind

2 fl oz (65 ml) whipping cream

3 oz (85 g) finely ground almonds

2 tbsp icing sugar

3 With an electric mixer, cream the
butter or margarine and brown sugar
together until light and fluffy. Beat in
the vanilla and lemon rind.

4 ▲ With the mixer on low speed,
add the flour mixture alternately with
the cream, beginning and ending with
flour. Stir in the ground almonds.

5 ▲ Shape the dough into ¾ in
(2 cm) balls. Place them on ungreased
baking trays about 1 in (2.5 cm) apart.
Bake until the biscuits are golden
brown underneath, 15–20 minutes.

6 Let the biscuits cool on the baking
trays about 1 minute before
transferring them to a wire rack to
cool completely. Before serving,
sprinkle them lightly with icing sugar.

Chocolate and Coconut Slices

MAKES 24

6 oz (175 g) digestive biscuits, crushed

2 oz (55 g) caster sugar

⅛ tsp salt

4 oz (115 g) butter or margarine, melted

3 oz (85 g) desiccated coconut

9 oz (260 g) plain chocolate chips

8 fl oz (250 ml) sweetened condensed
milk

4 oz (115 g) chopped walnuts

1 Preheat a 350°F/180°C/Gas 4 oven.

2 ▼ In a bowl, combine the crushed
biscuits, sugar, salt and butter or
margarine. Press the mixture evenly
over the bottom of an ungreased 13 ×
9 in (33 × 23 cm) baking dish.

3 ▲ Sprinkle the coconut over the
biscuit base, then scatter over the
chocolate chips. Pour the condensed
milk evenly over the chocolate.
Sprinkle the walnuts on top.

4 Bake 30 minutes. Unmould
onto a wire rack and let cool,
preferably overnight. When cooled,
cut into slices.

Spicy Pepper Biscuits (top), Chocolate and Coconut Slices

Shortbread

MAKES 8

5¹/₂ oz (150 g) unsalted butter, at room temperature
3¹/₂ oz (100 g) caster sugar
6¹/₄ oz (180 g) plain flour
2 oz (55 g) rice flour
¹/₄ teaspoon baking powder
¹/₈ teaspoon salt

1 Preheat the oven to 325°F/170°C/ Gas 3. Grease a shallow 8 in (20 cm) cake tin, preferably with a removable bottom.

2 With an electric mixer, cream the butter and sugar together until light and fluffy. Sift over the flours, baking powder and salt and mix well.

3 ▲ Press the dough neatly into the prepared tin, smoothing the surface with the back of a spoon.

4 Prick all over with a fork, then score into 8 equal wedges.

5 ▲ Bake until golden, 40–45 minutes. Leave in the tin until cool enough to handle, then turn out and recut the wedges while still hot. Store in an airtight container.

Flapjacks

MAKES 8

2 oz (55 g) butter
1 rounded tablespoon golden syrup
2³/₄ oz (80 g) dark brown sugar
3¹/₂ oz (100 g) quick-cooking porridge oats
¹/₈ teaspoon salt

1 ▲ Preheat a 350°F/180°C/Gas 4 oven. Line an 8 in (20 cm) cake tin with greaseproof paper and grease.

2 ▼ Place the butter, golden syrup and sugar in a saucepan over a low heat. Cook, stirring, until melted and combined.

~ VARIATION ~

If wished, add 1 teaspoon ground ginger to the melted butter.

3 ▲ Remove from the heat and add the oats and salt. Stir to blend.

4 Spoon into the prepared tin and smooth the surface. Place in the centre of the oven and bake until golden brown, 20–25 minutes. Leave in the tin until cool enough to handle, then turn out and cut into wedges while still hot.

Shortbread (top), Flapjacks

Chocolate Delights

MAKES 50

1 oz (30 g) plain chocolate
1 oz (30 g) bitter cooking chocolate
8 oz (225 g) plain flour
¹/₂ tsp salt
8 oz (225 g) unsalted butter, at room temperature
8 oz (225 g) caster sugar
2 eggs
1 tsp vanilla essence
4 oz (115 g) finely chopped walnuts

1 Melt the chocolates in the top of a double boiler, or in a heatproof bowl set over a pan of gently simmering water. Set aside.

2 ▼ In a small bowl, sift together the flour and salt. Set aside.

3 With an electric mixer, cream the butter until soft. Add the sugar and continue beating until the mixture is light and fluffy.

4 Mix the eggs and vanilla, then gradually stir into the butter mixture.

5 ▲ Stir in the chocolate, then the flour. Stir in the nuts.

6 ▲ Divide the mixture into 4 equal parts, and roll each into 2 in (5 cm) diameter logs. Wrap tightly in foil and refrigerate or freeze until firm.

7 Preheat a 375°F/190°C/Gas 5 oven. Grease 2 baking sheets.

8 With a sharp knife, cut the logs into ¹/₄ in (5mm) slices. Place the rounds on the prepared sheets and bake until lightly coloured, about 10 minutes. Transfer to a rack to cool.

> ### ~ VARIATION ~
>
> For two-tone biscuits, melt only half the chocolate. Combine all the ingredients, except the chocolate, as above. Divide the mixture in half. Add the chocolate to one half. Roll out the plain mixture to a flat sheet. Roll out the chocolate mixture, place on top of the plain one and roll up. Wrap, slice and bake as described.

Cinnamon Treats

MAKES 50

9 oz (250 g) plain flour
¹/₂ tsp salt
2 tsp ground cinnamon
8 oz (225 g) unsalted butter, at room temperature
8 oz (225 g) caster sugar
2 eggs
1 tsp vanilla essence

1 In a bowl, sift together the flour, salt and cinnamon. Set aside.

2 ▲ With an electric mixer, cream the butter until soft. Add the sugar and continue beating until the mixture is light and fluffy.

3 Beat the eggs and vanilla, then gradually stir into the butter mixture.

4 ▲ Stir in the dry ingredients.

5 ▲ Divide the mixture into 4 equal parts, then roll each into 2 in (5 cm) diameter logs. Wrap tightly in foil and refrigerate or freeze until firm.

6 Preheat a 375°F/190°C/Gas 5 oven. Grease 2 baking sheets.

7 ▼ With a sharp knife, cut the logs into ¹/₄ in (5 mm) slices. Place the rounds on the prepared sheets and bake until lightly coloured, about 10 minutes. With a metal spatula, transfer to a rack to cool.

Coffee Ice Cream Sandwiches

MAKES 8

4 oz (115 g) butter or margarine, at room temperature

2 oz (55 g) caster sugar

4 oz (115 g) plain flour

2 tbsp instant coffee

icing sugar, for sprinkling

16 fl oz (450 ml) coffee ice cream

2 tbsp cocoa powder, for sprinkling

1 Lightly grease 2–3 baking trays.

2 With an electric mixer or wooden spoon, beat the butter or margarine until soft. Beat in the caster sugar.

3 ▲ Add the flour and coffee and mix by hand to form an evenly blended dough. Wrap in a plastic bag and refrigerate at least 1 hour.

4 Lightly sprinkle the work surface with icing sugar. Knead the dough on the sugared surface for a few minutes to soften it slightly.

5 ▼ Using a rolling pin dusted with icing sugar, roll out the dough to ⅛ in (3 mm) thickness. With a 2½ in (6 cm) fluted pastry cutter, cut out 16 rounds. Transfer the rounds to the prepared baking trays. Refrigerate for at least 30 minutes.

6 Preheat a 300°F/150°C/Gas 2 oven. Bake the biscuits until they are lightly golden, about 30 minutes. Let them cool and firm up before removing them from the trays to a wire rack to cool completely.

7 Remove the ice cream from the freezer and let soften 10 minutes at room temperature.

8 ▲ With a metal spatula, spread the ice cream evenly on the flat side of eight of the biscuits, leaving the edges clear. Top with the remaining biscuits, flat-side down.

9 Arrange the ice cream sandwiches on a baking tray. Cover and freeze at least 1 hour, longer if a firmer sandwich is desired. Sift the cocoa powder over the tops before serving.

Hazelnut Squares

MAKES 9

2 oz (55 g) plain chocolate

2½ oz (70 g) butter or margarine

8 oz (225 g) caster sugar

2 oz (55 g) plain flour

½ tsp baking powder

2 eggs, beaten

½ tsp vanilla essence

4 oz (115 g) skinned hazelnuts, roughly chopped

1 Preheat the oven to 350°F/180°C/ Gas 4. Grease an 8 in (20 cm) square baking tin.

2 ▲ In a heatproof bowl set over a pan of barely simmering water, or in a double boiler, melt the chocolate and butter or margarine. Remove the bowl from the heat.

3 ▲ Add the sugar, flour, baking powder, eggs, vanilla and half the hazelnuts to the melted mixture and stir well with a wooden spoon.

4 ▼ Pour the mixture into the prepared tin. Bake 10 minutes, then sprinkle the reserved hazelnuts over the top. Return to the oven and continue baking until firm to the touch, about 25 minutes.

5 ▲ Let cool in the tin, set on a wire rack, for 10 minutes, then unmould onto the rack and let cool completely. Cut into squares for serving.

Peanut Butter Biscuits

MAKES 24

5 oz (140 g) plain flour

1/2 teaspoon bicarbonate of soda

1/2 teaspoon salt

4 oz (115 g) butter, at room temperature

5³/4 oz (165 g) light brown sugar

1 egg

1 teaspoon vanilla essence

9¹/2 oz (265 g) crunchy peanut butter

1 Sift together the flour, bicarbonate of soda and salt and set aside.

2 With an electric mixer, cream the butter and sugar together until light and fluffy.

3 In another bowl, mix the egg and vanilla, then gradually beat into the butter mixture.

4 ▲ Stir in the peanut butter and blend thoroughly. Stir in the dry ingredients. Refrigerate for at least 30 minutes, or until firm.

5 Preheat the oven to 350°F/180°C/ Gas 4. Grease 2 baking sheets.

6 Spoon out rounded teaspoonfuls of the dough and roll into balls.

7 ▲ Place the balls on the prepared sheets and press flat with a fork into circles about 2¹/2 in (6 cm) in diameter, making a criss-cross pattern. Bake until lightly coloured, 12–15 minutes. Transfer to a rack to cool.

~ VARIATION ~

Add 3 oz (85 g) peanuts, coarsely chopped, with the peanut butter.

Chocolate Chip Cookies

MAKES 24

4 oz (115 g) butter or margarine, at room temperature

1³/4 oz (50 g) caster sugar

3³/4 oz (110 g) dark brown sugar

1 egg

1/2 teaspoon vanilla essence

6 oz (170 g) plain flour

1/2 teaspoon bicarbonate of soda

1/8 teaspoon salt

6 oz (170 g) chocolate chips

2 oz (55 g) walnuts, chopped

1 Preheat the oven to 350°F/180°C/ Gas 4. Grease 2 large baking sheets.

2 ▼ With an electric mixer, cream the butter or margarine and two sugars together until light and fluffy.

3 In another bowl, mix the egg and vanilla, then gradually beat into the butter mixture. Sift over the flour, bicarbonate of soda and salt and stir.

4 ▲ Add the chocolate chips and walnuts, and mix to combine well.

5 Place heaped teaspoonfuls of the dough 2 in (5 cm) apart on the prepared sheets. Bake until lightly coloured, 10–15 minutes. Transfer to a rack to cool.

Peanut Butter Biscuits (top), Chocolate Chip Cookies

Apple-sauce Biscuits

MAKES 36

3½oz (90g) sugar
2oz (50g) butter or vegetable fat, at room temperature
6fl oz (175ml) thick apple sauce
⅛ teaspoon grated lemon rind
4oz (115g) flour
½ teaspoon baking powder
¼ teaspoon bicarbonate of soda
¼ teaspoon salt
½ teaspoon ground cinnamon
½ cup chopped walnuts

~ COOK'S TIP ~
If the apple sauce is runny, put it in a strainer over a bowl and let it drain for 10 minutes.

1 Preheat oven to 190°C/375°F/Gas 5.

2 In a medium bowl, beat together the sugar and butter or vegetable fat until well mixed. Beat in the apple sauce and lemon rind.

3 ▲ Sift the flour, baking powder, bicarbonate of soda, salt and cinnamon into the mixture, and stir to blend. Fold in the chopped walnuts.

4 ▲ Drop teaspoonfuls of the dough on a lightly greased baking sheet, spacing them about 2 in (5 cm) apart.

5 Bake the biscuits in the centre of the oven until they are golden brown, 8–10 minutes. Transfer the biscuits to a wire rack to cool.

Toffee Bars

MAKES 32

1lb (450g) soft light brown sugar, firmly packed
1lb (450g) butter or margarine, at room temperature
2 egg yolks
1½ teaspoons vanilla essence
1lb (450g) plain or wholemeal flour
½ teaspoon salt
4oz (115g) milk chocolate, broken in pieces
4oz (115g) chopped walnuts or pecans

1 Preheat the oven to 180°C/350°F/Gas 4.

2 Beat together the sugar and butter or margarine until light and fluffy. Beat in the egg yolks and vanilla. Stir in the flour and salt.

3 ▼ Spread the dough in a greased 13 × 9 × 2 in (33 × 23 × 5 cm) baking tin. Bake until lightly browned, 25–30 minutes. The texture will be soft.

4 ▲ Remove from the oven and immediately place the chocolate pieces on the hot biscuit base. Let stand until the chocolate softens, then spread it evenly with a spatula. Sprinkle with the nuts.

5 While still warm, cut into bars about 2 × 1½ in (5 × 4 cm).

Apple-sauce Biscuits (top), Toffee Bars

Chocolate Chip Brownies

MAKES 24

4 oz (115 g) plain chocolate
4 oz (115 g) butter
3 eggs
7 oz (200 g) sugar
¹/₂ teaspoon vanilla essence
pinch of salt
5 oz (140 g) plain flour
6 oz (170 g) chocolate chips

1 ▼ Preheat a 350°F/180°C/Gas 4 oven. Line a 13 × 9 in (33 × 23 cm) tin with greaseproof paper and grease.

2 ▲ Melt the chocolate and butter in the top of a double boiler, or in a heatproof bowl set over a pan of gently simmering water.

3 ▲ Beat together the eggs, sugar, vanilla and salt. Stir in the chocolate mixture. Sift over the flour and fold in. Add the chocolate chips.

4 ▲ Pour the mixture into the prepared tin and spread evenly. Bake until just set, about 30 minutes. Do not overbake; the brownies should be slightly moist inside. Cool in the pan.

5 To turn out, run a knife all around the edge and invert onto a baking sheet. Remove the paper. Place another sheet on top and invert again so the brownies are right-side up. Cut into squares for serving.

Marbled Brownies

MAKES 24

8 oz (225 g) plain chocolate
3 oz (85 g) butter
4 eggs
10½ oz (300 g) sugar
5 oz (140 g) plain flour
½ teaspoon salt
1 teaspoon baking powder
2 teaspoons vanilla essence
4 oz (115 g) walnuts, chopped
FOR THE PLAIN MIXTURE
2 oz (55 g) butter, at room temperature
6 oz (170 g) cream cheese
3½ oz (100 g) sugar
2 eggs
1 oz (30 g) plain flour
1 teaspoon vanilla essence

1 Preheat a 350°F/180°C/Gas 4 oven. Line a 13 × 9 in (33 × 23 cm) tin with greaseproof paper and grease.

2 Melt the chocolate and butter over very low heat, stirring constantly. Set aside to cool.

3 Meanwhile, beat the eggs until light and fluffy. Gradually add the sugar and continue beating until blended. Sift over the flour, salt and baking powder and fold to combine.

4 ▲ Stir in the cooled chocolate mixture. Add the vanilla and walnuts. Measure and set aside 16 fl oz (450 ml) of the chocolate mixture.

5 ▲ For the plain mixture, cream the butter and cream cheese with an electric mixer.

6 Add the sugar and continue beating until blended. Beat in the eggs, flour and vanilla.

7 Spread the unmeasured chocolate mixture in the tin. Pour over the plain mixture. Drop spoonfuls of the reserved chocolate mixture on top.

8 ▲ With a metal palette knife, swirl the mixtures to marble. Do not blend completely. Bake until just set, 35–40 minutes. Turn out when cool and cut into squares for serving.

Nutty Chocolate Squares

MAKES 16

2 eggs

2 tsp vanilla essence

1/8 tsp salt

6 oz (170 g) pecan nuts, coarsely chopped

2 oz (55 g) plain flour

2 oz (55 g) caster sugar

4 fl oz (125 ml) golden syrup

3 oz (85 g) plain chocolate, finely chopped

1½ oz (45 g) butter

16 pecan halves, for decorating

1 Preheat a 325°F/170°C/Gas 3 oven. Line the bottom and sides of an 8 in (20 cm) square baking tin with greaseproof paper and grease lightly.

2 ▼ Whisk together the eggs, vanilla and salt. In another bowl, mix together the pecans and flour. Set both aside.

3 In a saucepan, bring the sugar and golden syrup to a boil. Remove from the heat and stir in the chocolate and butter and blend thoroughly with a wooden spoon.

4 ▲ Mix in the beaten eggs, then fold in the pecan mixture.

5 Pour the mixture into the prepared tin and bake until set, about 35 minutes. Cool in the tin for 10 minutes before unmoulding. Cut into 2 in (5 cm) squares and press pecan halves into the tops while warm. Cool completely on a rack.

Raisin Brownies

MAKES 16

4 oz (115 g) butter or margarine

2 oz (55 g) cocoa powder

2 eggs

8 oz (225 g) caster sugar

1 tsp vanilla essence

1½ oz (45 g) plain flour

3 oz (85 g) chopped walnuts

3 oz (85 g) raisins

1 Preheat the oven to 350°F/ 180°C/Gas 4. Line the bottom and sides of an 8 in (20 cm) square baking tin with greaseproof paper and grease the paper.

2 ▼ Gently melt the butter or margarine in a small saucepan. Remove from the heat and stir in the cocoa powder.

3 With an electric mixer, beat the eggs, sugar and vanilla together until light. Add the cocoa mixture and stir to blend.

4 ▲ Sift the flour over the cocoa mixture and gently fold in. Add the walnuts and raisins and scrape the mixture into the prepared tin.

5 Bake in the centre of the oven for 30 minutes. Do not overbake. Leave in the tin to cool before cutting into 2 in (5 cm) squares and removing. The brownies should be soft and moist.

Nutty Chocolate Squares (top), Raisin Brownies

Chocolate Walnut Bars

MAKES 24

2 oz (55 g) walnuts
2¼ oz (60 g) caster sugar
3¾ oz (110 g) plain flour, sifted
3 oz (85 g) cold unsalted butter, cut into pieces
FOR THE TOPPING
1 oz (30 g) unsalted butter
3 fl oz (85 ml) water
1 oz (30 g) unsweetened cocoa powder
3½ oz (100 g) caster sugar
1 teaspoon vanilla essence
⅛ teaspoon salt
2 eggs
icing sugar, for dusting

1 Preheat a 350°F/180°C/Gas 4 oven. Grease the bottom and sides of an 8 in (20 cm) square baking tin.

2 ▼ Grind the walnuts with a few tablespoons of the sugar in a food processor, blender or coffee grinder.

3 In a bowl, combine the ground walnuts, remaining sugar and flour. With your fingertips, rub in the butter until the mixture resembles coarse breadcrumbs. Alternatively, process all the ingredients in a food processor until the mixture resembles coarse breadcrumbs.

4 ▲ Pat the walnut mixture into the bottom of the prepared tin in an even layer. Bake for 25 minutes.

5 ▲ Meanwhile, for the topping, melt the butter with the water. Whisk in the cocoa and sugar. Remove from the heat, stir in the vanilla and salt and let cool for 5 minutes. Whisk in the eggs until blended.

6 ▲ Pour the topping over the crust when baked.

7 Return to the oven and bake until set, about 20 minutes. Set the tin on a rack to cool. Cut into 2½ × 1 in (6 × 2.5 cm) bars and dust with icing sugar. Store in the refrigerator.

Pecan Squares

MAKES 36

8 oz (225 g) plain flour
pinch of salt
4 oz (115 g) granulated sugar
8 oz (225 g) cold butter or margarine, chopped
1 egg
finely grated rind of 1 lemon
FOR THE TOPPING
6 oz (175 g) butter
3 oz (75 g) honey
2 oz (50 g) granulated sugar
4 oz (115 g) dark brown sugar
5 tablespoons whipping cream
1 lb (450 g) pecan halves

1 Preheat the oven to 375°F/190°C/ Gas 5. Lightly grease a 15¹/₂ × 10¹/₂ × 1 in (37 × 27 × 2.5 cm) Swiss roll tin.

2 ▲ Sift the flour and salt into a mixing bowl. Stir in the sugar. Cut and rub in the butter or margarine until the mixture resembles coarse crumbs. Add the egg and lemon rind and blend with a fork until the mixture just holds together.

3 ▼ Spoon the mixture into the prepared tin. With floured fingertips, press into an even layer. Prick the pastry all over with a fork and chill for 10 minutes.

4 Bake the pastry crust for 15 minutes. Remove the tin from the oven, but keep the oven on while making the topping.

5 ▲ To make the topping, melt the butter, honey and both sugars. Bring to the boil. Boil, without stirring, for 2 minutes. Off the heat, stir in the cream and pecans. Pour over the crust, return to the oven and bake for 25 minutes. Leave to cool.

6 When cool, run a knife around the edge. Invert on to a baking sheet, place another sheet on top and invert again. Dip a sharp knife into very hot water and cut into squares for serving.

Figgy Bars

MAKES 48

12 oz (350 g) dried figs
3 eggs
6 oz (170 g) caster sugar
3 oz (85 g) plain flour
1 tsp baking powder
1/2 tsp ground cinnamon
1/4 tsp ground cloves
1/4 tsp grated nutmeg
1/4 tsp salt
3 oz (85 g) finely chopped walnuts
2 tbsp brandy or cognac
icing sugar, for dusting

1 Preheat a 325°F/170°C/Gas 3 oven.

2 Line a 12 × 8 × 1½ in (30 × 20 × 3 cm) tin with greaseproof paper and grease the paper.

3 ▲ With a sharp knife, chop the figs roughly. Set aside.

4 In a bowl, whisk the eggs and sugar until well blended. In another bowl, sift together the dry ingredients, then fold into the egg mixture in several batches.

5 ▼ Stir in the figs, walnuts and brandy or cognac.

6 Scrape the mixture into the prepared tin and bake until the top is firm and brown, 35–40 minutes. It should still be soft underneath.

7 Let cool in the tin for 5 minutes, then unmould and transfer to a sheet of greaseproof paper lightly sprinkled with icing sugar. Cut into bars.

Lemon Bars

MAKES 36

2 oz (55 g) icing sugar
6 oz (170 g) plain flour
1/2 tsp salt
6 oz (170 g) butter, cut in small pieces
FOR THE TOPPING
4 eggs
12 oz (350 g) caster sugar
grated rind of 1 lemon
4 fl oz (125 ml) fresh lemon juice
6 fl oz (175 ml) whipping cream
icing sugar, for dusting

1 Preheat a 325°F/170°C/Gas 3 oven.

2 Grease a 13 × 9 in (33 × 23 cm) baking tin.

3 Sift the sugar, flour and salt into a bowl. With a pastry blender, cut in the butter until the mixture resembles coarse breadcrumbs.

4 ▲ Press the mixture into the bottom of the prepared tin. Bake until golden brown, about 20 minutes.

5 Meanwhile, for the topping, whisk the eggs and sugar together until blended. Add the lemon rind and juice and mix well.

6 ▲ Lightly whip the cream and fold into the egg mixture. Pour over the still warm base, return to the oven, and bake until set, about 40 minutes.

7 Cool completely before cutting into bars. Dust with icing sugar.

Figgy Bars (top), Lemon Bars

Apricot Specials

MAKES 12

3¹/₂ oz (100 g) light brown sugar

3 oz (85 g) plain flour

3 oz (85 g) cold unsalted butter, cut in pieces

FOR THE TOPPING

5 oz (140 g) dried apricots

8 fl oz (250 ml) water

grated rind of 1 lemon

2¹/₂ oz (75 g) caster sugar

2 tsp cornflour

2 oz (55 g) chopped walnuts

1 Preheat a 350°F/180°C/Gas 4 oven.

2 ▲ In a bowl, combine the brown sugar and flour. With a pastry blender, cut in the butter until the mixture resembles coarse breadcrumbs.

3 ▲ Transfer to an 8 in (20 cm) square baking tin and press level. Bake for 15 minutes. Remove from the oven but leave the oven on.

4 Meanwhile, for the topping, combine the apricots and water in a saucepan and simmer until soft, about 10 minutes. Strain the liquid and reserve. Chop the apricots.

5 ▲ Return the apricots to the saucepan and add the lemon rind, caster sugar, cornflour, and 4 tablespoons of the soaking liquid. Cook for 1 minute.

6 ▲ Cool slightly before spreading the topping over the base. Sprinkle over the walnuts and continue baking for 20 minutes more. Let cool in the tin before cutting into bars.

Almond-Topped Squares

MAKES 18

3 oz (75 g) butter
2 oz (50 g) granulated sugar
1 egg yolk
grated rind and juice of ¹/₂ lemon
¹/₂ teaspoon vanilla essence
2 tablespoons whipping cream
4 oz (115 g) plain flour
FOR THE TOPPING
8 oz (225 g) granulated sugar
3 oz (75 g) sliced almonds
4 egg whites
¹/₂ teaspoon ground ginger
¹/₂ teaspoon ground cinnamon

1 ▲ Preheat the oven to 375°F/ 190°C/Gas 5. Line a 13 × 9 in (33 × 23 cm) Swiss roll tin with greaseproof paper and grease the paper.

2 Cream the butter and sugar. Beat in the egg yolk, lemon rind and juice, vanilla essence and cream.

3 ▲ Gradually stir in the flour. Gather into a ball of dough.

4 With lightly floured fingers, press the dough into the prepared tin. Bake for 15 minutes. Remove from the oven but leave the oven on.

5 ▲ To make the topping, combine all the ingredients in a heavy saucepan. Cook, stirring until the mixture comes to the boil.

6 Continue boiling until just golden, about 1 minute. Pour over the dough, spreading evenly.

7 ▲ Return to the oven and bake for about 45 minutes. Remove and score into bars or squares. Cool completely before cutting into squares and serving.

Spiced Raisin Bars

MAKES 30

3³/₄ oz (110 g) plain flour

1¹/₂ teaspoons baking powder

1 teaspoon ground cinnamon

¹/₂ teaspoon grated nutmeg

¹/₄ teaspoon ground cloves

¹/₄ teaspoon ground allspsice

7¹/₂ oz (215 g) raisins

4 oz (115 g) butter or margarine, at room temperature

3¹/₂ oz (100 g) sugar

2 eggs

5³/₄ oz (165 g) molasses

2 oz (55 g) walnuts, chopped

1 Preheat a 350°F/180°C/Gas 4 oven. Line a 13 × 9 in (33 × 23 cm) tin with greaseproof paper and grease.

2 Sift together the flour, baking powder and spices.

3 ▲ Place the raisins in another bowl and toss with a few tablespoons of the flour mixture.

4 ▲ With an electric mixer, cream the butter or margarine and sugar together until light and fluffy. Beat in the eggs, 1 at a time, then the molasses. Stir in the flour mixture, raisins and walnuts.

5 Spread evenly in the tin. Bake until just set, 15–18 minutes. Let cool in the tin before cutting into bars.

Toffee Meringue Bars

MAKES 12

2 oz (55 g) butter

7¹/₂ oz (215 g) dark brown sugar

1 egg

¹/₂ teaspoon vanilla essence

2¹/₂ oz (70 g) plain flour

¹/₂ teaspoon salt

¹/₄ teaspoon grated nutmeg

FOR THE TOPPING

1 egg white

¹/₈ teaspoon salt

1 tablespoon golden syrup

3¹/₂ oz (100 g) caster sugar

2 oz (55 g) walnuts, finely chopped

1 ▲ Combine the butter and brown sugar in a saucepan and heat until bubbling. Set aside to cool.

2 Preheat the oven to 350°F/180°C/ Gas 4. Line the bottom and sides of an 8 in (20 cm) square cake tin with greaseproof paper and grease.

3 Beat the egg and vanilla into cooled sugar mixture. Sift over the flour, salt and nutmeg and fold in. Spread in the bottom of the tin.

4 ▲ For the topping, beat the egg white with the salt until it holds soft peaks. Beat in the golden syrup, then the sugar and continue beating until the mixture holds stiff peaks. Fold in the nuts and spread on top. Bake for 30 minutes. Cut into bars when cool.

Spiced Raisin Bars (top), Toffee Meringue Bars

Strawberry Shortcake

SERVES 6

1 lb (450 g) strawberries, hulled and halved or quartered, depending on size

3 tbsp icing sugar

8 fl oz (250 ml) whipping cream

mint leaves, for garnishing

FOR THE SHORTCAKE

8 oz (225 g) plain flour

3 oz (85 g) caster sugar

1 tbsp baking powder

½ tsp salt

8 fl oz (250 ml) whipping cream

1 Preheat a 400°F/200°C/Gas 6 oven. Lightly grease a baking tray.

2 ▲ For the shortcake, sift the flour into a mixing bowl. Add 2 oz (55 g) of the caster sugar, the baking powder and salt. Stir well.

3 ▲ Gradually add the cream, tossing lightly with a fork until the mixture forms clumps.

4 ▲ Gather the clumps together, but do not knead the dough. Shape the dough into a 6 in (15 cm) log. Cut into 6 slices and place them on the prepared baking tray.

5 ▲ Sprinkle with the remaining 1 oz (30 g) caster sugar. Bake until light golden brown, about 15 minutes. Let cool on a wire rack.

6 ▲ Meanwhile, combine one-quarter of the strawberries with the icing sugar. Mash with a fork. Stir in the remaining strawberries. Let stand 1 hour at room temperature.

7 ▲ In a bowl, whip the cream until soft peaks form.

8 ▲ To serve, slice each shortcake in half horizontally using a serrated knife. Put the bottom halves on individual dessert plates. Top each half with some of the whipped cream. Divide the strawberries among the 6 shortcakes. Replace the tops and garnish with mint. Serve with the remaining whipped cream.

> **~ COOK'S TIP ~**
>
> For best results when whipping cream, refrigerate the bowl and beaters until thoroughly chilled. If using an electric mixer, increase speed gradually, and turn the bowl while beating to incorporate as much air as possible.

BUNS & TEA BREADS

EASY TO MAKE AND SATISFYING TO
EAT, THESE BUNS AND TEA BREADS
WILL FILL THE HOUSE WITH
MOUTHWATERING SCENTS AND LURE
YOUR FAMILY AND FRIENDS TO
LINGER OVER BREAKFAST, COFFEE OR
TEA – AND THEY ARE GREAT FOR
SNACKS OR LUNCH.

Raisin Bran Buns

MAKES 15

2 oz (55 g) butter or margarine
1½ oz (45 g) plain flour
2 oz (55 g) wholewheat flour
1½ tsp bicarbonate of soda
⅛ tsp salt
1 tsp ground cinnamon
1 oz (30 g) bran
3 oz (85 g) raisins
2½ oz (65 g) dark brown sugar
2 oz (55 g) caster sugar
1 egg
8 fl oz (250 ml) buttermilk
juice of ½ lemon

1 Preheat a 400°F/200°C/Gas 6 oven. Grease 15 bun-tray cups.

2 ▲ Place the butter or margarine in a saucepan and melt over gentle heat. Set aside.

3 In a mixing bowl, sift together the flours, bicarbonate of soda, salt and cinnamon.

4 ▲ Add the bran, raisins and sugars and stir until blended.

5 In another bowl, mix together the egg, buttermilk, lemon juice and melted butter.

6 ▲ Add the buttermilk mixture to the dry ingredients and stir lightly and quickly just until moistened; do not mix until smooth.

7 ▲ Spoon the mixture into the prepared bun tray, filling the cups almost to the top. Half-fill any empty cups with water.

8 Bake until golden, 15–20 minutes. Serve warm or at room temperature.

Raspberry Crumble Buns

MAKES 12

6 oz (170 g) plain flour
2 oz (55 g) caster sugar
1¾ oz (50 g) light brown sugar
2 tsp baking powder
⅛ tsp salt
1 tsp ground cinnamon
4 oz (115 g) butter, melted
1 egg
4 fl oz (125 ml) milk
5 oz (140 g) fresh raspberries
grated rind of 1 lemon
FOR THE CRUMBLE TOPPING
1 oz (30 g) finely chopped pecan nuts or walnuts
2 oz (55 g) dark brown sugar
3 tbsp plain flour
1 tsp ground cinnamon
3 tbsp butter, melted

1 Preheat a 350°F/180°C/Gas 4 oven. Lightly grease a 12-cup bun tray or use paper cases.

2 Sift the flour into a bowl. Add the sugars, baking powder, salt and cinnamon and stir to blend.

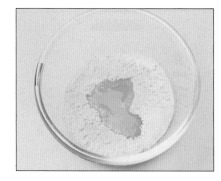

3 ▲ Make a well in the centre. Place the butter, egg and milk in the well and mix until just combined. Stir in the raspberries and lemon rind. Spoon the mixture into the prepared bun tray, filling the cups almost to the top.

4 ▼ For the crumble topping, mix the nuts, dark brown sugar, flour and cinnamon in a bowl. Add the melted butter and stir to blend.

5 ▲ Spoon some of the crumble over each bun. Bake until browned, about 25 minutes. Transfer to a rack to cool slightly. Serve warm.

Carrot Buns

MAKES 12

6 oz (170 g) margarine, at room temperature

3¹/₂ oz (100 g) dark brown sugar

1 egg, at room temperature

1 tbsp water

8 oz (225 g) carrots, grated

5 oz (140 g) plain flour

1 tsp baking powder

¹/₂ tsp bicarbonate of soda

1 tsp ground cinnamon

¹/₄ tsp grated nutmeg

¹/₂ tsp salt

1 Preheat a 350°F/180°C/Gas 4 oven. Grease a 12-cup bun tray or use paper cases.

2 With an electric mixer, cream the margarine and sugar until light and fluffy. Beat in the egg and water.

3 ▲ Stir in the carrots.

4 Sift over the flour, baking powder, bicarbonate of soda, cinnamon, nutmeg and salt. Stir to blend.

5 ▼ Spoon the mixture into the prepared bun tray, filling the cups almost to the top. Bake until the tops spring back when touched lightly, about 35 minutes. Let stand 10 minutes before transferring to a rack.

Dried Cherry Buns

MAKES 16

8 fl oz (250 ml) plain yoghurt

6 oz (170 g) dried cherries

4 oz (115 g) butter, at room temperature

6 oz (170 g) caster sugar

2 eggs, at room temperature

1 tsp vanilla essence

7 oz (200 g) plain flour

2 tsp baking powder

1 tsp bicarbonate of soda

¹/₈ tsp salt

1 In a mixing bowl, combine the yoghurt and cherries. Cover and let stand for 30 minutes.

2 Preheat a 350°F/180°C/Gas 4 oven. Grease 16 bun-tray cups or use paper cases.

3 With an electric mixer, cream the butter and sugar together until light and fluffy.

4 ▼ Add the eggs, 1 at a time, beating well after each addition. Add the vanilla and the cherry mixture and stir to blend. Set aside.

5 ▲ In another bowl, sift together the flour, baking powder, bicarbonate soda and salt. Fold into the cherry mixture in 3 batches.

6 Fill the prepared cups two-thirds full. For even baking, half-fill any empty cups with water. Bake until the tops spring back when touched lightly, about 20 minutes. Transfer to a rack to cool.

Carrot Buns (top), Dried Cherry Buns

Blueberry Muffins

MAKES 12

6¹/₄ oz (180 g) plain flour
2¹/₄ oz (60 g) sugar
2 teaspoons baking powder
¹/₄ teaspoon salt
2 eggs
2 oz (55 g) butter, melted
6 fl oz (175 ml) milk
1 teaspoon vanilla essence
1 teaspoon grated lemon rind
6 oz (170 g) fresh blueberries

1 Preheat a 400°F/200°C/Gas 6 oven.

2 ▼ Grease a 12-cup muffin tin or use paper cases.

3 ▲ Sift the flour, sugar, baking powder and salt into a bowl.

4 In another bowl, whisk the eggs until blended. Add the melted butter, milk, vanilla and lemon rind and stir to combine.

5 Make a well in the dry ingredients and pour in the egg mixture. With a large metal spoon, stir just until the flour is moistened, not until smooth.

6 ▲ Fold in the blueberries.

7 ▲ Spoon the batter into the cups, leaving room for the muffins to rise.

8 Bake until the tops spring back when touched lightly, 20–25 minutes. Let cool in the pan for 5 minutes before turning out.

Apple and Cranberry Muffins

MAKES 12

2 oz (55 g) butter or margarine
1 egg
3¹/₂ oz (100 g) sugar
grated rind of 1 large orange
4 fl oz (125 ml) freshly squeezed orange juice
5 oz (140 g) plain flour
1 teaspoon baking powder
¹/₂ teaspoon bicarbonate of soda
1 teaspoon ground cinnamon
¹/₂ teaspoon grated nutmeg
¹/₂ teaspoon ground allspice
¹/₄ teaspoon ground ginger
¹/₄ teaspoon salt
1–2 dessert apples
6 oz (170 g) cranberries
2 oz (55 g) walnuts, chopped
icing sugar, for dusting (optional)

1   Preheat the oven to 350°F/180°C/Gas 4. Grease a 12-cup muffin tin or use paper cases.

2   Melt the butter or margarine over gentle heat. Set aside to cool.

3 ▲   Place the egg in a mixing bowl and whisk lightly. Add the melted butter or margarine and whisk to combine.

4   Add the sugar, orange rind and juice. Whisk to blend, then set aside.

5   In a large bowl, sift together the flour, baking powder, bicarbonate of soda, cinnamon, nutmeg, allspice, ginger and salt. Set aside.

6 ▲   Quarter, core and peel the apples. With a sharp knife, chop coarsely.

7   Make a well in the dry ingredients and pour in the egg mixture. With a spoon, stir until just blended.

8 ▲   Add the apples, cranberries and walnuts and stir to blend.

9   Fill the cups three-quarters full and bake until the tops spring back when touched lightly, 25–30 minutes. Transfer to a rack to cool. Dust with icing sugar, if desired.

Chocolate Chip Muffins

MAKES 10

4 oz (115 g) butter or margarine, at room temperature

2¹/₂ oz (70 g) caster sugar

1 oz (30 g) dark brown sugar

2 eggs, at room temperature

7¹/₂ oz (215 g) plain flour

1 teaspoon baking powder

4 fl oz (125 ml) milk

6 oz (170 g) plain chocolate chips

1 Preheat the oven to 375°F/190°C/ Gas 5. Grease 10 muffin cups or use paper cases.

2 ▼ With an electric mixer, cream the butter until soft. Add both sugars and beat until light and fluffy. Beat in the eggs, 1 at a time.

3 Sift together the flour and baking powder, twice. Fold into the butter mixture, alternating with the milk.

4 ▲ Divide half the mixture between the muffin cups. Sprinkle several chocolate chips on top, then cover with a spoonful of the batter. To ensure even baking, half-fill any empty cups with water.

5 Bake until lightly coloured, about 25 minutes. Let stand 5 minutes before turning out.

Chocolate Walnut Muffins

MAKES 12

6 oz (170 g) unsalted butter

5 oz (140 g) plain chocolate

7 oz (200 g) caster sugar

2 oz (55 g) dark brown sugar

4 eggs

1 teaspoon vanilla essence

¹/₄ teaspoon almond essence

3³/₄ oz (110 g) plain flour

1 tablespoon unsweetened cocoa powder

4 oz (115 g) walnuts, chopped

1 Preheat the oven to 350°F/180°C/ Gas 4. Grease a 12-cup muffin pan or use paper cases.

2 ▼ Melt the butter with the chocolate in the top of a double boiler or in a heatproof bowl set over a pan of hot water. Transfer to a large mixing bowl.

3 Stir both the sugars into the chocolate mixture. Mix in the eggs, 1 at a time, then add the vanilla and almond essences.

4 Sift over the flour and cocoa.

5 ▲ Fold in and stir in the walnuts.

6 Fill the prepared cups almost to the top and bake until a skewer inserted in the centre barely comes out clean, 30–35 minutes. Let stand 5 minutes before turning out onto a rack to cool completely.

Chocolate Chip Muffins (top), Chocolate Walnut Muffins

Oat and Raisin Muffins

MAKES 12

3 oz (85 g) rolled oats
8 fl oz (250 ml) buttermilk
4 oz (120 g) butter, at room temperature
3½ oz (100 g) dark brown sugar
1 egg, at room temperature
4 oz (120 g) flour
1 teaspoon baking powder
½ teaspoon bicarbonate of soda
¼ teaspoon salt
1 oz (30 g) raisins

1 ▲ In a bowl, combine the oats and buttermilk and let soak for 1 hour.

2 ▲ Lightly grease a 12-cup muffin tin or use paper cases.

~ COOK'S TIP ~

If buttermilk is not available, add 1 teaspoon lemon juice or vinegar to milk. Let the mixture stand for a few minutes to curdle.

3 ▲ Preheat the oven to 400°F/ 200°C/Gas 6. With an electric mixer, cream the butter and sugar until light and fluffy. Beat in the egg.

4 In another bowl, sift the flour, baking powder, bicarbonate of soda and salt. Stir into the butter mixture, alternating with the oat mixture. Fold in the raisins. Do not overmix.

5 Fill the prepared cups two-thirds full. Bake until a skewer inserted in the centre comes out clean, 20–25 minutes. Transfer to a rack to cool.

Pumpkin Muffins

MAKES 14

4 oz (120 g) butter or margarine, at room temperature
5 oz (150 g) dark brown sugar
4 tablespoons molasses
1 egg, at room temperature, beaten
8 oz (225 g) cooked or canned pumpkin
8 oz (225 g) flour
¼ teaspoon salt
1 teaspoon bicarbonate of soda
1½ teaspoons ground cinnamon
1 teaspoon grated nutmeg
1 oz (30 g) currants or raisins

1 Preheat the oven to 400°F/200°C/ Gas 6. Grease 14 muffin cups or use paper cases.

2 With an electric mixer, cream the butter or margarine until soft. Add the sugar and molasses and beat until light and fluffy.

3 ▲ Add the egg and pumpkin and stir until well blended.

4 Sift over the flour, salt, bicarbonate of soda, cinnamon and nutmeg. Fold just enough to blend; do not overmix.

5 ▼ Fold in the currants or raisins.

6 Spoon the mixture into the prepared muffin cups, filling them three-quarters full.

7 Bake until the tops spring back when touched lightly, 12–15 minutes. Serve warm or cold.

Oat and Raisin Muffins (top), Pumpkin Muffins

Prune Muffins

MAKES 12

1 egg
8 fl oz (250 ml) milk
4 fl oz (125 ml) vegetable oil
1 3/4 oz (50 g) caster sugar
1 oz (30 g) dark brown sugar
10 oz (285 g) plain flour
2 teaspoons baking powder
1/2 teaspoon salt
1/4 teaspoon grated nutmeg
4 oz (115 g) cooked stoned prunes, chopped

1   Preheat a 400°F/200°C/Gas 6 oven. Grease a 12-cup muffin tin.

2   Break the egg into a mixing bowl and beat with a fork. Beat in the milk and oil.

3 ▼   Stir in the sugars. Set aside.

4   Sift the flour, baking powder, salt and nutmeg into a mixing bowl. Make a well in the centre, pour in the egg mixture and stir until moistened. Do not overmix; the batter should be slightly lumpy.

5 ▲   Fold in the prunes.

6   Fill the prepared cups two-thirds full. Bake until golden brown, about 20 minutes. Let stand 10 minutes before turning out. Serve warm or at room temperature.

Yogurt and Honey Muffins

MAKES 12

2 oz (55 g) butter
5 tablespoons clear honey
8 fl oz (250 ml) plain yogurt
1 large egg, at room temperature
grated rind of 1 lemon
2 fl oz (65 ml) lemon juice
5 oz (140 g) plain flour
6 oz (170 g) wholemeal flour
1 1/2 teaspoons bicarbonate of soda
1/8 teaspoon grated nutmeg

~ VARIATION ~

For Walnut Yogurt Honey Muffins, add 2 oz (55 g) chopped walnuts, folded in with the flour. This makes a more substantial muffin.

1   Preheat a 375°F/190°C/Gas 5 oven. Grease a 12-cup muffin tin or use paper cases.

2   In a saucepan, melt the butter and honey. Remove from the heat and set aside to cool slightly.

3 ▲   In a bowl, whisk together the yogurt, egg, lemon rind and juice. Add the butter and honey mixture. Set aside.

4 ▲   In another bowl, sift together the dry ingredients.

5   Fold the dry ingredients into the yogurt mixture to blend.

6   Fill the prepared cups two-thirds full. Bake until the tops spring back when touched lightly, 20–25 minutes. Let cool in the tin for 5 minutes before turning out. Serve warm or at room temperature.

Prune Muffins (top), Yogurt and Honey Muffins

Banana Muffins

MAKES 10

9 oz (250 g) plain flour
1 teaspoon baking powder
1 teaspoon bicarbonate of soda
1/4 teaspoon salt
1/2 teaspoon ground cinnamon
1/4 teaspoon grated nutmeg
3 large ripe bananas
1 egg
2 1/2 oz (70 g) dark brown sugar
2 fl oz (50 ml) vegetable oil
1 oz (30 g) raisins

1 ▼ Preheat the oven to 375°F/190°C/Gas 5. Lightly grease or line 10 deep muffin tins with paper cases.

2 Sift together the flour, baking powder, bicarbonate of soda, salt, cinnamon and nutmeg. Set aside.

3 ▲ With an electric mixer, beat the peeled bananas at moderate speed until mashed.

4 ▲ Beat in the egg, sugar and oil.

5 Add the dry ingredients and beat in gradually, on low speed. Mix just until blended. With a wooden spoon, stir in the raisins.

6 Fill the prepared cups two-thirds full. For even baking, half-fill any empty cups with water.

7 ▲ Bake until the tops spring back when touched lightly, 20–25 minutes. Transfer to a rack to cool.

Maple Pecan Muffins

MAKES 20

6 oz (170 g) pecans
12 oz (340 g) flour
1 teaspoon baking powder
1 teaspoon bicarbonate of soda
1/4 teaspoon salt
1/4 teaspoon ground cinnamon
3 1/2 oz (100 g) caster sugar
2 1/2 oz (70 g) light brown sugar
3 tablespoons maple syrup
5 oz (150 g) butter, at room temperature
3 eggs, at room temperature
1/2 pint (300 ml) buttermilk
60 pecan halves, for decorating

1   Preheat the oven to 350°F/180°C/ Gas 4. Lightly grease 24 deep muffin tins or use paper cases.

2 ▲ Spread the pecans on a baking sheet and toast in the oven for 5 minutes. When cool, chop coarsely and set aside.

3   In a bowl, sift together the flour, baking powder, bicarbonate of soda, salt and cinnamon. Set aside.

4 ▲ In a large mixing bowl, combine the caster sugar, light brown sugar, maple syrup and butter. Beat with an electric mixer until light and fluffy.

5   Add the eggs, 1 at a time, beating to incorporate thoroughly after each addition.

6 ▲ Pour half the buttermilk and half the dry ingredients into the butter mixture, then stir until blended. Repeat with the remaining buttermilk and dry ingredients.

7   Fold in the chopped pecans. Fill the prepared cups two-thirds full. Top with the pecan halves. For even baking, half-fill any empty cups with water.

8   Bake until puffed up and golden, 20–25 minutes. Let stand 5 minutes before unmoulding.

~ VARIATION ~

For Pecan Spice Muffins, substitute an equal quantity of golden syrup for the maple syrup. Increase the cinnamon to 1/2 teaspoon, and add 1 teaspoon ground ginger and 1/2 teaspoon grated nutmeg, sifted with the dry ingredients.

Banana and Pecan Muffins

MAKES 8

5 oz (150 g) plain flour

1½ teaspoons baking powder

2 oz (55 g) butter or margarine,
at room temperature

5 oz (150 g) caster sugar

1 egg

1 teaspoon vanilla essence

3 medium bananas, mashed

2 oz (55 g) pecans, chopped

5 tablespoons milk

~ **VARIATION** ~

Use an equal quantity of walnuts
instead of the pecans.

1 Preheat the oven to 375°F/190°C/
Gas 5. Lightly grease 8 deep muffin tins.

2 Sift the flour and baking powder
into a small bowl. Set aside.

3 ▲ With an electric mixer, cream
the butter or margarine and sugar
together. Add the egg and vanilla and
beat until fluffy. Mix in the banana.

4 ▼ Add the pecans. With the mixer
on low speed, beat in the flour
mixture alternately with the milk.

5 Spoon the mixture into the
prepared muffin cups, filling them
two-thirds full. Bake until golden
brown and a skewer inserted into the
centre of a muffin comes out clean,
20–25 minutes.

6 Let cool in the tin on a wire rack
for 10 minutes. To loosen, run a knife
gently around each muffin and
unmould on to the wire rack. Let cool
10 minutes longer before serving.

Blueberry and Cinnamon Muffins

MAKES 8

4 oz (120 g) plain flour

1 tablespoon baking powder

pinch of salt

2½ oz (70 g) light brown sugar

1 egg

6 fl oz (175 ml) milk

3 tablespoons vegetable oil

2 teaspoons ground cinnamon

4 oz (120 g) fresh or thawed frozen
blueberries

1 Preheat the oven to 375°F/190°C/
Gas 5. Lightly grease 8 deep muffin tins.

2 With an electric mixer, beat
the first 8 ingredients together
until smooth.

3 ▲ Fold in the blueberries.

4 ▲ Spoon the mixture into the
muffin cups, filling them two-thirds
full. Bake until a skewer inserted in
the centre of a muffin comes out
clean, about 25 minutes.

5 Let cool in the tins on a wire rack
for 10 minutes, then unmould the
muffins on to the wire rack and allow
to cool completely.

Banana and Pecan Muffins (top), Blueberry and Cinnamon Muffins

Raspberry Muffins

MAKES 10–12

4 oz (120 g) self-raising flour

4 oz (120 g) wholemeal self-raising flour

3 tablespoons caster sugar

½ teaspoon salt

2 eggs, beaten

7 fl oz (200 ml) milk

2 oz (55 g) butter, melted

6 oz (170 g) raspberries, fresh or frozen
(defrosted for less than 30 minutes)

1 ▼ Preheat the oven to 375°F/190°C/Gas 5. Lightly grease the muffin tins, or use paper cases. Sift the dry ingredients together, then tip back in the wholewheat flakes from the sieve.

2 ▲ Beat the eggs, milk and butter with the dry ingredients to give a thick batter. Add the raspberries.

3 ▲ Stir in the raspberries gently. (If you are using frozen raspberries, work quickly as the cold berries make the mixture solidify.) If you mix too much the raspberries begin to disintegrate and colour the dough. Spoon the mixture into the tins or paper cases.

4 Bake the muffins for 30 minutes, until well risen and just firm. Serve warm or cool.

Cherry Marmalade Muffins

MAKES 12

8 oz (225 g) self-raising flour
1 teaspoon mixed spice
3 oz (85 g) caster sugar
4 oz (120 g) glacé cherries, quartered
2 tablespoons orange marmalade
¼ pint (150 ml) skimmed milk
2 oz (55 g) soft sunflower margarine
marmalade, to brush

1 ▲   Preheat the oven to 400°F/200°C/Gas 6. Lightly grease 12 deep muffin tins with oil.

2 ▲   Sift together the flour and spice then stir in the sugar and cherries.

3   Mix the marmalade with the milk and beat into the dry ingredients with the margarine. Spoon into the greased tins. Bake for 20–25 minutes, until golden brown and firm.

4 ▼   Turn out on to a wire rack and brush the tops with warmed marmalade. Serve warm or cold.

~ VARIATION ~

To make Honey, Nut and Lemon Muffins, substitute 2 tablespoons clear honey for the orange marmalade, and the juice and finely grated rind of a lemon, and 2 oz (55 g) toasted, chopped hazelnuts, instead of the glacé cherries.

Blackberry and Almond Muffins

MAKES 12

11 oz (300 g) plain flour
2 oz (50 g) light brown sugar
4 teaspoons baking powder
pinch of salt
2¼ oz (60 g) chopped blanched almonds
3½ oz (100 g) fresh blackberries
2 eggs
7 fl oz (200 ml) milk
4 tablespoons melted butter, plus a little more to grease cups, if using
1 tablespoon sloe gin
1 tablespoon rosewater

1 ▼ Mix the flour, sugar, baking powder and salt in a bowl and stir in the almonds and blackberries, mixing them well to coat with the flour mixture. Preheat the oven to 400°F/200°C/Gas 6.

2 ▲ In another bowl, mix the eggs with the milk, then gradually add the butter, sloe gin and rosewater. Make a well in the centre of the bowl of dry ingredients and add the egg and milk mixture. Stir well.

3 Lightly grease 12 deep muffin tins. Spoon in the mixture and bake for 20–25 minutes or until browned. Turn out the muffins on to a wire rack to cool. Serve with butter.

~ **COOK'S TIP** ~

Other berries can be substituted for the blackberries, such as elderberries or blueberries.

~ **VARIATION** ~

For Blackberry and Apple Muffins, substitute 2 dessert apples, peeled, cored and diced for the almonds. Add 1 teaspoon ground coriander to the flour mixture, and instead of the sloe gin and rosewater, substitute 2 tablespoons of Crème de Mûre.

Bacon and Cornmeal Muffins

MAKES 14

8 bacon rashers
2 oz (55 g) butter
2 oz (55 g) margarine
4 oz (120 g) plain flour
1 tablespoon baking powder
1 teaspoon sugar
¼ teaspoon salt
8 oz (225 g) cornmeal
4 fl oz (125 ml) milk
2 eggs

1 Preheat the oven to 400°F/200°C/ Gas 6. Lightly grease 14 deep muffin tins or use paper cases.

2 ▲ Fry the bacon until crisp. Drain on kitchen paper, then chop into small pieces. Set aside.

3 Gently melt the butter and margarine and set aside.

4 ▲ Sift the flour, baking powder, sugar, and salt into a large mixing bowl. Stir in the cornmeal, then make a well in the centre.

5 In a saucepan, heat the milk to lukewarm. In a small bowl, lightly whisk the eggs, then add to the milk. Stir in the melted fats.

6 ▼ Pour the milk mixture into the centre of the well and stir until smooth and well blended.

7 ▲ Stir the bacon into the mixture, then spoon the mixture into the prepared cups, filling them half-full. Bake until risen and lightly coloured, about 20 minutes. Serve hot or warm.

Cheese Muffins

MAKES 9

2 oz (55 g) butter

7 oz (200 g) plain flour

2 teaspoons baking powder

2 tablespoons sugar

1/4 teaspoon salt

1 teaspoon paprika

2 eggs

4 fl oz (125 ml) milk

1 teaspoon dried thyme

2 oz (55 g) mature Cheddar cheese, cut into 1/2 in (1 cm) dice

1   Preheat the oven to 375°F/190°C/ Gas 5. Thickly grease 9 deep muffin tins or use paper cases.

2   Melt the butter and set aside.

3 ▼   In a mixing bowl, sift together the flour, baking powder, sugar, salt and paprika.

4 ▲   In another bowl, combine the eggs, milk, melted butter and thyme, and whisk to blend.

5   Add the milk mixture to the dry ingredients and stir just until moistened; do not mix until smooth.

6 ▲   Place a heaped spoonful of batter into the prepared cups. Drop a few pieces of cheese over each, then top with another spoonful of batter. For even baking, half-fill any empty muffin cups with water.

7 ▲   Bake until puffed and golden, about 25 minutes. Let stand 5 minutes before unmoulding on to a rack. Serve warm or at room temperature.

Sweet Potato Scones

MAKES ABOUT 24

5oz (150g) plain flour
4 teaspoons baking powder
1 teaspoon salt
1 tablespoon soft light brown sugar
2fl oz (50ml) mashed cooked sweet potatoes
¼ pint (150ml) milk
2oz (50g) butter or margarine, melted

1 Preheat the oven to 230°C/450°F/ Gas 8.

2 ▲ Sift the flour, baking powder and salt into a bowl. Add the sugar and stir to mix.

3 ▲ In a separate bowl, combine the sweet potatoes with the milk and melted butter or margarine. Mix well until evenly blended.

4 ▼ Stir the dry ingredients into the sweet potato mixture to make a dough. Turn on to a lightly floured surface and knead lightly, just to mix, for 1–2 minutes.

5 ▲ Roll or pat out the dough to ½ in (1 cm) thickness. Stamp out rounds with a 1½ in (4 cm) biscuit cutter.

6 Arrange the rounds on a greased baking sheet. Bake until puffed and lightly golden, about 15 minutes. Serve the scones warm.

Buttermilk Scones

MAKES 15

7 oz (200 g) plain flour

1 teaspoon salt

1 teaspoon baking powder

1/2 teaspoon bicarbonate of soda

4 tablespoons cold butter or margarine

6 fl oz (175 ml) buttermilk

1 Preheat the oven to 425°F/220°C/ Gas 7. Grease a baking sheet.

2 Sift the dry ingredients into a bowl. Rub in the butter or margarine with your fingertips until the mixture resembles breadcrumbs.

3 ▼ Gradually pour in the buttermilk, stirring with a fork to form a soft dough.

4 ▲ Roll out the dough until about 1/2 in (1 cm) thick. Stamp out rounds with a 2-inch (5 cm) biscuit cutter.

5 Place on the prepared baking sheet and bake until golden, 12–15 minutes. Serve warm or at room temperature.

Traditional Sweet Scones

MAKES 8

6 oz (170 g) flour

2 tablespoons sugar

3 teaspoons baking powder

1/8 teaspoon salt

5 tablespoons cold butter, cut in pieces

4 fl oz (125 ml) milk

1 Preheat the oven to 425°F/220°C/ Gas 7. Grease a baking sheet.

2 ▲ Sift the flour, sugar, baking powder, and salt into a bowl.

3 Cut in the butter with a pastry blender until the mixture resembles coarse crumbs.

4 Pour in the milk and stir with a fork to form a soft dough.

~ VARIATION ~

To make a delicious and speedy dessert, split the scones in half while still warm. Butter one half, top with lightly sugared fresh strawberries, raspberries or blueberries, and sandwich with the other half. Serve at once with dollops of whipped cream.

5 ▲ Roll out the dough about 1/4 in (1/2 cm) thick. Stamp out rounds using a 2 1/2 in (6 cm) biscuit cutter.

6 Place on the prepared sheet and bake until golden, about 12 minutes. Serve hot or warm, with butter and jam, to accompany tea or coffee.

Buttermilk Scones (top), Traditional Sweet Scones

Wholemeal Scones

MAKES 16

6 oz (170 g) cold butter

12 oz (350 g) wholemeal flour

5 oz (140 g) plain flour

2 tablespoons sugar

1/2 teaspoon salt

2 1/2 teaspoons bicarbonate of soda

2 eggs

6 fl oz (175 ml) buttermilk

1 1/4 oz (35 g) raisins

1 Preheat the oven to 400°F/200°C/Gas 6. Grease and flour a large baking sheet.

2 ▲ Cut the butter into small pieces.

3 Combine the dry ingredients in a bowl. Add the butter and rub in with your fingertips until the mixture resembles coarse breadcrumbs. Set aside.

4 In another bowl, whisk together the eggs and buttermilk. Set aside 2 tablespoons for glazing.

5 Stir the remaining egg mixture into the dry ingredients until it just holds together. Stir in the raisins.

6 Roll out the dough about 3/4 in (2 cm) thick. Stamp out circles with a biscuit cutter. Place on the prepared sheet and brush with the glaze.

7 Bake until golden, 12–15 minutes. Allow to cool slightly before serving. Split in two with a fork while still warm and spread with butter and jam, if wished.

Orange and Raisin Scones

MAKES 16

10 oz (285 g) plain flour

1 1/2 teaspoons baking powder

2 1/4 oz (60 g) sugar

1/2 teaspoon salt

2 1/2 oz (70 g) butter, diced

2 1/2 oz (70 g) margarine, diced

grated rind of 1 large orange

2 oz (55 g) raisins

4 fl oz (125 ml) buttermilk

milk, for glazing

1 Preheat the oven to 425°F/220°C/Gas 7. Grease and flour a large baking sheet.

2 Combine the dry ingredients in a large bowl. Add the butter and margarine and rub in with your fingertips until the mixture resembles coarse breadcrumbs.

3 ▲ Add the orange rind and raisins.

4 Gradually stir in the buttermilk to form a soft dough.

5 ▲ Roll out the dough about 3/4 in (2 cm) thick. Stamp out circles with a biscuit cutter.

6 ▲ Place on the prepared sheet and brush the tops with milk.

7 Bake until golden, 12–15 minutes. Serve hot or warm, with butter, or whipped or clotted cream, and jam.

> **~ COOK'S TIP ~**
>
> For light tender scones, handle the dough as little as possible. If you wish, split the scones when cool and toast them under a preheated grill. Butter them while still hot.

Wholemeal Scones (top), Orange and Raisin Scones

Sunflower Sultana Scones

MAKES 10–12

8 oz (225 g) self-raising flour

1 teaspoon baking powder

1 oz (30 g) soft sunflower margarine

2 tablespoons caster sugar

2 oz (55 g) sultanas

2 tablespoons sunflower seeds

5 oz (150 g) natural yogurt

about 2–3 tablespoons skimmed milk

1   Preheat the oven to 450°F/230°C/ Gas 8. Lightly oil a baking sheet. Sift the flour and baking powder into a bowl and rub in the margarine evenly.

2   Stir in the sugar, sultanas and half the sunflower seeds, then mix in the yogurt, with just enough milk to make a fairly soft, but not sticky dough.

3 ▼   Roll out on a lightly floured surface to about ³/₄ in (2 cm) thickness. Cut into 2¹/₂ in (6 cm) flower shapes or rounds with a biscuit cutter and lift on to the baking sheet.

4 ▲   Brush with milk and sprinkle with the reserved sunflower seeds, then bake for 10–12 minutes, until well risen and golden brown.

5   Cool the scones on a wire rack. Serve split and spread with butter and jam.

Prune and Peel Rock Buns

MAKES 12

8 oz (225 g) plain flour

2 teaspoons baking powder

3 oz (85 g) demerara sugar

2 oz (55 g) chopped ready-to-eat dried prunes

2 oz (55 g) chopped mixed peel

finely grated rind of 1 lemon

2 fl oz (50 ml) sunflower oil

5 tablespoons skimmed milk

~ **VARIATION** ~

For Spicy Rock Buns, substitute 2 oz (50 g) currants for the ready-to-eat dried prunes, 2 oz (50 g) raisins for the mixed peel, and add 1 teaspoon mixed spice, ¹/₄ teaspoon ground ginger, and ¹/₄ teaspoon ground cinnamon.

1 ▼   Preheat the oven to 400°F/ 200°C/Gas 6. Lightly oil a large baking sheet. Sift together the flour and baking powder, then stir in the sugar, prunes, peel and lemon rind.

2   Mix the oil and milk, then stir into the mixture, to make a dough which just binds together.

3 ▲   Spoon into rocky heaps on the baking sheet and bake for 20 minutes, until golden. Cool on a wire rack.

Sunflower Sultana Scones (top), Prune and Peel Rock Buns

...d Marjoram Scones

1 ▼ Sift the two kinds of flour into a bowl and add the salt. Cut the butter into small pieces, and rub into the flour until the mixture resembles fine breadcrumbs.

...our

...) self-raising flour

pinch of salt

1½ oz (45 g) butter

¼ teaspoon dry mustard

2 teaspoons dried marjoram

2–3 oz (55–85 g) Cheddar cheese, finely grated

4 fl oz (125 ml) milk, or as required

1 teaspoon sunflower oil

2 oz (50 g) pecan or walnuts, chopped

2 ▲ Add the mustard, marjoram and grated cheese, and mix in sufficient milk to make a soft dough. Knead the dough lightly.

3 Preheat the oven to 425°F/220°C/Gas 7. Roll out the dough on a floured surface to about a ¾ in (2 cm) thickness and cut out about 18 scones using a 2 in (5 cm) square cutter. Grease two baking sheets with a little sunflower oil, and place the scones on the trays.

4 Brush the scones with a little milk and sprinkle the chopped pecans or walnuts over the top. Bake for 12 minutes. Serve warm.

~ VARIATION ~

For Mixed Herb and Mustard Scones, use 2 tablespoons chopped fresh parsley or chives instead of the dried marjoram and 1 teaspoon Dijon mustard instead of the dry mustard. Substitute 2 oz (50 g) chopped pistachio nuts for the pecans or walnuts.

Cheese and Chive Scones

MAKES 9

4 oz (120 g) self-raising flour

5 oz (150 g) self-raising wholemeal flour

1/2 teaspoon salt

3 oz (85 g) feta cheese

1 tablespoon snipped fresh chives

1/4 pint (150 ml) skimmed milk, plus extra for glazing

1/4 teaspoon cayenne pepper

1 ▲ Pre-heat the oven to 400°F/ 200°C/Gas 6. Sift the flours and salt into a mixing bowl, adding any bran left over from the flour in the sieve.

2 ▲ Crumble the feta cheese and rub into the dry ingredients. Stir in the chives, then add the milk and mix to a soft dough.

3 ▼ Turn out the dough on to a floured surface and lightly knead until smooth. Roll out to 3/4 in (2 cm) thick and stamp out nine scones with a 2 1/2 in (6 cm) biscuit cutter.

4 ▲ Transfer the scones to a non-stick baking sheet. Brush with skimmed milk, then sprinkle over the cayenne pepper. Bake in the oven for 15 minutes, or until golden brown. Serve warm or cold.

Dill and Potato Cakes

MAKES 10

8 oz (225 g) self-raising flour

3 tablespoons butter, softened

pinch of salt

1 tablespoon finely chopped fresh dill

6 oz (170 g) mashed potato, freshly made

2–3 tablespoons milk, as required

1 ▼ Preheat the oven to 450°F/230°C/Gas 8. Sift the flour into a bowl, and add the butter, salt and dill. Mix in the mashed potato and enough milk to make a soft, pliable dough.

2 ▲ Roll out the dough on a well-floured surface until it is fairly thin. Cut into neat rounds using a 3 in (7.5 cm) cutter.

3 ▲ Grease a baking sheet, place the cakes on it, and bake for 20–25 minutes until risen and golden.

~ VARIATION ~

For Cheese and Herb Potato Cakes, stir in about 2 oz (55 g) crumbled blue cheese, and substitute 1 tablespoon snipped fresh chives for the dill. Mix in 3 tablespoons soured cream instead of the butter.

Parmesan Popovers

MAKES 6

2 oz (55 g) freshly grated Parmesan cheese
4 oz (120 g) plain flour
¼ teaspoon salt
2 eggs
4 fl oz (125 ml) milk
1 tablespoon melted butter or margarine

1 ▼ Preheat the oven to 450°F/230°C/Gas 8. Grease six deep bun or tartlet tins. Sprinkle each tin with 1 tablespoon of the grated Parmesan. Alternatively, you can use ramekins; heat them on a baking sheet in the oven, then grease and sprinkle with Parmesan just before filling.

2 Sift the flour and salt into a small bowl. Set aside.

3 ▲ In a mixing bowl, beat together the eggs, milk, and butter or margarine. Add the flour mixture and stir until smoothly blended.

4 ▼ Divide the mixture evenly among the tins, filling each one about half full. Bake for 15 minutes, then sprinkle the tops of the popovers with the remaining grated Parmesan cheese. Reduce the heat to 350°F/180°C/Gas 4 and continue baking until the popovers are firm and golden brown, 20–25 minutes.

5 ▲ Remove the popovers from the oven. To unmould, run a thin knife around the inside of each tin to loosen the popovers. Gently ease out, then transfer to a wire rack to cool.

Herb Popovers

MAKES 12

3 eggs

8 fl oz (250 ml) milk

1 oz (30 g) butter, melted

3 oz (85 g) plain flour

1/8 tsp salt

1 small sprig each mixed fresh herbs, such as chives, tarragon, dill and parsley

1 Preheat a 425°F/220°C/Gas 7 oven. Grease 12 small ramekins or individual baking cups.

2 With an electric mixer, beat the eggs until blended. Beat in the milk and melted butter.

3 Sift together the flour and salt, then beat into the egg mixture to combine thoroughly.

4 ▼ Strip the herb leaves from the stems and chop finely. Mix together and measure out 2 tablespoons. Stir the herbs into the batter.

5 ▲ Fill the prepared cups half-full.

6 Bake until golden, 25–30 minutes. Do not open the oven door during baking time or the popovers may collapse. For drier popovers, pierce each one with a knife after the 30 minute baking time and bake for 5 minutes more. Serve hot.

Cheese Popovers

MAKES 12

3 eggs

8 fl oz (250 ml) milk

1 oz (30 g) butter, melted

3 oz (85 g) plain flour

1/4 tsp salt

1/4 tsp paprika

1 oz (30 g) freshly grated Parmesan cheese

~ **VARIATION** ~

For traditional Yorkshire Pudding, omit the cheese and paprika, and use 4–6 tablespoons of beef dripping to replace the butter. Put them into the oven in time to serve warm as an accompaniment for roast beef.

1 Preheat a 425°F/220°C/Gas 7 oven. Grease 12 small ramekins.

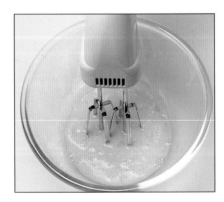

2 ▲ With an electric mixer, beat the eggs until blended. Beat in the milk and melted butter.

3 ▲ Sift together the flour, salt and paprika, then beat into the egg mixture. Add the cheese and stir.

4 Fill the prepared cups half-full and bake until golden, 25–30 minutes. Do not open the oven door or the popovers may collapse. For drier popovers, pierce each one with a knife after the 30 minute baking time and bake for 5 minutes more. Serve hot.

Herb Popovers (top), Cheese Popovers

Orange and Honey Tea Bread

MAKES 1 LOAF

13½ oz (385 g) plain flour

2½ teaspoons baking powder

½ teaspoon bicarbonate of soda

½ teaspoon salt

1 oz (30 g) margarine

8 fl oz (250 ml) clear honey

1 egg, at room temperature, lightly beaten

1½ tablespoons grated orange rind

6 fl oz (175 ml) freshly squeezed orange juice

4 oz (115 g) walnuts, chopped

1   Preheat a 325°F/170°C/Gas 3 oven.

2   Sift together the flour, baking powder, bicarbonate of soda and salt.

3   Line the bottom and sides of a 9 × 5 in (23 × 13 cm) loaf tin with greaseproof paper and grease.

4 ▲   With an electric mixer, cream the margarine until soft. Stir in the honey until blended, then stir in the egg. Add the orange rind and stir to combine thoroughly.

5 ▲   Fold the flour mixture into the honey and egg mixture in 3 batches, alternating with the orange juice. Stir in the walnuts.

6   Pour into the tin and bake until a skewer inserted in the centre comes out clean, 60–70 minutes. Let stand 10 minutes before turning out onto a rack to cool.

Apple Loaf

MAKES 1 LOAF

1 egg

8 fl oz (250 ml) bottled or homemade apple sauce

2 oz (55 g) butter or margarine, melted

3¾ oz (110 g) dark brown sugar

1¾ oz (50 g) caster sugar

10 oz (285 g) plain flour

2 teaspoons baking powder

½ teaspoon bicarbonate of soda

½ teaspoon salt

1 teaspoon ground cinnamon

½ teaspoon grated nutmeg

2½ oz (70 g) currants or raisins

2 oz (55 g) pecans or walnuts, chopped

1   Preheat a 350°F/180°C/Gas 4 oven. Line a 9 × 5 in (23 × 13 cm) loaf tin with greaseproof paper and grease.

2 ▲   Break the egg into a bowl and beat lightly. Stir in the apple sauce, butter or margarine and both sugars. Set aside.

3   In another bowl, sift together the flour, baking powder, bicarbonate of soda, salt, cinnamon and nutmeg. Fold dry ingredients into the apple sauce mixture in 3 batches.

4 ▼   Stir in the currants or raisins, and nuts.

5   Pour into the prepared tin and bake until a skewer inserted in the centre comes out clean, about 1 hour. Let stand 10 minutes. Turn out onto a rack and cool completely.

Orange and Honey Tea Bread (top), Apple Loaf

Malt Loaf

Makes 1 loaf

¼ pint (150 ml) warm skimmed milk
1 teaspoon (5 ml) dried yeast
pinch of caster sugar
12 oz (350 g) plain flour
½ teaspoon (1.5 ml) salt
2 tablespoons (30 ml) light muscovado sugar
6 oz (175 g) sultanas
1 tablespoons (15 ml) sunflower oil
3 tablespoons (45 ml) malt extract
For the glaze
2 tablespoons (30 ml) caster sugar
2 tablespoons (30 ml) water

~ COOK'S TIP ~

This is a rich and sticky loaf. If it lasts long enough to go stale, try toasting it for a delicious tea-time treat.

~ VARIATION ~

To make buns, divide the dough into 10 pieces, shape into rounds, leave to rise, then bake for about 15–20 minutes. Brush with the glaze while still hot.

1 ▲ Place the warm milk in a bowl. Sprinkle the yeast on top and add the sugar. Leave for 30 minutes until frothy. Stir the flour and salt into a mixing bowl, stir in the muscovado sugar and sultanas, and make a well.

2 ▲ Add the yeast mixture with the oil and malt extract. Gradually incorporate the flour and mix to a soft dough, adding a little extra milk if necessary.

3 ▲ Turn on to a floured surface and knead for about 5 minutes until smooth and elastic. Grease a 1 lb (450 g) loaf tin.

4 ▲ Shape the dough and place it in the prepared loaf tin. Cover with a damp dish towel and leave in a warm place for about 1–2 hours until the dough is well risen. Preheat the oven to 190°C/375°F/Gas 5.

5 ▲ Bake the loaf for 30–35 minutes, or until it sounds hollow when it is tapped underneath.

6 ▲ Meanwhile, prepare the glaze by dissolving the sugar in the water in a small pan. Bring to the boil, stirring, then lower the heat and simmer for 1 minute. Place the loaf on a wire rack and brush with the glaze while still hot. Leave the loaf to cool before serving.

Lemon and Walnut Tea Bread

MAKES 1 LOAF

4 oz (115 g) butter or margarine, at room temperature

3¹/₂ oz (100 g) sugar

2 eggs, at room temperature, separated

grated rind of 2 lemons

2 tablespoons lemon juice

7¹/₂ oz (215 g) plain flour

2 teaspoons baking powder

4 fl oz (125 ml) milk

2 oz (55 g) walnuts, chopped

¹/₈ teaspoon salt

1 Preheat a 350°F/180°C/Gas 4 oven. Line a 9 × 5 in (23 × 13 cm) loaf tin with greaseproof paper and grease.

2 With an electric mixer, cream the butter or margarine with the sugar until light and fluffy.

3 ▲ Beat in the egg yolks.

4 Add the lemon rind and juice and stir until blended. Set aside.

5 ▲ In another bowl, sift together the flour and baking powder, 3 times. Fold into the butter mixture in 3 batches, alternating with the milk. Fold in the walnuts. Set aside.

6 ▲ Beat the egg whites and salt until stiff peaks form. Fold a large dollop of the egg whites into the walnut mixture to lighten it. Fold in the remaining egg whites carefully until just blended.

7 ▲ Pour the batter into the prepared tin and bake until a skewer inserted in the centre of the loaf comes out clean, 45–50 minutes. Let stand 5 minutes before turning out onto a rack to cool completely.

Banana Bread

MAKES 1 LOAF

7 oz (200 g) plain flour
2¼ teaspoons baking powder
½ teaspoon salt
¾ teaspoon ground cinnamon (optional)
4 tablespoons wheat germ
2½ oz (75 g) butter or margarine, at room temperature
4 oz (115 g) caster sugar
¾ teaspoon grated lemon zest
3 ripe bananas, mashed
2 eggs, beaten to mix

1   Preheat a 350°F/180°C/Gas 4 oven. Grease and flour an 8½ × 4½ in (21 × 11 cm) loaf tin.

2 ▲   Sift the flour, baking powder, salt and cinnamon, if using, into a bowl. Stir in the wheat germ.

3 ▲   In another bowl, combine the butter or margarine with the sugar and lemon zest. Beat until the mixture is light and fluffy.

4 ▲   Add the mashed bananas and eggs and mix well.

5   Add the dry ingredients and blend quickly and evenly.

~ VARIATION ~

For Banana Walnut Bread, add 2–3 oz (55–85 g) finely chopped walnuts with the dry ingredients.

---

6 ▼   Spoon into the prepared loaf tin. Bake for 50–60 minutes or until a wooden skewer inserted in the centre comes out clean.

7   Cool in the pan for about 5 minutes, then turn out on to a wire rack to cool completely.

Pineapple and Apricot Cake

SERVES 10–12

6 oz (170 g) unsalted butter

5 oz (150 g) caster sugar

3 eggs, beaten

few drops of vanilla essence

8 oz (225 g) plain flour, sifted

1/2 teaspoon salt

1 1/2 teaspoons baking powder

8 oz (225 g) ready-to-eat dried apricots, chopped

4 oz (120 g) each chopped crystallized ginger and crystallized pineapple

grated rind and juice of 1/2 orange

grated rind and juice of 1/2 lemon

a little milk

1 ▲ Preheat the oven to 350°F/180°C/Gas 4. Double line an 8 in (20 cm) round or 7 in (18 cm) square cake tin. Cream the butter and sugar together until light and fluffy.

2 Gradually beat the eggs into the creamed mixture with the vanilla essence, beating well after each addition. Sift together the flour, salt and baking powder, and add a little with the last of the egg, then fold in the rest.

3 ▲ Fold in the fruit, crystallized fruit and fruit rinds gently, then add sufficient fruit juice and milk to give a fairly soft dropping consistency.

4 ▲ Spoon into the prepared tin and smooth the top with a wet spoon. Bake for 20 minutes, then reduce the heat to 325°F/160°C/Gas 3 for a further 1 1/2 –2 hours, or until firm to the touch and a skewer comes out of the centre clean. Leave the cake to cool in the tin, turn out and wrap in fresh paper before storing in an airtight tin.

~ COOK'S TIP ~

This is not a long-keeping cake, but it does freeze, well-wrapped in greaseproof paper and then foil.

Date and Nut Malt Loaf

1 Sift the flours and salt into a large bowl, adding any bran from the sieve. Stir in the sugar and yeast.

2 ▲ Mix the butter or margarine with the treacle and malt extract. Stir over a low heat until melted. Leave to cool, then combine with the milk.

3 Stir the liquid into the dry ingredients and knead for 15 minutes until the dough is elastic. (If you have a dough blade on your food processor, follow the manufacturer's instructions for timings.)

4 ▲ Knead in the fruits and nuts. Transfer the dough to an oiled bowl, cover with clear film, and leave in a warm place for about 1½ hours, until the dough has doubled in size.

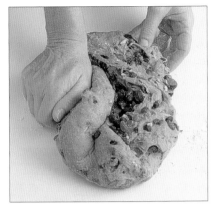

5 ▲ Grease two 1 lb (450 g) loaf tins. Knock back the dough and knead lightly. Divide in half, form into loaves and place in the tins. Cover and leave in a warm place for about 30 minutes, until risen. Meanwhile, preheat the oven to 190°C/375°F/Gas 5.

6 Bake for 35–40 minutes, until well risen and sounding hollow when tapped underneath. Cool on a wire rack. Brush with honey while warm.

MAKES 2 LOAVES

11 oz (300 g) strong plain flour
10 oz (275 g) strong plain wholemeal flour
1 teaspoon (5 ml) salt
3 oz (75 g) soft brown sugar
1 teaspoon (15 ml) easy-blend dried yeast
2oz (50 g) butter or margarine
1 tablespoon (15 ml) black treacle
4 tablespoons (60 ml) malt extract
scant 8fl oz (250 ml) tepid milk
4oz (115 g) chopped dates
3oz (75 g) sultanas
3oz (75 g) raisins
2oz (50 g) chopped nuts
2 tablespoons (30 ml) clear honey, to glaze

~ COOK'S TIP ~

This moist loaf is perfect for packed lunches.

Banana Orange Loaf

For the best banana flavour and a really good, moist texture, make sure the bananas are very ripe for this cake.

MAKES 1 LOAF

2 tablespoons (30 ml) sunflower oil

3½ oz (90 g) wholemeal plain flour

3½ oz (90 g) plain flour

1 teaspoon (5 ml) baking powder

1 teaspoon (5 ml) ground mixed spice

3 tablespoons (45 ml) flaked hazelnuts, toasted

2 large ripe bananas

1 egg

2 tablespoons (30 ml) clear honey

finely grated rind and juice of 1 small orange

4 orange slices, halved

2 teaspoons (10 ml) icing sugar

1 Preheat the oven to 180°C/350°F/ Gas 4.

2 ▲ Brush a 1¾ pint (1 litre) loaf tin with sunflower oil and line the base with non-stick baking paper.

3 ▲ Sift the flours with the baking powder and spice, adding any bran that is caught in the sieve. Stir in the toasted hazelnuts.

4 ▲ Peel and mash the bananas. Beat together with the egg, oil, honey and the orange rind and juice. Stir evenly into the dry ingredients.

5 Spoon into the prepared tin and smooth the top. Bake for 40–45 minutes, or until firm and golden brown. Turn out and cool on a wire rack. Sprinkle the orange slices with the icing sugar and grill until golden brown. Use to decorate the cake.

~ COOK'S TIP ~

If you plan to keep the loaf for more than two or three days, omit the orange slices, brush with honey and sprinkle with flaked hazelnuts.

Apple, Apricot and Walnut Loaf

Serve warm and store what is left in an airtight tin.

1 ▲ Preheat the oven to 180°C/ 350°F/Gas 4. Line and grease a 2lb (900 g) loaf tin.

2 ▲ Sift the flour, baking powder and salt into a large mixing bowl, then tip the bran remaining in the sieve into the mixture. Add the margarine, sugar, eggs, orange rind and juice. Stir, then beat with a hand-held electric beater until smooth.

3 ▲ Stir in the walnuts and apricots. Peel, quarter, and core the apple, chop it roughly and add it to the mixture. Stir, then spoon into the prepared tin and level the top.

MAKES 1 LOAF

8 oz (225 g) plain wholemeal flour
1 teaspoon (5 ml) baking powder
pinch of salt
4 oz (115 g) sunflower margarine
6 oz (175 g) soft light brown sugar
2 size 2 eggs, lightly beaten
grated rind and juice of 1 orange
2 oz (50 g) chopped walnuts
2 oz (50 g) ready-to-eat dried apricots, chopped
1 large cooking apple

4 Bake for 1 hour, or until a skewer inserted into the centre comes out clean. Cool in the tin for 5 minutes, then turn the loaf out on to a wire rack and peel off the lining paper.

Banana and Ginger Tea Bread

Serve this tea bread in slices with low-fat spread. The stem ginger adds an interesting flavour.

MAKES 1 LOAF

6 oz (175 g) self-raising flour
1 teaspoon (5 ml) baking powder
1½ oz (40 g) soft margarine
2oz (50 g) dark muscovado sugar
2oz (50 g) drained stem ginger, chopped
4 tablespoons (60 ml) skimmed milk
2 ripe bananas, mashed

1 ▲ Preheat the oven to 180°C/350°F/Gas 4. Grease and line a 1 lb (450 g) loaf tin. Sift the flour and baking powder into a mixing bowl.

2 ▲ Rub in the margarine until the mixture resembles breadcrumbs.

3 ▲ Stir in the sugar. Add the ginger, milk and bananas and mix.

4 ▲ Spoon into the prepared tin and bake for 40–45 minutes, or until an inserted skewer comes out clean. Run a palette knife around the edges to loosen, then turn the tea bread on to a wire rack and leave to cool.

Pear and Sultana Tea Bread

This is an ideal tea bread to make when pears are plentiful – an excellent use for windfalls.

1 ▲ Preheat the oven to 180°C/ 350°F/Gas 4. Grease and line a 1 lb (450 g) loaf tin with baking paper. Mix the oats with the sugar, pour over the pear or apple juice and oil, mix well and leave for 15 minutes.

2 ▲ Quarter, core and coarsely grate the pears. Add the fruit to the oat mixture with the flour, sultanas, baking powder, mixed spice and egg, then mix together thoroughly.

3 ▲ Spoon the mixture into the prepared loaf tin and level the top. Bake for 50–60 minutes or until a skewer inserted into the centre comes out clean.

4 ▲ Transfer the tea bread on to a wire rack and peel off the lining paper. Leave to cool completely.

~ COOK'S TIP ~

Health food shops sell concentrated pear and apple juice, ready for diluting as required.

MAKES 1 LOAF
1 oz (25 g) rolled oats
2 oz (50 g) light muscovado sugar
2 tablespoons (30 ml) pear or apple juice
2 tablespoons (30 ml) sunflower oil
1 large or 2 small pears
4 oz (115 g) self-raising flour
4 oz (115 g) sultanas
½ teaspoon (2.5 ml) baking powder
2 teaspoons (10 ml) mixed spice
1 egg

Cardamom and Saffron Tealoaf

An aromatic sweet bread ideal for afternoon tea or lightly toasted for breakfast. Using the sachets of fast-action or easy-blend yeasts make tealoaf-making so simple.

MAKES 1 LOAF

good pinch of saffron strands

1¼ pints (750 ml) lukewarm milk

1 oz (30 g) butter

32 oz (900 g) strong plain flour

2 teaspoons fast-action yeast

1½ oz (30 g) caster sugar

6 cardamom pods, split open and seeds extracted

4 oz (115 g) raisins

2 tablespoons clear honey, plus extra for brushing

1 egg, beaten

~ COOK'S TIP ~

Slice this loaf when cold and spread with butter. It is also good lightly toasted.

1 ▲ Crush the saffron into a cup containing a little of the warm milk and leave to infuse for 5 minutes.

2 Rub the butter into the flour, then mix in the yeast, sugar and cardamom seeds (these may need rubbing to separate them). Stir in the raisins.

3 ▲ Beat the remaining milk with the honey and egg, then mix this into the flour with the saffron milk and strands, stirring well until a firm dough is formed. You may not need all the milk; it depends on the flour.

4 ▲ Turn out the dough and knead it on a lightly floured board for about 5 minutes until smooth.

5 Return the dough to the mixing bowl, cover with oiled clear film and leave in a warm place until doubled in size. This could take between 1–3 hours. Grease a 2 lb (1 kg) loaf tin. Turn the dough out on to a floured board again, punch it down, knead for 3 minutes, then shape it into a fat roll and fit it into the greased loaf tin.

6 Cover with a sheet of lightly oiled clear film and stand in a warm place until the dough begins to rise again. Preheat the oven to 200°C/400°F/ Gas 6. Bake the loaf for 25 minutes until golden brown and firm on top. Turn out of the tin and as it cools, brush the top with honey.

Bilberry Tea Bread

MAKES 8 PIECES

2 oz (55 g) butter or margarine, at room temperature

6 oz (170 g) caster sugar

1 egg, at room temperature

4 fl oz (125 ml) milk

8 oz (225 g) plain flour

2 tsp baking powder

½ tsp salt

10 oz (285 g) fresh bilberries, or blueberries

FOR THE TOPPING

4 oz (115 g) sugar

1½ oz (45 g) plain flour

½ tsp ground cinnamon

2 oz (55 g) butter, cut in pieces

1 Preheat a 375°F/190°C/Gas 5 oven. Grease a 9 in (23 cm) baking dish.

2 With an electric mixer, cream the butter or margarine with the sugar until light and fluffy. Add the egg, beat to combine, then mix in the milk until blended.

3 ▼ Sift over the flour, baking powder and salt and stir just enough to blend the ingredients.

4 ▲ Add the berries and stir.

5 Transfer to the baking dish.

6 ▲ For the topping, place the sugar, flour, cinnamon and butter in a mixing bowl. Cut in with a pastry blender until the mixture resembles coarse breadcrumbs.

7 ▲ Sprinkle the topping over the mixture in the baking dish.

8 Bake until a skewer inserted in the centre comes out clean, about 45 minutes. Serve warm or cold.

Glazed Banana Spice Loaf

MAKES 1 LOAF

1 large ripe banana

4 oz (115 g) butter, at room temperature

5¹/₂ oz (150 g) caster sugar

2 eggs, at room temperature

7¹/₂ oz (215 g) plain flour

1 teaspoon salt

1 teaspoon bicarbonate of soda

¹/₂ teaspoon grated nutmeg

¹/₄ teaspoon ground allspice

¹/₄ teaspoon ground cloves

6 fl oz (175 ml) soured cream

1 teaspoon vanilla essence

FOR THE GLAZE

4 oz (115 g) icing sugar

1–2 tablespoons lemon juice

1   Preheat a 350°F/180°C/Gas 4 oven. Line an 8¹/₂ × 4¹/₂ in (21.5 × 11.5 cm) loaf tin with greaseproof and grease.

2 ▼   With a fork, mash the banana in a bowl. Set aside.

3   With an electric mixer, cream the butter and sugar until light and fluffy. Add the eggs, 1 at a time, beating to blend well after each addition.

4   Sift together the flour, salt, bicarbonate of soda, nutmeg, allspice and cloves. Add to the butter mixture and stir to combine well.

5 ▲   Add the soured cream, banana, and vanilla and mix just enough to blend. Pour into the prepared tin.

6 ▲   Bake until the top springs back when touched lightly, 45–50 minutes. Let cool in the pan for 10 minutes. Turn out onto a wire rack to cool.

7 ▲   For the glaze, combine the icing sugar and lemon juice, then stir until smooth.

8   To glaze, place the cooled loaf on a rack set over a baking sheet. Pour the glaze over the top of the loaf and allow to set.

Chocolate Chip Walnut Loaf

MAKES 1 LOAF

3½ oz (100 g) caster sugar
3½ oz (100 g) flour
1 teaspoon baking powder
4 tablespoons cornflour
4½ oz (130 g) butter, at room temperature
2 eggs, at room temperature
1 teaspoon vanilla extract
2 tablespoons currants or raisins
1 oz (30 g) walnuts, finely chopped
grated rind of ½ lemon
3 tablespoons plain chocolate chips
icing sugar, for dusting

1 Preheat the oven to 350°F/180°C/ Gas 4. Grease and line an 8½ × 4½ in (22 × 12 cm) loaf tin.

2 ▲ Sprinkle 1½ tablespoons of the caster sugar into the pan and tilt to distribute the sugar in an even layer over the bottom and sides. Shake out any excess.

~ VARIATION ~

For the best results, the eggs should be at room temperature. If they are too cold when folded into the creamed butter mixture, they may separate. If this happens, add a spoonful of the flour to help stabilize the mixture.

3 ▼ Sift together the flour, baking powder and cornflour into a mixing bowl, 3 times. Set aside.

4 With an electric mixer, cream the butter until soft. Add the remaining sugar and continue beating until light and fluffy. Add the eggs, 1 at a time, beating to incorporate thoroughly after each addition.

5 Gently fold the dry ingredients into the butter mixture, in 3 batches; do not overmix.

6 ▲ Fold in the vanilla, currants or raisins, walnuts, lemon rind, and chocolate chips until just blended.

7 Pour the mixture into the prepared tin and bake until a cake tester inserted in the centre comes out clean, 45–50 minutes. Let cool in the tin for 5 minutes before transferring to a rack to cool completely. Dust over an even layer of icing sugar before serving.

uity Tea Bread

MAKES 1 LOAF

8 oz (225 g) plain flour

4 oz (115 g) caster sugar

1 tbsp baking powder

1/2 tsp salt

grated rind of 1 large orange

5 1/2 fl oz (170 ml) fresh orange juice

2 eggs, lightly beaten

3 oz (85 g) butter or margarine, melted

4 oz (115 g) fresh cranberries, or
  bilberries

2 oz (55 g) chopped walnuts

1 Preheat a 350°F/180°C/Gas 4 oven. Line a 9 × 5 in (23 × 13 cm) loaf tin with greaseproof paper and grease.

2 Sift the flour, sugar, baking powder and salt into a mixing bowl.

3 ▼ Stir in the orange rind.

4 ▲ Make a well in the centre and add the orange juice, eggs and melted butter or margarine. Stir from the centre until the ingredients are blended; do not overmix.

5 ▲ Add the berries and walnuts and stir until blended.

6 Transfer the mixture to the prepared tin and bake until a skewer inserted in the centre comes out clean, 45–50 minutes.

7 ▲ Let cool in the tin for 10 minutes before transferring to a rack to cool completely. Serve thinly sliced, toasted or plain, with butter or cream cheese and jam.

Dried Fruit Loaf

MAKES 1 LOAF

1 lb (450 g) mixed dried fruit, such as currants, raisins, chopped dried apricots and dried cherries
10 fl oz (300 ml) cold strong tea
7 oz (200 g) dark brown sugar
grated rind and juice of 1 small orange
grated rind and juice of 1 lemon
1 egg, lightly beaten
7 oz (200 g) plain flour
1 tbsp baking powder
1/8 tsp salt

1 ▲ In a bowl, mix the dried fruit with the tea and soak overnight.

2 Preheat a 350°F/180°C/Gas 4 oven. Line the bottom and sides of a 9 × 5 in (23 × 13 cm) loaf tin with greaseproof paper and grease the paper.

3 ▲ Strain the fruit, reserving the liquid. In a bowl, combine the brown sugar, grated orange and lemon rind, and fruit.

4 ▼ Pour the orange and lemon juice into a measuring jug; if the quantity is less than 8 fl oz (250 ml), top up with the soaking liquid.

5 Stir the citrus juices and egg into the dried fruit mixture.

6 In another bowl, sift together the flour, baking powder and salt. Stir into the fruit mixture until blended.

7 Transfer to the prepared tin and bake until a skewer inserted in the centre comes out clean, about 1¼ hours. Let stand 10 minutes before unmoulding.

Mango Tea Bread

MAKES 2 LOAVES

10 oz (285 g) plain flour

2 teaspoons bicarbonate of soda

2 teaspoons ground cinnamon

$^1/_2$ teaspoon salt

4 oz (115 g) margarine, at room temperature

3 eggs, at room temperature

$10^1/_2$ oz (300 g) sugar

4 fl oz (125 ml) vegetable oil

1 large ripe mango, peeled and chopped

$3^1/_4$ oz (90 g) desiccated coconut

$2^1/_2$ oz (70 g) raisins

1   Preheat the oven to 350°F/180°C/ Gas 4. Line the bottom and sides of 2 9 × 5 in (23 × 13 cm) loaf tins with greaseproof paper and grease.

2   Sift together the flour, bicarbonate of soda, cinnamon and salt. Set aside.

3   With an electric mixer, cream the margarine until soft.

4 ▼   Beat in the eggs and sugar until light and fluffy. Beat in the oil.

5   Fold the dry ingredients into the creamed ingredients in 3 batches.

6   Fold in the mangoes, two-thirds of the coconut and the raisins.

7 ▲   Spoon the batter into the pans.

8   Sprinkle over the remaining coconut. Bake until a skewer inserted in the centre comes out clean, 50–60 minutes. Let stand for 10 minutes before turning out onto a rack to cool completely.

Courgette Tea Bread

MAKES 1 LOAF

2 oz (55 g) butter

3 eggs

8 fl oz (250 ml) vegetable oil

$10^1/_2$ oz (300 g) sugar

2 medium unpeeled courgettes, grated

10 oz (285 g) plain flour

2 teaspoons bicarbonate of soda

1 teaspoon baking powder

1 teaspoon salt

1 teaspoon ground cinnamon

1 teaspoon grated nutmeg

$^1/_4$ teaspoon ground cloves

4 oz (115 g) walnuts, chopped

1   Preheat the oven to 350°F/180°C/ Gas 4.

2   Line the bottom and sides of a 9 × 5 in (23 × 13 cm) loaf tin with greaseproof paper and grease.

3 ▲   In a saucepan, melt the butter over low heat. Set aside.

4   With an electric mixer, beat the eggs and oil together until thick. Beat in the sugar. Stir in the melted butter and courgettes. Set aside.

5 ▲   In another bowl, sift all the dry ingredients together 3 times. Carefully fold into the courgette mixture. Fold in the walnuts.

6   Pour into the tin and bake until a skewer inserted in the centre comes out clean, 60–70 minutes. Let stand 10 minutes before turning out onto wire rack to cool completely.

Mango Tea Bread (top), Courgette Tea Bread

PIES & TARTS

HERE IS EVERY SORT OF FILLING –
FROM ORCHARD FRUITS TO AUTUMN
NUTS, TANGY CITRUS TO LUSCIOUS
CHOCOLATE – FOR THE MOST
MEMORABLE PIES AND TARTS. SOME
ARE PLAIN AND SOME ARE FANCY,
BUT ALL ARE DELICIOUS.

Traditional Apple Pie

SERVES 8

about 2 lb (900 g) tart eating apples,
   such as Granny Smith, peeled, cored
   and sliced

1 tbsp fresh lemon juice

1 tsp vanilla essence

4 oz (115 g) caster sugar

½ tsp ground cinnamon

1½ oz (45 g) butter or margarine

1 egg yolk

2 tsp whipping cream

FOR THE PASTRY

8 oz (225 g) plain flour

1 tsp salt

6 oz (170 g) lard or vegetable fat

4–5 tbsp iced water

1 tbsp quick-cooking tapioca

1 Preheat a 450°F/230°C/Gas 8 oven.

2 For the pastry, sift the flour and salt into a bowl. Using a pastry blender, cut in the fat until the mixture resembles coarse breadcrumbs.

3 ▲ Sprinkle in the water, 1 tablespoon at a time, tossing lightly with your fingertips or with a fork until the pastry forms a ball.

4 ▲ Divide the pastry in half and shape each half into a ball. On a lightly floured surface, roll out one of the balls to a circle about 12 in (30 cm) in diameter.

5 ▲ Use it to line a 9 in (23 cm) pie tin, easing the dough in and being careful not to stretch it. Trim off the excess pastry and use the trimmings for decorating. Sprinkle the tapioca over the bottom of the pie shell.

6 ▲ Roll out the remaining pastry to ⅛ in (3 mm) thickness. With a sharp knife, cut out 8 large leaf-shapes. Cut the trimmings into small leaf shapes. Score the leaves with the back of the knife to mark veins.

7 ▲ In a bowl, toss the apples with the lemon juice, vanilla, sugar and cinnamon. Fill the pastry case with the apple mixture and dot with the butter or margarine.

8 ▲ Arrange the large pastry leaves in a decorative pattern on top. Decorate the edge with small leaves.

9 ▲ Mix together the egg yolk and cream and brush over the leaves to glaze them.

10 Bake 10 minutes, then reduce the heat to 350°F/180°C/Gas 4 and continue baking until the pastry is golden brown, 35–45 minutes. Let the pie cool in the tin, set on a wire rack.

Apple and Cranberry Lattice Pie

SERVES 8

grated rind of 1 orange

3 tablespoons fresh orange juice

2 large, tart cooking apples

6 oz (170 g) cranberries

2¹/₂ oz (70 g) raisins

1 oz (30 g) walnuts, chopped

7¹/₂ oz (215 g) caster sugar

4 oz (115 g) dark brown sugar

2 tablespoons plain flour

FOR THE CRUST

10 oz (285 g) plain flour

¹/₂ teaspoon salt

3 oz (85 g) cold butter, cut into pieces

3 oz (85 g) cold vegetable fat or lard, cut into pieces

2–4 fl oz (65–125 ml) iced water

1 ▼ For the crust, sift the flour and salt into a bowl. Add the butter and fat and rub in with your fingertips until the mixture resembles coarse breadcrumbs. With a fork, stir in just enough water to bind the dough. Gather into 2 equal balls, wrap in cling film, and refrigerate for at least 20 minutes.

2 ▲ Put the orange rind and juice into a mixing bowl. Peel and core the apples and grate into the bowl. Stir in the cranberries, raisins, walnuts, all except 1 tablespoon of the caster sugar, the brown sugar and flour.

3 Place a baking sheet in the oven and preheat to 400°F/200°C/Gas 6.

4 On a lightly floured surface, roll out 1 ball of dough about ¹/₈ in (3mm) thick. Transfer to a 9 in (23 cm) pie plate and trim. Spoon the cranberry and apple mixture into the shell.

5 ▲ Roll out the remaining dough to a circle about 11 in (28 cm) in diameter. With a serrated pastry wheel, cut the dough into 10 strips, ³/₄ in (2 cm) wide. Place 5 strips horizontally across the top of the tart at 1 in (2.5 cm) intervals. Weave in 5 vertical strips and trim. Sprinkle the top with the remaining sugar.

6 Bake the pie for 20 minutes. Reduce the heat to 350°F/180°C/Gas 4 and bake for about 15 minutes more, until the crust is golden and the filling is bubbling.

Rhubarb and Cherry Pie

SERVES 8

1 lb (450 g) rhubarb, cut into 1 in (2.5 cm) pieces
1 lb (450 g) canned stoned tart red or black cherries, drained
10 oz (285 g) caster sugar
1 oz (30 g) quick-cooking tapioca
FOR THE PASTRY
10 oz (285 g) plain flour
1 tsp salt
3 oz (85 g) cold butter, cut in pieces
2 oz (55 g) cold vegetable fat or lard, cut in pieces
2–4 fl oz (65–125 ml) iced water
milk, for glazing

1 ▲ For the pastry, sift the flour and salt into a bowl. Add the butter and fat to the dry ingredients and cut in with a pastry blender until the mixture resembles coarse breadcrumbs.

2 With a fork, stir in just enough water to bind the pastry. Gather into 2 balls, 1 slightly larger than the other. Wrap the pastry in greaseproof paper and refrigerate for at least 20 minutes.

3 Preheat a baking sheet in the centre of a 400°F/200°C/Gas 6 oven.

4 On a lightly floured surface, roll out the larger pastry ball to a thickness of about 1/8 in (3 mm).

5 ▼ Roll the pastry around the rolling pin and transfer to a 9 in (23 cm) pie dish. Trim the edge to leave a 1/2 in (1 cm) overhang.

6 Refrigerate the pastry case while making the filling.

7 In a mixing bowl, combine the rhubarb, cherries, sugar and tapioca and spoon into the pie shell.

8 ▲ Roll out the remaining pastry and cut out leaf shapes.

9 Transfer the pastry lid to the pie and trim to leave a 3/4 in (2 cm) overhang. Fold the top edge under the bottom and flute. Roll small balls from the scraps. Mark veins in the pastry leaves and place on top with the balls.

10 Glaze the top and bake until golden, 40–50 minutes.

Rhubarb Pie

SERVES 6

6oz (175g) plain flour
½ teaspoon salt
2 teaspoons caster sugar
3oz (75g) cold butter or vegetable fat
2fl oz (50ml) or more iced water
2 tablespoons whipping cream
FOR THE FILLING
2lb (900g) fresh rhubarb, cut in ½–1 in (1–2.5 cm) pieces
2 tablespoons cornflour
1 egg
10½oz (285g) caster sugar
1 tablespoon grated orange rind

1 ▲ For the pastry, sift the flour, salt, and sugar into a bowl. Using a pastry blender or two knives, cut the butter or fat into the dry ingredients as quickly as possible until the mixture resembles coarse breadcrumbs.

2 Sprinkle with the iced water and mix until the dough holds together. If the dough is too crumbly, add a little more water, 1 tablespoon at a time.

~ COOK'S TIP ~

Be sure to cut off and discard the green rhubarb leaves from the pink stalks as they are toxic and not edible.

3 ▲ Gather the dough into a ball, flatten into a disc, wrap in grease-proof paper, and chill for at least 20 minutes.

4 ▲ Roll out the dough between two sheets of greaseproof paper to a thickness of about ⅛ in (3 mm). Use to line a 9 in (23 cm) pie dish. Trim all round, leaving a ½ in (1 cm) overhang. Fold the overhang under the edge and flute. Refrigerate the pie shell and dough trimmings for 30 minutes.

5 ▲ For the filling, place the rhubarb in a bowl and sprinkle with the cornflour. Toss to coat.

6 Preheat oven to 220°C/425°F/Gas 7.

7 In a small bowl, beat the egg with the sugar. Mix in the orange rind.

8 ▲ Stir the sugar mixture into the rhubarb and mix well. Spoon the fruit into the pie shell.

9 ▲ Roll out the dough trimmings. Stamp out decorative shapes with a biscuit cutter or cut shapes with a small knife, using a template made out of card as a guide, if wished.

10 Arrange the shapes on top of the pie. Brush the trimmings and the rim of the pie with cream.

11 Bake for 30 minutes. Reduce the heat to 160°C/325°F/Gas 3 and continue baking until the pastry is golden brown and the rhubarb is tender, about 15–20 minutes more.

Plum Pie

SERVES 8

2 lb (900 g) red or purple plums
grated rind of 1 lemon
1 tbsp fresh lemon juice
4–6 oz (115–170 g) caster sugar
3 tbsp quick-cooking tapioca
$^1/_8$ tsp salt
$^1/_2$ tsp ground cinnamon
$^1/_4$ tsp grated nutmeg
FOR THE PASTRY
10 oz (285 g) plain flour
1 tsp salt
3 oz (85 g) cold butter, cut in pieces
2 oz (55 g) cold vegetable fat or lard, cut in pieces
2–4 fl oz (65–125 ml) iced water
milk, for glazing

1 ▼ For the pastry, sift the flour and salt into a bowl. Add the butter and fat and cut in with a pastry blender until the mixture resembles coarse breadcrumbs.

2 Stir in just enough water to bind the pastry. Gather into 2 balls, 1 slightly larger than the other. Wrap and refrigerate for 20 minutes.

3 Preheat a baking sheet in the centre of a 425°F/220°C/Gas 7 oven.

4 On a lightly floured surface, roll out the larger pastry ball to about $^1/_8$ in (3 mm) thick. Transfer to a 9 in (23 cm) pie dish and trim the edge.

5 ▲ Halve the plums, discard the stones, and cut into large pieces. Mix all the filling ingredients together (if the plums are very tart, use extra sugar). Transfer to the pastry case.

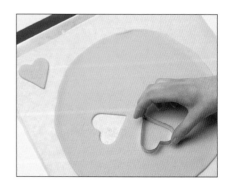

6 ▲ Roll out the remaining pastry and place on a baking tray lined with greaseproof paper. With a cutter, stamp out 4 hearts. Transfer the pastry lid to the pie using the paper.

7 Trim to leave a $^3/_4$ in (2 cm) overhang. Fold the top edge under the bottom and pinch to seal. Arrange the hearts on top. Brush with the milk. Bake for 15 minutes. Reduce the heat to 350°F/180°C/Gas 4 and bake 30–35 minutes more. If the crust browns too quickly, protect with a sheet of foil.

Lattice Berry Pie

SERVES 8

1 lb (450 g) berries, such as bilberries, blueberries, blackcurrants etc
4 oz (115 g) caster sugar
3 tbsp cornflour
2 tbsp fresh lemon juice
1 oz (30 g) butter, diced
FOR THE PASTRY
10 oz (285 g) plain flour
¾ tsp salt
4 oz (115 g) cold butter, cut in pieces
1½ oz (45 g) cold vegetable fat or lard, cut in pieces
5–6 tbsp iced water
1 egg beaten with 1 tbsp water, for glazing

1 For the pastry, sift the flour and salt into a bowl. Add the butter and fat and cut in with a pastry blender until the mixture resembles coarse breadcrumbs. With a fork, stir in just enough water to bind the pastry. Form into 2 balls, wrap in greaseproof paper, and refrigerate for 20 minutes.

2 On a lightly floured surface, roll out one ball about ⅛ in (3 mm) thick. Transfer to a 9 in (23 cm) pie dish and trim to leave a ½ in (1 cm) overhang. Brush the bottom with egg glaze.

3 ▲ Mix all the filling ingredients together, except the butter (reserve a few berries for decoration). Spoon into the pastry case and dot with the butter. Brush the egg glaze around the rim of the pastry case.

4 Preheat a baking sheet in the centre of a 425°F/220°C/Gas 7 oven.

5 ▼ Roll out the remaining pastry on a baking tray lined with grease-proof paper. With a serrated pastry wheel, cut out 24 thin pastry strips. Roll out the scraps and cut out leaf shapes. Mark veins in the leaves with the point of a knife.

6 ▲ Weave the strips in a close lattice, then transfer to the pie using the paper. Press the edges to seal and trim. Arrange the pastry leaves around the rim. Brush with egg glaze.

7 Bake for 10 minutes. Reduce the heat to 350°F/180°C/Gas 4 and bake until the pastry is golden, 40–45 minutes more. Decorate with berries.

Cherry Pie

SERVES 8

2 lb (900 g) fresh Morello cherries, stoned, or 2 × 1 lb (450 g) cans or jars, drained and stoned

2½ oz (70 g) caster sugar

1 oz (30 g) plain flour

1½ tbsp fresh lemon juice

¼ tsp almond essence

1 oz (30 g) butter or margarine

FOR THE PASTRY

8 oz (225 g) plain flour

1 tsp salt

6 oz (175 g) lard or vegetable fat

4–5 tbsp iced water

1 For the pastry, sift the flour and salt into a mixing bowl. Using a pastry blender, cut in the fat until the mixture resembles coarse breadcrumbs.

2 ▲ Sprinkle in the water, 1 tablespoon at a time, tossing lightly with your fingertips or a fork until the pastry forms a ball.

3 Divide the pastry in half and shape each half into a ball. On a lightly floured surface, roll out one of the balls to a circle about 12 in (30 cm) in diameter.

4 ▲ Use it to line a 9 in (23 cm) pie tin, easing the pastry in and being careful not to stretch it. With scissors, trim off excess pastry, leaving a ½ in (1 cm) overhang around the pie rim.

5 ▲ Roll out the remaining pastry to ⅛ in (3 mm) thickness. Cut out 11 strips ½ in (1 cm) wide.

6 ▲ In a mixing bowl, combine the cherries, sugar, flour, lemon juice and almond essence. Spoon the mixture into the pastry case and dot with the butter or margarine.

7 ▲ To make the lattice, place 5 of the pastry strips evenly across the filling. Fold every other strip back. Lay the first strip across in the opposite direction. Continue in this pattern, folding back every other strip each time you add a cross strip.

8 ▲ Trim the ends of the lattice strips even with the case overhang. Press together so that the edge rests on the pie-tin rim. With your thumbs, flute the edge. Refrigerate 15 minutes.

9 Preheat a 425°F/220°C/Gas 7 oven.

10 Bake the pie 30 minutes, covering the edge of the pastry case with foil, if necessary, to prevent over-browning. Let cool, in the tin, on a wire rack.

Peach Leaf Pie

SERVES 8

2 lb 8 oz (1.2 kg) ripe peaches
juice of 1 lemon
3½ oz (100 g) sugar
3 tablespoons cornflour
¼ teaspoon grated nutmeg
½ teaspoon ground cinnamon
1 oz (30 g) butter, diced
FOR THE CRUST
10 oz (285 g) plain flour
¾ teaspoon salt
4 oz (115 g) cold butter, cut into pieces
2¼ oz (60 g) cold vegetable fat or lard, cut into pieces
5–6 tablespoons iced water
1 egg beaten with 1 tablespoon water, for glazing

1 For the pastry, sift the flour and salt into a bowl. Add the butter and fat and rub in with your fingertips until the mixture resembles coarse breadcrumbs.

2 ▲ With a fork, stir in just enough water to bind the dough. Gather into 2 balls, one slightly larger than the other. Wrap in clear film and refrigerate for at least 20 minutes.

3 Place a baking sheet in the oven and preheat to 425°F/220°C/Gas 7.

4 ▲ Drop a few peaches at a time into boiling water for 20 seconds, then transfer to a bowl of cold water. When cool, peel off the skins.

5 Slice the peaches and combine with the lemon juice, sugar, cornstarch and spices. Set aside.

6 ▲ On a lightly floured surface, roll out the larger dough ball about ⅛ in (3 mm) thick. Transfer to a 9 in (23 cm) pie tin and trim. Refrigerate.

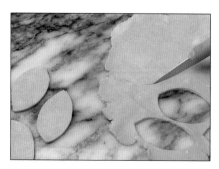

7 ▲ Roll out the remaining dough ¼ in (5 mm) thick. Cut out leaf shapes 3 in (8 cm) long, using a template if needed. Mark veins with a knife. With the scraps, roll a few balls.

8 ▲ Brush the bottom of the pastry shell with egg glaze. Add the peaches, piling them higher in the centre. Dot with the butter.

9 ▲ To assemble, start from the outside edge and cover the peaches with a ring of leaves. Place a second ring of leaves above, staggering the positions. Continue with rows of leaves until covered. Place the balls in the centre. Brush with glaze.

10 Bake for 10 minutes. Lower the heat to 350°F/180°C/Gas 4 and bake for 35–40 minutes more.

~ COOK'S TIP ~

Baking the pie on a preheated baking sheet helps to make the bottom crust crisp. The moisture from the filling keeps the bottom crust more humid than the top, but this baking method helps to compensate for the top crust being better exposed to the heat source.

Maryland Peach and Blueberry Pie

SERVES 8

8oz (225g) flour
½ teaspoon salt
2 teaspoons sugar
5oz (150g) cold butter or margarine
1 egg yolk
2fl oz (50ml) or more iced water
2 tablespoons milk, for glazing
FOR THE FILLING
7 fresh peaches, peeled and sliced
8oz (225g) fresh blueberries
5oz (150g) sugar
2 tablespoons fresh lemon juice
1½oz (40g) plain flour
⅛ teaspoon grated nutmeg
1oz (25g) butter or margarine, cut in pea-size pieces

1 For the pastry, sift the flour, salt, and sugar into a bowl. Using a pastry blender or two knives, cut the butter or margarine into the dry ingredients as quickly as possible until the mixture resembles coarse breadcrumbs.

2 Mix the egg yolk with the iced water and sprinkle over the flour mixture. Combine with a fork until the dough holds together. If the dough is too crumbly, add a little more water, 1 tablespoon at a time. Gather the dough into a ball and flatten into a disk. Wrap in greaseproof paper and refrigerate for at least 20 minutes.

3 Roll out two-thirds of the dough between two sheets of greaseproof paper to a thickness of about ⅛ in (3 mm). Use to line a 9 in (23 cm) pie pan. Trim the edge, leaving a ½ in (1 cm) overhang. Fold the overhang under to form the edge. Using a fork, press the edge to the rim of the pie dish.

4 ▲ Gather the trimmings and remaining dough into a ball, and roll out to a thickness of about ¼ in (5 mm). Using a serrated pastry wheel or sharp knife, cut strips ½ in (1 cm) wide. Refrigerate both the pastry case and the strips of dough for 20 minutes.

5 Preheat a 200°C/400°F/Gas 6 oven.

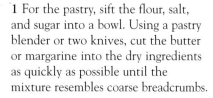

6 ▲ Line the pastry case with greaseproof paper and fill with dried beans. Bake until the case is just set, 7–10 minutes. Remove from the oven and carefully lift out the paper with the beans. Prick the bottom of the pastry case all over with a fork, then return to the oven and bake for 5 minutes more. Let the pastry case cool slightly before filling. Leave the oven on.

7 ▲ In a mixing bowl, combine the peach slices with the blueberries, sugar, lemon juice, flour and nutmeg. Spoon the fruit mixture evenly into the pastry case. Dot with the pieces of butter or margarine.

8 ▲ Weave a lattice top with the chilled pastry strips, pressing the ends to the baked pastry case edge. Brush the strips with the milk.

9 Bake the pie for 15 minutes. Reduce the heat to 180°C/350°F/Gas 4, and continue baking until the filling is tender and bubbling and the pastry lattice is golden, about 30 minutes more. If the pastry gets too brown, cover loosely with a piece of foil. Serve the pie warm or at room temperature.

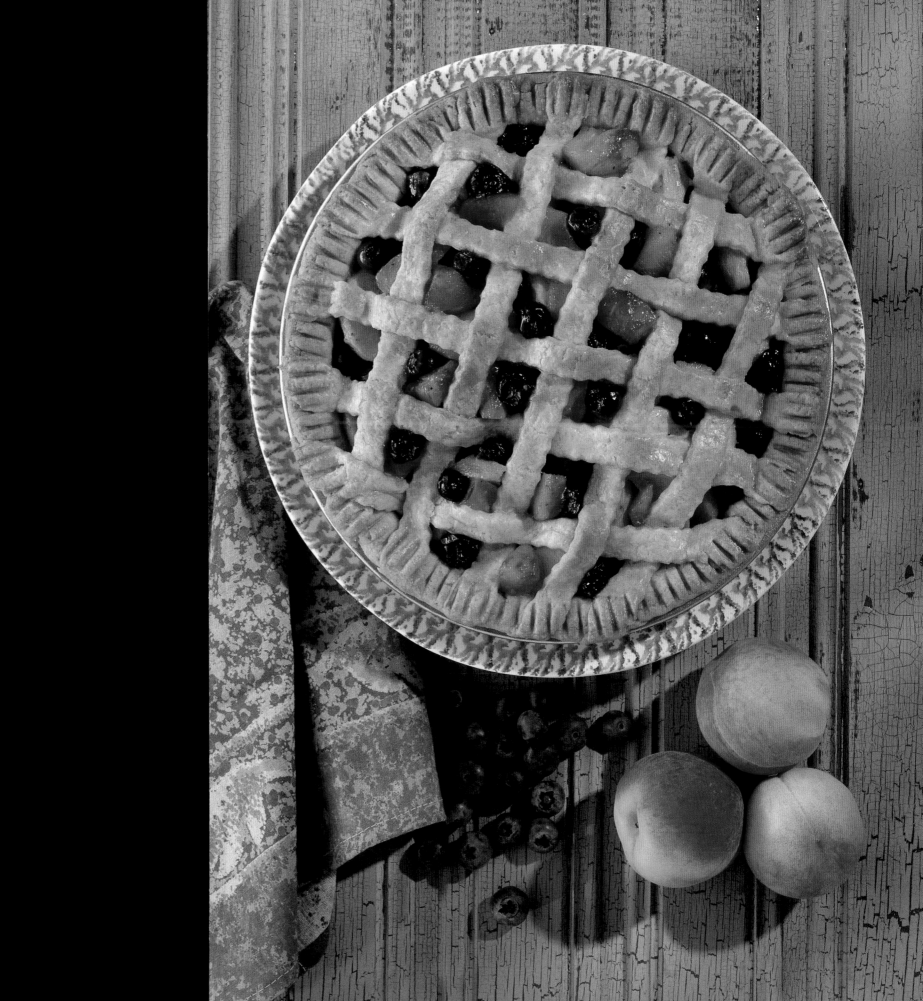

Blueberry Pie

Serves 6–8

basic or rich shortcrust for a two-crust
   pie (page 222, shortcrust variations)

1¼ lb (575 g) blueberries

5½ oz (160 g) caster sugar

3 tablespoons plain flour

1 teaspoon grated orange zest

¼ teaspoon grated nutmeg

2 tablespoons orange juice

1 teaspoon lemon juice

1 Preheat a 375°F/190°C/Gas 5 oven.

2 ▲ Roll out half of the pastry and use to line a 9 in (23 cm) pie tin that is about 2 in (5 cm) deep.

3 ▲ Combine the blueberries, 5 oz (145 g) of the sugar, the flour, orange zest and nutmeg in a bowl. Toss the mixture gently to coat the fruit evenly with the dry ingredients.

4 ▼ Pour the blueberry mixture into the pastry case and spread it evenly. Sprinkle over the citrus juices.

5 ▲ Roll out the remaining pastry and cover the pie. Cut out small decorative shapes or cut 2–3 slits for steam vents. Finish the edge.

6 ▲ Brush the top lightly with water and sprinkle evenly with the remaining caster sugar.

7 Bake for about 45 minutes or until the pastry is golden brown. Serve warm or at room temperature.

Walnut and Pear Lattice Pie

SERVES 6–8

nut shortcrust for a two-crust pie (page 222, pastry variations), using walnuts

2 lb (900 g) pears, peeled, cored and thinly sliced

2 oz (55 g) caster sugar

1 oz (30 g) plain flour

½ teaspoon grated lemon zest

1 oz (30 g) raisins or sultanas

1 oz (30 g) walnuts, chopped

½ teaspoon ground cinnamon

2 oz (55 g) icing sugar

1 tablespoon lemon juice

about 2 teaspoons cold water

1 Preheat a 375°F/190°C/Gas 5 oven.

2 Roll out half of the pastry dough and use to line a 9 in (23 cm) tin that is about 2 in (5 cm) deep.

3 ▲ Combine the pears, caster sugar, flour and lemon zest in a bowl. Toss gently until the fruit is evenly coated with the dry ingredients. Mix in the raisins, nuts and cinnamon.

~ COOK'S TIP ~

For a simple cutout lattice top, roll out the dough for the top into a circle. Using a small pastry cutter, cut out shapes in a pattern, spacing them evenly and not too close together.

4 ▲ Put the pear filling into the pastry case and spread it evenly.

5 Roll out the remaining pastry dough and use to make a lattice top.

6 Bake for 55 minutes or until the pastry is golden brown.

7 Combine the icing sugar, lemon juice and water in a bowl and stir until smoothly blended.

8 ▼ Remove the pie from the oven. Drizzle the icing sugar glaze evenly over the top of the pie, on pastry and filling. Leave the pie to cool, set on a wire rack, before serving.

Mince Pies

MAKES 36

6 oz (170 g) finely chopped blanched almonds

5 oz (140 g) dried apricots, finely chopped

6 oz (170 g) raisins

5 oz (140 g) currants

5 oz (140 g) glacé cherries, chopped

5 oz (140 g) cut mixed peel, chopped

4 oz (115 g) finely chopped beef suet

grated rind and juice of 2 lemons

grated rind and juice of 1 orange

7 oz (200 g) dark brown sugar

4 cooking apples, peeled, cored and chopped

2 tsp ground cinnamon

1 tsp grated nutmeg

1/2 tsp ground cloves

8 fl oz (250 ml) brandy

8 oz (225 g) cream cheese

2 tbsp caster sugar

icing sugar, for dusting (optional)

FOR THE PASTRY

15 oz (420 g) plain flour

5 oz (140 g) icing sugar

12 oz (350 g) cold butter, cut in pieces

grated rind and juice of 1 orange

milk, for glazing

1 Mix the nuts, dried and preserved fruit, suet, citrus rind and juice, brown sugar, apples and spices.

2 ▲ Stir in the brandy. Cover and leave in a cool place for 2 days.

3 For the pastry, sift the flour and icing sugar into a bowl. Cut in the butter until the mixture resembles coarse breadcrumbs.

4 ▲ Add the orange rind. Stir in just enough orange juice to bind. Gather into a ball, wrap in greaseproof paper, and refrigerate for at least 20 minutes.

5 Preheat a 425°F/220°C/Gas 7 oven. Grease 2–3 bun trays. Beat together the cream cheese and sugar.

6 ▲ Roll out the pastry 1/4 in (5 mm) thick. With a fluted pastry cutter, stamp out 36 3 in (8 cm) rounds.

~ COOK'S TIP ~

The mincemeat mixture may be packed into sterilized jars and sealed. It will keep refrigerated for several months. Add a few tablespoonfuls to give apple pies a lift, or make small mincemeat-filled parcels using filo pastry.

7 ▲ Transfer the rounds to the bun tray. Fill halfway with mincemeat. Top with a teaspoonful of the cream cheese mixture.

8 ▲ Roll out the remaining pastry and stamp out 36 2 in (5 cm) rounds with a fluted cutter. Brush the edges of the pies with milk, then set the rounds on top. Cut a small steam vent in the top of each pie.

9 ▲ Brush lightly with milk. Bake until golden, 15–20 minutes. Let cool for 10 minutes before unmoulding. Dust with icing sugar, if wished.

...ar and Apple Crumble Pie

SERVES 8

3 firm pears
4 cooking apples
6 oz (170 g) caster sugar
2 tbsp cornflour
1/8 tsp salt
grated rind of 1 lemon
2 tbsp fresh lemon juice
3 oz (85 g) raisins
3 oz (85 g) plain flour
1 tsp ground cinnamon
3 oz (85 g) cold butter, cut in pieces
FOR THE PASTRY
5 oz (140 g) plain flour
1/2 tsp salt
2 1/2 oz (70 g) cold vegetable fat or lard, cut in pieces
2 tbsp iced water

1 For the pastry, combine the flour and salt in a bowl. Add the fat and cut in with a pastry blender until the mixture resembles coarse breadcrumbs. Stir in just enough water to bind the pastry. Gather into a ball and transfer to a lightly floured surface. Roll out 1/8 in (3 mm) thick.

2 ▲ Transfer to a shallow 9 in (23 cm) pie dish and trim to leave a 1/2 in (1 cm) overhang. Fold the overhang under for double thickness. Flute the edge. Refrigerate.

3 Preheat a baking sheet in the centre of a 450°F/230°C/Gas 8 oven.

4 ▲ Peel and core the pears. Slice them into a bowl. Peel, core and slice the apples. Add to the pears. Stir in one-third of the sugar, the cornflour, salt and lemon rind. Add the lemon juice and raisins and stir to blend.

5 For the crumble topping, combine the remaining sugar, flour, cinnamon, and butter in a bowl. Blend with your fingertips until the mixture resembles coarse breadcrumbs. Set aside.

6 ▲ Spoon the fruit filling into the pastry case. Sprinkle the crumbs lightly and evenly over the top.

7 Bake for 10 minutes, then reduce the heat to 350°F/180°C/Gas 4. Cover the top of the pie loosely with a sheet of foil and continue baking until browned, 35–40 minutes more.

Open Apple Pie

SERVES 8

3 lb (1.4 kg) sweet-tart firm eating or cooking apples
1³/₄ oz (50 g) sugar
2 teaspoons ground cinnamon
grated rind and juice of 1 lemon
1 oz (30 g) butter, diced
2–3 tablespoons honey
FOR THE CRUST
10 oz (285 g) plain flour
¹/₂ teaspoon salt
4 oz (115 g) cold butter, cut into pieces
2¹/₄ oz (60 g) cold vegetable fat or lard, cut into pieces
5–6 tablespoons iced water

1 For the crust, sift the flour and salt into a bowl. Add the butter and fat and rub in with your fingertips until the mixture resembles coarse breadcrumbs.

2 ▲ With a fork, stir in just enough water to bind the dough. Gather into a ball, wrap in clear film, and refrigerate for at least 20 minutes.

3 Place a baking sheet in the centre of the oven and preheat to 400°F/200°C/Gas 6.

4 ▼ Peel, core, and slice the apples. Combine the sugar and cinnamon in a bowl. Add the apples, lemon rind and juice and stir.

5 On a lightly floured surface, roll out the dough to a circle about 12 in (30 cm) in diameter. Transfer to a 9 in (23 cm) diameter deep pie dish; leave the dough hanging over the edge. Fill with the apple slices.

6 ▲ Fold in the edges and crimp loosely for a decorative border. Dot the apples with diced butter.

7 Bake on the hot sheet until the pastry is golden and the apples are tender, about 45 minutes.

8 Melt the honey in a saucepan and brush over the apples to glaze. Serve warm or at room temperature.

Brethren's Cider Pie

SERVES 6

6oz (175g) plain flour
¼ teaspoon salt
2 teaspoons sugar
4oz (115g) cold butter or margarine
2fl oz (50ml) or more iced water
FOR THE FILLING
1 pint (600ml) unfiltered apple juice
½oz (15g) butter
8fl oz (250ml) maple syrup
2fl oz (50ml) water
¼ teaspoon salt
2 eggs, at room temperature, separated
1 teaspoon grated nutmeg

1 ▲ For the pastry, sift the flour, salt, and sugar into a bowl. Using a pastry blender or two knives, cut the butter or margarine into the dry ingredients as quickly as possible until the mixture resembles coarse breadcrumbs.

2 Sprinkle the iced water over the flour mixture. Combine with a fork until the dough holds together. If the dough is too crumbly, add a little more water, 1 tablespoon at a time. Gather the dough into a ball and flatten into a disk. Wrap in greaseproof paper and refrigerate for at least 20 minutes.

3 ▲ Meanwhile, place the apple juice in a heavy pan. Boil until only 6fl oz (175ml) remains. Leave to cool.

4 ▲ Roll out the dough between two sheets of greaseproof paper to a thickness of about ⅛ in (3 mm). Use to line a 9 in (23 cm) pie dish.

5 ▲ Trim the edge, leaving a ½ in (1 cm) overhang. Fold the overhang under to form the edge. Using a fork, press the edge to the rim of the dish and press up from under with your fingers at intervals for a ruffle effect. Refrigerate for 20 minutes.

6 Preheat a 180°C/350°F/Gas 4 oven.

7 ▲ For the filling, add the butter, maple syrup, water and salt to the juice and simmer gently for 5–6 minutes. Remove the pan from the heat and leave to cool slightly. Beat the egg yolks and whisk them into the pan.

8 ▲ In a large bowl, beat the egg whites until they form stiff peaks. Add the juice mixture and fold gently together until evenly blended.

9 ▲ Pour into the prepared pastry case. Dust with the grated nutmeg.

10 Bake until the pastry is golden brown and the filling is well set, 30–35 minutes. Serve warm.

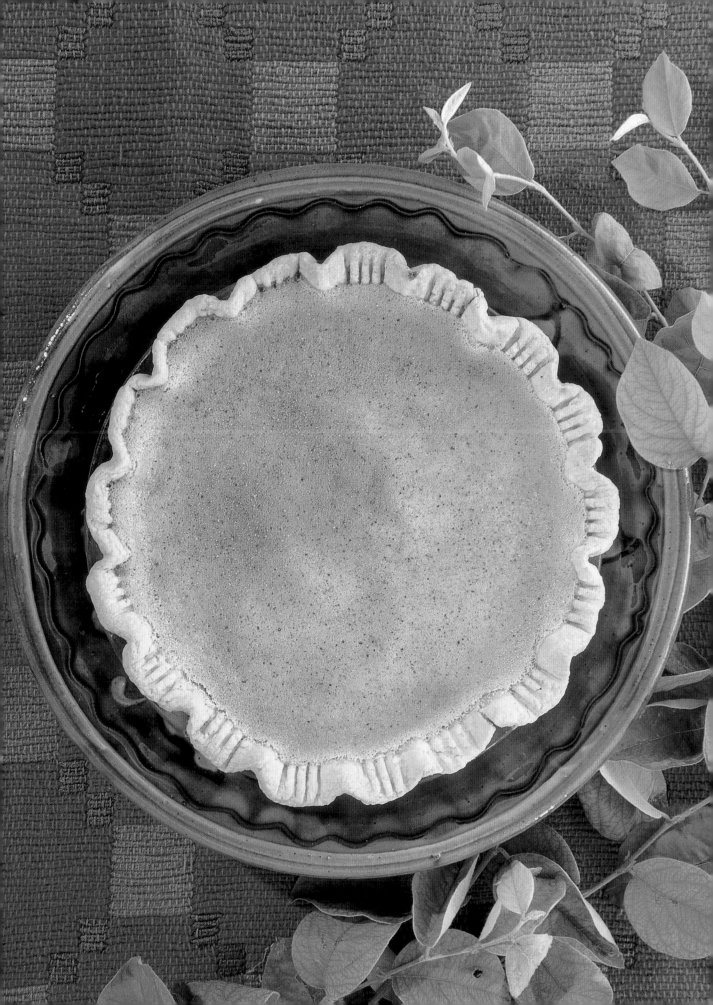

Caramelized Upside-Down Pear Pie

SERVES 8

5–6 firm, ripe pears
6 oz (170 g) sugar
4 oz (115 g) unsalted butter
whipped cream, for serving
FOR THE PASTRY
4 oz (115 g) plain flour
¹/₄ teaspoon salt
4¹/₂ oz (125 g) cold butter, cut into pieces
1¹/₂ oz (45 g) cold vegetable fat, cut into pieces
4 tablespoons iced water

2 ▲ Quarter, peel and core the pears. Place in a bowl and toss with a few tablespoons of the sugar.

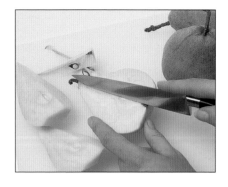

3 ▲ In a 10¹/₂ in (27 cm) ovenproof frying pan, melt the butter over moderately high heat. Add the remaining sugar. When it starts to colour, arrange the pears evenly around the edge and in the centre.

5 ▲ Let the fruit cool. Roll out a circle of dough slightly larger than the diameter of the pan. Place the dough on top of the pears, tucking it around the edges. Transfer the pan to the oven and bake for 15 minutes, then reduce the heat to 350°F/180°C/ Gas 4. Bake until golden, about 15 minutes more.

1 ▲ For the pastry, combine the flour and salt in a bowl. Add the butter and vegetable fat and cut in with a pastry blender until the mixture resembles coarse crumbs. With a fork, stir in enough iced water to bind the dough. Gather into a ball, wrap in clear film and refrigerate for at least 20 minutes. Preheat the oven to 400°F/200°C/Gas 6.

4 ▲ Continue cooking, uncovered, until caramelized, about 20 minutes.

~ VARIATION ~

For Caramelized Upside-Down Apple Pie, replace the pears with 8–9 firm, tart apples. There may seem to be too many apples, but they shrink slightly as they cook.

---

6 ▲ Let the pie cool in the pan for about 3–4 minutes. Run a knife around the edge of the pan to loosen the pie, ensuring that the knife reaches down to the bottom of the pan. Invert a plate on top and, protecting your hands with oven gloves, hold plate and pan firmly, and turn them both over quickly.

7 Lift off the pan. If any pears stick to the pan, remove them gently with a metal spatula and replace them carefully on the pie. Serve warm, with the whipped cream passed separately.

Lemon Meringue Pie

SERVES 8

grated rind and juice of 1 large lemon
8 fl oz (250 ml) plus 1 tbsp cold water
4 oz (115 g) plus 6 tbsp caster sugar
1 oz (30 g) butter
3 tbsp cornflour
3 eggs, separated
$\frac{1}{8}$ tsp salt
$\frac{1}{8}$ tsp cream of tartar
FOR THE PASTRY
5 oz (140 g) plain flour
$\frac{1}{2}$ tsp salt
$2\frac{1}{2}$ oz (70 g) cold vegetable fat or lard, cut in pieces
2 tbsp iced water

1 For the pastry, sift the flour and salt into a bowl. Add the fat and cut in with a pastry blender until the mixture resembles coarse breadcrumbs. With a fork, stir in just enough water to bind the mixture. Gather the pastry into a ball.

2 ▲ On a lightly floured surface, roll out the pastry about $\frac{1}{8}$ in (3 mm) thick. Transfer to a 9 in (23 cm) pie dish and trim the edge to leave a $\frac{1}{2}$ in (2 cm) overhang.

3 ▲ Fold the overhang under and crimp the edge. Refrigerate the pastry case for at least 20 minutes.

4 Preheat a 400°F/200°C/Gas 6 oven.

5 ▲ Prick the case all over with a fork. Line with crumpled greaseproof paper and fill with baking beans. Bake for 12 minutes. Remove the paper and beans and continue baking until golden, 6–8 minutes more.

6 In a saucepan, combine the lemon rind and juice, 8 fl oz (250 ml) of the water, 4 oz (115 g) of the sugar, and butter. Bring the mixture to a boil.

7 Meanwhile, in a mixing bowl, dissolve the cornflour in the remaining water. Add the egg yolks.

8 ▲ Add the egg yolks to the lemon mixture and return to the boil, whisking continuously until the mixture thickens, about 5 minutes.

9 Cover the surface with greaseproof paper and let cool.

10 ▲ For the meringue, using an electric mixer beat the egg whites with the salt and cream of tartar until they hold stiff peaks. Add the remaining sugar and beat until glossy.

11 ▲ Spoon the lemon mixture into the pastry case and level. Spoon the meringue on top, smoothing it up to the pastry rim to seal. Bake until golden, 12–15 minutes.

Lime Meringue Pie

SERVES 8

3 egg yolks

12 fl oz (350 ml) sweetened condensed milk

finely grated rind and juice of 4 limes

7 egg whites

⅛ tsp salt

squeeze of fresh lemon juice

4 oz (115 g) sugar

½ tsp vanilla essence

FOR THE PASTRY

5½ oz (165 g) plain flour

½ tsp salt

4 oz (115 g) lard or vegetable fat

2–3 tbsp iced water

1 Preheat a 425°F/220°C/Gas 7 oven.

2 ▲ For the pastry, sift the flour and salt into a mixing bowl. Using a pastry blender or 2 knives, cut in the fat until the mixture resembles coarse breadcrumbs. Sprinkle in the water, 1 tablespoon at a time, tossing lightly with a fork until the mixture forms a ball.

~ COOK'S TIP ~

When beating egg whites with an electric mixer, start slowly, and increase speed after they become frothy. Turn the bowl constantly.

3 ▲ On a lightly floured surface, roll out the pastry. Use it to line a 9 in (23 cm) pie tin, easing in the pastry. Make a fluted edge.

4 Using a fork, prick the bottom and sides of the pastry case all over. Bake until lightly browned, 10–15 minutes. Let cool, in the tin, on a wire rack. Reduce oven temperature to 350°F/180°C/Gas 4.

5 ▲ With an electric mixer on high speed, beat the yolks and condensed milk. Stir in the lime rind and juice.

6 ▲ In another clean bowl, beat 3 of the egg whites until stiff. Fold into the lime mixture.

7 ▲ Spread the lime filling in the pastry case. Bake 10 minutes.

8 ▲ Meanwhile, beat the remaining egg whites with the salt and lemon juice until soft peaks form. Beat in the sugar, 1 tablespoon at a time, until stiff peaks form. Add the vanilla.

9 ▲ Remove the pie from the oven. Using a metal spatula, spread the meringue over the lime filling, making a swirled design and covering the surface completely.

10 Bake until the meringue is lightly browned and the pastry is golden brown, about 12 minutes longer. Let cool, in the tin, on a wire rack.

Glacé Fruit Pie

SERVES 10

1 tablespoon rum
2 oz (55 g) mixed glacé fruit, chopped
16 fl oz (450 ml) milk
4 teaspoons gelatin
3½ oz (100 g) sugar
½ teaspoon salt
3 eggs, separated
8 fl oz (250 ml) whipping cream
chocolate curls, for decorating
FOR THE CRUST
6 oz (170 g) digestive biscuits, crushed
2½ oz (70 g) butter, melted
1 tablespoon sugar

1 For the crust, mix the crushed digestive biscuits, butter and sugar. Press evenly and firmly over the bottom and side of a 9 in (23 cm) pie plate. Refrigerate until firm.

2 ▲ In a bowl, stir together the rum and glacé fruit. Set aside.

3 Pour 4 fl oz (125 ml) of the milk into a small bowl. Sprinkle over the gelatin and let stand 5 minutes to soften.

4 ▲ In the top of a double boiler, combine 1¾ oz (50 g) of the sugar, the remaining milk and salt. Stir in the gelatin mixture. Cook over hot water, stirring, until gelatin dissolves.

5 Whisk in the egg yolks and cook, stirring, until thick enough to coat a spoon. Do not boil. Pour the custard over the glacé fruit mixture. Set in a bowl of ice water to cool.

6 Whip the cream lightly. Set aside.

7 With an electric mixer, beat the egg whites until they hold soft peaks. Add the remaining sugar and beat just enough to blend. Fold in a large dollop of the egg whites into the cooled gelatin mixture. Pour into the remaining egg whites and carefully fold together. Fold in the cream.

8 ▲ Pour into the pie shell and chill until firm. Decorate the top with chocolate curls.

Pumpkin Pie

SERVES 8

1 lb (450 g) cooked or canned pumpkin
8 fl oz (250 ml) whipping cream
2 eggs
4 oz (115 g) dark brown sugar
4 tablespoons golden syrup
1½ teaspoons ground cinnamon
1 teaspoon ground ginger
¼ teaspoon ground cloves
½ teaspoon salt
FOR THE PASTRY
6 oz (170 g) plain flour
½ teaspoon salt
3 oz (85 g) cold butter, cut into pieces
1½ oz (45 g) cold vegetable fat, cut into pieces
3–4 tablespoons iced water

1 For the pastry, sift the flour and salt into a bowl. Cut in the butter and fat until it resembles coarse crumbs. Bind with iced water. Wrap in clear film and refrigerate for 20 minutes.

2 Roll out the dough and line a 9 in (23 cm) pie tin. Trim off the overhang. Roll out the trimmings and cut out leaf shapes. Wet the rim of the pastry case with a brush dipped in water.

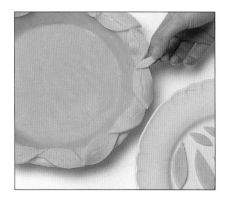

3 ▲ Place the dough leaves around the rim of the pastry case. Chill for about 20 minutes. Preheat the oven to 400°F/200°C/Gas 6.

4 ▲ Line the pastry case with greaseproof paper. Fill with baking beans and bake for 12 minutes. Remove paper and beans and bake until golden, 6–8 minutes more. Reduce the heat to 375°F/190°C/Gas 5.

5 ▼ Beat together the pumpkin, cream, eggs, sugar, golden syrup, spices and salt. Pour into the pastry case and bake until set, 40 minutes.

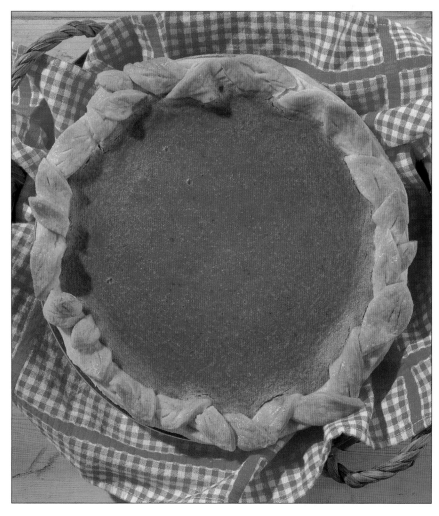

Chess Pie

SERVES 8

2 eggs
3 tablespoons whipping cream
4 oz (115 g) dark brown sugar
2 tablespoons granulated sugar
2 tablespoons plain flour
1 tablespoon whisky
1½ oz (45 g) butter, melted
2 oz (55 g) chopped walnuts
3 oz (85 g) stoned dates
whipped cream, for serving
FOR THE PASTRY
3 oz (85 g) cold butter
1½ oz (45 g) cold vegetable fat
6 oz (170 g) plain flour
½ teaspoon salt
3–4 tablespoons iced water

1 ▲ For the pastry, cut the butter and fat into small pieces.

2 Sift the flour and salt into a bowl. With a pastry blender, cut in the butter and fat until the mixture resembles coarse crumbs. Stir in just enough water to bind. Gather into a ball, wrap in greaseproof paper and refrigerate for at least 20 minutes.

3 Place a baking sheet in the oven and preheat it to 375°F/190°C/Gas 5.

4 Roll out the dough thinly and line a 9 in (23 cm) pie tin. Trim the edge. Roll out the trimmings, cut thin strips and plait them. Brush the edge of the pastry case with water and fit the pastry plaits around the rim.

5 ▲ In a mixing bowl, whisk together the eggs and cream.

6 Add both sugars and beat until well combined. Sift over 1 tablespoon of the flour and stir in. Add the whisky, the melted butter and the walnuts. Stir to combine.

7 ▲ Mix the dates with the remaining tablespoon of flour and stir into the walnut mixture.

8 Pour into the pastry case and bake until the pastry is golden and the filling puffed up, about 35 minutes. Serve at room temperature, with whipped cream, if liked.

Shoofly Pie

SERVES 8

4 oz (115 g) plain flour
4 oz (115 g) dark brown sugar
1/4 teaspoon each salt, ground ginger, cinnamon, mace and grated nutmeg
3 oz (85 g) cold butter, cut into pieces
2 eggs
4 fl oz (125 ml) molasses
4 fl oz (125 ml) boiling water
1/2 teaspoon bicarbonate of soda
FOR THE PASTRY
4 oz (115 g) cream cheese, at room temperature, cut into pieces
4 oz (115 g) cold butter, at room temperature, cut into pieces
4 oz (115 g) plain flour

1 For the pastry, put the cream cheese and butter in a mixing bowl. Sift over the flour.

2 ▲ Cut in with a pastry blender until the dough just holds together. Wrap in clear film and refrigerate for at least 30 minutes.

3 Put a baking sheet in the centre of the oven and preheat the oven to 375°F/190°C/Gas 5.

4 In a bowl, mix the flour, sugar, salt and spices. Rub in the butter with your fingertips until the mixture resembles coarse crumbs. Set aside.

5 On a lightly floured surface, roll out the dough and line a 9 in (23 cm) pie tin. Trim the overhanging pastry and flute the rim.

6 ▲ Spoon a third of the crumbed mixture into the pastry case.

7 ▲ To complete the filling, whisk the eggs with the molasses in a large bowl until combined.

8 Pour the boiling water into a small bowl. Stir in the bicarbonate of soda; the mixture will foam. Immediately whisk into the egg mixture. Pour carefully into the pastry case and sprinkle the remaining crumbed mixture evenly over the top.

9 Stand on the hot baking sheet and bake until browned, about 35 minutes. Leave to cool to room temperature, then serve.

Rich Chocolate Pie

SERVES 8

3 oz (85 g) plain chocolate

2 oz (55 g) butter or margarine

3 tbsp golden syrup

3 eggs, beaten

5 oz (140 g) caster sugar

1 tsp vanilla essence

4 oz (115 g) milk chocolate

16 fl oz (500 ml) whipping cream

FOR THE PASTRY

5½ oz (165 g) plain flour

½ tsp salt

4 oz (115 g) lard or vegetable fat

2–3 tbsp iced water

1 Preheat a 425°F/220°C/Gas 7 oven.

2 For the pastry, sift the flour and salt into a mixing bowl. Using a pastry blender, cut in the fat until the mixture resembles coarse breadcrumbs. Sprinkle in the water, 1 tablespoon at a time. Toss lightly with a fork until the pastry forms a ball.

3 On a lightly floured surface, roll out the pastry. Use to line an 8 or 9 in (20 or 23 cm) pie tin, easing in the pastry and being careful not to stretch it. Make a fluted edge.

4 Using a fork, prick the bottom and sides of the pastry case all over. Bake until lightly browned, 10–15 minutes. Let cool, in the tin, on a wire rack.

5 ▲ In a heatproof bowl set over a pan of simmering water, or in a double boiler, melt the plain chocolate, the butter or margarine and golden syrup. Remove the bowl from the heat and stir in the eggs, sugar and vanilla.

6 Reduce the oven temperature to 350°F/180°C/Gas 4. Pour the chocolate mixture into the case. Bake until the filling is set, 35–40 minutes. Let cool in the tin, set on a rack.

7 ▲ For the decoration, use the heat of your hands to soften the chocolate bar slightly. Draw the blade of a swivel-headed vegetable peeler along the side of the chocolate bar to shave off short, wide curls. Chill the chocolate curls until needed.

8 Before serving, lightly whip the cream until soft peaks form. Using a rubber spatula, spread the cream over the surface of the chocolate filling. Decorate with the chocolate curls.

Chocolate Chiffon Pie

SERVES 8

7 oz (200 g) plain chocolate
8 fl oz (250 ml) milk
1 tablespoon gelatin
3½ oz (100 g) sugar
2 extra-large eggs, separated
1 teaspoon vanilla essence
12 fl oz (350 ml) whipping cream
⅛ teaspoon salt
whipped cream and chocolate curls, for decorating

FOR THE CRUST

7 oz (200 g) digestive biscuits, crushed
3 oz (85 g) butter, melted

1 Place a baking sheet in the oven and preheat to 350°F/180°C/ Gas 4.

2 For the crust, mix the crushed digestive biscuits and butter in a bowl. Press evenly over the bottom and side of a 9 in (23 cm) pie plate. Bake for 8 minutes. Let cool.

3 Chop the chocolate, then grate in a food processor or blender. Set aside.

4 Place the milk in the top of a double boiler. Sprinkle over the gelatin. Let stand 5 minutes to soften.

5 ▲ Set the top of a double boiler over hot water. Add 1½ oz (45 g) sugar, the chocolate and the egg yolks. Stir until dissolved. Add the vanilla essence.

6 ▲ Set the top of the double boiler in a bowl of ice and stir until the mixture reaches room temperature. Remove from the ice and set aside.

7 Whip the cream lightly. Set aside. With an electric mixer, beat the egg whites and salt until they hold soft peaks. Add the remaining sugar and beat only enough to blend.

8 Fold a dollop of egg whites into the chocolate mixture, then pour back into the whites and fold in.

9 ▲ Fold in the whipped cream and pour into the pie shell. Put in the freezer until just set, about 5 minutes. If the centre sinks, fill with any remaining mixture. Refrigerate for 3–4 hours. Decorate with whipped cream and chocolate curls. Serve cold.

Black Bottom Pie

SERVES 8

2 teaspoons gelatin
3 tablespoons cold water
2 eggs, separated
5 oz (140 g) caster sugar
¹/₂ oz (15 g) cornflour
¹/₂ teaspoon salt
16 fl oz (450 ml) milk
2 oz (55 g) plain chocolate, finely chopped
2 tablespoons rum
¹/₄ teaspoon cream of tartar
chocolate curls, for decorating
FOR THE CRUST
6 oz (170 g) gingersnaps, crushed
2¹/₂ oz (70 g) butter, melted

1 Preheat a 350°F/180°C/Gas 4 oven.

2 For the crust, mix the crushed gingersnaps and melted butter.

3 ▲ Press the mixture evenly over the bottom and side of a 9 in (23 cm) pie plate. Bake for 6 minutes.

4 Sprinkle the gelatin over the water and let stand to soften.

5 Beat the egg yolks in a large mixing bowl and set aside.

6 In a saucepan, combine half the sugar, the cornflour and salt. Gradually stir in the milk. Boil for 1 minute, stirring constantly.

7 ▲ Whisk the hot milk mixture into the yolks, then pour all back into the saucepan and return to the boil, whisking. Cook for 1 minute, still whisking. Remove from the heat.

8 ▲ Measure out 8 oz (225 g) of the hot custard mixture and pour into a bowl. Add the chopped chocolate to the custard mixture, and stir until melted. Stir in half the rum and pour into the pie shell.

9 ▲ Whisk the softened gelatin into the plain custard until it has dissolved, then stir in the remaining rum. Set the pan in cold water until it reaches room temperature.

10 ▲ With an electric mixer, beat the egg whites and cream of tartar until they hold stiff peaks. Add the remaining sugar gradually, beating or whisking thoroughly at each addition.

11 ▲ Fold the custard into the egg whites, then spoon over the chocolate mixture in the pie shell. Refrigerate until set, about 2 hours.

12 Decorate the top with chocolate curls. Keep the pie refrigerated until ready to serve.

> ### ~ COOK'S TIP ~
>
> To make chocolate curls, melt 8 oz (225 g) plain chocolate over hot water, stir in 1 tablespoon of vegetable fat and mould in a small foil-lined loaf tin. For large curls, soften the bar between your hands and scrape off curls from the wide side with a vegetable peeler; for small curls, grate from the narrow side using a box grater.

Brown Sugar Pie

SERVES 8

6oz (175g) plain flour
½ teaspoon salt
2 teaspoons granulated sugar
3oz (75g) cold butter
2fl oz (50ml) or more iced water
FOR THE FILLING
1oz (25g) plain flour, sifted
8oz (225g) soft light brown sugar
½ teaspoon vanilla essence
12fl oz (350ml) whipping cream
1½oz (40g) butter, cut in tiny pieces
⅛ teaspoon grated nutmeg

1 Sift the flour, salt, and sugar into a bowl. Using a pastry blender or two knives, cut in the butter until it resembles coarse breadcrumbs.

2 ▲ Sprinkle with the water and mix until the dough holds together. If it is too crumbly, add more water, 1 tablespoon at a time. Gather into a ball and flatten. Wrap in greaseproof paper and refrigerate for 20 minutes.

3 Roll out the dough about ⅛ in (3 mm) thick and line a 9 in (23 cm) pie dish. Trim the edge, leaving a ½ in (1 cm) overhang. Fold it under and flute the edge. Refrigerate for 30 minutes.

4 Preheat a 220°C/425°F/Gas 7 oven.

5 Line the pastry case with a piece of greaseproof paper that is 2 in (5 cm) larger all around than the diameter of the pan. Fill the case with dried beans. Bake until the pastry has just set, 8–10 minutes. Remove from the oven and lift out the paper and beans. Prick the bottom of the pastry case all over with a fork. Return to the oven and bake for 5 minutes more. Let the pastry case cool slightly before filling. Turn the oven down to 190°C/375°F/Gas 5.

6 ▲ In a small bowl, mix together the flour and sugar using a fork. Spread this mixture in an even layer on the bottom of the pastry case.

7 ▲ Stir the vanilla into the cream. Pour the flavoured cream over the flour and sugar mixture and gently swirl with a fork to mix. Dot with the butter. Sprinkle the nutmeg on top.

8 Cover the edge of the pie with foil strips to prevent overbrowning. Set on a baking sheet and bake until the filling is golden brown and firm to the touch, about 45 minutes. Serve the pie at room temperature.

Creamy Banana Pie

SERVES 6

7 oz (200 g) ginger biscuits, finely crushed

2½ oz (70 g) butter or margarine, melted

½ tsp grated nutmeg or ground cinnamon

6 oz (175 g) ripe bananas, mashed

12 oz (350 g) cream cheese, at room temperature

2 fl oz (65 ml) thick plain yogurt or soured cream

3 tbsp dark rum or 1 tsp vanilla essence

FOR THE TOPPING

8 fl oz (250 ml) whipping cream

3–4 bananas

1 Preheat a 375°F/190°C/Gas 5 oven.

2 ▲ In a mixing bowl, combine the crushed biscuits, butter or margarine and spice. Mix thoroughly with a wooden spoon.

3 ▲ Press the biscuit mixture into a 9 in (23 cm) pie dish, building up thick sides with a neat edge. Bake 5 minutes. Let cool, in the dish.

4 ▼ With an electric mixer, beat the mashed bananas with the cream cheese. Fold in the yogurt or soured cream and rum or vanilla. Spread the filling in the biscuit base. Refrigerate at least 4 hours or overnight.

5 ▲ For the topping, whip the cream until soft peaks form. Spread on the pie filling. Slice the bananas and arrange on top in a decorative pattern.

Georgia Peanut Butter Pie

SERVES 8

4oz (115g) fine digestive crumbs

2oz (50g) soft light brown sugar,
    firmly packed

3oz (75g) butter or margarine, melted

whipped cream or ice cream,
    for serving

FOR THE FILLING

3 egg yolks

3½oz (90g) granulated sugar

2oz (50g) soft light brown sugar,
    firmly packed

2oz (50g) cornflour

⅛ teaspoon salt

1 pint (600ml) evaporated milk

1oz (25g) unsalted butter or margarine

1½ teaspoons vanilla essence

4oz (115g) chunky peanut butter,
    preferably made from freshly ground
    peanuts

3oz (75g) icing sugar

1 Preheat a 180°C/350°F/Gas 4 oven.

2 ▲ Combine the crumbs, sugar, and butter or margarine in a bowl and blend well. Spread the mixture in a well-greased 9 in (23 cm) pie dish, pressing evenly over the bottom and sides with your fingertips.

3 Bake the crumb crust for 10 minutes. Remove from the oven and leave to cool. Leave the oven on.

4 ▲ For the filling, combine the egg yolks, granulated and brown sugars, cornflour and salt in a heavy saucepan.

5 Slowly whisk in the milk. Cook over a medium heat, stirring constantly, until the mixture thickens, about 8–10 minutes. Reduce the heat to very low and cook until very thick, 3–4 minutes more.

6 ▲ Beat in the butter or margarine. Stir in the vanilla. Remove from the heat. Cover the surface closely with clear film and leave to cool.

~ VARIATIONS ~

If preferred, use an equal amount of finely crushed ginger biscuits in place of digestives for the crumb crust. Or make the pie with a ready-made biscuit crust.

7 ▲ In a small bowl, combine the peanut butter with the icing sugar, working with your fingers to blend the ingredients to the consistency of fine crumbs.

8 ▲ Sprinkle all but 3 tablespoons of the peanut butter crumbs evenly over the bottom of the crumb crust.

9 ▲ Pour in the filling, spreading it in an even layer. Sprinkle with the remaining crumbs. Bake for 15 minutes.

10 Let the pie cool for 1 hour. Serve with whipped cream or ice cream.

Lime Tart

SERVES 8

3 large egg yolks

1 × 14 oz (400 g) can sweetened condensed milk

1 tbsp grated lime rind

4 fl oz (125 ml) fresh lime juice

green food colouring (optional)

4 fl oz (125 ml) whipping cream

FOR THE BASE

4 oz (115 g) digestive biscuits, crushed

2¹/₂ oz (70 g) butter or margarine, melted

1 Preheat a 350°F/180°C/Gas 4 oven.

2 ▲ For the base, place the crushed biscuits in a bowl and add the butter or margarine. Mix to combine.

~ VARIATION ~

Use lemons instead of limes, with yellow food colouring.

3 Press the mixture evenly over the bottom and sides of a 9 in (23 cm) pie dish. Bake for 8 minutes. Let cool.

4 ▲ Beat the yolks until thick. Beat in the milk, lime rind and juice and colouring, if using. Pour into the pastry case and refrigerate until set, about 4 hours. To serve, whip the cream. Pipe a lattice pattern on top.

Fruit Tartlets

MAKES 8

6 fl oz (175 ml) red currant jelly

1 tbsp fresh lemon juice

6 fl oz (175 ml) whipping cream

1¹/₂ lb (700 g) fresh fruit, such as strawberries, raspberries, kiwi fruit, peaches, grapes or currants, peeled and sliced as necessary

FOR THE PASTRY

5 oz (140 g) cold butter, cut in pieces

2¹/₂ oz (65 g) dark brown sugar

3 tbsp cocoa powder

7 oz (200 g) plain flour

1 egg white

1 For the pastry, combine the butter, brown sugar and cocoa over low heat. When the butter is melted, remove from the heat and sift over the flour. Stir, then add just enough egg white to bind the mixture. Gather into a ball, wrap in greaseproof paper, and refrigerate for 30 minutes.

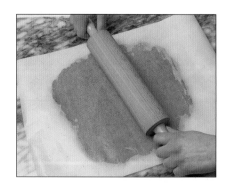

2 ▲ Grease 8 3 in (8 cm) tartlet tins. Roll out the pastry between 2 sheets of greaseproof paper. Stamp out 8 4 in (10 cm) rounds with a fluted cutter.

3 Line the tartlet tins. Prick the bottoms. Refrigerate for 15 minutes. Preheat a 350°F/180°C/Gas 4 oven.

4 Bake until firm, 20–25 minutes. Cool, then remove from the tins.

5 ▲ Melt the jelly with the lemon juice. Brush a thin layer in the bottom of the tartlets. Whip the cream and spread a thin layer in the tartlet cases. Arrange the fruit on top. Brush with the glaze and serve.

Lime Tart (top), Fruit Tartlets

Chocolate Lemon Tart

SERVES 8–10

8³/₄ oz (240 g) caster sugar

6 eggs

grated rind of 2 lemons

5¹/₂ fl oz (170 ml) fresh lemon juice

5¹/₂ fl oz (170 ml) whipping cream

chocolate curls, for decorating

FOR THE CRUST

6¹/₄ oz (180 g) plain flour

2 tablespoons unsweetened cocoa powder

1 oz (30 g) icing sugar

¹/₂ teaspoon salt

4 oz (115 g) butter or margarine

1 tablespoon water

1 ▲ Grease a 10 in (25 cm) tart tin.

2 For the crust, sift the flour, cocoa powder, icing sugar and salt into a bowl. Set aside.

3 ▲ Melt the butter and water over a low heat. Pour over the flour mixture and stir with a wooden spoon until the dough is smooth and the flour has absorbed all the liquid.

4 Press the dough evenly over the base and side of the prepared tart tin. Refrigerate the tart shell while preparing the filling.

5 Preheat a baking sheet in a 375°F/190°C/Gas 5 oven.

6 ▲ Whisk the sugar and eggs until the sugar is dissolved. Add the lemon rind and juice and mix well. Add the cream. Taste the mixture and add more lemon juice or sugar if needed. It should taste tart but also sweet.

7 Pour the filling into the tart shell and bake on the hot sheet until the filling is set, 20–25 minutes. Cool on a rack. When cool, decorate with the chocolate curls.

Lemon Almond Tart

SERVES 8

5¹/₂ oz (150 g) whole blanched almonds

3¹/₂ oz (100 g) sugar

2 eggs

grated rind and juice of 1¹/₂ lemons

4 oz (115 g) butter, melted

strips of lemon rind, for decorating

FOR THE CRUST

6¹/₄ oz (180 g) plain flour

1 tablespoon sugar

¹/₂ teaspoon salt

¹/₂ teaspoon baking powder

3 oz (85 g) cold unsalted butter, cut into pieces

3–4 tablespoons whipping cream

1 For the crust, sift the flour, sugar, salt and baking powder into a bowl. Add the butter and rub in with your fingertips until the mixture resembles coarse breadcrumbs.

2 ▲ With a fork, stir in just enough cream to bind the dough.

3 Gather into a ball and transfer to a lightly floured surface. Roll out the dough about ¹/₈ in (3 mm) thick and carefully transfer to a 9 in (23 cm) tart tin. Trim and prick the base all over with a fork. Refrigerate for at least 20 minutes.

4 Preheat a baking sheet in a 400°F/ 200°C/Gas 6 oven.

5 Line the tart shell with crumpled greaseproof paper and fill with dried beans. Bake for 12 minutes. Remove the paper and beans and continue baking until golden, 6–8 minutes more. Reduce the oven temperature to 350°F/180°C/Gas 4.

6 ▲ Grind the almonds finely with 1 tablespoon of the sugar in a food processor, blender, or coffee grinder.

7 ▲ Set a mixing bowl over a pan of hot water. Add the eggs and the remaining sugar, and beat with an electric mixer until the mixture is thick enough to leave a ribbon trail when the beaters are lifted.

8 Stir in the lemon rind and juice, butter and ground almonds.

9 Pour into the prebaked shell. Bake until the filling is golden and set, about 35 minutes. Decorate with lemon rind.

Orange Tart

SERVES 8

7 oz (200 g) sugar

8 fl oz (250 ml) fresh orange juice, strained

2 large navel oranges

5½ oz (150 g) whole blanched almonds

2 oz (55 g) butter

1 egg

1 tablespoon plain flour

3 tablespoons apricot jam

FOR THE CRUST

7½ oz (215 g) plain flour

½ teaspoon salt

2 oz (55 g) cold butter, cut into pieces

1½ oz (45 g) cold margarine, cut into pieces

3–4 tablespoons iced water

1 For the crust, sift the flour and salt into a bowl. Add the butter and margarine and rub in with your fingertips until the mixture resembles coarse breadcrumbs. Stir in just enough water to bind the dough. Gather into a ball, wrap in clear film, and refrigerate for at least 20 minutes.

2 On a lightly floured surface, roll out the dough ¼ in (5 mm) thick and transfer to an 8 in (20 cm) tart tin. Trim off the overhang. Refrigerate until needed.

3 In a saucepan, combine 5½ oz (150 g) of the sugar and the orange juice and boil until thick and syrupy, about 10 minutes.

4 ▲ Cut the oranges into ¼ in (5 mm) slices. Do not peel. Add to the syrup. Simmer gently for 10 minutes, or until glazed. Transfer to a rack to dry. When cool, cut in half. Reserve the syrup. Place a baking sheet in the oven and heat to 400°F/200°C/Gas 6.

5 Grind the almonds finely in a food processor, blender or coffee grinder. With an electric mixer, cream the butter and remaining sugar until light and fluffy. Beat in the egg and 2 table-spoons of the orange syrup. Stir in the almonds and flour.

6 Melt the jam over low heat, then brush over the tart shell. Pour in the almond mixture. Bake until set, about 20 minutes. Let cool.

7 ▲ Arrange overlapping orange slices on top. Boil the remaining syrup until thick. Brush on top to glaze.

Rich Orange Cheesecake

SERVES 8

1½ lb (700 g) full-fat soft cheese, at room temperature
7 oz (200 g) caster sugar
2 tablespoons plain flour
3 eggs
4 oz (115 g) butter, melted
1 teaspoon vanilla essence
1 tablespoon grated orange zest
8 in (20 cm) biscuit case, made with digestive biscuits and orange zest, chilled
4 sweet oranges, peeled and segmented
squeeze of lemon juice
1–2 tablespoons orange liqueur (optional)

1 Preheat a 300°F/150°C/Gas 2 oven.

2 ▲ Combine the soft cheese, sugar and flour in a bowl. Beat until the mixture is light and fluffy.

3 ▲ Add the eggs, butter, vanilla essence and orange zest and beat until smoothly blended.

4 ▲ Pour the filling into the biscuit case. Set the springform tin on a baking sheet.

5 Bake for 1–1¼ hours or until the filling is gently set (it will continue to firm up as it cools). If the top browns too quickly, cover with foil. Turn off the oven and open the door.

6 Leave the cheesecake to cool in the oven. When it is cold, cover and refrigerate overnight.

7 Mix together the orange segments, lemon juice and liqueur, if using. Serve with the cheesecake.

~ VARIATIONS ~

For Lemon Cheesecake, use 1½ teaspoons lemon zest instead of orange in the filling. For a lighter cheesecake, use a mixture of ricotta or curd cheese and full-fat soft cheese, worked in a food processor until smooth.

Blueberry-Hazelnut Cheesecake

SERVES 6–8

12oz (350g) blueberries

1 tablespoon honey

3oz (75g) granulated sugar

1 teaspoon plus 1 tablespoon fresh
lemon juice

6oz (175g) cream cheese, at room
temperature

1 egg

1 teaspoon hazelnut liqueur (optional)

4fl oz (120ml) whipping cream

FOR THE BASE

5¾oz (170g) ground hazelnuts

3oz (75g) plain flour

⅛ teaspoon salt

2oz (50g) butter, at room temperature

5½oz (65g) soft light brown sugar,
firmly packed

1 egg yolk

1 ▲ For the base, put the hazelnuts in
a large bowl. Sift in the flour and salt,
and stir to mix. Set aside.

~ COOK'S TIP ~

The cheesecake can be
prepared a day in advance, but
add the fruit shortly before
serving. Instead of covering the
top completely, leave spaces to
make a design, if wished.

2 Beat the butter with the brown
sugar until light and fluffy. Beat in the
egg yolk. Gradually fold in the nut
mixture, in three batches.

3 ▲ Press the mixture into a greased
9 in (23 cm) pie dish, spreading it
evenly against the sides. Form a rim
around the top edge that is slightly
thicker than the sides. Cover and
refrigerate for at least 30 minutes.

4 Preheat a 180°C/350°F/Gas 4 oven.

5 ▲ Meanwhile, for the topping,
combine the blueberries, honey,
1 tablespoon of the granulated sugar,
and 1 teaspoon lemon juice in a heavy
saucepan. Cook the mixture over a low
heat, stirring occasionally, until the
berries have given off some liquid but
still retain their shape, 5–7 minutes.
Remove from the heat and set aside.

6 Place the base in the oven and bake
15 minutes. Remove and leave to cool
while making the filling.

7 ▲ Beat together the cream cheese
and remaining granulated sugar until
light and fluffy. Add the egg,
remaining lemon juice, the liqueur,
if using, and the cream and beat until
thoroughly incorporated.

8 ▲ Pour the cheese mixture into the
base and spread evenly. Bake until
just set, 20–25 minutes.

9 Let the cheesecake cool completely
on a wire rack, then cover and
refrigerate for at least 1 hour.

10 Spread the blueberry mixture
evenly over the top of the cheesecake.
Serve the cheesecake at a cool room
temperature.

Chocolate Cheesecake Tart

SERVES 8

12 oz (350 g) cream cheese

4 tbsp whipping cream

8 oz (225 g) caster sugar

2 oz (55 g) cocoa powder

1/2 tsp ground cinnamon

3 eggs

whipped cream, for decorating

chocolate curls, for decorating

FOR THE BASE

3 oz (85 g) digestive biscuits, crushed

1 1/2 oz (45 g) crushed amaretti biscuits (if unavailable, use extra crushed digestive biscuits)

3 oz (85 g) butter, melted

1 Preheat a baking sheet in the centre of a 350°F/180°C/Gas 4 oven.

2 For the base, mix the crushed biscuits and butter in a bowl.

3 ▲ With a spoon, press the mixture over the bottom and sides of a 9 in (23 cm) pie dish. Bake for 8 minutes. Let cool. Keep the oven on.

4 With an electric mixer, beat the cheese and cream together until smooth. Beat in the sugar, cocoa and cinnamon until blended.

5 ▼ Add the eggs, 1 at a time, beating just enough to blend.

6 Pour into the biscuit base and bake on the hot sheet for 25–30 minutes. The filling will sink down as it cools. Decorate with whipped cream and chocolate curls.

Frozen Strawberry Tart

SERVES 8

8 oz (225 g) cream cheese

8 fl oz (250 ml) soured cream

1 lb 4 oz (575 g) frozen strawberries, thawed and sliced

FOR THE BASE

4 oz (115 g) digestive biscuits, crushed

1 tbsp caster sugar

2 1/2 oz (70 g) butter, melted

1 ▲ For the base, mix together the biscuits, sugar and butter.

2 Press the mixture evenly and firmly over the bottom and sides of a 9 in (23 cm) pie dish. Freeze until firm.

3 ▼ Blend together the cream cheese and soured cream. Reserve 6 tablespoons of the strawberries. Add the rest to the cream cheese mixture.

4 Pour the filling into the biscuit base and freeze 6–8 hours until firm. To serve, spoon some of the reserved berries and juice on top.

~ VARIATION ~

For Frozen Raspberry Tart, use raspberries in place of the strawberries and prepare the same way, or try other frozen fruit.

Chocolate Cheesecake Pie (top), Frozen Strawberry Tart

Kiwi Ricotta Cheese Tart

SERVES 8

3 oz (75 g) blanched almonds, ground
3¹/₂ oz (130 g) sugar
2 lb (900 g) ricotta cheese
8 fl oz (250 ml) whipping cream
1 egg and 3 egg yolks
1 tablespoon plain flour
pinch of salt
2 tablespoons rum
grated rind of 1 lemon
2¹/₂ tablespoons lemon juice
2 tablespoons honey
5 kiwi fruit
FOR THE PASTRY
5 oz (150 g) plain flour
1 tablespoon sugar
¹/₂ teaspoon salt
¹/₂ teaspoon baking powder
6 tablespoons butter
1 egg yolk
3–4 tablespoons whipping cream

1 For the pastry, mix together the flour, sugar, salt and baking powder in a large bowl. Cut the butter into cubes and gradually rub it into the pastry mixture. Mix in the egg yolk and cream. Stir in just enough to bind the pastry.

2 ▲ Transfer to a lightly floured surface, flatten slightly, wrap and refrigerate for 30 minutes. Preheat the oven to 425°F/220°C/Gas 7.

3 ▲ On a lightly floured surface, roll out the dough to a ¹/₈ in (3 mm) thickness. Transfer to a 9 in (23 cm) springform tin. Crimp the edge.

4 ▲ Prick the pastry with a fork. Line with greaseproof paper and fill with dried beans. Bake for 10 minutes. Remove the paper and beans and bake for 6–8 minutes more until golden. Leave to cool. Reduce the temperature to 350°F/180°C/Gas 4.

5 ▲ Mix the almonds with 1 tablespoon of the sugar in a food processor or blender.

6 Beat the ricotta until creamy. Add the cream, egg, yolks, remaining sugar, flour, salt, rum, lemon rind and 2 tablespoons of lemon juice. Combine.

7 ▲ Stir in the ground almonds until well blended.

8 Pour into a pastry case and bake for 1 hour. Chill, loosely covered for 2–3 hours. Unmould and put on a plate.

9 Combine the honey and remaining lemon juice for the glaze.

10 ▲ Peel the kiwis. Halve them lengthwise, then slice. Arrange the slices in rows across the top of the tart. Just before serving, brush with the honey glaze.

Raspberry Tart

SERVES 8

4 egg yolks

2¹/₂ oz (70 g) caster sugar

3 tbsp plain flour

10 fl oz (300 ml) milk

¹/₈ tsp salt

¹/₂ tsp vanilla essence

1 lb (450 g) fresh raspberries

5 tbsp red currant jelly

1 tbsp fresh orange juice

FOR THE PASTRY

6¹/₂ oz (190 g) plain flour

¹/₂ tsp baking powder

¹/₄ tsp salt

1 tbsp sugar

grated rind of ¹/₂ orange

3 oz (85 g) cold butter, cut in pieces

1 egg yolk

3–4 tbsp whipping cream

1 For the pastry, sift the flour, baking powder and salt into a bowl. Stir in the sugar and orange rind. Add the butter and cut in with a pastry blender until the mixture resembles coarse breadcrumbs. Stir in the egg yolk and just enough cream to bind the dough. Gather into a ball, wrap in greaseproof paper and refrigerate.

2 For the custard filling, beat the egg yolks and sugar until thick and lemon coloured. Gradually stir in the flour.

3 In a saucepan, bring the milk and salt just to the boil, then remove from the heat. Whisk into the egg yolk mixture, return to the pan and continue whisking over moderately high heat until just bubbling. Cook for 3 minutes to thicken. Transfer immediately to a bowl. Add the vanilla and stir to blend.

4 ▲ Cover with greaseproof paper to prevent a skin from forming.

5 ▲ Preheat a 400°F/200°C/Gas 6 oven. On a floured surface, roll out the pastry ¹/₈ in (3 mm) thick, transfer to a 10 in (25 cm) pie dish and trim. Prick the bottom with a fork and line with crumpled greaseproof paper. Fill with baking beans and bake for 15 minutes. Remove the paper and beans. Continue baking until golden, 6–8 minutes more. Let cool.

6 ▲ Spread an even layer of the pastry cream filling in the pastry case and arrange the raspberries on top. Melt the jelly and orange juice in a pan and brush on top to glaze.

Treacle Tart

SERVES 4–6

6 fl oz (175 ml) golden syrup
3 oz (85 g) fresh white breadcrumbs
grated rind of 1 lemon
2 tbsp fresh lemon juice
FOR THE PASTRY
6 oz (170 g) plain flour
1/2 tsp salt
3 oz (85 g) cold butter, cut in pieces
1 1/2 oz (45 g) cold margarine, cut in pieces
3–4 tbsp iced water

1 For the pastry, combine the flour and salt in a bowl. Add the butter and margarine and cut in with a pastry blender until the mixture resembles coarse breadcrumbs.

2 ▲ With a fork, stir in just enough water to bind the pastry. Gather into a ball, wrap in greaseproof paper, and refrigerate for at least 20 minutes.

3 On a lightly floured surface, roll out the pastry to a thickness of 1/8 in (3 mm). Transfer to an 8 in (20 cm) pie dish and trim off the overhang. Refrigerate for at least 20 minutes. Reserve the trimmings for the lattice top.

4 Preheat a baking sheet at the top of a 400°F/200°C/Gas 6 oven.

5 In a saucepan, warm the syrup until thin and runny.

6 ▲ Remove from the heat and stir in the breadcrumbs and lemon rind. Let sit for 10 minutes so the bread can absorb the syrup. Add more breadcrumbs if the mixture is thin. Stir in the lemon juice and spread evenly in the pastry case.

7 Roll our the pastry trimmings and cut into 10–12 thin strips.

8 ▼ Lay half the strips on the filling, then lay the remaining strips at an angle over them to form a lattice.

9 Place on the hot sheet and bake for 10 minutes. Lower the heat to 375°F/190°C/Gas 5. Bake until golden, about 15 minutes more. Serve warm or cold.

Coconut Cream Tart

SERVES 8

5 oz (140 g) desiccated coconut
5 oz (140 g) caster sugar
4 tbsp cornflour
1/8 tsp salt
1 pt (625 ml) milk
2 fl oz (65 ml) whipping cream
2 egg yolks
1 oz (30 g) unsalted butter
2 tsp vanilla essence
FOR THE PASTRY
5 oz (140 g) plain flour
1/4 tsp salt
1 1/2 oz (45 g) cold butter, cut in pieces
1 oz (30 g) cold vegetable fat or lard
2–3 tbsp iced water

4 ▲ Spread 2 oz (55 g) of the coconut on a baking sheet and toast in the oven until golden, 6–8 minutes, stirring often. Set aside for decorating.

5 Put the sugar, cornflour and salt in a saucepan. In a bowl, whisk the milk, cream and egg yolks. Add the egg mixture to the saucepan.

6 ▼ Cook over a low heat, stirring, until the mixture comes to the boil. Boil for 1 minute, then remove from the heat. Add the butter, vanilla and remaining coconut.

7 Pour into the prebaked pastry case. When cool, sprinkle toasted coconut in a ring in the centre.

1 For the pastry, sift the flour and salt into a bowl. Add the butter and fat and cut in with a pastry blender until the mixture resembles coarse breadcrumbs.

2 ▲ With a fork, stir in just enough water to bind the pastry. Gather into a ball, wrap in greaseproof paper and refrigerate for 20 minutes.

3 Preheat a 425°F/220°C/Gas 7 oven. Roll out the pastry 1/8 in (3 mm) thick. Line a 9 in (23 cm) pie dish. Trim and flute the edges. Prick the bottom. Line with crumpled greaseproof and fill with baking beans. Bake 10–12 minutes. Remove paper and beans, reduce heat to 350°F/180°C/Gas 4 and bake until brown, 10–15 minutes.

Brandy Alexander Tart

SERVES 8

4 fl oz (125 ml) cold water
1 tablespoon powdered gelatine
4 oz (115 g) sugar
3 eggs, separated
4 tablespoons brandy
4 tablespoons crème de cacao
pinch of salt
10 fl oz (300 ml) whipping cream
chocolate curls, for decorating
FOR THE BISCUIT CRUST
8 oz (225 g) digestive biscuits, crumbed
2¹/₂ oz (70 g) butter, melted
1 tablespoon sugar

1 Preheat the oven to 375°F/190°C/ Gas 5.

2 For the crust, mix the biscuit crumbs with the butter and sugar in a bowl.

3 ▲ Press the crumbs evenly on to the bottom and sides of a 9 in (23 cm) tart tin. Bake until just brown, about 10 minutes. Cool on a rack.

4 Place the water in the top of a double boiler set over hot water. Sprinkle over the powdered gelatine and leave to stand for 5 minutes to soften. Add half the sugar and the egg yolks. Whisk constantly over a very low heat until the gelatine dissolves and the mixture has thickened slightly. Do not allow the mixture to boil.

5 ▲ Remove from the heat and stir in the brandy and crème de cacao.

6 Set the pan over iced water and stir occasionally until it cools and thickens; it should not set firmly.

7 With an electric mixer, beat the egg whites and salt until they hold stiff peaks. Beat in the remaining sugar. Spoon a dollop of whites into the yolk mixture and fold in to lighten.

8 ▼ Pour the egg yolk mixture over the remaining whites and fold together.

9 Whip the cream until soft peaks form, then gently fold into the filling. Spoon into the baked biscuit case and chill until set, 3–4 hours. Decorate the top with chocolate curls before serving.

Velvety Mocha Tart

SERVES 8

2 tsp instant espresso coffee
2 tbsp hot water
12 fl oz (350 ml) whipping cream
6 oz (170 g) plain chocolate
1 oz (30 g) bitter cooking chocolate
4 fl oz (125 ml) whipped cream, for decorating
chocolate-covered coffee beans, for decorating

FOR THE BASE

5 oz (140 g) chocolate wafers, crushed
2 tbsp caster sugar
2½ oz (70 g) butter, melted

1 ▲ For the base, mix the crushed chocolate wafers and sugar together, then stir in the melted butter.

2 Press the mixture evenly over the bottom and sides of a 9 in (23 cm) pie dish. Refrigerate until firm.

3 In a bowl, dissolve the coffee in the water and set aside.

4 Pour the cream into a mixing bowl. Set the bowl in hot water to warm the cream, bringing it closer to the temperature of the chocolate.

5 Melt both the chocolates in the top of a double boiler, or in a heatproof bowl set over a pan of hot water. Remove from the heat when nearly melted and stir to continue melting. Set the bottom of the pan in cool water to reduce the temperature. Be careful not to splash any water on the chocolate or it will become grainy.

6 ▲ With an electric mixer, whip the cream until it is lightly fluffy. Add the dissolved coffee and whip until the cream just holds its shape.

7 ▲ When the chocolate is at room temperature, fold it gently into the cream with a large metal spoon.

8 Pour into the chilled biscuit base and refrigerate until firm. To serve, pipe a ring of whipped cream rosettes around the edge, then place a chocolate-covered coffee bean in the centre of each rosette.

Chocolate Pear Tart

SERVES 8

4 oz (115 g) plain chocolate, grated
3 large firm, ripe pears
1 egg
1 egg yolk
4 fl oz (125 ml) single cream
1/2 tsp vanilla essence
3 tbsp caster sugar
FOR THE PASTRY
5 oz (140 g) plain flour
1/8 tsp salt
2 tbsp sugar
4 oz (115 g) cold unsalted butter, cut into pieces
1 egg yolk
1 tbsp fresh lemon juice

1 For the pastry, sift the flour and salt into a bowl. Add the sugar and butter. Cut in with a pastry blender until the mixture resembles coarse breadcrumbs. Stir in the egg yolk and lemon juice until the mixture forms a ball. Wrap in greaseproof paper, and refrigerate for at least 20 minutes.

2 Preheat a baking sheet in the centre of a 400°F/200°C/Gas 6 oven.

3 On a lightly floured surface, roll out the pastry 1/8 in (3 mm) thick. Transfer to a 10 in (25 cm) tart dish and trim.

4 ▲ Sprinkle the bottom of the case with the grated chocolate.

5 ▲ Peel, halve and core the pears. Cut in thin slices crosswise, then fan them out slightly.

6 Transfer the pear halves to the tart with the help of a metal spatula and arrange on top of the chocolate like the spokes of a wheel.

7 ▼ Whisk together the egg and egg yolk, cream and vanilla. Ladle over the pears, then sprinkle with sugar.

8 Bake for 10 minutes. Reduce the heat to 350°F/180°C/Gas 4 and cook until the custard is set and the pears begin to caramelize, about 20 minutes more. Serve warm.

Maple Walnut Tart

SERVES 8

3 eggs

1/8 tsp salt

2 oz (55 g) caster sugar

2 oz (55 g) butter or margarine, melted

8 fl oz (250 ml) pure maple syrup

4 oz (115 g) chopped walnuts

whipped cream, for decorating

FOR THE PASTRY

2 1/2 oz (70 g) plain flour

2 1/2 oz (70 g) wholewheat flour

1/8 tsp salt

2 oz (55 g) cold butter, cut in pieces

1 1/2 oz (45 g) cold vegetable fat or lard, cut in pieces

1 egg yolk

2–3 tbsp iced water

1 ▼ For the pastry, mix the flours and salt in a bowl. Add the butter and fat and cut in with a pastry blender until the mixture resembles coarse breadcrumbs. With a fork, stir in the egg yolk and just enough water to bind the pastry. Form into a ball.

2 Wrap in greaseproof paper and refrigerate for 20 minutes.

3 Preheat a 425°F/220°C/Gas 7 oven.

4 On a lightly floured surface, roll out the pastry about 1/8 in (3 mm) thick and transfer to a 9 in (23 cm) pie dish. Trim the edge. To decorate, roll out the trimmings. With a small heart-shaped cutter, stamp out enough hearts to go around the rim of the pie. Brush the edge with water, then arrange the pastry hearts all around.

5 ▲ Prick the bottom with a fork. Line with crumpled greaseproof paper and fill with baking beans. Bake for 10 minutes. Remove the paper and beans and continue baking until golden brown, 3–6 minutes more.

6 In a bowl, whisk the eggs, salt and sugar together. Stir in the butter and maple syrup.

7 ▲ Set the pastry case on a baking sheet. Pour in the filling, then sprinkle the nuts over the top.

8 Bake until just set, for about 35 minutes. Cool on a rack. Decorate with whipped cream, if wished.

Pecan Tart

SERVES 8

3 eggs
¹/₈ tsp salt
7 oz (200 g) dark brown sugar
4 fl oz (125 ml) golden syrup
2 tbsp fresh lemon juice
3 oz (85 g) butter, melted
5 oz (140 g) chopped pecan nuts
2 oz (55 g) pecan halves
FOR THE PASTRY
6 oz (170 g) plain flour
1 tbsp caster sugar
1 tsp baking powder
¹/₂ tsp salt
3 oz (85 g) cold unsalted butter, cut in pieces
1 egg yolk
3–4 tbsp whipping cream

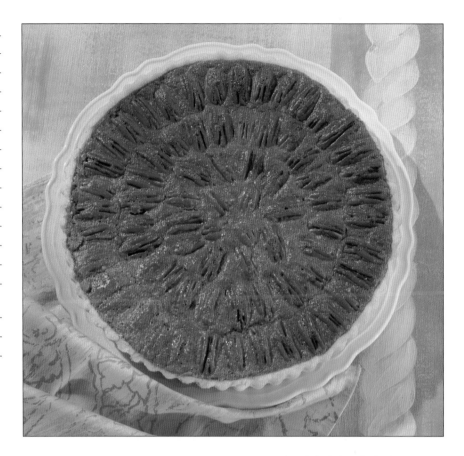

1 For the pastry, sift the flour, sugar, baking powder and salt into a bowl. Add the butter and cut in with a pastry blender until the mixture resembles coarse breadcrumbs.

2 ▼ In a bowl, beat together the egg yolk and cream until blended.

~ COOK'S TIP ~

Serve this tart warm, accompanied by ice cream or whipped cream, if wished.

3 ▲ Pour the cream mixture into the flour mixture and stir with a fork.

4 Gather the pastry into a ball. On a lightly floured surface, roll out ¹/₈ in (3 mm) thick and transfer to a 9 in (23 cm) pie dish. Trim the overhang and flute the edge with your fingers. Refrigerate for at least 20 minutes.

5 Preheat a baking sheet in the middle of a 400°F/200°C/Gas 6 oven.

6 In a bowl, lightly whisk the eggs and salt. Add the sugar, syrup, lemon juice and butter. Mix well and stir in the chopped nuts.

7 ▲ Pour into the pastry case and arrange the pecan halves in concentric circles on top.

8 Bake for 10 minutes. Reduce the heat to 325°F/170°C/Gas 3 and continue baking for 25 minutes.

Peach Tart with Almond Cream

SERVES 8–10

4 large ripe peaches
4 oz (115 g) blanched almonds
2 tbsp plain flour
3½ oz (100 g) unsalted butter, at room temperature
4 oz (115 g) plus 2 tbsp caster sugar
1 egg
1 egg yolk
½ tsp vanilla essence, or 2 tsp rum
FOR THE PASTRY
6½ oz (190 g) plain flour
¾ tsp salt
3½ oz (100 g) cold unsalted butter, cut in pieces
1 egg yolk
2½–3 tbsp iced water

1 ▲ For the pastry, sift the flour and salt into a bowl.

2 Add the butter and cut in with a pastry blender until the mixture resembles coarse breadcrumbs. Stir in the egg yolk and just enough water to bind the pastry. Gather into a ball, wrap in greaseproof paper, and refrigerate for at least 20 minutes.

3 Preheat a baking sheet in the centre of a 400°F/200°C/Gas 6 oven.

4 ▲ On a floured surface, roll out the pastry ⅛ in (3mm) thick. Transfer to a 10 in (25 cm) pie dish. Trim the edge, prick the bottom and refrigerate.

5 ▲ Score the bottoms of the peaches. Drop the peaches, 1 at a time, into boiling water. Boil for 20 seconds, then dip in cold water. Peel off the skins using a sharp knife.

6 ▲ Grind the almonds finely with the flour in a food processor, blender or grinder. With an electric mixer, cream the butter and 4 oz (115 g) of the sugar until light and fluffy. Gradually beat in the egg and yolk. Stir in the almonds and vanilla or rum. Spread in the pastry case.

7 ▲ Halve the peaches and remove the stones. Cut crosswise in thin slices and arrange on top of the almond cream like the spokes of a wheel; keep the slices of each peach-half together. Fan out by pressing down gently at a slight angle.

8 ▲ Bake until the pastry begins to brown, 10–15 minutes. Lower the heat to 350°F/180°C/Gas 4 and continue baking until the almond cream sets, about 15 minutes more. Ten minutes before the end of the cooking time, sprinkle with the remaining 2 tablespoons of sugar.

~ **VARIATION** ~

For a Nectarine and Apricot Tart with Almond Cream, replace the peaches with nectarines, prepared and arranged the same way. Peel and chop 3 fresh apricots. Fill the spaces between the fanned-out nectarines with 1 tablespoon of chopped apricots. Bake as above.

Almond Syrup Tart

SERVES 6

3 oz (85 g) fresh white breadcrumbs

8 oz (225 g) golden syrup

finely grated zest of ½ lemon

2 teaspoons lemon juice

9 in (23 cm) pastry case, made with basic, nut or rich shortcrust pastry

1 oz (30 g) flaked almonds

1 Preheat a 200°C/400°F/Gas 6 oven.

2 ▲ In a mixing bowl, combine the breadcrumbs with the golden syrup and the lemon zest and juice.

3 Spoon into the pastry case and spread out evenly.

4 ▲ Sprinkle the flaked almonds evenly over the top.

5 ▼ Brush the pastry with milk to glaze, if you like. Bake for 25–30 minutes or until the pastry and filling are golden brown.

6 Remove to a wire rack to cool. Serve warm or cold, with cream, custard or ice cream.

~ VARIATIONS ~

For Walnut Syrup Tart, replace the almonds with chopped walnuts. For Ginger Syrup Tart, mix 1 teaspoon ground ginger with the breadcrumbs before adding the syrup and lemon zest and juice. Omit the nuts if liked. For Coconut Syrup Tart, replace 1 oz (30 g) of the breadcrumbs with 1½ oz (45 g) desiccated coconut.

Apple Maple Dumplings

SERVES 8

18oz (475g) plain flour
2 teaspoons salt
12oz (350g) vegetable fat
2–8fl oz (50–250ml) iced water
8 firm eating apples
1 egg white
4½oz (130g) sugar
3 tablespoons whipping cream
½ teaspoon vanilla essence
8fl oz (250ml) maple syrup
whipped cream, for serving

1 Sift the flour and salt into a large bowl. Using a pastry blender or two knives, cut in the fat until the mixture resembles coarse breadcrumbs. Sprinkle with 6fl oz (175ml) water and mix until the dough holds together. If it is too crumbly, add a little more water. Gather into a ball. Wrap in greaseproof paper and refrigerate for at least 20 minutes.

2 Preheat a 220°C/425°F/Gas 7 oven.

3 Peel the apples. Remove the cores, without cutting through the base.

4 ▲ Roll out the dough thinly. Cut squares almost large enough to enclose the apples. Brush the squares with egg white. Set an apple in the centre of each square of dough.

5 Combine the sugar, cream and vanilla in a small bowl. Spoon some into the hollow in each apple.

6 ▼ Pull the points of the dough squares up around the apples and moisten the edges where they overlap. Mould the dough round the apples, pleating the top. Do not cover the centre hollows. Crimp the edges tightly to seal.

7 Set the apples in a large greased baking dish, at least ¾ in (2 cm) apart. Bake for 30 minutes. Lower the oven temperature to 180°C/350°F/ Gas 4 and continue baking until the pastry is golden brown and the apples are tender, about 20 minutes more.

8 Transfer the dumplings to a serving dish. Mix the maple syrup with the juices in the baking dish and drizzle over the dumplings.

9 Serve the dumplings hot with whipped cream.

Apple Strudel

SERVES 10–12

3 oz (85 g) raisins
2 tbsp brandy
5 eating apples, such as Granny Smith or Cox's
3 large cooking apples
3¹/₂ oz (100 g) dark brown sugar
1 tsp ground cinnamon
grated rind and juice of 1 lemon
1 oz (30 g) dry breadcrumbs
2 oz (55 g) chopped pecans or walnuts
12 sheets frozen filo pastry, thawed
6 oz (170 g) butter, melted
icing sugar, for dusting

1 Soak the raisins in the brandy for at least 15 minutes.

2 ▼ Peel, core and thinly slice the apples. In a bowl, combine the sugar, cinnamon and lemon rind. Stir in the apples and half the breadcrumbs.

3 Add the raisins, nuts and lemon juice and stir until blended.

4 Preheat a 375°F/190°C/Gas 5 oven. Grease 2 baking sheets.

5 ▲ Carefully unfold the filo sheets. Keep the unused sheets covered with greaseproof paper. Lift off 1 sheet, place on a clean surface and brush with melted butter. Lay a second sheet on top and brush with butter. Continue until you have a stack of 6 buttered sheets.

6 Sprinkle a few tablespoons of breadcrumbs over the last sheet and spoon half the apple mixture at the bottom edge of the strip.

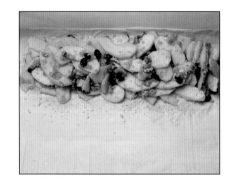

7 ▲ Starting at the apple-filled end, roll up the pastry, as for a Swiss roll. Place on a baking sheet, seam-side down, and carefully fold under the ends to seal. Repeat the procedure to make a second strudel. Brush both with butter.

8 Bake the strudels for 45 minutes. Let cool slightly. Using a small sieve, dust with a fine layer of icing sugar. Serve warm.

Cherry Strudel

SERVES 8

2¹/₂ oz (70 g) fresh breadcrumbs
6 oz (170 g) butter, melted
7 oz (200 g) sugar
1 tablespoon ground cinnamon
1 teaspoon grated lemon rind
1 lb (450 g) sour cherries, stoned
8 sheets filo pastry
icing sugar, for dusting

1 In a frying pan, lightly fry the fresh breadcrumbs in 2¹/₂ oz (70 g) of the melted butter until golden. Set aside to cool.

2 ▲ In a large mixing bowl, toss together the sugar, cinnamon and lemon rind.

3 Stir in the cherries.

4 Preheat the oven to 375°F/190°C/Gas 5. Grease a baking sheet.

5 Carefully unfold the filo sheets. Keep the unused sheets covered with damp kitchen paper. Lift off one sheet, place on a flat surface lined with parchment paper. Brush the pastry with melted butter. Sprinkle about an eighth of the breadcrumbs evenly over the surface.

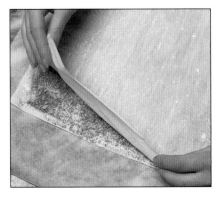

6 ▲ Lay a second sheet of filo on top, brush with butter and sprinkle with crumbs. Continue until you have a stack of 8 buttered, crumbed sheets.

7 Spoon the cherry mixture at the bottom edge of the strip. Starting at the cherry-filled end, roll up the dough as for a Swiss roll. Use the paper to help flip the strudel onto the baking sheet, seam-side down.

8 ▼ Carefully fold under the ends to seal in the fruit. Brush the top with any remaining butter.

9 Bake the strudel for 45 minutes. Let cool slightly. Using a small sieve, dust with a fine layer of icing sugar.

Chicken-Mushroom Pie

SERVES 6

½oz (15g) dried porcini mushrooms
2oz (50g) butter
½oz (15g) flour
8fl oz (250ml) hot chicken stock
2fl oz (50ml) whipping cream or milk
salt and pepper
1 onion, roughly chopped
2 carrots, sliced
2 celery sticks, roughly chopped
2oz (50g) fresh mushrooms, quartered
1lb (450g) cooked chicken meat, cubed
2oz (50g) shelled fresh or frozen peas
beaten egg, for glazing
FOR THE CRUST
8oz (225g) plain flour
¼ teaspoon salt
4oz (115g) cold butter, cut in pieces
3oz (75g) vegetable fat
4–8 tablespoons iced water

1 ▲ For the crust, sift the flour and salt into a bowl. With a pastry blender or two knives, cut in the butter and fat until the mixture resembles coarse breadcrumbs. Sprinkle with 6 tablespoons iced water and mix until the dough holds together. If the dough is too crumbly, add a little more water, 1 tablespoon at a time. Gather the dough into a ball and flatten into a disk. Wrap in greaseproof paper and refrigerate for at least 30 minutes.

2 Place the porcini mushrooms in a small bowl. Add hot water to cover and soak until soft, about 30 minutes. Lift out of the water with a slotted spoon to leave any grit behind and drain. Discard the soaking water.

3 Preheat a 190°C/375°F/Gas 5 oven.

4 ▲ Melt 1oz (25g) of the butter in a heavy saucepan. Whisk in the flour and cook until bubbling, whisking constantly. Add the stock and cook over a moderate heat, whisking, until the mixture boils. Cook for 2–3 minutes more. Whisk in the cream or milk. Season with salt and pepper. Set aside.

5 ▲ Heat the remaining butter in a large non-stick frying pan until foamy. Add the onion and carrots and cook until softened, about 5 minutes. Add the celery and fresh mushrooms and cook for 5 minutes more. Stir in the chicken, peas, and drained porcini mushrooms.

6 Add the chicken mixture to the cream sauce and stir to mix. Taste for seasoning. Transfer to a 2.8 litre (3¾ pint) rectangular pie dish.

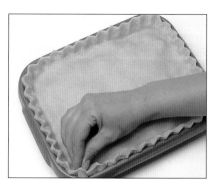

7 ▲ Roll out the dough to about ⅛ in (3 mm) thickness. Cut out a rectangle about 1 in (2.5 cm) larger all round than the dish. Lay the rectangle of dough over the filling. Make a decorative edge, crimping the dough by pushing the index finger of one hand between the thumb and index finger of the other.

8 Cut several vents to allow steam to escape. Brush with the egg glaze.

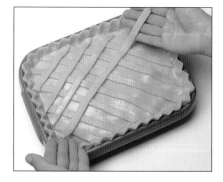

9 ▲ Press together the dough trimmings, then roll out again. Cut into strips and lay them over the top. Glaze again. If desired, roll small balls of dough and set them in the "windows" in the lattice.

10 Bake until the pastry top is browned, about 30 minutes. Serve the pie hot from the dish.

Ricotta and Basil Tart

SERVES 8–10

2 oz (55 g) basil leaves
1 oz (30 g) flat-leaf parsley
4 fl oz (125 ml) extra-virgin olive oil
salt and pepper
2 eggs
1 egg yolk
1 lb 12 oz (800 g) ricotta cheese
3¹/₂ oz (100 g) black olives, stoned
2¹/₄ oz (60 g) Parmesan cheese, freshly grated
FOR THE CRUST
6¹/₂ oz (180 g) plain flour
¹/₂ teaspoon salt
3 oz (85 g) cold butter, cut into pieces
1¹/₂ oz (45 g) cold margarine, cut into pieces
3–4 tablespoon iced water

1 ▲ For the crust, combine the flour and salt in a bowl. Add the butter and margarine.

2 Rub in with your fingertips until the mixture resembles coarse breadcrumbs. With a fork, stir in just enough water to bind the dough. Gather into a ball, wrap in clear film, and refrigerate for at least 20 minutes.

3 Preheat a baking sheet in a 375°F/190°C/Gas 5 oven.

4 Roll out the dough ¹/₈ in (3 mm) thick and transfer to a 10 in (25 cm) tart tin. Prick the base with a fork and line with greaseproof paper. Fill with dried beans and bake for 12 minutes. Remove the paper and beans and bake until golden, 3–5 minutes more. Lower the heat to 350°F/180°C/Gas 4.

5 ▲ In a food processor, combine the basil, parsley and olive oil. Season well with salt and pepper and process until finely chopped.

6 In a bowl, whisk the eggs and yolk to blend. Gently fold in the ricotta.

7 ▲ Fold in the basil mixture and olives until well combined. Stir in the Parmesan and adjust the seasoning.

8 Pour into the prebaked shell and bake until set, 30–35 minutes.

Onion and Anchovy Tart

SERVES 8

4 tablespoons olive oil

2 lb (900 g) onions, sliced

1 teaspoon dried thyme

salt and pepper

2–3 tomatoes, sliced

24 small black olives, stoned

1 × 2 oz (55 g) can anchovy fillets,
    drained and sliced

6 sun-dried tomatoes, cut into slivers

FOR THE CRUST

6¼ oz (180 g) plain flour

½ teaspoon salt

4 oz (115 g) cold butter, cut into pieces

1 egg yolk

2–3 tablespoons iced water

1 ▲ For the crust, sift the flour and salt into a bowl. Rub in the butter with your fingertips until the mixture resembles coarse breadcrumbs. Stir in the yolk and enough water to bind.

2 ▲ Roll out the dough to a thickness of about ⅛ in (3 mm). Transfer to a 9 in (23 cm) tart tin and trim the edge. Chill in the refrigerator until needed.

3 ▲ Heat the oil in a frying pan. Add the onions, thyme and seasoning. Cook over low heat, covered, for 25 minutes. Uncover and continue cooking until soft. Let cool. Preheat the oven to 400°F/200°C/Gas 6.

4 ▼ Spoon the onions into the tart shell and top with the tomato slices. Arrange the olives in rows. Make a lattice pattern, alternating lines of anchovies and sun-dried tomatoes. Bake until golden, 20–25 minutes.

Mushroom Quiche

SERVES 8

1 lb (450 g) mushrooms

2 tablespoons olive oil

1 tablespoon butter

1 clove garlic, finely chopped

1 tablespoon lemon juice

salt and pepper

2 tablespoons finely chopped parsley

3 eggs

12 fl oz (300 ml) whipping cream

2¼ oz (60 g) Parmesan cheese, grated

FOR THE CRUST

6¼ (180 g) plain flour

½ teaspoon salt

3 oz (85 g) cold butter, cut into pieces

1½ oz (45 g) cold margarine, cut into pieces

3–4 tablespoons iced water

1 For the crust, sift the flour and salt into a bowl. Rub in the butter and margarine until the mixture resembles coarse breadcrumbs. Stir in just enough water to bind.

2 Gather into a ball, wrap in clear film and refrigerate for 20 minutes.

3 Preheat a baking sheet in a 375°F/190°C/Gas 5 oven.

4 Roll out the dough ⅛ in (3 mm) thick. Transfer to a 9 in (23 cm) tart tin and trim. Prick the base all over with a fork. Line with greaseproof paper and fill with dried beans. Bake for 12 minutes. Remove the paper and beans and continue baking until golden, about 5 minutes more.

5 ▲ Wipe the mushrooms with damp kitchen paper to remove any dirt. Trim the ends of the stalks, place on a cutting board, and slice thinly.

6 Heat the oil and butter in a frying pan. Stir in the mushrooms, garlic and lemon juice. Season with salt and pepper. Cook until the mushrooms render their liquid, then raise the heat and cook until dry.

7 ▼ Stir in the parsley and add more salt and pepper if necessary.

8 Whisk the eggs and cream together, then stir in the mushrooms. Sprinkle the cheese over the bottom of the prebaked shell and pour the mushroom filling over the top.

9 Bake until puffed and brown, about 30 minutes. Serve the quiche warm.

Bacon and Cheese Quiche

SERVES 8

4 oz (115 g) medium-thick bacon slices

3 eggs

12 fl oz (350 ml) whipping cream

3½ oz (100 g) Gruyère cheese, grated

⅛ teaspoon grated nutmeg

salt and pepper

FOR THE CRUST

6¼ oz (180 g) plain flour

½ teaspoon salt

3 oz (85 g) cold butter, cut into pieces

1½ oz (45 g) cold margarine, cut into pieces

3–4 tablespoons iced water

1 Make the crust as directed in steps 1–4 above. Maintain the oven temperature at 375°F/190°C/Gas 5.

2 ▲ Fry the bacon until crisp. Drain, then crumble into small pieces. Sprinkle in the pastry shell.

3 ▲ Beat together the eggs, cream, cheese, nutmeg, salt and pepper. Pour over the bacon and bake until puffed and brown, about 30 minutes. Serve the quiche warm.

Mushroom Quiche (top), Bacon and Cheese Quiche

Asparagus, Sweetcorn and Red Pepper Quiche

SERVES 6

8 oz (225 g) fresh asparagus, woody stalks removed

1 oz (30 g) butter or margarine

1 small onion, finely chopped

1 red pepper, seeded and finely chopped

4 oz (115 g) drained canned sweetcorn, or frozen sweetcorn, thawed

2 eggs

8 fl oz (250 ml) single cream

2 oz (55 g) Cheddar cheese, grated

salt and pepper

FOR THE PASTRY

6½ oz (190 g) plain flour

½ tsp salt

4 oz (115 g) lard or vegetable fat

2–3 tbsp iced water

1 Preheat a 400°F/200°C/Gas 6 oven.

2 For the pastry, sift the flour and salt into a mixing bowl. Using a pastry blender or 2 knives, cut in the fat until the mixture resembles coarse breadcrumbs. Sprinkle in the water, 1 tablespoon at a time, tossing lightly with your fingertips or a fork until the dough forms a ball.

3 ▲ On a lightly floured surface, roll out the dough. Use it to line a 10 in (25 cm) quiche dish or loose-bottomed tart tin, easing the pastry in and being careful not to stretch it. Trim off excess pastry.

4 ▲ Line the pastry case with greaseproof paper and weigh it down with pastry weights or dried beans. Bake 10 minutes. Remove the paper and weight or beans and bake until the pastry is set and beige in colour, about 5 minutes longer. Let cool.

5 Trim the stem ends of 8 of the asparagus spears to make them 4 in (10 cm) in length. Set aside.

6 ▲ Finely chop the asparagus trimmings and any remaining spears. Place in the bottom of the case.

7 ▲ Melt the butter or margarine in a frying pan. Add the onion and red pepper and cook until softened, about 5 minutes. Stir in the sweetcorn and cook 2 minutes longer.

8 Spoon the sweetcorn mixture over the chopped asparagus.

9 ▲ In a small bowl, beat the eggs with the cream. Stir in the cheese and salt and pepper to taste. Pour into the pastry case.

10 ▲ Arrange the reserved asparagus spears like the spokes of a wheel on top of the filling.

11 Bake until the filling is set, about 25–30 minutes.

~ VARIATION ~

To make individual tarts, roll out the pastry and use to line a 12-cup bun tray. For the filling, cut off and reserve the asparagus tips and chop the tender part of the stalks. Mix the asparagus and the cooked vegetables into the egg mixture with the cheese. Spoon the filling into the pastry cases and bake as directed, decreasing baking time by about 8–10 minutes.

Cheesy Tomato Quiche

10 medium tomatoes

1 × 2 oz (55 g) can anchovy fillets, drained and finely chopped

4 fl oz (125 ml) whipping cream

7 oz (200 g) mature Cheddar cheese, grated

1 oz (30 g) wholemeal breadcrumbs

1/2 teaspoon dried thyme

salt and pepper

FOR THE CRUST

71/2 oz (215 g) plain flour

4 oz (115 g) cold butter, cut into pieces

1 egg yolk

2–3 tablespoons iced water

1 Preheat the oven to 400°F/200°C/ Gas 6.

2 For the crust, sift the flour into a bowl. Rub in the butter with your fingertips until the mixture resembles coarse breadcrumbs.

3 ▲ With a fork, stir in the egg yolk and enough water to bind the dough.

4 Roll out the dough about 1/8 in (3 mm) thick and transfer to a 9 in (23 cm) tart tin. Refrigerate until needed.

5 ▲ Score the bottoms of the tomatoes. Plunge in boiling water for 1 minute. Remove and peel off the skin with a knife. Cut in quarters and remove the seeds with a spoon.

6 ▲ In a bowl, mix the anchovies and cream. Stir in the cheese.

7 Sprinkle the breadcrumbs in the tart. Arrange the tomatoes on top. Season with thyme, salt and pepper.

8 ▲ Spoon the cheese mixture on top. Bake until golden, 25–30 minutes. Serve warm.

Quiche Lorraine

SERVES 6

8 oz (225 g) smoked streaky bacon rashers, chopped

9 in (23 cm) flan case, partially baked blind

3 eggs

2 egg yolks

12 fl oz (360 ml) whipping cream

4 fl oz (120 ml) milk

salt and pepper

1 Preheat a 200°C/400°F/Gas 6 oven.

2 ▲ Fry the bacon in a frying pan until it is crisp and golden brown. Drain the bacon on paper towels.

3 ▲ Scatter the bacon in the partially baked flan case.

4 In a bowl, whisk together the eggs, egg yolks, cream and milk. Season with salt and pepper.

5 ▼ Pour the egg mixture into the flan case.

6 Bake for 35–40 minutes or until the filling is set and golden brown and the pastry is golden. Serve warm or at room temperature.

~ VARIATIONS ~

Add 3 oz (85 g) grated Gruyère cheese with the bacon. Replace the bacon with diced cooked ham, if desired. For a vegetarian quiche, omit the bacon. Slice 1 lb (450 g) courgettes and fry in a little oil until lightly browned on both sides. Drain on paper towels, then arrange in the flan case. Scatter 2 oz (55 g) grated cheese on top. Make the egg mixture with 4 eggs, 8 fl oz (240 ml) cream, 4 tablespoons milk, 1/8 teaspoon grated nutmeg, salt and pepper.

Pizza

MAKES 2

1 lb 2 oz (500 g) plain flour
1 tsp salt
2 tsp active dry yeast
10 fl oz (300 ml) lukewarm water
2–4 fl oz (65–125 ml) extra-virgin olive oil
tomato sauce, grated cheese, olives and herbs, for topping

1   Combine the flour and salt in a large mixing bowl. Make a well in the centre and add the yeast, water and 2 tablespoons of the olive oil. Leave for 15 minutes to dissolve the yeast.

2   With your hands, stir until the dough just holds together. Transfer to a floured surface and knead until smooth and elastic. Avoid adding too much flour while kneading.

3 ▲   Brush the inside of a clean bowl with 1 tablespoon of the oil. Place the dough in the bowl and roll around to coat with the oil. Cover with a plastic bag and leave to rise in a warm place until more than doubled in volume, about 45 minutes.

4   Divide the dough into 2 balls. Preheat a 400°F/200°C/Gas 6 oven.

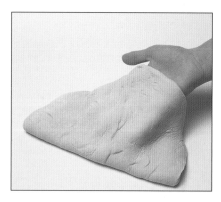

5 ▲   Roll each ball into a 10 in (25 cm) circle. Flip the circles over and onto your palm. Set each circle on the work surface and rotate, stretching the dough as you turn, until it is about 12 in (30 cm) in diameter.

6 ▲   Brush 2 pizza pans with oil. Place the dough circles in the pans and neaten the edges. Brush with oil.

7 ▲   Cover with the toppings and bake until golden, 10–12 minutes.

Onion, Olive and Anchovy Pizza

SERVES 4

6 tbsp olive oil

1 lb (450 g) onions, thinly sliced

3 garlic cloves, crushed

1 bay leaf

2 tsp dried thyme

salt and pepper

2 cans anchovy fillets, drained and blotted dry on kitchen paper

12 olives, mixed black and green

FOR THE PIZZA DOUGH

4 oz (115 g) wholewheat flour

3 oz (85 g) plain flour

1¼ tsp active dry yeast

⅛ tsp sugar

5 fl oz (150 ml) tepid water

2 tbsp olive oil

½ tsp salt

1 For the pizza dough, in a food processor combine the flours, yeast and sugar. With the motor running, pour in the tepid water. Turn the motor off. Add the oil and salt. Process until a ball of dough is formed.

2 Put the dough in an oiled bowl and turn it to coat with oil. Cover and let rise until doubled in size.

3 ▲ Heat 3 tablespoons of the oil in a frying pan. Add the onions, garlic and herbs. Cook over a low heat until the onions are very soft and the moisture has evaporated, about 45 minutes. Season with salt and pepper.

4 Preheat the oven to the highest setting. Oil a 13 × 9 in (33 × 23 cm) baking tray.

5 ▼ Transfer the risen dough onto a lightly floured surface. Punch down the dough and knead it briefly. Roll it out into a rectangle to fit the baking tray. Lay the dough on the tray and press it up the edges of the tray.

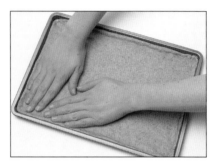

6 Brush the dough with 1 tablespoon olive oil. Discard the bay leaf, and spoon the onion mixture onto the dough. Spread it out evenly, leaving a ½ in (1 cm) border around the edge.

7 ▲ Arrange the anchovies and olives on top of the onions. Drizzle the remaining 2 tablespoons olive oil over the top.

8 Bake the pizza until the edges are puffed and browned, 15–20 minutes.

Broccoli and Goat Cheese Pizza

SERVES 2–3

8 oz (225 g) broccoli florets

2 tbsp cornmeal, or polenta

4 fl oz (125 ml) fresh tomatoes, skinned, cooked and sieved

6 cherry tomatoes, halved

12 black olives, stoned

4 oz (115 g) goat cheese, cut into pieces

1½ oz (45 g) Parmesan cheese, grated

1 tbsp olive oil

FOR THE PIZZA DOUGH

8–9 oz (225–250 g) plain flour

1 package active dry yeast (¼ oz/7.5 g)

⅛ tsp sugar

5 fl oz (150 ml) tepid water

2 tbsp olive oil

½ tsp salt

1 For the pizza dough, combine 3 oz (85 g) of the flour, the yeast and sugar in a food processor. With the motor running, pour in the water. Turn the motor off. Add the oil, 5 oz (140 g) of the remaining flour and the salt.

2 ▲ Process until a ball of dough is formed, adding more water, 1 teaspoon at a time, if the dough is too dry, or the remaining flour, 1 tablespoon at a time, if it is too wet.

3 ▲ Put the dough in an oiled bowl and turn it so the ball of dough is oiled all over. Cover the bowl and let the dough rise in a warm place until doubled in size, about 1 hour.

4 ▲ Meanwhile, cook the broccoli florets in boiling salted water or steam them until just tender, about 5 minutes. Drain well and set aside.

5 Preheat the oven to the highest setting. Oil a 12 in (30 cm) round pizza pan and sprinkle with the cornmeal.

6 When the dough has risen, turn out onto a lightly floured surface. Punch down the dough to deflate it, and knead it briefly.

~ COOK'S TIP~

If it is more convenient, the pizza dough can be used as soon as it is made, without any rising.

7 ▲ Roll out the dough to a 12 in (30 cm) round. Lay the dough on the pizza pan and press it down evenly.

8 ▲ Spread the tomato sauce evenly onto the pizza base, leaving a rim of dough uncovered around the edge about ½ in (1 cm) wide.

9 ▲ Arrange the broccoli florets, tomatoes, and olives on the tomato sauce and sprinkle with the cheeses. Drizzle the olive oil over the top.

10 Bake until the cheese melts and the edge of the pizza base is puffed and browned, 10–15 minutes.

CAKES & GATEAUX

AS DELICIOUS AS THEY ARE
BEAUTIFUL, THESE CAKES AND
GÂTEAUX ARE PERFECT TO SERVE
AT TEATIME OR FOR DESSERT.
DELIGHTFUL PARTY CAKES MAKE
SPECIAL OCCASIONS MEMORABLE.

Apple Ring Cake

SERVES 12

7 eating apples, such as Cox's or Granny Smith
12 fl oz (350 ml) vegetable oil
1 lb (450 g) caster sugar
3 eggs
15 oz (420 g) plain flour
1 tsp salt
1 tsp bicarbonate of soda
1 tsp ground cinnamon
1 tsp vanilla essence
4 oz (115 g) chopped walnuts
6 oz (170 g) raisins
icing sugar, for dusting

1 Preheat a 350°F/180°C/Gas 4 oven. Grease a 9 in (23 cm) ring mould.

2 ▲ Quarter, peel, core and slice the apples into a bowl. Set aside.

3 With an electric mixer, beat the oil and sugar together until blended. Add the eggs and continue beating until the mixture is creamy.

4 Sift together the flour, salt, bicarbonate of soda and cinnamon.

5 ▼ Fold the flour mixture into the egg mixture with the vanilla. Stir in the apples, walnuts and raisins.

6 Pour into the tin and bake until the cake springs back when touched lightly, about 1¼ hours. Let stand for 15 minutes, then unmould and transfer to a cooling rack. Dust with a layer of icing sugar before serving.

Orange Cake

SERVES 6

6 oz (170 g) plain flour
1½ tsp baking powder
⅛ tsp salt
4 oz (115 g) butter or margarine
4 oz (115 g) caster sugar
grated rind of 1 large orange
2 eggs, at room temperature
2 tbsp milk
FOR THE SYRUP AND DECORATION
4 oz (115 g) caster sugar
8 fl oz (250 ml) fresh orange juice, strained
3 orange slices, for decorating

1 Preheat the oven to 350°F/ 180°C/Gas 4. Line an 8 in (20 cm) cake tin with greaseproof paper and grease the paper.

2 ▲ Sift the flour, salt and baking powder onto greaseproof paper.

3 With an electric mixer, cream the butter or margarine until soft. Add the sugar and orange rind and continue beating until light and fluffy. Beat in the eggs, 1 at a time. Fold in the flour in 3 batches, then add the milk.

4 Spoon into the tin and bake until the cake pulls away from the sides, about 30 minutes. Remove from the oven but leave in the tin.

5 Meanwhile, for the syrup, dissolve the sugar in the orange juice over a low heat. Add the orange slices and simmer for 10 minutes. Remove and drain. Let the syrup cool.

6 ▲ Prick the cake all over with a fine skewer. Pour the syrup over the hot cake. It may seem at first that there is too much syrup for the cake to absorb, but it will soak it all up. Unmould when completely cooled and decorate with small triangles of the orange slices arranged on top.

Apple Ring Cake (top), Orange Cake

Angel Cake

SERVES 12–14

4¹/₂ oz (125 g) sifted plain flour

2 tablespoons cornflour

10¹/₂ oz (300 g) caster sugar

10–11 oz (285–310 g) egg whites (about 10–11 eggs)

1¹/₄ teaspoons cream of tartar

¹/₄ teaspoon salt

1 teaspoon vanilla essence

¹/₄ teaspoon almond essence

icing sugar, for dusting

1 Preheat the oven to 325°F/170°C/ Gas 3.

2 ▼ Sift the flours before measuring, then sift them 4 times with 3¹/₂ oz (100 g) of the sugar.

3 With an electric mixer, beat the egg whites until foamy. Sift over the cream of tartar and salt and continue to beat until the whites hold soft peaks when the beaters are lifted.

4 ▲ Add the remaining sugar in 3 batches, beating well after each addition. Stir in the vanilla and almond essences.

5 ▲ Add the flour mixture, in 2 batches, and fold in with a large metal spoon after each addition.

6 Transfer to an ungreased 10 in (25 cm) tube tin and bake until just browned on top, about 1 hour.

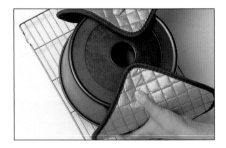

7 ▲ Turn the tin upside down onto a cake rack and let cool for 1 hour. If the cake does not turn out, run a knife around the edge to loosen it. Invert on a serving plate.

8 When cool, lay a star-shaped template on top of the cake, sift over icing sugar and remove template.

Marbled Ring Cake

SERVES 16

4 oz (115 g) plain chocolate
12 oz (350 g) plain flour
1 tsp baking powder
1 lb (450 g) butter, at room temperature
1 lb 10 oz (740 g) caster sugar
1 tbsp vanilla essence
10 eggs, at room temperature
icing sugar, for dusting

1 ▲ Preheat a 350°F/180°C/Gas 4 oven. Line a 10 × 4 in (25 × 10 cm) ring mould with greaseproof paper and grease the paper. Dust with flour.

2 ▲ Melt the chocolate in the top of a double boiler, or in a heatproof bowl set over a pan of hot water. Stir occasionally. Set aside.

3 In a bowl, sift together the flour and baking powder. In another bowl, cream the butter, sugar and vanilla with an electric mixer until light and fluffy. Add the eggs, 2 at a time, then gradually incorporate the flour mixture on low speed.

4 ▲ Spoon half of the mixture into the prepared tin.

5 ▲ Stir the chocolate into the remaining mixture, then spoon into the tin. With a metal spatula, swirl the mixtures for a marbled effect.

6 Bake until a skewer inserted in the centre comes out clean, about 1 hour 45 minutes. Cover with foil halfway through baking. Let stand for 15 minutes, then unmould and transfer to a cooling rack. To serve, dust with icing sugar.

Carrot Cake

SERVES 10

1 lb (450 g) caster sugar

8 fl oz (250 ml) vegetable oil

4 eggs

about 8 oz (225 g) carrots, finely grated

8 oz (225 g) plain flour

1½ tsp bicarbonate of soda

1½ tsp baking powder

1 tsp ground allspice

1 tsp ground cinnamon

FOR THE ICING

8 oz (225 g) icing sugar

8 oz (225 g) cream cheese, at room temperature

2 oz (55 g) butter or margarine, at room temperature

2 tsp vanilla essence

6 oz (175 g) chopped walnuts or pecans

1 Preheat a 375°F/190°C/Gas 5 oven.

2 Butter and flour 2 × 9 in (23 cm) round cake tins.

3 ▲ In a mixing bowl, combine the caster sugar, vegetable oil, eggs, and carrots. Beat for 2 minutes.

4 Sift the dry ingredients into another bowl. Add in 4 equal batches to the carrot mixture, mixing well after each addition.

5 ▲ Divide the cake mixture evenly between the prepared cake tins. Bake until a skewer inserted in the centre of the cake comes out clean, 35–45 minutes.

6 Let cool in the tins on wire racks for 10 minutes, then unmould the cakes from the tins onto the wire racks and let cool completely.

7 For the icing, combine everything but the nuts in a bowl and beat until smooth.

8 ▲ To assemble, set 1 cake layer on a serving plate and spread with one-third of the icing. Place the second cake layer on top. Spread the remaining icing all over the top and sides of the cake, swirling it to make a decorative finish. Sprinkle the nuts around the top edge.

Madeira Cake

SERVES 12

8 oz (225 g) plain flour

1 tsp baking powder

8 oz (225 g) butter or margarine, at room temperature

8 oz (225 g) caster sugar

grated rind of 1 lemon

1 tsp vanilla essence

4 eggs

1 Preheat a 325°F/170°C/Gas 3 oven. Grease a 9 × 5 in (23 × 13 cm) loaf tin.

2 Sift the flour and baking powder into a small bowl. Set aside.

3 ▲ With an electric mixer, cream the butter or margarine, adding the sugar 2 tablespoons at a time, until light and fluffy. Stir in the lemon rind and vanilla.

4 ▲ Add the eggs one at a time, beating for 1 minute after each addition.

5 ▼ Add the flour mixture and stir until just combined.

6 ▲ Pour the cake mixture into the tin and tap lightly. Bake until a metal skewer inserted in the centre comes out clean, about 1¼ hours.

7 Let cool in the tin on a wire rack for 10 minutes, then unmould the cake from the tin onto the wire rack and let cool completely.

Lemon Yogurt Ring

SERVES 12

8 oz (225 g) butter, at room temperature

10¹/₂ oz (300 g) caster sugar

4 eggs, at room temperature, separated

2 teaspoons grated lemon rind

3 fl oz (85 ml) lemon juice

8 fl oz (250 ml) plain yogurt

10 oz (285 g) plain flour

2 teaspoons baking powder

1 teaspoon bicarbonate of soda

¹/₂ teaspoon salt

FOR THE GLAZE

4 oz (115 g) icing sugar

2 tablespoons lemon juice

3–4 tablespoons plain yogurt

1 Preheat a 350°F/180°C/Gas 4 oven. Grease a 4²/₃ pt (3 litre) bundt or fluted tube tin and dust with flour.

2 With an electric mixer, cream the butter and caster sugar until light and fluffy. Add the egg yolks, 1 at a time, beating well after each addition.

3 ▲ Add the lemon rind, juice and yogurt and stir to blend.

4 Sift together the flour, baking powder and bicarbonate of soda. In another bowl, beat the egg whites and salt until they hold stiff peaks.

5 ▲ Fold the dry ingredients into the butter mixture, then fold in a dollop of egg whites. Fold in the remaining whites until blended.

6 Pour into the tin and bake until a skewer inserted in the centre comes out clean, about 50 minutes. Let stand 15 minutes, then turn out and cool on a rack.

7 For the glaze, sift the icing sugar into a bowl. Stir in the lemon juice and just enough yogurt to make a smooth glaze.

8 ▲ Set the cooled cake on the rack over a sheet of greaseproof paper or a baking sheet. Pour over the glaze and let it drip down the sides. Allow the glaze to set before serving.

Banana Lemon Layer Cake

SERVES 8–10

9oz (250g) flour
1¼ teaspoons baking powder
½ teaspoon salt
4oz (115g) butter, at room temperature
7oz (200g) granulated sugar
4oz (115g) soft light brown sugar, firmly packed
2 eggs
½ teaspoon grated lemon rind
3 medium very ripe bananas, mashed
1 teaspoon vanilla essence
2fl oz (50 ml) milk
3oz (75g) chopped walnuts

FOR THE FROSTING

4oz (115g) butter, at room temperature
18oz (475g) icing sugar
¼ teaspoon grated lemon rind
3–5 tablespoons fresh lemon juice

1 Preheat the oven to 180°C/350°F/ Gas 4. Grease two 9 in (23 cm) round cake tins, and line the bottoms with disks of buttered greaseproof paper.

2 Sift the flour with the baking powder and salt.

3 ▲ In a large mixing bowl, cream the butter with the sugars until light and fluffy. Beat in the eggs, one at a time. Stir in the lemon rind.

4 ▲ In a small bowl, mix the bananas with the vanilla and milk. Add the banana mixture and the dry ingredients to the butter mixture alternately in two or three batches and stir until just blended. Fold in the nuts.

5 Divide the batter between the cake tins and spread it out evenly. Bake until a skewer inserted in the centre comes out clean, 30–35 minutes. Leave to stand for 5 minutes before unmoulding on to a wire rack. Peel off the greaseproof paper.

6 For the frosting, cream the butter until smooth, then gradually beat in the sugar. Stir in the lemon rind and enough juice to make a spreadable consistency.

7 ▼ Set one of the cake layers on a serving plate. Cover with about one-third of the frosting. Top with the second cake layer. Spread the remaining frosting evenly over the top and sides of the cake.

Light Fruit Cake

MAKES 2 LOAVES

8 oz (225 g) prunes
8 oz (225 g) dates
8 oz (225 g) currants
8 oz (225 g) sultanas
8 fl oz (250 ml) dry white wine
8 fl oz (250 ml) rum
12 oz (350 g) plain flour
2 tsp baking powder
1 tsp ground cinnamon
¹/₂ tsp grated nutmeg
8 oz (225 g) butter, at room temperature
8 oz (225 g) caster sugar
4 eggs, at room temperature, lightly beaten
1 tsp vanilla essence

1 Stone the prunes and dates and chop finely. Place in a bowl with the currants and sultanas.

2 ▲ Stir in the wine and rum and let stand, covered, for 48 hours. Stir occasionally.

3 Preheat a 300°F/150°C/Gas 2 oven with a tray of hot water in the bottom. Line 2 9 × 5 in (23 × 13 cm) tins with greaseproof paper and grease.

4 Sift together the flour, baking powder, cinnamon, and nutmeg.

5 ▲ With an electric mixer, cream the butter and sugar together until light and fluffy.

6 Gradually add the eggs and vanilla. Fold in the flour mixture in 3 batches. Fold in the dried fruit mixture and its soaking liquid.

7 ▲ Divide the mixture between the tins and bake until a skewer inserted in the centre comes out clean, about 1¹/₂ hours.

8 Let stand 20 minutes, then unmould and transfer to a cooling rack. Wrap in foil and store in an air-tight container. If possible, leave for at least 1 week before serving to allow the flavours to mellow.

Rich Fruit Cake

SERVES 12

5 oz (140 g) currants
6 oz (170 g) raisins
2 oz (55 g) sultanas
2 oz (55 g) glacé cherries, halved
3 tbsp sweet sherry
6 oz (170 g) butter
7 oz (200 g) dark brown sugar
2 size 1 eggs, at room temperature
7 oz (200 g) plain flour
2 tsp baking powder
2 tsp each ground ginger, allspice, and cinnamon
1 tbsp golden syrup
1 tbsp milk
2 oz (55 g) cut mixed peel
4 oz (115 g) chopped walnuts
FOR THE DECORATION
8 oz (225 g) caster sugar
4 fl oz (125 ml) water
1 lemon, thinly sliced
1/2 orange, thinly sliced
4 fl oz (125 ml) orange marmalade
glacé cherries

1 One day before preparing, combine the currants, raisins, sultanas and cherries in a bowl. Stir in the sherry. Cover and let stand overnight to soak.

2 Preheat a 300°F/150°C/Gas 2 oven. Line a 9 × 3 in (23 × 8 cm) spring-form tin with greaseproof paper and grease. Place a tray of hot water on the bottom of the oven.

3 With an electric mixer, cream the butter and sugar until light and fluffy. Beat in the eggs, 1 at a time.

4 ▲ Sift the flour, baking powder and spices together 3 times. Fold into the butter mixture in 3 batches. Fold in the syrup, milk, dried fruit and liquid, mixed peel and nuts.

5 ▲ Spoon into the tin, spreading out so there is a slight depression in the centre of the mixture.

6 Bake until a skewer inserted in the centre comes out clean, 2¹/₂–3 hours. Cover with foil when the top is golden to prevent over-browning. Cool in the tin on a rack.

7 ▲ For the decoration, combine the sugar and water in a saucepan and bring to the boil. Add the lemon and orange slices and cook until crystallized, about 20 minutes. Work in batches, if necessary. Remove the fruit with a slotted spoon. Pour the remaining syrup over the cake and let cool. Melt the marmalade over low heat, then brush over the top of the cake. Decorate with the crystallized citrus slices and cherries.

Ginger Cake with Spiced Whipped Cream

SERVES 9

6 oz (170 g) plain flour

2 tsp baking powder

½ tsp salt

2 tsp ground ginger

2 tsp ground cinnamon

1 tsp ground cloves

¼ tsp grated nutmeg

2 eggs

8 oz (225 g) caster sugar

8 fl oz (250 ml) whipping cream

1 tsp vanilla essence

icing sugar, for sprinkling

FOR THE SPICED WHIPPED CREAM

6 fl oz (175 ml) whipping cream

1 tsp icing sugar

¼ tsp ground cinnamon

¼ tsp ground ginger

⅛ tsp grated nutmeg

1 Preheat a 350°F/180°C/Gas 4 oven. Grease a 9 in (23 cm) square baking tin.

2 Sift the flour, baking powder, salt and spices into a bowl. Set aside.

3 ▲ With an electric mixer, beat the eggs on high speed until very thick, about 5 minutes. Gradually beat in the caster sugar.

4 ▲ With the mixer on low speed, beat in the flour mixture alternately with the cream, beginning and ending with the flour. Stir in the vanilla.

5 ▲ Pour the cake mixture into the tin and bake until the top springs back when touched lightly, 35–40 minutes. Let cool in the tin on a wire rack for 10 minutes.

6 ▲ Meanwhile, to make the spiced whipped cream, combine the ingredients in a bowl and whip until the cream will hold soft peaks.

7 Sprinkle icing sugar over the hot cake, cut in 9 squares, and serve with spiced whipped cream.

Rich Sticky Gingerbread

MAKES AN 8 IN (20 CM) SQUARE CAKE

8 oz (225 g) plain flour
pinch of salt
1 teaspoon bicarbonate of soda
2 teaspoons ground ginger
1 teaspoon mixed spice
4 oz (115 g) butter or margarine
4 oz (115 g) golden syrup
4 oz (115 g) black treacle
2 oz (55 g) soft dark brown sugar
2 eggs, beaten
4 fl oz (120 ml) milk
4 oz (115 g) sultanas or chopped stem ginger (optional)

FOR THE ICING (OPTIONAL)

4 oz (115 g) icing sugar
about 4 teaspoons water

1 ▲ Preheat a 350°F/180°C/Gas 4 oven. Grease and line an 8 in (20 cm) square cake tin.

2 ▲ Sift the flour, salt, bicarbonate of soda and spices into a bowl.

3 Put the butter or margarine, golden syrup, treacle and brown sugar in a saucepan and warm over a gentle heat, stirring occasionally, until the fat has melted and the mixture is smooth. Remove from the heat and leave to cool slightly.

4 ▼ Make a well in the centre of the dry ingredients and add the melted mixture, the beaten eggs and milk. Beat with a wooden spoon until the mixture is smooth. Add the sultanas or ginger, if using.

5 Turn the cake mixture into the prepared tin. Bake for about 1 hour. To test if the gingerbread is done, press it lightly in the centre; it should spring back. Allow to cool in the tin for 5 minutes before turning out on to a wire rack to cool completely.

6 ▲ If icing the gingerbread, sift the icing sugar into a bowl and add 3 teaspoons of the water. Stir to mix, then add more water 1 teaspoon at a time until the icing is smooth and has a pouring consistency. Pour the icing over the gingerbread and leave to set before serving.

Walnut Layer Cake

SERVES 8

8oz (225g) plain flour

1 tablespoon baking powder

½ teaspoon salt

4oz (115g) butter or margarine,
    at room temperature

7oz (200g) granulated sugar

2 eggs

1 teaspoon grated orange rind

1 teaspoon vanilla essence

4oz (115g) ground walnuts

6fl oz (175ml) milk

black walnut halves, for decoration

FOR THE FROSTING

4oz (115g) butter

6oz (175g) soft light brown sugar,
    firmly packed

3 tablespoons maple syrup

2fl oz (50ml) milk

6–8oz (175–225g) icing sugar, sifted

1 ▲ Grease two 8 × 2 in (20 × 5 cm) cake tins and line the bottom of each with a disk of buttered greaseproof paper. Preheat the oven to 190°C/375°F/Gas 5.

2 Sift together the flour, baking powder and salt.

~ VARIATION ~

If black walnuts are not available, substitute ordinary walnuts, or use pecans instead.

3 ▲ Beat the butter or margarine to soften, then gradually beat in the granulated sugar until light and fluffy. Beat in the eggs, one at a time. Add the orange rind and vanilla and beat to mix well.

4 ▲ Stir in the ground walnuts. Add the flour alternately with the milk, stirring only enough to blend after each addition.

5 ▲ Divide the mixture between the prepared cake tins. Bake until a skewer inserted in the centre comes out clean, about 25 minutes. Cool in the cake tins for 5 minutes before unmoulding on to a wire rack.

6 ▲ For the frosting, melt the butter in a medium saucepan. Add the brown sugar and maple syrup and boil for 2 minutes, stirring constantly.

7 ▲ Add the milk. Bring back to the boil and stir in 1oz (25g) of the icing sugar. Remove from the heat and allow to cool until lukewarm. Gradually beat in the remaining icing sugar. Set the pan in a bowl of iced water and stir until the frosting is thick enough to spread.

8 ▲ Spread some of the frosting on one of the cake layers. Set the other layer on top. Spread the remaining frosting over the top and sides of the cake. Decorate with walnut halves.

Coffee-Iced Ring

SERVES 16

10 oz (285 g) plain flour	
1 tbsp baking powder	
1 tsp salt	
12 oz (350 g) caster sugar	
4 fl oz (125 ml) vegetable oil	
7 eggs, at room temperature, separated	
6 fl oz (175 ml) cold water	
2 tsp vanilla essence	
2 tsp grated lemon rind	
1/2 tsp cream of tartar	

FOR THE ICING

5 1/2 oz (165 g) unsalted butter, at room temperature	
1 lb 4 oz (575 g) icing sugar	
4 tsp instant coffee dissolved in 4 tbsp hot water	

1 Preheat a 325°F/170°C/Gas 3 oven.

2 ▼ Sift the flour, baking powder and salt into a bowl. Stir in 8 oz (225 g) of the sugar. Make a well in the centre and add in the following order: oil, egg yolks, water, vanilla and lemon rind. Beat with a whisk or metal spoon until smooth.

3 With an electric mixer, beat the egg whites with the cream of tartar until they hold soft peaks. Add the remaining 4 oz (115 g) of sugar and beat until they hold stiff peaks.

4 ▲ Pour the flour mixture over the whites in 3 batches, folding well after each addition.

5 Transfer the mixture to a 10 × 4 in (25 × 10 cm) ring mould and bake until the top springs back when touched lightly, about 1 hour.

6 ▲ When baked, remove from the oven and immediately hang the cake upside-down over the neck of a funnel or a narrow bottle. Let cool. To remove the cake, run a knife around the inside to loosen, then turn the tin over and tap the sides sharply. Invert the cake onto a serving plate.

7 For the icing, beat together the butter and icing sugar with an electric mixer until smooth. Add the coffee and beat until fluffy. With a metal spatula, spread over the sides and top of the cake.

Forgotten Gâteau

SERVES 6

6 egg whites, at room temperature

1/2 teaspoon cream of tartar

1/8 teaspoon salt

10 1/2 oz (300 g) caster sugar

1 teaspoon vanilla essence

6 fl oz (175 ml) whipping cream

FOR THE SAUCE

12 oz (350 g) fresh or thawed frozen
   raspberries

2–3 tablespoons icing sugar

1 Preheat a 450°F/230°C/Gas 8 oven.
Grease a 2 1/3 pt (1.5 litre) ring mould.

2 ▲ With an electric mixer, beat the
egg whites, cream of tartar and salt
until they hold soft peaks. Gradually
add the sugar and beat until glossy and
stiff. Fold in the vanilla.

3 ▲ Spoon into the prepared mould
and smooth the top level.

4 Place in the oven, then turn the
oven off. Leave overnight; do not
open the oven door at any time.

5 ▼ To serve, gently loosen the edge
with a sharp knife and turn out onto a
serving plate. Whip the cream until
firm. Spread it over the top and upper
sides of the meringue and decorate
with any meringue crumbs.

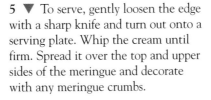

6 ▲ For the sauce, purée the fruit,
then strain. Sweeten to taste.

~ COOK'S TIP ~

This recipe is not suitable for fan
assisted and solid fuel ovens.

Nut and Apple Gâteau

SERVES 8

4 oz (115 g) pecan nuts or walnuts
2 oz (55 g) plain flour
2 tsp baking powder
1/4 tsp salt
2 large cooking apples
3 eggs
8 oz (225 g) caster sugar
1 tsp vanilla essence
6 fl oz (175 ml) whipping cream

1 Preheat a 325°F/170°C/Gas 3 oven. Line 2 9 in (23 cm) cake tins with greaseproof paper and grease the paper. Spread the nuts on a baking sheet and bake for 10 minutes.

2 Finely chop the nuts. Reserve 1 1/2 tablespoons and place the rest in a mixing bowl. Sift over the flour, baking powder and salt and stir.

3 ▲ Quarter, core and peel the apples. Cut into 1/8 in (3 mm) dice, then stir into the nut-flour mixture.

4 ▲ With an electric mixer, beat the eggs until frothy. Gradually add the sugar and vanilla and beat until a ribbon forms, about 8 minutes. Gently fold in the flour mixture.

5 Pour into the tins and level the tops. Bake until a skewer inserted in the centre comes out clean, about 35 minutes. Let stand 10 minutes.

6 ▲ To loosen, run a knife around the inside edge of each layer. Let cool.

7 ▲ Whip the cream until firm. Spread half over the cake. Top with the second cake. Pipe whipped cream rosettes on top and sprinkle over the reserved nuts before serving.

Almond Cake

SERVES 4–6

8 oz (225 g) blanched whole almonds, plus more for decorating
1 oz (30 g) butter
3 oz (85 g) icing sugar
3 eggs
½ tsp almond essence
1 oz (30 g) plain flour
3 egg whites
1 tbsp caster sugar

1 ▲ Preheat a 325°F/170°C/Gas 3 oven. Line a 9 in (23 cm) round cake tin with greaseproof paper and grease.

2 ▲ Spread the almonds in a baking tray and toast for 10 minutes. Cool, then coarsely chop 8 oz (225 g).

3 Melt the butter and set aside.

4 Preheat a 400°F/200°C/Gas 6 oven.

5 Grind the chopped almonds with half the icing sugar in a food processor, blender or grinder. Transfer to a mixing bowl.

6 ▲ Add the whole eggs and remaining icing sugar. With an electric mixer, beat until the mixture forms a ribbon when the beaters are lifted. Mix in the butter and almond essence. Sift over the flour and fold in gently.

7 With an electric mixer, beat the egg whites until they hold soft peaks. Add the caster sugar and beat until stiff and glossy.

8 ▲ Fold the whites into the almond mixture in 4 batches.

9 Spoon the mixture into the prepared tin and bake in the centre of the oven until golden brown, about 15–20 minutes. Decorate the top with the remaining toasted whole almonds. Serve warm.

Walnut Coffee Gâteau

Serves 8–10

5 oz (140 g) walnuts
5¹/₂ oz (150 g) sugar
5 eggs, separated
2 oz (55 g) dry breadcrumbs
1 tablespoon unsweetened cocoa powder
1 tablespoon instant coffee
2 tablespoons rum or lemon juice
¹/₈ teaspoon salt
6 tablespoons redcurrant jelly
chopped walnuts, for decorating
For the frosting
8 oz (225 g) plain chocolate
1¹/₄ pt (750 ml) whipping cream

3 ▲ Grind the nuts with 3 tablespoons of the sugar in a food processor, blender, or coffee grinder.

4 With an electric mixer, beat the egg yolks and remaining sugar until thick and lemon-coloured.

5 ▲ Fold in the walnuts. Stir in the breadcrumbs, cocoa, coffee and rum or lemon juice.

6 ▲ In another bowl, beat the egg whites with the salt until they hold stiff peaks. Fold carefully into the walnut mixture with a rubber scraper.

1 ▲ For the frosting, combine the chocolate and cream in the top of a double boiler, or in a heatproof bowl set over simmering water. Stir until the chocolate melts. Let cool, then cover and refrigerate overnight or until the mixture is firm.

2 Preheat the oven to 350°F/180°C/ Gas 4. Line a 9 × 2 in (23 × 5 cm) cake tin with greaseproof paper and grease.

7 Pour the meringue batter into the prepared tin and bake until the top of the cake springs back when touched lightly, about 45 minutes. Let the cake stand for 5 minutes, then turn out and cool on a rack.

8 ▲ When cool, slice the cake in half horizontally.

9 With an electric mixer, beat the chocolate frosting mixture on low speed until it becomes lighter, about 30 seconds. Do not overbeat or it may become grainy.

10 ▲ Warm the jelly in a saucepan until melted, then brush over the cut cake layer. Spread with some of the chocolate frosting, then sandwich with the remaining cake layer. Brush the top of the cake with jelly, then cover the side and top with the remaining chocolate frosting. Make a starburst pattern by pressing gently with a table knife in lines radiating from the centre. Sprinkle the chopped walnuts around the edge.

Coconut Cake

SERVES 10

6 oz (175 g) icing sugar
4 oz (115 g) plain flour
12 fl oz (375 ml) egg whites (about 12)
1½ tsp cream of tartar
8 oz (225 g) caster sugar
¼ tsp salt
2 tsp almond essence
3½ oz (100 g) desiccated coconut
FOR THE ICING
2 egg whites
4 oz (115 g) caster sugar
¼ tsp salt
2 tbsp cold water
2 tsp almond essence
7 oz (200 g) desiccated coconut, toasted

1 ▲ Preheat a 350°F/180°C/Gas 4 oven. Sift the icing sugar and flour into a bowl. Set aside.

2 With an electric mixer, beat the egg whites with the cream of tartar on medium speed until very thick. Turn the mixer to high speed and beat in the caster sugar, 2 tablespoons at a time, reserving 2 tablespoons.

3 ▲ Continue beating until stiff and glossy. Swiftly beat in the reserved 2 tablespoons of sugar, with the salt and almond essence.

4 ▲ One heaped teaspoon at a time, sprinkle the flour mixture over the meringue, quickly folding until just combined. Fold in the desiccated coconut in 2 batches.

5 ▲ Transfer the cake mixture to an ungreased 10 in (25 cm) non-stick tube tin, and cut gently through the mixture with a metal spatula. Bake until the top of the cake springs back when touched lightly, 30–35 minutes.

6 ▲ As soon as the cake is done, turn the tin upside down and suspend its funnel over the neck of a funnel or bottle. Let cool, about 1 hour.

7 ▲ For the icing, combine the egg whites, sugar, salt and water in a heatproof bowl. Beat with an electric mixer until blended. Set the bowl over a pan of boiling water and continue beating on medium speed until the icing is stiff, about 3 minutes. Remove the pan from the heat and stir in the almond essence.

8 ▲ Unmould the cake onto a serving plate. Spread the icing gently over the top and sides of the cake. Sprinkle with the toasted coconut.

Lemon Coconut Layer Cake

SERVES 8–10

6 oz (175 g) plain flour
1/4 teaspoon salt
7 eggs
12 oz (350 g) caster sugar
1 tablespoon grated orange rind
grated rind of 1 1/2 lemons
juice of 1 lemon
2 1/2 oz (65 g) desiccated coconut
1 tablespoon cornflour
4 fl oz (120 ml) water
1 1/2 oz (40 g) butter
FOR THE ICING
3 oz (75 g) unsalted butter
6 oz (175 g) icing sugar
grated rind of 1 1/2 lemon
2 tablespoons lemon juice
7 oz (200 g) desiccated coconut

1 Preheat the oven to 350°F/180°C/ Gas 4. Line three 8 in (20 cm) cake tins with greaseproof paper and grease. In a bowl, sift together the flour and salt and set aside.

2 ▲ Place six of the eggs in a large heatproof bowl set over hot water. With an electric mixer, beat until frothy. Gradually beat in 8 oz (225 g) caster sugar until the mixture doubles in volume and leaves a ribbon trail when the beaters are lifted, about 10 minutes.

3 ▲ Remove the bowl from the hot water. Fold in the orange rind, half the grated lemon rind and 1 tablespoon of the lemon juice until blended. Fold in the coconut.

4 Sift over the flour mixture in three batches, gently folding in thoroughly after each addition.

5 ▲ Divide the mixture between the prepared tins.

6 Bake until the cakes pull away from the sides of the tins, 20–25 minutes. Leave to stand for 5 minutes, then turn out to cool on a rack.

7 In a bowl, blend the cornflour with a little cold water to dissolve. Whisk in the remaining egg until just blended. Set aside.

8 ▲ In a saucepan, combine the remaining lemon rind and juice, the water, remaining sugar and butter.

9 Over a medium heat, bring the mixture to the boil. Whisk in the eggs and cornflour mixture, and return to the boil. Whisk continuously until thick, about 5 minutes. Remove from the heat and pour into a bowl. Cover with clear film and set aside to cool.

10 ▲ For the icing, cream the butter and icing sugar until smooth. Stir in the lemon rind and enough lemon juice to obtain a thick, spreadable consistency.

11 Sandwich the three cake layers with the lemon custard mixture. Spread the icing over the top and sides. Cover the cake with the coconut, pressing it in gently.

Coconut Lime Gâteau

SERVES 8 OR MORE

8 oz (225 g) plain flour
2½ teaspoons baking powder
¼ teaspoon salt
8 oz (225 g) butter, at room temperature
8 oz (225 g) caster sugar
grated zest of 2 limes
4 eggs
4 tablespoons fresh lime juice (from about 2 limes)
3 oz (85 g) desiccated coconut
1 recipe quantity American frosting (page 239)

1 Preheat a 350°F/180°C/Gas 4 oven. Grease two 9 in (23 cm) sandwich tins and line the bottoms with greased greaseproof paper.

2 Sift together the flour, baking powder and salt.

3 In a large bowl, beat the butter until it is soft and pliable. Add the sugar and lime zest and beat until the mixture is pale and fluffy. Beat in the eggs, one at a time.

4 ▲ Using a wooden spoon fold in the sifted dry ingredients in small portions, alternating with the lime juice. When the mixture is smooth, stir in two-thirds of the coconut.

5 ▲ Divide the mixture between the prepared tins and spread it evenly to the sides. Bake for 30–35 minutes (test with a skewer).

6 ▲ Remove the cakes from the oven and set them, in their tins, on a wire rack. Cool for 10 minutes. Then turn out and peel off the lining paper. Cool completely on the rack.

7 ▲ Spread the remaining coconut in another cake tin. Bake until golden brown, stirring occasionally. Watch carefully so that the coconut does not get too dark. Cool.

8 ▲ Put one of the cakes, base up, on a serving plate. Spread a layer of frosting evenly over the cake.

9 ▲ Set the second layer on top, base down. Spread the remaining frosting all over the top and round the sides of the cake.

10 ▲ Scatter the toasted coconut over the top of the cake and leave to set before serving.

Cranberry Upside-Down Cake

SERVES 8

12–14 oz (350–400 g) fresh cranberries
2 oz (55 g) butter
5 oz (140 g) sugar
FOR THE CAKE MIXTURE
2¹/₂ oz (70 g) plain flour
1 teaspoon baking powder
3 eggs
4 oz (115 g) sugar
grated rind of 1 orange
1¹/₂ oz (45 g) butter, melted

1 Preheat the oven to 350°F/180°C/ Gas 4. Place a baking sheet on the middle shelf of the oven.

2 Wash the cranberries and pat dry. Thickly smear the butter on the bottom and sides of a 9 × 2 in (23 × 5 cm) round cake tin. Add the sugar and swirl the tin to coat evenly.

3 ▲ Add the cranberries and spread in an even layer over the bottom of the tin.

4 For the cake mixture, sift the flour and baking powder twice. Set aside.

5 ▲ Combine the eggs, sugar and orange rind in a heatproof bowl set over a pan of hot but not boiling water. With an electric mixer, beat until the eggs leave a ribbon trail when the beaters are lifted.

6 Add the flour mixture in 3 batches, folding in well after each addition. Gently fold in the melted butter, then pour over the cranberries.

7 Bake for 40 minutes. Leave to cool for 5 minutes, then run a knife around the inside edge to loosen.

8 ▲ While the cake is still warm, invert a plate on top of the tin. Protecting your hands with oven gloves, hold plate and tin firmly and turn them both over quickly. Lift off the tin carefully.

Pineapple Upside-Down Cake

SERVES 8

4 oz (115 g) butter
7 oz (200 g) dark brown sugar
16 oz (450 g) canned pineapple slices, drained
4 eggs, separated
grated rind of 1 lemon
1/8 tsp salt
4 oz (115 g) caster sugar
3 oz (85 g) plain flour
1 tsp baking powder

1 Preheat a 350°F/180°C/Gas 4 oven.

2 Melt the butter in a 10 in (25 cm) ovenproof cast-iron frying pan. Remove 1 tablespoon of the melted butter and set aside.

3 ▲ Add the brown sugar to the pan and stir until blended. Place the drained pineapple slices on top in one layer. Set aside.

4 In a bowl, whisk together the egg yolks, reserved butter and lemon rind until well blended. Set aside.

5 ▼ With an electric mixer, beat the egg whites with the salt until stiff. Fold in the caster sugar, 2 tablespoons at a time. Fold in the egg yolk mixture.

6 Sift the flour and baking powder together. Carefully fold into the egg mixture in 3 batches.

7 ▲ Pour the mixture over the pineapple and smooth level.

8 Bake until a skewer inserted in the centre comes out clean, about 30 minutes.

9 While still hot, place a serving plate on top of the pan, bottom-side up. Holding them tightly together with oven gloves, quickly flip over. Serve hot or cold.

~ **VARIATION** ~

For Dried Apricot Upside-Down Cake, replace the pineapple slices with 8 oz (225 g) of dried apricots. If they need softening, simmer the apricots in about 4 fl oz (125 ml) orange juice until plump and soft. Drain the apricots and discard any remaining cooking liquid.

Spice Cake with Cream Cheese Frosting

SERVES 10–12

10 fl oz (300 ml) milk
2 tablespoons golden syrup
2 teaspoons vanilla essence
3 oz (85 g) walnuts, chopped
6 oz (170 g) butter, at room temperature
10½ oz (300 g) sugar
1 egg, at room temperature
3 egg yolks, at room temperature
10 oz (285 g) plain flour
1 tablespoon baking powder
1 teaspoon grated nutmeg
1 teaspoon ground cinnamon
½ teaspoon ground cloves
¼ teaspoon ground ginger
¼ teaspoon ground allspice
FOR THE FROSTING
6 oz (170 g) cream cheese
1 oz (30 g) unsalted butter
70 oz (200 g) icing sugar
2 tablespoons finely chopped stem ginger
2 tablespoons syrup from stem ginger
stem ginger pieces, for decorating

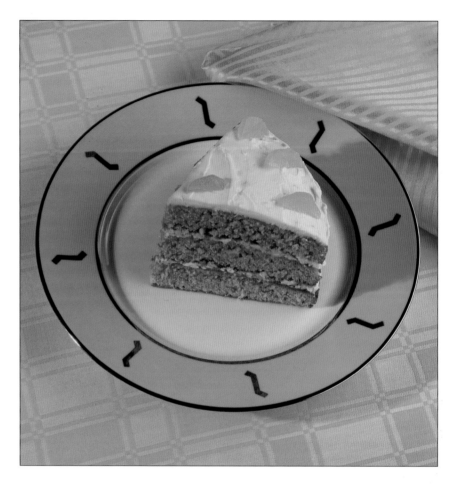

1 Preheat a 350°F/180°C/Gas 4 oven. Line 3 8 in (20 cm) cake tins with greaseproof paper and grease. In a bowl, combine the milk, golden syrup, vanilla and walnuts.

2 ▼ With an electric mixer, cream the butter and sugar until light and fluffy. Beat in the egg and egg yolks. Add the milk mixture and stir well.

3 Sift together the flour, baking powder and spices 3 times.

4 ▲ Add the flour mixture in 4 batches, and fold in carefully after each addition.

5 Divide the cake mixture between the tins. Bake until the cakes spring back when touched lightly, about 25 minutes. Let stand 5 minutes, then turn out and cool on a rack.

6 ▼ For the frosting, combine all the ingredients and beat with an electric mixer. Spread the frosting between the layers and over the top. Decorate with pieces of stem ginger.

Soured Cream Crumble Cake

SERVES 12–14

4 oz (115 g) butter, at room temperature

4¹/₂ oz (125 g) caster sugar

3 eggs, at room temperature

7¹/₂ oz (215 g) plain flour

1 teaspoon bicarbonate of soda

1 teaspoon baking powder

8 fl oz (250 ml) soured cream

FOR THE TOPPING

8 oz (225 g) dark brown sugar

2 teaspoons ground cinnamon

4 oz (115 g) walnuts, finely chopped

2 oz (55 g) cold butter, cut into pieces

1 Preheat a 350°F/180°C/Gas 4 oven. Line the bottom of a 9 in (23 cm) square cake tin with greaseproof paper and grease.

2 ▲ For the topping, place the brown sugar, cinnamon and walnuts in a bowl. Mix with your fingertips, then add the butter and continue working with your fingertips until the mixture resembles breadcrumbs.

3 To make the cake, cream the butter with an electric mixer until soft. Add the sugar and continue beating until the mixture is light and fluffy.

4 Add the eggs, 1 at a time, beating well after each addition.

5 In another bowl, sift the flour, bicarbonate of soda and baking powder together 3 times.

6 ▲ Fold the dry ingredients into the butter mixture in 3 batches, alternating with the soured cream. Fold until blended after each addition.

7 ▲ Pour half of the batter into the prepared tin and sprinkle over half of the walnut crumb topping mixture.

8 Pour the remaining batter on top and sprinkle over the remaining walnut crumb mixture.

9 Bake until browned, 60–70 minutes. Let stand 5 minutes, then turn out and cool on a rack.

Carrot Cake with Maple Butter Icing

SERVES 12

1 lb (450 g) carrots, peeled
6 oz (170 g) plain flour
2 tsp baking powder
1/2 tsp bicarbonate of soda
1 tsp salt
2 tsp ground cinnamon
4 eggs
2 tsp vanilla essence
4 oz (115 g) dark brown sugar
2 oz (55 g) caster sugar
10 fl oz (300 ml) sunflower oil
4 oz (115 g) finely chopped walnuts
3 oz (85 g) raisins
walnut halves, for decorating (optional)

FOR THE ICING

3 oz (85 g) unsalted butter, at room temperature
12 oz (350 g) icing sugar
2 fl oz (65 ml) maple syrup

1 Preheat a 350°F/180°C/Gas 4 oven. Line an 11 × 8 in (28 × 20 cm) tin with greaseproof paper and grease.

2 ▲ Grate the carrots and set aside.

3 Sift the flour, baking powder, bicarbonate of soda, salt and cinnamon into a bowl. Set aside.

4 With an electric mixer, beat the eggs until blended. Add the vanilla, sugars and oil; beat to incorporate. Add the dry ingredients, in 3 batches, folding in well after each addition.

5 ▲ Add the carrots, walnuts and raisins and fold in thoroughly.

6 Pour the mixture into the prepared tin and bake until the cake springs back when touched lightly, 40–45 minutes. Let stand 10 minutes, then unmould and transfer to a rack.

7 ▼ For the icing, cream the butter with half the icing sugar until soft. Add the syrup, then beat in the remaining sugar until blended.

8 Spread the icing over the top of the cake. Using the tip of a palette knife, make decorative ridges in the icing. Cut into squares. Decorate with walnut halves, if wished.

Peach Torte

SERVES 8

4 oz (115 g) plain flour
1 teaspoon baking powder
pinch of salt
4 oz (115 g) unsalted butter, at room temperature
6 oz (170 g) sugar
2 eggs, at room temperature
6–7 peaches
sugar and lemon juice, for sprinkling
whipped cream, for serving (optional)

1 Preheat the oven to 350°F/180°C/ Gas 4. Grease a 10 in (25 cm) spring-form tin.

2 ▲ Sift together the flour, baking powder and salt. Set aside.

3 With an electric mixer, cream the butter and sugar until light and fluffy. Beat in the eggs, then fold in the dry ingredients until blended.

4 ▲ Spoon the mixture into the tin and smooth it to make an even layer over the bottom.

5 ▼ To skin the peaches, drop several at a time into a pan of gently boiling water. Boil for 10 seconds, then remove with a slotted spoon. Peel off the skin with the aid of a sharp knife. Cut the peaches in half and discard the stones.

6 ▲ Arrange the peach halves on top of the mixture. Sprinkle lightly with sugar and lemon juice.

7 Bake until golden brown and set, 50–60 minutes. Serve warm, with whipped cream, if liked.

Plum Crumble Cake

SERVES 8–10

5 oz (140 g) butter or margarine, at room temperature

5 oz (140 g) caster sugar

4 eggs, at room temperature

1¹/₂ tsp vanilla essence

5 oz (140 g) plain flour

1 tsp baking powder

1¹/₂ lb (700 g) red plums, halved and stoned

FOR THE TOPPING

4 oz (115 g) plain flour

4¹/₂ oz (130 g) light brown sugar

1¹/₂ tsp ground cinnamon

3 oz (85 g) butter, cut in pieces

1 Preheat a 350°F/180°C/Gas 4 oven.

2 For the topping, combine the flour, light brown sugar and cinnamon in a bowl. Add the butter and work the mixture lightly with your fingertips until it resembles coarse breadcrumbs. Set aside.

3 ▲ Line a 10 × 2 in (25 × 5 cm) tin with greaseproof paper and grease.

4 Cream the butter and sugar until light and fluffy.

5 ▲ Beat in the eggs, 1 at a time. Stir in the vanilla.

6 In a bowl, sift together the flour and baking powder, then fold into the butter mixture in 3 batches.

7 ▲ Pour the mixture into the tin. Arrange the plums on top.

8 ▲ Sprinkle the topping over the plums in an even layer.

9 Bake until a skewer inserted in the centre comes out clean, about 45 minutes. Let cool in the tin.

10 To serve, run a knife around the inside edge and invert onto a plate. Invert again onto a serving plate so the topping is right-side up.

~ VARIATION ~

This cake can also be made with the same quantity of apricots, peeled if preferred, or stoned cherries, or use a mixture of fruit, such as red or yellow plums, greengages and apricots.

Yule Log Cake

SERVES 8 OR MORE

4 eggs, separated

5 oz (145 g) caster sugar

1 teaspoon vanilla essence

pinch of cream of tartar (if needed)

4 oz (115 g) plain flour, sifted

8 fl oz (240 ml) whipping cream

10 oz (300 g) plain or bittersweet
   chocolate, chopped

2 tablespoons rum or Cognac

1 Preheat a 375°F/190°C/Gas 5 oven. Grease, line and flour a 16 × 11 in (40 × 28 cm) Swiss roll tin.

2 Put the egg yolks in a large bowl. Reserve 2 tablespoons sugar; add the remainder to the egg yolks. Whisk until pale and thick. Add the vanilla.

3 In another bowl, scrupulously clean and grease-free, whisk the egg whites (with the cream of tartar if not using a copper bowl) until they will hold soft peaks. Add the reserved sugar and continue whisking until the whites are glossy and will hold stiff peaks.

4 Gently fold half the flour into the egg yolk mixture. Add one-quarter of the egg whites and fold in to lighten the mixture. Fold in the remaining flour, then the remaining egg whites.

5 ▲ Spread the mixture in the prepared tin. Bake for 15 minutes.

6 Turn on to paper sprinkled with caster sugar. Roll up and cool.

7 Bring the cream to the boil in a small saucepan. Put the chocolate in a bowl, add the cream and stir until the chocolate has melted.

8 ▲ Beat the chocolate mixture until it is fluffy and has thickened to a spreading consistency. Spoon one-third of the chocolate mixture into another bowl. Mix in rum or Cognac.

9 Unroll the cake. Spread the rum and chocolate mixture evenly over the surface. Roll up the cake again.

10 Cut off about one-quarter of the cake, at an angle. Place it against the side of the larger piece of cake, to resemble a branch from a tree trunk.

11 ▼ Spread the remaining chocolate mixture all over the cake. Mark with the prongs of a fork to resemble bark. Before serving, add small Christmas decorations and sprigs of holly if liked, and dust with a little icing sugar 'snow'.

Orange and Walnut Swiss Roll

SERVES 8

4 eggs, separated
4 oz (115 g) caster sugar
4 oz (115 g) very finely chopped walnuts
1/8 tsp cream of tartar
1/8 tsp salt
icing sugar, for dusting
FOR THE FILLING
10 fl oz (300 ml) whipping cream
1 tbsp caster sugar
grated rind of 1 orange
1 tbsp orange liqueur, such as Grand Marnier

1 Preheat a 350°F/180°C/Gas 4 oven. Line a 12 × 9½ in (30 × 24 cm) Swiss roll tin with greaseproof paper and grease the paper.

2 With an electric mixer, beat the egg yolks and sugar until thick.

3 ▲ Stir in the walnuts.

4 In another bowl, beat the egg whites with the cream of tartar and salt until they hold stiff peaks. Fold gently but thoroughly into the walnut mixture.

5 Pour the mixture into the prepared tin and spread level with a spatula. Bake for 15 minutes.

6 Run a knife along the inside edge to loosen, then invert the cake onto a sheet of greaseproof paper dusted with icing sugar.

7 ▲ Peel off the baking paper. Roll up the cake while it is still warm with the help of the sugared paper. Set aside to cool.

8 For the filling, whip the cream until it holds soft peaks. Stir together the caster sugar and orange rind, then fold into the whipped cream. Add the liqueur.

9 ▲ Gently unroll the cake. Spread the inside with a layer of orange whipped cream, then re-roll. Keep refrigerated until ready to serve. Dust the top with icing sugar just before serving.

Chocolate Swiss Roll

SERVES 10

8 oz (225 g) plain chocolate
3 tbsp water
2 tbsp rum, brandy or strong coffee
7 eggs, separated
6 oz (170 g) caster sugar
1/8 tsp salt
12 fl oz (350 ml) whipping cream
icing sugar, for dusting

1 Preheat a 350°F/180°C/Gas 4 oven. Line a 15 × 13 in (38 × 33 cm) Swiss roll tin with greaseproof paper and grease the paper.

2 ▲ Combine the chocolate, water and rum or other flavouring in the top of a double boiler, or in a heatproof bowl set over hot water. Heat until melted. Set aside.

3 With an electric mixer, beat the egg yolks and sugar until thick.

4 ▲ Stir in the melted chocolate.

5 In another bowl, beat the egg whites and salt until they hold stiff peaks. Fold a large dollop of egg whites into the yolk mixture to lighten it, then carefully fold in the rest of the whites.

6 ▼ Pour the mixture into the pan; smooth evenly with a metal spatula.

7 Bake for 15 minutes. Remove from the oven, cover with greaseproof paper and a damp cloth. Let stand for 1–2 hours.

8 With an electric mixer, whip the cream until stiff. Set aside.

9 Run a knife along the inside edge to loosen, then invert the cake onto a sheet of greaseproof paper that has been dusted with icing sugar.

10 Peel off the baking paper. Spread with an even layer of whipped cream, then roll up the cake with the help of the sugared paper.

11 Refrigerate for several hours. Before serving, dust with an even layer of icing sugar.

Traditional Chocolate Cake

SERVES 10

4 oz (115 g) plain chocolate
9 fl oz (275 ml) milk
7 oz (200 g) light brown sugar
1 egg yolk
9 oz (260 g) plain flour
1 tsp bicarbonate of soda
½ tsp salt
5 oz (140 g) butter or margarine, at room temperature
9 oz (260 g) caster sugar
3 eggs
1 tsp vanilla essence
FOR THE ICING
8 oz (225 g) plain chocolate
¼ tsp salt
6 fl oz (175 ml) soured cream

1 Preheat a 350°F/180°C/Gas 4 oven. Line 2 × 8–9 in (20–23 cm) round cake tins with greaseproof paper.

2 ▲ In a heatproof bowl set over a pan of simmering water, or in a double boiler, combine the chocolate, one-third of the milk, the brown sugar and egg yolk. Cook, stirring, until smooth and thickened. Let cool.

3 ▲ Sift the flour, bicarbonate of soda and salt into a bowl. Set aside.

4 ▲ With an electric mixer, cream the butter or margarine with the caster sugar until light and fluffy. Beat in the whole eggs, one at a time. Mix in the vanilla.

5 On low speed, beat the flour mixture into the butter mixture alternately with the remaining milk, beginning and ending with flour.

6 ▲ Pour in the chocolate mixture and mix until just combined.

7 Divide the cake mixture evenly between the cake tins. Bake until a skewer inserted in the centre comes out clean, 35–40 minutes.

8 Let cool in the tins on wire racks for 10 minutes, then unmould the cakes from the tins onto the wire racks and let cool completely.

9 ▲ For the icing, melt the chocolate in a heatproof bowl set over a pan of hot, not boiling, water, or in the top of a double boiler. Remove the bowl from the heat and stir in the salt and soured cream. Let cool slightly.

10 ▲ Set 1 cake layer on a serving plate and spread with one-third of the icing. Place the second cake layer on top. Spread the remaining icing all over the top and sides of the cake, swirling it to make a decorative finish.

Chocolate Frosted Layer Cake

1 Preheat a 350°F/180°C/Gas 4 oven. Line 2 8 in (20 cm) round cake tins with greaseproof paper and grease. Dust the tins with flour and shake to evenly distribute. Tap to dislodge excess flour.

2 With an electric mixer, cream the butter or margarine until soft. Gradually add the sugar and continue beating until light and fluffy.

3 ▲ Lightly beat the egg yolks, then mix into the creamed butter and sugar with the vanilla.

4 Sift the flour with the baking powder 3 times. Set aside.

5 In another bowl, beat the egg whites with the salt until they hold stiff peaks. Set aside.

6 ▲ Gently fold the dry ingredients into the butter mixture in 3 batches, alternating with the milk.

7 Add a large dollop of the whites and fold in to lighten the mixture. Carefully fold in the remaining whites until just blended.

8 Divide the batter between the tins and bake until the cakes pull away from the sides of the tins, for about 30 minutes. Let stand 5 minutes. Turn out and cool on a rack.

9 ▲ For the frosting, melt the chocolate in the top of a double boiler or a bowl set over hot water. When cool, stir in the soured cream and salt.

10 Sandwich the layers with frosting, then spread on the top and side.

Devil's Food Cake with Orange Frosting

SERVES 8–10

2 oz (55 g) unsweetened cocoa powder

6 fl oz (175 ml) boiling water

6 oz (170 g) butter, at room temperature

12 oz (350 g) dark brown sugar

3 eggs, at room temperature

10 oz (285 g) plain flour

1½ teaspoons bicarbonate of soda

¼ teaspoon baking powder

4 fl oz (125 ml) soured cream

orange rind strips, for decoration

FOR THE FROSTING

10½ oz (300 g) caster sugar

2 egg whites

4 tablespoons frozen orange juice concentrate

1 tablespoon lemon juice

grated rind of 1 orange

1 Preheat a 350°F/180°C/Gas 4 oven. Line 2 9 in (23 cm) cake tins with greaseproof paper and grease. In a bowl, mix the cocoa and water until smooth. Set aside.

2 With an electric mixer, cream the butter and sugar until light and fluffy. Add the eggs, 1 at a time, beating well after each addition.

3 ▲ When the cocoa mixture is lukewarm, add to the butter mixture.

4 ▼ Sift together the flour, soda and baking powder twice. Fold into the cocoa mixture in 3 batches, alternating with the soured cream.

5 Pour into the tins and bake until the cakes pull away from the sides of the tins, 30–35 minutes. Let stand for 15 minutes. Turn out onto a rack.

6 Thinly slice the orange rind strips. Blanch in boiling water for 1 minute.

7 ▲ For the frosting, place all the ingredients in the top of a double boiler or in a bowl set over hot water. With an electric mixer, beat until the mixture holds soft peaks. Continue beating off the heat until thick enough to spread.

8 Sandwich the cake layers with frosting, then spread over the top and side. Arrange the blanched orange rind strips on top of the cake.

Best-Ever Chocolate Sandwich

SERVES 12–14

4 oz (115 g) unsalted butter
4 oz (115 g) plain flour
2 oz (55 g) cocoa powder
1 tsp baking powder
1/8 tsp salt
6 eggs
8 oz (225 g) caster sugar
2 tsp vanilla essence
FOR THE ICING
8 oz (225 g) plain chocolate, chopped
3 oz (85 g) unsalted butter
3 eggs, separated
8 fl oz (250 ml) whipping cream
3 tbsp caster sugar

1 Preheat a 350°F/180°C/Gas 4 oven. Line 3 8 × 1 1/2 in (20 × 3 cm) round tins with greaseproof paper and grease.

2 ▲ Dust evenly with flour and spread with a brush. Set aside.

~ **VARIATION** ~

For a simpler icing, combine 8 fl oz (250 ml) whipping cream with 8 oz (225 g) finely chopped plain chocolate in a saucepan. Stir over a low heat until the chocolate has melted. Cool and whisk to spreading consistency.

3 ▲ Melt the butter over a low heat. With a spoon, skim off any foam that rises to the surface. Set aside.

4 ▲ Sift the flour, cocoa, baking powder and salt together 3 times and set aside.

5 Place the eggs and sugar in a large heatproof bowl set over a pan of hot water. With an electric mixer, beat until the mixture doubles in volume and is thick enough to leave a ribbon trail when the beaters are lifted, about 10 minutes. Add the vanilla.

6 ▲ Sift over the dry ingredients in 3 batches, folding in carefully after each addition. Fold in the butter.

7 Divide the mixture between the tins and bake until the cakes pull away from the sides of the tin, about 25 minutes. Transfer to a rack.

8 For the icing, melt the chopped chocolate in the top of a double boiler, or in a heatproof bowl set over hot water.

9 ▲ Off the heat, stir in the butter and egg yolks. Return to a low heat and stir until thick. Remove from the heat and set aside.

10 Whip the cream until firm; set aside. In another bowl, beat the egg whites until stiff. Add the sugar and beat until glossy.

11 Fold the cream into the chocolate mixture, then carefully fold in the egg whites. Refrigerate for 20 minutes to thicken the icing.

12 ▲ Sandwich the cake layers with icing, stacking them carefully. Spread the remaining icing evenly over the top and sides of the cake.

Mississippi Mud Cake

SERVES 8–10

8oz (225g) plain flour
⅛ teaspoon salt
1 teaspoon baking powder
½ pint (300ml) strong brewed coffee
2fl oz (50ml) bourbon or brandy
5oz (150g) unsweetened chocolate
½lb (225g) butter or margarine
14oz (400g) caster sugar
2 eggs, at room temperature
1½ teaspoons vanilla essence
unsweetened cocoa powder
sweetened whipped cream or ice cream, for serving

1 Preheat the oven to 140°C/275°F/ Gas 1.

2 Sift the flour, salt and baking powder together.

3 ▼ Combine the coffee, bourbon or brandy, chocolate, and butter or margarine in the top of a double boiler. Heat until the chocolate and butter have melted and the mixture is smooth, stirring occasionally.

4 ▲ Pour the chocolate mixture into a large bowl. Using an electric mixer on low speed, gradually beat in the sugar. Continue beating until the sugar has dissolved.

5 Increase the speed to medium and add the sifted dry ingredients. Mix well, then beat in the eggs and vanilla until thoroughly blended.

6 Pour the batter into a well-greased 5 pint (3 litre) ring mould that has been dusted lightly with cocoa powder. Bake until a skewer inserted in the cake comes out clean, about 1 hour 20 minutes.

7 ▲ Leave to cool in the mould for 15 minutes, then unmould on to a wire rack. Leave to cool completely.

8 When the cake is cold, dust it lightly with cocoa powder. Serve with sweetened whipped cream or ice cream, if desired.

Blueberry Cake

SERVES 10

8oz (225g) plain flour
1 tablespoon baking powder
1 teaspoon salt
6oz (175g) butter or margarine, at room temperature
5oz (150g) granulated sugar
1 egg
8fl oz (250ml) milk
½ teaspoon grated lemon rind
8oz (225g) fresh or frozen blueberries, well drained
4oz (115g) icing sugar
2 tablespoons fresh lemon juice

1 Preheat a 180°C/350°F/Gas 4 oven.

2 ▲ Sift the flour with the baking powder and salt.

3 ▲ In a large bowl, beat the butter or margarine with the granulated sugar until light and fluffy. Beat in the egg and milk. Fold in the flour mixture, mixing well until evenly blended to a batter. Mix in the lemon rind.

4 ▼ Spread half the batter in a greased 13 × 9 × 2 in (33 × 23 × 5 cm) ovenproof dish. Sprinkle with 4oz (115g) of the berries. Top with the remaining batter and sprinkle with the rest of the berries. Bake until golden brown and a skewer inserted in the centre comes out clean, 35–45 minutes.

5 ▲ Mix the icing sugar gradually into the lemon juice to make a smooth glaze with a pourable consistency. Drizzle the glaze over the top of the warm cake and allow it to set before serving, still warm or at room temperature.

Chocolate Cinnamon Cake with Banana Sauce

SERVES 6

4oz (115g) plain chocolate, chopped
4oz (115g) unsalted butter, at room temperature
1 tablespoon instant coffee powder
5 eggs, separated
7oz (200g) granulated sugar
4oz (115g) flour
2 teaspoons ground cinnamon
FOR THE SAUCE
4 ripe bananas
2oz (50g) soft light brown sugar, firmly packed
1 tablespoon fresh lemon juice
6fl oz (175ml) whipping cream
1 tablespoon rum (optional)

1 Preheat the oven to 180°C/350°F/ Gas 4. Grease an 8 in (20 cm) round cake tin.

2 ▲ Combine the chocolate and butter in the top of a double boiler or in a heatproof bowl set over hot water. Stir until melted. Remove from the heat and stir in the coffee. Set aside.

3 Beat the egg yolks with the granulated sugar until thick and lemon-coloured. Add the chocolate mixture and beat just to blend the mixtures evenly.

4 Sift together the flour and cinnamon into a bowl.

5 ▲ In another bowl, beat the egg whites until they hold stiff peaks.

6 ▲ Fold a dollop of whites into the chocolate mixture to lighten it. Fold in the remaining whites in three batches, alternating with the sifted flour.

7 ▲ Pour the mixture into the prepared tin. Bake until a skewer inserted in the centre comes out clean, 40–50 minutes. Unmould the cake on to a wire rack.

8 Preheat the grill.

9 ▲ For the sauce, slice the bananas into a shallow, heatproof dish. Add the brown sugar and lemon juice and stir to blend. Place under the grill and cook, stirring occasionally, until the sugar is caramelized and bubbling, about 8 minutes.

10 ▲ Transfer the bananas to a bowl and mash with a fork until almost smooth. Stir in the cream and rum, if using. Serve the cake and sauce warm.

~ VARIATION ~

For a special occasion, top the cake slices with a scoop of ice cream (rum-raisin, chocolate, or vanilla) before adding the banana sauce. With this addition, the dessert will make at least eight portions.

Rich Chocolate Nut Cake

SERVES 10

8 oz (225 g) butter
8 oz (225 g) plain chocolate
4 oz (115 g) cocoa powder
12 oz (350 g) caster sugar
6 eggs
3 fl oz (85 ml) brandy or cognac
8 oz (225 g) finely chopped hazelnuts
FOR THE GLAZE
2 oz (55 g) butter
5 oz (140 g) bitter cooking chocolate
2 tbsp milk
1 tsp vanilla essence

1 Preheat a 350°F/180°C/Gas 4 oven. Line a 9 × 2 in (23 × 5 cm) round tin with greaseproof paper and grease.

2 Melt the butter and chocolate together in the top of a double boiler, or in a heatproof bowl set over hot water. Set aside to cool.

3 ▼ Sift the cocoa into a bowl. Add the sugar and eggs and stir until just combined. Pour in the melted chocolate mixture and brandy.

4 Fold in three-quarters of the nuts, then pour the mixture into the prepared tin.

5 ▲ Set the tin inside a large tin and pour 1 in (2.5 cm) of hot water into the outer tin. Bake until the cake is firm to the touch, about 45 minutes. Let stand 15 minutes, then unmould and transfer to a cooling rack.

6 Wrap the cake in greaseproof paper and refrigerate for 6 hours.

7 For the glaze, combine the butter, chocolate, milk and vanilla in the top of a double boiler or in a heatproof bowl set over hot water, until melted.

8 Place a piece of greaseproof paper under the cake, then drizzle spoonfuls of glaze along the edge to drip down and coat the sides. Pour the remaining glaze on top of the cake.

9 ▲ Cover the sides of the cake with the remaining nuts, gently pressing them on with the palm of your hand.

Chocolate Layer Cake

SERVES 8–10

4 oz (115 g) plain chocolate
6 oz (170 g) butter
1 lb (450 g) caster sugar
3 eggs
1 tsp vanilla essence
6 oz (170 g) plain flour
1 tsp baking powder
4 oz (115 g) chopped walnuts
FOR THE TOPPING
12 fl oz (350 ml) whipping cream
8 oz (225 g) plain chocolate
1 tbsp vegetable oil

1 Preheat a 350°F/180°C/Gas 4 oven. Line two 8 in (20 cm) cake tins, at least 1¾ in (4.5 cm) deep, with grease-proof paper and grease.

2 Melt the chocolate and butter together in the top of a double boiler, or in a heatproof bowl set over a saucepan of hot water.

3 ▲ Transfer to a mixing bowl and stir in the sugar. Add the eggs and vanilla and mix until well blended.

4 ▲ Sift over the flour and baking powder. Stir in the walnuts.

5 Divide the mixture between the prepared tins and spread level.

6 Bake until a skewer inserted in the centre comes out clean, for about 30 minutes. Let stand 10 minutes, then unmould and transfer to a rack.

7 When the cakes are cool, whip the cream until firm. With a long serrated knife, carefully slice each cake in half horizontally.

8 Sandwich the layers with some of the whipped cream and spread the remainder over the top and sides of the cake. Refrigerate until needed.

9 ▼ For the chocolate curls, melt the chocolate and oil in the top of a double boiler or a bowl set over hot water. Transfer to a non-porous surface. Spread to a ³/₈ in (1 cm) thick rectangle. Just before the chocolate sets, hold the blade of a straight knife at an angle to the chocolate and scrape across the surface to make curls. Place on top of the cake.

~ VARIATION ~

To make Chocolate Ice Cream Layer Cake, sandwich the cake layers with softened vanilla ice cream. Freeze before serving.

Sachertorte

SERVES 8–10

4 oz (115 g) plain chocolate
3 oz (85 g) unsalted butter, at room temperature
2 oz (55 g) sugar
4 eggs, separated
1 extra egg white
¼ teaspoon salt
2½ oz (70 g) plain flour, sifted
FOR THE TOPPING
5 tablespoons apricot jam
8 fl oz (250 ml) plus 1 tablespoon water
½ oz (15 g) unsalted butter
6 oz (170 g) plain chocolate
3 oz (85 g) sugar
ready-made chocolate decorating icing (optional)

1 Preheat the oven to 325°F/170°C/ Gas 3. Line a 9 × 2 in (23 × 5 cm) cake tin with greaseproof paper and grease.

2 ▲ Melt the chocolate in the top of a double boiler, or in a heatproof bowl set over hot water. Set aside.

3 With an electric mixer, cream the butter and sugar until light and fluffy. Stir in the chocolate.

4 ▲ Beat in the yolks, 1 at a time.

5 In another bowl, beat the egg whites with the salt until stiff.

6 ▲ Fold a dollop of whites into the chocolate mixture to lighten it. Fold in the remaining whites in 3 batches, alternating with the sifted flour.

7 ▲ Pour into the tin and bake until a cake tester comes out clean, about 45 minutes. Turn out onto a rack.

8 ▲ Meanwhile, melt the jam with 1 tablespoon of the water over low heat, then strain for a smooth consistency.

9 For the frosting, melt the butter and chocolate in the top of a double boiler or a bowl set over hot water.

10 ▲ In a heavy saucepan, dissolve the sugar in the remaining water over low heat. Raise the heat and boil until it reaches 225°F/107°C (thread stage) on a sugar thermometer. Immediately plunge the bottom of the pan into cold water for 1 minute. Pour into the chocolate mixture and stir to blend. Let cool for a few minutes.

11 To assemble, brush the warm jam over the cake. Starting in the centre, pour over the frosting and work outward in a circular movement. Tilt the rack to spread; use a palette knife to smooth the side of the cake. Leave to set overnight. If wished, decorate with chocolate icing.

Boston Cream Pie

Serves 8

8oz (225g) plain flour

1 tablespoon baking powder

½ teaspoon salt

4oz (115g) butter, at room
temperature

7oz (200g) granulated sugar

2 eggs

1 teaspoon vanilla essence

6fl oz (175ml) milk

For the filling

8fl oz (250ml) milk

3 egg yolks

3½oz (90g) granulated sugar

1oz (25g) flour

½oz (15g) butter

1 tablespoon brandy or 1 teaspoon
vanilla essence

For the chocolate glaze

1oz (25g) plain chocolate

1oz (25g) butter or margarine

2oz (50g) icing sugar, plus extra
for dusting

½ teaspoon vanilla essence

about 1 tablespoon hot water

1 Preheat the oven to 190°C/375°F/
Gas 5.

2 Grease two 8 × 2 in (20 × 5 cm)
round cake tins, and line the bottoms
with rounds of buttered greaseproof
paper.

3 Sift the flour with the baking
powder and salt.

4 Beat the butter and granulated
sugar together until light and fluffy.
Add the eggs one at a time, beating
well after each addition. Stir in the
vanilla. Add the milk and dry
ingredients alternately, mixing only
enough to blend thoroughly. Do not
over-beat the mixture.

5 Divide the cake mixture between
the prepared tins and spread it out
evenly. Bake until a skewer inserted
in the centre comes out clean, about
25 minutes.

6 Meanwhile, make the filling. Heat
the milk in a small saucepan to
boiling point. Remove from the heat.

7 ▲ In a heatproof mixing bowl,
beat the egg yolks until smooth.
Gradually add the granulated sugar
and continue beating until pale
yellow. Beat in the flour.

8 ▲ Pour the hot milk into the egg
yolk mixture in a steady stream, beating
constantly. When all the milk has
been added, place the bowl over
a pan of boiling water, or pour the
mixture into the top of a double boiler.
Heat, stirring constantly, until thickened.
Cook 2 minutes more, then remove
from the heat. Stir in the butter and
brandy or vanilla. Allow to cool.

9 ▲ When the cakes have cooled, use
a large sharp knife to slice off the
domed top to make a flat surface.
Place one cake on a serving plate and
spread on the filling in a thick layer.
Set the other cake on top, cut side
down. Smooth the edge of the filling
layer so it is flush with the sides of the
cake layers.

10 ▲ For the glaze, melt the
chocolate with the butter or
margarine in the top of a double
boiler. When smooth, remove from
the heat and beat in the sugar to
make a thick paste. Add the vanilla.
Beat in a little of the hot water. If the
glaze does not have a spreadable
consistency, add more water,
1 teaspoon at a time.

11 Spread the glaze evenly over the
top of the cake, using a palette knife.
Dust the top with icing sugar. Because
of the custard filling, refrigerate any
leftover cake.

Caramel Layer Cake

SERVES 8–10

10 oz (285 g) plain flour
1¹/₂ teaspoons baking powder
6 oz (170 g) butter, at room temperature
5¹/₂ oz (150 g) caster sugar
4 eggs, at room temperature, beaten
1 teaspoon vanilla essence
8 tablespoons milk
whipped cream, for decorating
caramel threads, for decorating (optional, see below)

FOR THE FROSTING

10¹/₂ oz (300 g) dark brown sugar
8 fl oz (250 ml) milk
1 oz (30 g) unsalted butter
3–5 tablespoons whipping cream

1 Preheat a 350°F/180°C/Gas 4 oven. Line 2 8 in (20 cm) cake tins with greaseproof paper and grease lightly.

2 ▲ Sift the flour and baking powder together 3 times. Set aside.

~ COOK'S TIP ~

To make caramel threads, combine 2¹/₂ oz (70 g) sugar and 2 fl oz (65 ml) water in a heavy saucepan. Boil until light brown. Dip the pan in cold water to halt cooking. Trail from a spoon on an oiled baking sheet.

3 With an electric mixer, cream the butter and caster sugar until light and fluffy.

4 ▲ Slowly mix in the beaten eggs. Add the vanilla. Fold in the flour mixture, alternating with the milk.

5 ▲ Divide the batter between the prepared tins and spread evenly, hollowing out the centres slightly.

6 Bake until the cakes pull away from the sides of the tin, about 30 minutes. Let stand 5 minutes, then turn out and cool on a rack.

7 ▲ For the frosting, combine the brown sugar and milk in a saucepan.

8 Bring to the boil, cover and cook for 3 minutes. Remove lid and continue to boil, without stirring, until the mixture reaches 238°F/119°C (soft ball stage) on a sugar thermometer.

9 ▲ Immediately remove the pan from the heat and add the butter, but do not stir it in. Let cool until lukewarm, then beat until the mixture is smooth and creamy.

10 Stir in enough cream to obtain a spreadable consistency. If necessary, refrigerate to thicken more.

11 ▲ Spread a layer of frosting on top of one cake. Sandwich with the second cake, then spread the top and sides with the rest of the frosting and smooth the surface.

12 To decorate, pipe whipped cream rosettes around the edge. If using, place a mound of caramel threads in the centre before serving.

Whiskey Cake

MAKES 1 LOAF

6 oz (170 g) chopped walnuts
3 oz (85 g) raisins, chopped
3 oz (85 g) currants
4 oz (115 g) plain flour
1 tsp baking powder
1/4 tsp salt
4 oz (115 g) butter
8 oz (225 g) caster sugar
3 eggs, at room temperature, separated
1 tsp grated nutmeg
1/2 tsp ground cinnamon
3 fl oz (85 ml) Irish whiskey or bourbon
icing sugar, for dusting

1 ▼ Preheat a 325°F/170°C/Gas 3 oven. Line a 9 × 5 in (23 × 13 cm) loaf tin with greaseproof paper. Grease the paper and sides of the pan.

2 ▲ Place the walnuts, raisins, and currants in a bowl. Sprinkle over 2 tablespoons of the flour, mix and set aside. Sift together the remaining flour, baking powder and salt.

3 ▲ Cream the butter and sugar until light and fluffy. Beat in the egg yolks.

4 Mix the nutmeg, cinnamon and whiskey. Fold into the butter mixture, alternating with the flour mixture.

5 ▲ In another bowl, beat the egg whites until stiff. Fold into the whiskey mixture until just blended. Fold in the walnut mixture.

6 Bake until a skewer inserted in the centre comes out clean, about 1 hour. Let cool in the pan. Dust with icing sugar over a template.

American Berry Shortcake

SERVES 8

½ pint (300 ml) whipping cream
1 oz (30 g) icing sugar, sifted
1½ lb (700 g) strawberries or mixed berries, halved or sliced if large
2 oz (55 g) caster sugar, or to taste
FOR THE SHORTCAKE
10 oz (300 g) plain flour
2 teaspoons baking powder
2½ oz (75 g) caster sugar
4 oz (115 g) butter
5 tablespoons milk
1 size-1 egg

1 Preheat a 450°F/230°C/Gas 8 oven. Grease an 8 in (20 cm) round cake tin.

2 For the shortcake, sift the flour, baking powder and sugar into a bowl. Add the butter and rub in until the mixture resembles fine crumbs. Combine the milk and egg. Add to the crumb mixture and stir just until evenly mixed to a soft dough.

3 Put the dough in the prepared tin and pat out to an even layer. Bake for 15–20 minutes or until a wooden skewer inserted in the centre comes out clean. Leave to cool slightly.

5 Put the berries in a bowl. Sprinkle with the caster sugar and toss together lightly. Cover and set aside for the berries to give up some juice.

6 ▼ Remove the cooled shortcake from the tin. With a long, serrated knife, split the shortcake horizontally into two equal layers.

4 ▲ Whip the cream until it starts to thicken. Add the icing sugar and continue whipping until the cream will hold soft peaks.

7 ▲ Put the bottom layer on a serving plate. Top with half of the berries and most of the cream. Set the second layer on top and press down gently. Spoon the remaining berries over the top layer (or serve them separately) and add the remaining cream in small, decorative dollops.

Lady Baltimore Cake

SERVES 8–10

10 oz (285 g) plain flour
2¹/₂ teaspoons baking powder
¹/₂ teaspoon salt
4 eggs
12 oz (350 g) sugar
grated rind of 1 large orange
8 fl oz (250 ml) fresh orange juice
8 fl oz (250 ml) vegetable oil
18 pecan halves, for decorating
FOR THE FROSTING
2 egg whites
12 oz (350 g) sugar
5 tablespoons cold water
¹/₄ teaspoon cream of tartar
1 teaspoon vanilla essence
2 oz (55 g) pecans, finely chopped
3 oz (85 g) raisins, chopped
3 dried figs, finely chopped

1 Preheat the oven to 350°F/180°C/ Gas 4. Grease 2 9 in (23 cm) round cake tins and line with greaseproof paper. Grease the paper. In a bowl, sift together the flour, baking powder and salt. Set aside.

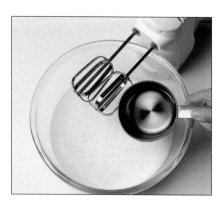

2 ▲ With an electric mixer, beat the eggs and sugar until thick and lemon-coloured. Beat in the orange rind and juice, then the oil.

3 On low speed, beat in the flour mixture in 3 batches. Divide the cake mixture between the tins.

4 ▲ Bake until a skewer inserted in the centre comes out clean, about 30 minutes. Leave to stand for 15 minutes, then run a knife around the inside of the cakes and transfer them to racks to cool completely.

5 ▲ For the frosting, combine the egg whites, sugar, water and cream of tartar in the top of a double boiler, or in a heatproof bowl set over boiling water. With an electric mixer, beat until glossy and thick. Off the heat, add the vanilla essence and continue beating until thick. Fold in the pecans, raisins and figs.

6 Spread a layer of frosting on top of one cake. Sandwich with the second cake, then spread the top and sides with the rest of the frosting. Arrange the pecan halves on top.

Raspberry-Hazelnut Meringue Cake

SERVES 8

5 oz (140 g) hazelnuts
4 egg whites
⅛ teaspoon salt
7 oz (200 g) sugar
½ teaspoon vanilla essence
FOR THE FILLING
10 fl oz (300 ml) whipping cream
1 lb 8 oz (700 g) raspberries

1 Preheat a 350°F/180°C/Gas 4 oven. Line the bottom of 2 8 in (20 cm) cake tins with greaseproof paper and grease.

2 Spread the hazelnuts on a baking sheet and bake until lightly toasted, about 8 minutes. Let cool slightly.

3 ▲ Rub the hazelnuts vigorously in a clean tea towel to remove most of the skins.

4 Grind the nuts in a food processor, blender, or coffee grinder until they are the consistency of coarse sand.

5 Reduce oven to 300°F/150°C/Gas 2.

6 With an electric mixer, beat the egg whites and salt until they hold stiff peaks. Beat in 2 tablespoons of the sugar, then fold in the remaining sugar, a few tablespoons at a time, with a rubber scraper. Fold in the vanilla and the hazelnuts.

7 ▲ Divide the batter between the prepared tins and spread level.

8 Bake for 1¼ hours. If the meringues brown too quickly, protect with a sheet of foil. Let stand 5 minutes, then carefully run a knife around the inside edge of the tins to loosen. Turn out onto a rack to cool.

9 For the filling, whip the cream just until firm.

10 ▲ Spread half the cream in an even layer on one meringue round and top with half the raspberries.

11 Top with the other meringue round. Spread the remaining cream on top and arrange the remaining raspberries over the cream. Refrigerate for 1 hour to facilitate cutting.

Classic Cheesecake

SERVES 8

2 oz (55 g) digestive biscuits, crushed

2 lb (900 g) cream cheese, at room temperature

8¾ oz (240 g) sugar

grated rind of 1 lemon

3 tablespoons lemon juice

1 teapoon vanilla essence

4 eggs, at room temperature

1 Preheat the oven to 325°F/170°C/ Gas 3. Grease an 8 in (20 cm) springform tin. Place on a round of foil 4–5 in (10–12.5 cm) larger than the diameter of the tin. Press it up the sides to seal tightly.

2 Sprinkle the crushed biscuits in the base of the tin. Press to form an even layer.

3 With an electric mixer, beat the cream cheese until smooth. Add the sugar, lemon rind and juice, and vanilla, and beat until blended. Beat in the eggs, 1 at a time. Beat just enough to blend thoroughly.

4 ▲ Pour into the prepared tin. Set the tin in a larger baking tray and place in the oven. Pour enough hot water in the outer tray to come 1 in (2.5 cm) up the side of the tin.

5 Bake until the top of the cake is golden brown, about 1½ hours. Let cool in the tin.

6 ▼ Run a knife around the edge to loosen, then remove the rim of the tin. Refrigerate for at least 4 hours before serving.

Chocolate Cheesecake

SERVES 10–12

10 oz (285 g) plain chocolate

2 lb 8 oz (1.2 kg) cream cheese, at room temperature

7 oz (200 g) sugar

2 teaspoons vanilla essence

4 eggs, at room temperature

6 fl oz (175 ml) soured cream

1 tablespoon cocoa powder

FOR THE BASE

7 oz (200 g) chocolate biscuits, crushed

3 oz (85 g) butter, melted

½ teaspoon ground cinnamon

1 Preheat a 350°F/180°C/Gas 4 oven. Grease the bottom and sides of a 9 × 3 in (23 × 7.5 cm) springform tin.

2 ▲ For the base, mix the crushed biscuits with the butter and cinnamon. Press evenly onto the bottom of the tin.

3 Melt the chocolate in the top of a double boiler, or in a heatproof bowl set over hot water. Set aside.

4 Beat the cream cheese until smooth, then beat in the sugar and vanilla. Add the eggs, 1 at a time.

5 Stir the soured cream into the cocoa powder to form a paste. Add to the cream cheese mixture. Stir in the melted chocolate.

6 ▼ Pour into the crust. Bake for 1 hour. Let cool in the tin; remove rim. Refrigerate before serving.

Classic Cheesecake (top), Chocolate Cheesecake

Lemon Mousse Cheesecake

SERVES 10–12

2½ lb (1.2 kg) cream cheese, at room temperature

12 oz (350 g) caster sugar

1½ oz (45 g) plain flour

4 eggs, at room temperature, separated

4 fl oz (125 ml) fresh lemon juice

grated rind of 2 lemons

4 oz (115 g) digestive biscuits, crushed

1 Preheat a 325°F/170°C/Gas 3 oven. Line a 10 × 2 in (25 × 5 cm) round cake tin with greaseproof paper and grease the paper.

2 With an electric mixer, beat the cream cheese until smooth. Gradually add 10 oz (285 g) of the sugar, and beat until light. Beat in the flour.

3 ▲ Add the egg yolks, and lemon juice and rind, and beat until smooth and well blended.

4 In another bowl, beat the egg whites until they hold soft peaks. Add the remaining sugar and beat until stiff and glossy.

5 ▲ Add the egg whites to the cheese mixture and gently fold in.

6 Pour the mixture into the prepared tin, then place the tin in a larger baking tin. Place in the oven and pour hot water in the outer tin to come 1 in (2.5 cm) up the side.

7 Bake until golden, 60–65 minutes. Let cool in the pan on a rack. Cover and refrigerate for at least 4 hours.

8 To unmould, run a knife around the inside edge. Place a flat plate, bottom-side up, over the pan and invert onto the plate. Smooth the top with a metal spatula.

9 ▲ Sprinkle the biscuits over the top in an even layer, pressing down slightly to make a top crust.

10 To serve, cut slices with a sharp knife dipped in hot water.

Marbled Cheesecake

SERVES 10

2 oz (55 g) unsweetened cocoa powder	
5 tablespoons hot water	
2 lb (900 g) cream cheese, at room temperature	
7 oz (200 g) sugar	
4 eggs	
1 teaspoon vanilla essence	
2¹/₂ oz (70 g) digestive biscuits, crushed	

1 Preheat a 350°F/180°C/Gas 4 oven. Line an 8 × 3 in (20 × 8 cm) cake tin with greaseproof paper and grease.

2 Sift the cocoa powder into a bowl. Pour over the hot water and stir to dissolve. Set aside.

3 With an electric mixer, beat the cheese until smooth and creamy. Add the sugar and beat to incorporate. Beat in the eggs, one at a time. Do not overmix.

4 Divide the mixture evenly between 2 bowls. Stir the chocolate mixture into one, then add the vanilla to the remaining mixture.

5 ▲ Pour a cupful of the plain mixture into the centre of the tin; it will spread out into an even layer. Slowly pour over a cupful of chocolate mixture in the centre.

6 ▲ Repeat alternating cupfuls of the batters in a circular pattern until both are used up.

7 Set the tin in a larger baking tray and pour in hot water to come 1¹/₂ in (3 cm) up the sides of the cake tin.

8 Bake until the top of the cake is golden, about 1¹/₂ hours. It will rise during baking but will sink later. Let cool in the tin on a rack.

9 To turn out, run a knife around the inside edge. Place a flat plate, bottom-side up, over the tin and invert onto the plate.

10 ▼ Sprinkle the crushed biscuits evenly over the base, gently place another plate over them, and invert again. Cover and refrigerate for at least 3 hours, or overnight. To serve, cut slices with a sharp knife dipped in hot water.

Chocolate Fairy Cakes

MAKES 24

4 oz (115 g) good-quality plain chocolate, cut into small pieces

1 tablespoon water

10 oz (300 g) plain flour

1 teaspoon baking powder

½ teaspoon bicarbonate of soda

pinch of salt

10 oz (300 g) caster sugar

6 oz (170 g) butter or margarine, at room temperature

¼ pint (150 ml) milk

1 teaspoon vanilla essence

3 eggs

1 recipe quantity buttercream, flavoured to taste

1 Preheat a 350°F/180°C/Gas 4 oven. Grease and flour 24 deep bun tins, about 2¾ in (6.5 cm) in diameter, or use paper cases in the tins.

2 ▲ Put the chocolate and water in a bowl set over a pan of almost simmering water. Heat until melted and smooth, stirring. Remove from the heat and leave to cool.

3 Sift the flour, baking powder, bicarbonate of soda, salt and sugar into a large bowl. Add the chocolate mixture, butter, milk and vanilla essence.

4 ▲ With an electric mixer on medium-low speed, beat until smoothly blended. Increase the speed to high and beat for 2 minutes. Add the eggs and beat for 2 minutes.

5 Divide the mixture evenly among the prepared bun tins.

6 Bake for 20–25 minutes or until a skewer inserted into the centre of a cake comes out clean. Cool in the tins for 10 minutes, then turn out to cool completely on a wire rack.

7 ▼ Ice the top of each cake with buttercream, swirling it into a peak in the centre.

Chocolate Orange Sponge Drops

MAKES ABOUT 14

2 eggs

2 oz (55 g) caster sugar

½ teaspoon grated orange zest

2 oz (55 g) plain flour

4 tablespoons fine shred orange
  marmalade

1½ oz (45 g) plain chocolate, cut into
  small pieces

1 Preheat a 400°F/200°C/Gas 6 oven.
Line 3 baking sheets with baking
parchment.

2 ▲ Put the eggs and sugar in a large
bowl and set over a pan of just
simmering water. Whisk until the
mixture is thick and pale.

3 ▲ Remove the bowl from the pan
of water and continue whisking until
the mixture is cool. Whisk in the
grated orange zest.

4 Sift the flour over the whisked
mixture and fold it in gently with a
rubber spatula.

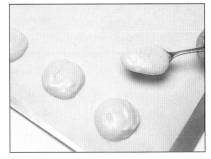

5 ▲ Using a dessertspoon, put
spoonfuls of the mixture on the
prepared baking sheets, leaving space
around each spoonful to allow for
spreading. The mixture will make
28–30 drops.

6 Bake for about 8 minutes or until
golden. Cool for a few minutes on the
baking sheets, then transfer to a wire
rack to cool completely.

7 Sandwich pairs of sponge drops
together with the orange marmalade.

8 ▼ Melt the chocolate in a double
saucepan over simmering water until
smooth. Using a small spoon, drizzle
chocolate over the tops of the sponge
drops, or pipe it in fine lines using a
small greaseproof paper piping bag.
Leave to set before serving.

Iced Fancies

MAKES 16

4 oz (115 g) butter, at room temperature
8 oz (225 g) caster sugar
2 eggs, at room temperature
6 oz (170 g) plain flour
1/4 tsp salt
1 1/2 tsp baking powder
4 fl oz (125 ml) plus 1 tbsp milk
1 tsp vanilla essence
FOR ICING AND DECORATING
2 large egg whites
14 oz (400 g) sifted icing sugar
1–2 drops glycerine
juice of 1 lemon
food colourings
hundreds and thousands, for decorating
crystallized lemon and orange slices, for decorating

1 Preheat a 375°F/190°C/Gas 5 oven.

2 ▲ Line 16 bun-tray cups with fluted paper baking cases, or grease.

~ COOK'S TIP ~

Ready-made cake decorating products are widely available, and may be used, if preferred, instead of the recipes given for icing and decorating. Coloured icing in ready-to-pipe tubes is useful.

---

3 With an electric mixer, cream the butter and sugar until light and fluffy. Add the eggs, 1 at a time, beating well after each addition.

4 Sift together the flour, salt and baking powder. Stir into the butter mixture, alternating with the milk. Stir in the vanilla.

5 ▲ Fill the cups half-full and bake until the tops spring back when touched lightly, about 20 minutes. Let the cakes stand in the tray for 5 minutes, then unmould and transfer to a rack to cool completely.

6 For the icing, beat the egg whites until stiff but not dry. Gradually add the sugar, glycerine and lemon juice, and continue beating for 1 minute. The consistency should be spreadable. If necessary, thin with a little water or add more sifted icing sugar.

7 ▲ Divide the icing between several bowls and tint with food colourings. Spread different coloured icings over the cooled cakes.

8 ▲ Decorate the cakes as wished, with sugar decorations such as hundreds and thousands.

9 ▲ Other decorations include crystallized orange and lemon slices. Cut into small pieces and arrange on top of the cakes. Alternatively, use other suitable sweets.

10 ▲ To make freehand iced decorations, fill paper piping bags with different colour icings. Pipe on faces, or make other designs.

Heart Cake

MAKES 1 CAKE

8 oz (225 g) butter or margarine, at room temperature
8 oz (225 g) caster sugar
4 eggs, at room temperature
6 oz (170 g) plain flour
1 tsp baking powder
½ tsp bicarbonate of soda
2 tbsp milk
1 tsp vanilla essence
FOR ICING AND DECORATING
3 egg whites
12 oz (350 g) caster sugar
2 tbsp cold water
2 tbsp fresh lemon juice
¼ tsp cream of tartar
pink food colouring
3–4 oz (85–115 g) icing sugar

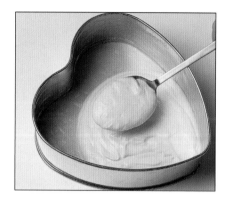

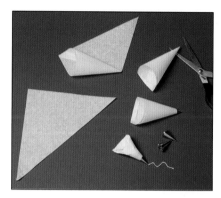

1 Preheat a 350°F/180°C/Gas 4 oven. Line an 8 in (20 cm) heart-shaped tin with greaseproof paper and grease.

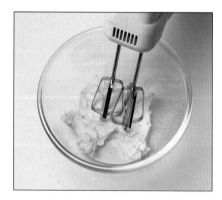

2 ▲ With an electric mixer, cream the butter or margarine and sugar until light and fluffy. Add the eggs, 1 at a time, beating thoroughly after each addition.

3 Sift the flour, baking powder and baking soda together. Fold the dry ingredients into the butter mixture in 3 batches, alternating with the milk. Stir in the vanilla.

4 ▲ Spoon the mixture into the prepared tin and bake until a skewer inserted in the centre comes out clean, 35–40 minutes. Let the cake stand in the tin for 5 minutes, then unmould and transfer to a rack to cool completely.

5 For the icing, combine 2 of the egg whites, the caster sugar, water, lemon juice and cream of tartar in the top of a double boiler or in a bowl set over simmering water. With an electric mixer, beat until thick and holding soft peaks, about 7 minutes. Remove from the heat and continue beating until the mixture is thick enough to spread. Tint the icing with the pink food colouring.

6 ▲ Put the cake on a board, about 12 in (30 cm) square, covered in foil or in paper suitable for contact with food. Spread the icing evenly on the cake. Smooth the top and sides. Leave to set for 3–4 hours, or overnight.

7 ▲ For the paper piping bags, fold an 11 × 8 in (28 × 20 cm) sheet of greaseproof paper in half diagonally, then cut into 2 pieces along the fold mark. Roll over the short side, so that it meets the right-angled corner and forms a cone. To form the piping bag, hold the cone in place with one hand, wrap the point of the long side of the triangle around the cone, and tuck inside, folding over twice to secure. Snip a hole in the pointed end and slip in a small metal piping nozzle to extend about ¼ in (5 mm).

8 For the piped decorations, place 1 tablespoon of the remaining egg white in a bowl and whisk until frothy. Gradually beat in enough icing sugar to make a stiff mixture suitable for piping.

9 ▲ Spoon into a paper piping bag to half-fill. Fold over the top and squeeze to pipe decorations on the top and sides of the cake.

Snake Cake

SERVES 10–12

8 oz (225 g) butter or margarine, at room temperature

grated rind and juice of 1 small orange

8 oz (225 g) sugar

4 eggs, at room temperature, separated

6 oz (170 g) plain flour

1 teaspoon baking powder

pinch of salt

FOR THE ICING AND DECORATING

1 oz (30 g) butter, at room temperature

12 oz (350 g) icing sugar

5 oz (140 g) plain chocolate

pinch of salt

4 fl oz (125 ml) soured cream

1 egg white

green and blue food colourings

1 Preheat the oven to 375°F/190°C/Gas 5. Grease 2 8¹/₂ oz (22 cm) ring tins and dust them with flour.

2 Cream the butter or margarine, orange rind and sugar until light. Beat in the egg yolks, 1 at a time.

3 Sift the flour and baking powder. Fold into the butter mixture, alternating with the orange juice.

4 ▲ In another bowl, beat the egg whites and salt until stiff.

5 Fold a large dollop of the egg whites into the creamed butter mixture to lighten it, then gently fold in the remaining whites.

6 Divide the mixture between the prepared tins and bake until a skewer inserted in the centre comes out clean, about 25 minutes. Leave to stand for 5 minutes, then turn out on to a wire rack to cool.

7 Prepare a board, 24 × 8 in (60 × 20 cm), covered in paper suitable for contact with food, or in foil.

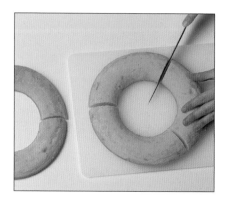

8 ▲ Cut the cakes into 3 even pieces. Trim to level the flat side, if necessary, and shape the head by cutting off wedges from the front. Shape the tail in the same way.

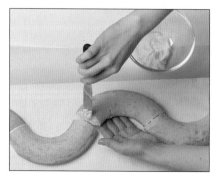

9 ▲ For the buttercream, mix the butter with 1¹/₂ oz (45 g) of the icing sugar. Use to join the cake sections and arrange on the board.

10 ▲ For the chocolate icing, melt the chocolate. Stir in the salt and soured cream. When cool, spread over the cake and smooth the surface.

11 ▲ For the decoration, beat the egg white until frothy. Add enough of the remaining icing sugar to obtain a thick mixture. Divide among several bowls and add food colourings.

12 ▲ Fill paper piping bags with icing and pipe decorations along the top of the cake.

Sun Cake

SERVES 10–12

4 oz (115 g) unsalted butter
6 eggs
8 oz (225 g) caster sugar
4 oz (115 g) plain flour
1/2 tsp salt
1 tsp vanilla essence
FOR ICING AND DECORATING
1 oz (30 g) unsalted butter, at room temperature
1 lb (450 g) sifted icing sugar
4 fl oz (125 ml) apricot jam
2 tbsp water
2 large egg whites
1–2 drops glycerine
juice of 1 lemon
yellow and orange food colourings

1 Preheat a 350°F/180°C/Gas 4 oven. Line 2 8 × 2 in (20 × 5 cm) round cake tins, then grease and flour.

2 In a saucepan, melt the butter over very low heat. Skim off any foam that rises to the surface, then set aside.

3 ▲ Place a heatproof bowl over a saucepan of hot water. Add the eggs and sugar. Beat with an electric mixer until the mixture doubles in volume and is thick enough to leave a ribbon trail when the beaters are lifted, 8–10 minutes.

4 Sift the flour and salt together 3 times. Sift over the egg mixture in 3 batches, folding in well after each addition. Fold in the melted butter and vanilla.

5 Divide the mixture between the tins. Level the surfaces and bake until the cakes shrink slightly from the sides of the tins, 25–30 minutes. Let stand 5 minutes, then unmould and transfer to a cooling rack.

6 Prepare a board, 16 in (40 cm) square, covered in paper suitable for contact with food, or in foil.

7 ▲ For the sunbeams, cut one of the cakes into 8 equal wedges. Cut away a rounded piece from the base of each so that they fit nearly up against the sides of the whole cake.

8 ▲ For the butter icing, mix the butter and 1 oz (30 g) of the icing sugar. Use to attach the sunbeams.

9 ▲ Melt the jam with the water and brush over the cake. Place on the board and straighten, if necessary.

10 ▲ For the icing, beat the egg whites until stiff but not dry. Gradually add 14 oz (400 g) icing sugar, the glycerine and lemon juice, and continue beating for 1 minute. If necessary, thin with water or thicken with a little more sugar. Tint with yellow food colouring and spread over the cake.

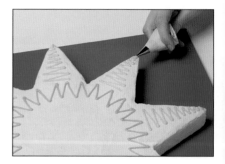

11 ▲ Divide the remaining icing in half and tint with more food colouring to obtain bright yellow and orange. Pipe decorative zigzags on the sunbeams and a face in the middle.

Jack-O'-Lantern Cake

SERVES 8–10

6 oz (170 g) plain flour

2¹/₂ teaspoons baking powder

pinch of salt

4 oz (115 g) butter, at room
   temperature

8 oz (225 g) sugar

3 egg yolks, at room temperature,
   well beaten

1 teaspoon grated lemon rind

6 fl oz (175 ml) milk

FOR THE CAKE COVERING

1 lb 4 oz–1 lb 8 oz (565–700 g) icing
   sugar

2 egg whites

2 tablespoons liquid glucose

orange and black food colourings

1 Preheat the oven to 375°F/190°C/
Gas 5. Line an 8 in (20 cm) round
cake tin with greaseproof paper
and grease.

2 Sift together the flour, baking
powder and salt. Set aside.

3 With an electric mixer, cream the
butter and sugar until light and fluffy.
Gradually beat in the egg yolks, then
add the lemon rind. Fold in the flour
mixture in 3 batches, alternating
with the milk.

4 Spoon the mixture into the
prepared tin. Bake until a skewer
inserted in the centre comes out
clean, about 35 minutes. Leave to
stand, then turn out on to a rack.

~ COOK'S TIP ~

If preferred, use ready-made
roll-out cake covering,
available at cake decorating
supply shops. Knead in food
colouring, if required.

5 For the icing, sift 1 lb 4 oz (565 g)
of the icing sugar into a bowl. Make
a well in the centre, add 1 egg white,
the glucose and orange food colouring.
Stir until a dough forms.

6 ▲ Transfer to a clean work
surface dusted with icing sugar and
knead briefly.

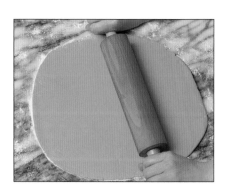

7 ▲ Carefully roll out the orange
cake covering to a thin sheet.

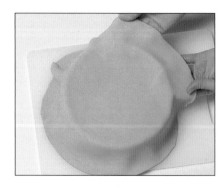

8 ▲ Place the sheet on top of the
cooled cake and smooth the sides.
Trim the excess icing and reserve.

9 ▲ From the trimmings, cut shapes
for the top. Tint the remaining cake
covering trimmings with black food
colouring. Roll out thinly and cut
shapes for the face.

10 ▲ Brush the undersides with
water and arrange the face on top of
the cake.

11 ▲ Place 1 tablespoon of the
remaining egg white in a bowl and
stir in enough icing sugar to make a
thick icing. Tint with black food
colouring, fill a paper piping bag and
complete the decoration.

Stars and Stripes Cake

SERVES 20

8 oz (225 g) butter or margarine, at room temperature
8 oz (225 g) dark brown sugar
8 oz (225 g) granulated sugar
5 eggs, at room temperature
10 oz (285 g) plain flour
2 teaspoons baking powder
1 teaspoon bicarbonate of soda
1 teaspoon ground cinnamon
1 teaspoon ground ginger
$^1/_2$ teaspoon ground allspice
$^1/_4$ teaspoon ground cloves
$^1/_4$ teaspoon salt
12 fl oz (350 ml) buttermilk
3 oz (85 g) raisins
FOR THE CAKE COVERING
1 oz (30 g) butter
2 lb 4 oz–2 lb 10 oz (1–1.3 kg) icing sugar
3 egg whites
4 tablespoons liquid glucose
red and blue food colourings

1 Preheat the oven to 350°F/180°C/ Gas 4. Line a 12 × 9 in (30 × 23 cm) baking tin with greaseproof paper and lightly grease.

2 With an electric mixer, cream the butter or margarine and sugars until light and fluffy. Gradually beat in the eggs, 1 at a time, beating well after each addition.

3 Sift together the flour, baking powder, bicarbonate of soda, spices and salt. Fold into the butter mixture in 3 batches, alternating with the buttermilk. Stir in the raisins.

4 Pour the mixture into the prepared tin and bake until the cake springs back when touched lightly, about 35 minutes. Leave to stand for 10 minutes, then turn out on to a wire rack.

5 Make buttercream for assembling the cake by mixing the butter with $1^1/_2$ oz (45 g) of the icing sugar.

6 ▲ When the cake is cool, cut a curved shape from the top.

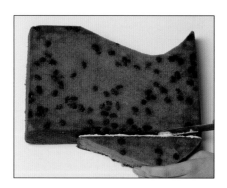

7 ▲ Attach it to the bottom of the cake with the buttercream.

8 Prepare a board, about 16 × 12 in (40 × 30 cm), covered in paper suitable for contact with food, or in foil. Transfer the cake to the board.

9 For the cake covering, sift 2 lb 4 oz (1 kg) of the icing sugar into a bowl. Add 2 of the egg whites and the liquid glucose. Stir until the mixture forms a dough.

10 Cover and set aside half of the covering. On a clean work surface lightly dusted with icing sugar, roll out the remaining covering to a sheet. Carefully transfer to the cake. Smooth the sides and trim any excess from the bottom edges.

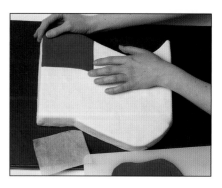

11 ▲ Tint one quarter of the remaining covering blue and tint the rest red. Roll out the blue to a thin sheet and cut out the background for the stars. Place on the cake.

12 ▲ Roll out the red covering, cut out stripes and place on the cake.

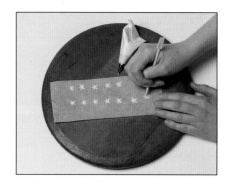

13 ▲ For the stars, mix 1 tablespoon of the egg white with just enough icing sugar to thicken. Pipe small stars on to a sheet of greaseproof paper and leave to set. When dry, peel them off and place on the blue background.

LOW-FAT CAKES & BAKES

ALL THE CAKES AND BAKES IN THIS
CHAPTER ARE LOW IN FAT, IN MANY
CASES CONTAIN LITTLE OR NO
EGGS, AND OFTEN SUGAR IS
REDUCED BY USING FRUITS TO
SWEETEN THE MIXTURE.
EVERYONE WILL LOVE THESE
BAKED GOODS – THEY'RE BURSTING
WITH FLAVOUR AND SUITED TO
ALL OCCASIONS.

Spiced Apple Cake

Grated apple and chopped dates give this cake a natural sweetness.

SERVES 8

8 oz (225 g) self-raising wholemeal flour
1 teaspoon (5 ml) baking powder
2 teaspoons (10 ml) ground cinnamon
6 oz (175 g) chopped dates
3 oz (75 g) light muscovado sugar
1 tablespoon (15 ml) pear and apple spread
4 fl oz (120 ml) apple juice
2 eggs
6 tablespoons (90 ml) sunflower oil
2 eating apples, cored and grated
1 tablespoon (15 ml) chopped walnuts

1 ▲ Preheat the oven to 180°C/ 350°F/Gas 4. Grease and line a deep round 8 in (20 cm) cake tin. Sift the flour, baking powder and cinnamon into a mixing bowl, then mix in the dates and make a well in the centre.

2 ▲ Mix the sugar with the pear and apple spread in a small bowl. Gradually stir in the apple juice. Add to the dry ingredients with the eggs, oil and grated apples. Mix thoroughly.

3 ▲ Spoon the mixture into the prepared cake tin, sprinkle liberally with the walnuts and bake for 60–65 minutes or until a skewer inserted into the centre of the cake comes out clean. Transfer to a wire rack, remove the lining paper and leave to cool.

NUTRITION NOTES
Per portion

Energy	331Kcals/13895kJ
Fat	11.41g
Saturated Fat	1.68g
Cholesterol	48.13mg
Fibre	2.5g

Spiced Date and Walnut Cake

A classic flavour combination, which makes a very easy low-fat, high-fibre cake.

1 Preheat the oven to 180°C/350°F/ Gas 4. Grease and line a 2 lb (900 g) loaf tin with greaseproof paper.

2 ▲ Sift together the flour and spice, adding back any bran from the sieve. Stir in the dates and walnuts.

3 ▲ Mix the oil, sugar and milk, then stir evenly into the dry ingredients.

4 ▲ Spoon into the prepared tin and arrange the walnut halves on top. Bake the cake for about 45–50 minutes, or until golden brown and firm. Turn out the cake, remove the lining paper and leave to cool.

SERVES 10

11 oz (300 g) wholemeal self-raising flour
2 teaspoons (10 ml) mixed spice
5 oz (150 g) chopped dates
2 oz (50 g) chopped walnuts
4 tablespoons (60 ml) sunflower oil
4 oz (115 g) dark muscovado sugar
½ pint (300 ml) skimmed milk
walnut halves, to decorate

NUTRITION NOTES
Per portion
Energy	265Kcals/1114kJ
Fat	9.27g
Saturated Fat	1.14g
Cholesterol	0.6mg
Fibre	3.51g

~ COOK'S TIP ~
Pecan nuts can be used in place of the walnuts in this cake.

Greek Honey and Lemon Cake

Moist and tangy, a delicious tea-time treat.

MAKES 16 SLICES

1½ oz (40 g) sunflower margarine

4 tablespoons (60 ml) clear honey

finely grated rind and juice of
    1 lemon

¼ pint (150 ml) skimmed milk

5 oz (150 g) plain flour

1½ teaspoons (7.5 ml) baking powder

½ teaspoon (2.5 ml) grated nutmeg

2 oz (50 g) semolina

2 egg whites

2 teaspoons (10 ml) sesame seeds

1 Preheat the oven to 200°C/400°F/
Gas 6. Lightly oil a 7½ in (19 cm)
square deep cake tin and line the
base with non-stick baking paper.

2 ▲ Gently melt the margarine and
3 tablespoons (45 ml) of the honey.
Reserve 1 tablespoon (15 ml) lemon
juice, then stir in the rest with the
rind and milk. Transfer to a bowl.

3 ▲ Add the flour, baking powder
and nutmeg, and stir through.
Gradually beat the semolina into the
mixture. Whisk the egg whites until
soft peaks form, then fold them in.

4 ▲ Spoon into the tin and sprinkle
with sesame seeds. Bake the cake for
25–30 minutes, until golden brown.
Mix together the reserved honey and
lemon juice and drizzle over the cake
while warm. Cool in the tin, then
cut into fingers to serve.

NUTRITION NOTES
Per portion

Energy	82Kcals/342kJ
Fat	2.62g
Saturated Fat	0.46g
Cholesterol	0.36mg
Fibre	0.41g

Cranberry and Apple Ring

Tangy cranberries add an unusual flavour to this low-fat cake. It is best eaten very fresh.

SERVES 8

8 oz (225 g) self-raising flour
1 teaspoon (5 ml) ground cinnamon
3 oz (75 g) light muscovado sugar
1 crisp eating apple, cored and diced
3 oz (75 g) fresh or frozen cranberries
4 tablespoons (60 ml) sunflower oil
¾ pint (150 ml) apple juice
cranberry jelly and apple slices, to decorate

1 ▲ Preheat the oven to 180°C/ 350°F/Gas 4. Lightly grease a 1¼ pint (1 litre) ring mould with oil.

2 Sift together the flour and ground cinnamon, then stir in the sugar.

4 ▲ Spoon the mixture into the prepared ring mould and bake for about 35–40 minutes, or until the cake is firm to the touch. Turn out and leave to cool completely.

5 To serve, drizzle warmed cranberry jelly over the cake and decorate with apple slices.

NUTRITION NOTES
Per portion

Energy	202Kcals/848kJ
Fat	5.91g
Saturated Fat	0.76g
Cholesterol	0
Fibre	1.55g

3 ▲ Toss together the diced apple and cranberries. Stir into the dry ingredients, then add the oil and apple juice and beat well.

~ COOK'S TIP ~

Fresh cranberries are available throughout the winter months and if you don't use them all at once, they can be frozen for up to a year.

Lemon Chiffon Cake

Lemon mousse provides a tangy filling for this light lemon sponge.

SERVES 8

2 eggs
3 oz (75 g) caster sugar
grated rind of 1 lemon
2 oz (50 g) sifted plain flour
lemon shreds, to decorate
FOR THE FILLING
2 eggs, separated
3 oz (75 g) caster sugar
grated rind and juice of 1 lemon
2 tablespoons (70 ml) water
1 tablespoon (15 ml) gelatine
4 fl oz (125 ml) low-fat fromage frais
FOR THE ICING
1 tablespoon (15 ml) lemon juice
4 oz (115 g) icing sugar, sifted

~ COOK'S TIP ~

The mousse should be just setting when the egg whites are added. Speed up this process by placing the bowl of mousse in iced water.

NUTRITION NOTES

Per portion

Energy	202Kcals/849kJ
Fat	2.81g
Saturated Fat	0.79g
Cholesterol	96.4mg
Fibre	0.2g

1 ▲ Preheat the oven to 180°C/ 350°F/Gas 4. Grease and line an 8 in (20 cm) loose-bottomed cake tin. Whisk the eggs, sugar and lemon rind together until mousse-like. Gently fold in the flour, then turn the mixture into the tin.

2 ▲ Bake for 20–25 minutes until the cake springs back when lightly pressed in the centre. Turn on to a wire rack. Once cold, split the cake in half horizontally and return the lower half to the clean cake tin.

3 ▲ Make the filling. Put the egg yolks, sugar, lemon rind and juice in a bowl. Beat with a hand-held electric whisk until thick, pale and creamy.

4 ▲ Pour the water into a heatproof bowl and sprinkle the gelatine on top. Leave until spongy, then stir over simmering water until dissolved. Cool, then whisk into the yolk mixture. Fold in the fromage frais. When the mixture begins to set, whisk the egg whites to soft peaks. Fold the egg whites into the mousse.

5 ▲ Pour the lemon mousse over the sponge in the cake tin, spreading it to the edges. Set the second layer of sponge on top and chill until set.

6 ▲ Slide a palette knife dipped in hot water between the tin and the cake to loosen it. Transfer to a plate. To make icing, add enough lemon juice to the icing sugar to make a mixture thick enough to coat the back of a wooden spoon. Pour over the cake. Decorate with lemon shreds.

Strawberry Gâteau

It's hard to believe that this delicious gâteau is low in fat, but it's true, so enjoy!

SERVES 6

2 eggs	
3 oz (75 g) caster sugar	
grated rind of ½ orange	
2 oz (50 g) plain flour	
strawberry leaves, to decorate (optional)	
icing sugar, for dusting	

FOR THE FILLING

10 oz (275 g) low-fat soft cheese	
grated rind of ½ orange	
2 tablespoons (30 ml) caster sugar	
4 tablespoons (60 ml) low-fat fromage frais	
8 oz (225 g) strawberries, halved	
1 oz (25 g) chopped almonds, toasted	

~ COOK'S TIP ~

Use other soft fruits in season, such as currants, raspberries, blackberries or blueberries, or try a mixture of different berries.

NUTRITION NOTES

Per portion

Energy	213Kcals/893kJ
Fat	6.08g
Saturated Fat	1.84g
Cholesterol	70.22mg
Fibre	1.02g

1 ▲ Preheat the oven to 190°C/ 375°F/Gas 5. Grease a 12 × 8 in (30 × 20 cm) Swiss roll tin and line with non-stick baking paper.

2 ▲ In a bowl, whisk the eggs, sugar and orange rind together with a hand-held electric whisk until thick and mousse-like (when the whisk is lifted, a trail should remain on the surface of the mixture for 15 seconds).

3 ▲ Fold in the flour with a metal spoon, being careful not to knock out any air. Turn into the prepared tin. Bake for 15–20 minutes, or until the cake springs back when lightly pressed. Turn the cake on to a wire rack, remove the lining paper and leave to cool.

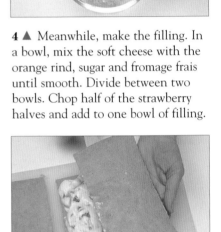

4 ▲ Meanwhile, make the filling. In a bowl, mix the soft cheese with the orange rind, sugar and fromage frais until smooth. Divide between two bowls. Chop half of the strawberry halves and add to one bowl of filling.

5 ▲ Cut the sponge widthways into three equal pieces and sandwich them together with the strawberry filling. Spread two-thirds of the plain filling over the sides of the cake and press on the toasted almonds.

6 ▲ Spread the rest of the filling over the top of the cake and decorate with strawberry halves, and strawberry leaves, if liked. Dust with icing sugar and transfer to a serving plate.

Tia Maria Gâteau

A feather-light coffee sponge with a creamy liqueur-flavoured filling.

SERVES 8

3 oz (75 g) plain flour

2 tablespoons (30 ml) instant coffee powder

3 eggs

4 oz (115 g) caster sugar

coffee beans, to decorate (optional)

FOR THE FILLING

6 oz (175 g) low-fat soft cheese

1 tablespoon (15 ml) clear honey

1 tablespoon (15 ml) Tia Maria liqueur

2 oz (50 g) stem ginger, roughly chopped

FOR THE ICING

8 oz (225 g) icing sugar, sifted

2 teaspoons (10 ml) coffee essence

1 tablespoon (15 ml) water

1 teaspoon (5 ml) reduced-fat cocoa powder

~ COOK'S TIP ~

When folding in the flour mixture in step 3, be careful not to remove the air, as it helps the cake to rise.

NUTRITION NOTES
Per portion
Energy	226Kcals/951kJ
Fat	3.14g
Saturated Fat	1.17g
Cholesterol	75.03mg
Fibre	0.64g

1 ▲ Preheat the oven to 190°C/ 375°F/Gas 5. Grease and line an 8 in (20 cm) deep round cake tin. Sift the flour and coffee powder together on to a sheet of greaseproof paper.

2 ▲ Whisk the eggs and sugar in a bowl with a hand-held electric whisk until thick and mousse-like (when the whisk is lifted, a trail should remain on the surface of the mixture for at least 15 seconds).

3 ▲ Gently fold in the flour mixture with a metal spoon. Turn the mixture into the prepared tin. Bake the sponge for 30–35 minutes or until it springs back when lightly pressed. Turn on to a wire rack to cool completely.

4 ▲ To make the filling, mix the soft cheese with the honey in a bowl. Beat until smooth, then stir in the Tia Maria and chopped stem ginger.

5 ▲ Split the cake in half horizontally and sandwich the two halves together with the Tia Maria filling.

6 Make the icing. In a bowl, mix the icing sugar and coffee essence with enough of the water to make a consistency that will coat the back of a wooden spoon. Pour three-quarters of the icing over the cake, spreading it evenly to the edges. Stir the cocoa into the remaining icing until smooth. Spoon into a piping bag fitted with a writing nozzle and pipe the mocha icing over the coffee icing. Decorate with coffee beans, if liked.

Chocolate Banana Cake

A chocolate cake that's deliciously low in fat – it is moist enough to eat without the icing if you want to cut down on calories.

SERVES 8

8 oz (225 g) self-raising flour

3 tablespoons (45 ml) fat-reduced cocoa powder

4 oz (115 g) light muscovado sugar

2 tablespoons (30 ml) malt extract

2 tablespoons (30 ml) golden syrup

2 eggs

4 tablespoons (60 ml) skimmed milk

4 tablespoons (60 ml) sunflower oil

2 large ripe bananas

FOR THE ICING

8 oz (225 g) icing

sugar, sifted

7 teaspoons (35 ml) fat-reduced cocoa powder, sifted

1–2 tablespoons (15–30 ml) warm water

NUTRITION NOTES
Per portion
Energy	411Kcals/1727kJ
Fat	8.791g
Saturated Fat	2.06g
Cholesterol	48.27mg
Fibre	2.06g

1 ▲ Preheat the oven to 160°C/325°F/Gas 3. Grease and line a deep round 8 in (20 cm) cake tin.

2 ▲ Sift the flour into a mixing bowl with the cocoa. Stir in the sugar.

3 ▲ Make a well in the centre and add the malt extract, golden syrup, eggs, milk and oil. Mash the bananas thoroughly and stir them into the mixture until well combined.

4 ▲ Pour the cake mixture into the prepared tin and bake for 1–1¼ hours or until the centre of the cake springs back when lightly pressed.

5 ▲ Remove the cake from the tin and leave on a wire rack to cool.

6 ▲ Reserve 2 oz (50 g) icing sugar and 1 teaspoon (5 ml) cocoa powder. Make a dark icing by beating the remaining sugar and cocoa powder with enough of the warm water to make a thick icing. Pour it over the cake and spread evenly. Make a light icing by mixing the remaining icing sugar and cocoa powder with a few drops of water. Drizzle this icing across the top of the cake.

Chocolate and Orange Angel Cake

This light-as-air sponge with its fluffy icing is virtually fat-free, yet tastes heavenly.

Serves 10

1 oz (25 g) plain flour
½ oz (15 g) reduced-fat cocoa powder
½ oz (15 g) cornflour
pinch of salt
5 egg whites
½ teaspoon (2.5 ml) cream of tartar
4 oz (115 g) caster sugar
blanched and shredded rind of 1 orange, to decorate

For the icing

7 oz (200 g) caster sugar
1 egg white

NUTRITION NOTES
Per portion

Energy	153Kcals/644kJ
Fat	0.27g
Saturated Fat	0.13g
Cholesterol	0
Fibre	0.25g

1 ▲ Preheat the oven to 180°C/ 350°F/Gas 4. Sift the flour, cocoa powder, cornflour and salt together three times. Beat the egg whites in a large clean, dry bowl until foamy. Add the cream of tartar, then whisk.

2 ▲ Add the caster sugar to the egg whites a spoonful at a time, whisking after each addition. Sift a third of the flour and cocoa mixture over the meringue and gently fold in. Repeat, sifting and folding in the flour and cocoa mixture two more times.

3 ▲ Spoon the mixture into a non-stick 8 in (20 cm) ring mould and level the top. Bake for 35 minutes or until springy to the touch. Turn upside down on to a wire rack and leave to cool in the tin. Carefully ease out of the tin.

4 ▲ For the icing, mix the sugar with 5 tablespoons (75 ml) cold water. Stir over a low heat until dissolved. Boil until the syrup reaches 120°C/250°F on a sugar thermometer or when a drop of the syrup makes a soft ball when dripped into cold water. Remove from the heat.

5 ▲ Whisk the egg white until stiff. Add the syrup in a thin stream, whisking all the time. Continue to whisk until the mixture is very thick.

6 ▲ Spread the icing over the top and sides of the cooled cake. Sprinkle the orange rind over the top of the cake and serve.

ggless Christmas Cake

A deliciously clever way to create a low-calorie Christmas treat!

SERVES 12

3 oz (75 g) sultanas
3 oz (75 g) raisins
3 oz (75 g) currants
3 oz (75 g) halved glacé cherries
2 oz (50 g) cut mixed peel
8 fl oz (250 ml) apple juice
1 oz (25 g) toasted hazelnuts
2 tablespoons (30 ml) pumpkin seeds
2 pieces stem ginger in syrup, chopped
finely grated rind of 1 lemon
4 fl oz (120 ml) skimmed milk
4 fl oz (120 ml) sunflower oil
8 oz (225 g) self-raising flour
2 teaspoons (10 ml) mixed spice
3 tablespoons (45 ml) brandy or rum
apricot jam, for brushing

1 ▲ Place the sultanas, raisins, currants, halved cherries and mixed peel in a bowl and stir in the apple juice. Cover and leave to soak overnight.

2 Preheat the oven to 150°C/300°F/ Gas 2.

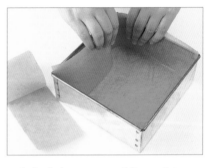

3 ▲ Lightly grease and line a 7 in (18 cm) square cake tin.

4 ▲ Add the hazelnuts, pumpkin seeds, ginger and lemon rind to the fruit. Stir in the milk, oil, sifted flour and spice, and the brandy or rum.

5 ▲ Spoon into the prepared tin and bake for 1½ hours, or until golden brown and firm to the touch. Turn out and cool on a wire rack. Brush with sieved apricot jam and decorate with glacé fruits, if desired.

NUTRITION NOTES
Per portion

Energy	225Kcals/946kJ
Fat	6.13g
Saturated Fat	0.89g
Cholesterol	0.2mg
Fibre	2.45g

Fruit and Nut Cake

A rich fruit cake that improves with keeping.

1 ▲ Preheat the oven to 160°C/325°F/Gas 3. Grease and line a deep round 8 in (20 cm) cake tin. Secure brown paper around the outside.

2 ▲ Sift the flours into a mixing bowl together with the mixed spice and make a well in the centre.

3 ▲ Put the apple and apricot spread in a small bowl. Gradually stir in the honey and molasses. Add to the dry ingredients with the oil, orange juice, eggs and dried fruit and mix.

4 ▲ Turn the mixture into the prepared tin and smooth the surface. Arrange the almonds and cherries in a pattern over the top. Bake for 2 hours or until a skewer comes out clean. Transfer to a wire rack until cold, then lift out of the tin and remove the paper.

SERVES 12–14

6 oz (175 g) self-raising wholemeal flour
6 oz (175 g) self-raising white flour
2 teaspoons (10 ml) mixed spice
1 tablespoon (15 ml) apple and apricot spread
3 tablespoons (45 ml) clear honey
1 tablespoon (15 ml) molasses
6 tablespoons (90 ml) sunflower oil
6 fl oz (175 ml) orange juice
2 eggs, beaten
1½ lb (675 g) mixed dried fruit
3 tablespoons (45 ml) split almonds
2 oz (50 g) glacé cherries, halved

NUTRITION NOTES
Per portion
Energy	333Kcals/14000kJ
Fat	8.54g
Saturated Fat	1.12g
Cholesterol	29.62mg
Fibre	3.08g

Banana Ginger Parkin

Parkin keeps well and really improves over time. Store it in a container for up to two months.

SERVES 12

7 oz (200 g) plain flour
2 tsp (10 ml) bicarbonate of soda
2 tsp (10 ml) ground ginger
5 oz (150 g) medium oatmeal
4 tbsp (60 ml) dark muscovado sugar
3 oz (75 g) sunflower margarine
5 oz (150 g) golden syrup
1 egg, beaten
3 ripe bananas, mashed
3 oz (75 g) icing sugar

NUTRITION NOTES
Per portion
Energy	277Kcals/1163kJ
Fat	6.9g
Saturated Fat	6.9g
Cholesterol	16.4mg
Fibre	1.72g

1 Preheat the oven to 160°C/325°F/ Gas 3. Grease and line a 7 × 11 in (18 × 28 cm) cake tin.

2 ▲ Sift together the flour, bicarbonate of soda and ginger, then stir in the oatmeal. Melt the sugar, margarine and syrup in a saucepan, then stir into the flour mixture. Beat in the egg and mashed bananas.

3 ▲ Spoon into the tin and bake for about 1 hour, or until firm to the touch. Allow to cool in the tin, then turn out and cut into squares.

4 ▲ Sift the icing sugar into a bowl and stir in just enough water to make a smooth, runny icing. Drizzle the icing over each square and top with a piece of stem ginger, if desired.

~ COOK'S TIP ~
This is a nutritious, energy-giving cake that is a really good choice for packed lunches as it doesn't break up too easily.

Nectarine Amaretto Cake

Amaretto liqueur adds a hint of luxury to this fruity cake.

1 ▲ Preheat the oven to 180°C/ 350°F/Gas 4. Grease an 8 in (20 cm) round, loose-bottomed cake tin. Whisk together the egg yolks, caster sugar, lemon rind and juice in a bowl until the mixture is thick and creamy.

2 Fold in the semolina, almonds and flour until smooth.

3 ▲ Whisk the egg whites in a bowl until fairly stiff. Use a metal spoon to stir a generous spoonful of the whites into the semolina mixture, then fold in the remaining egg whites. Spoon the mixture into the cake tin.

4 Bake for 30–35 minutes until the centre of the cake springs back when pressed lightly. Remove from the oven and loosen around the edge with a palette knife. Prick the top with a skewer. Leave to cool in the tin.

5 To make the syrup, heat the sugar and water in a small pan, stirring until the sugar is dissolved. Boil without stirring for 2 minutes. Add the Amaretto liqueur and drizzle the liqueur syrup over the cake in the tin.

6 ▲ Remove the cake from the tin and transfer to a serving plate. Decorate with sliced nectarines. Brush with warm apricot glaze.

SERVES 8

3 eggs, separated
6 oz (175 g) caster sugar
grated rind and juice of 1 lemon
2 oz (50 g) semolina
1 oz (25 g) ground almonds
1 oz (25 g) plain flour
2 nectarines, halved and stoned
4 tablespoons (60 ml) apricot glaze
FOR THE SYRUP
3 oz (45 g) caster sugar
6 tablespoons (90 ml) water
2 tablespoons (30 ml) Amaretto

NUTRITION NOTES
Per portion

Energy	264Kcals/1108kJ
Fat	5.7g
Saturated Fat	0.85g
Cholesterol	72.19mg
Fibre	1.08g

Banana and Gingerbread Slices

Very quick to make and deliciously moist due to the addition of bananas.

SERVES 20

4 oz (115 g) soft light brown sugar

10 oz (275 g) plain flour

4 teaspoons (20 ml) ground ginger

2 teaspoons (10 ml) mixed spice

1 teaspoon (5 ml) bicarbonate
of soda

4 tablespoons (60 ml) sunflower oil

2 tablespoons (30 ml) molasses or
black treacle

2 tablespoons (30 ml) malt extract

2 eggs

4 tablespoons (60 ml) orange juice

3 bananas

4 oz (115 g) raisins

~ VARIATION ~
To make Spiced Honey and
Banana Cake; omit the ground
ginger and add another
1 teaspoon (5 ml) mixed spice;
omit the malt extract and the
molasses or treacle and add
4 tablespoons (60 ml) strong-
flavoured clear honey instead;
and replace the raisins with
either sultanas, coarsely
chopped ready-to-eat dried
apricots, or semi-dried
pineapple. If you choose to use
the pineapple, then you could
also replace the orange juice
with fresh pineapple juice.

~ COOK'S TIP ~
This cake improves as it keeps,
so if you can, store it for a few
days before eating.

NUTRITION NOTES
Per portion

Energy	148Kcals/621kJ
Fat	3.07g
Saturated Fat	0.53g
Cholesterol	19.3mg
Fibre	0.79g

1 ▲ Preheat the oven to 180°C/350°F/
Gas 4. Lightly grease and line a
7 × 11 in (18 × 28 cm) baking tin.

2 ▲ Mix in the sugar with some of
the flour and sift it into the bowl.
Sift the remaining flour into the bowl
with the spices and bicarbonate of soda.

3 ▲ Make a well in the centre, add
the oil, molasses or black treacle,
malt extract, eggs and orange juice
and mix together thoroughly.

4 ▲ Mash the bananas, then add
them to the bowl with the raisins
and mix together well.

5 ▲ Pour the mixture into the
baking tin and bake for about 35–40
minutes, or until the centre springs
back when lightly pressed.

6 ▲ Leave the cake in the tin to
cool for 5 minutes, then turn out on
to a wire rack and leave to cool
completely. Cut into 20 slices.

Apricot and Orange Roulade

This elegant dessert is very good served with a spoonful of natural yogurt or crème fraîche.

SERVES 6

4 egg whites
4 oz (115 g) golden caster sugar
2 oz (50 g) plain flour
finely grated rind of 1 small orange
3 tablespoons (45 ml) orange juice
2 teaspoons (10 ml) icing sugar and shreds of orange zest, to decorate

FOR THE FILLING

4 oz (115 g) dried apricots
4 oz (115 g) orange juice

NUTRITION NOTES
Per portion
Energy	203Kcals/853kJ
Fat	10.52g
Saturated Fat	2.05g
Cholesterol	0
Fibre	2.53g

1 Preheat the oven to 200°C/400°F/ Gas 6. Grease a 9 × 13 in (23 × 33 cm) Swiss roll tin and line it with non-stick baking paper. Grease the paper.

2 ▲ For the roulade, place the egg whites in a large bowl and whisk them until they hold peaks. Gradually add the sugar, whisking hard between each addition.

3 Fold in the flour, orange rind and juice. Spoon the mixture into the prepared tin and spread it evenly.

4 Bake for about 15–18 minutes, or until the sponge is firm and light golden in colour. Turn out on to a sheet of non-stick baking paper and roll it up Swiss roll-style loosely from one short side. Leave to cool.

5 ▲ For the filling, roughly chop the apricots, and place them in a saucepan with the orange juice. Cover the tin and leave to simmer until most of the liquid has been absorbed. Purée the apricots.

6 ▲ Unroll the roulade and spread with the apricot mixture. Roll up, arrange strips of paper diagonally across the roll, sprinkle lightly with lines of icing sugar, remove the paper and scatter with orange zest to serve.

~ COOK'S TIP ~
Make and bake the sponge mixture a day in advance and keep it, rolled with the paper, in a cool place. Fill it with the fruit purée 2–3 hours before serving.

Strawberry Roulade

A creamy fruit filling is delicious in a light roulade.

1 Preheat the oven to 200°C/400°F/ Gas 6. Oil a 9 × 13 in (23 × 33 cm) Swiss roll tin and line with non-stick baking paper.

2 ▲ Place the egg whites in a large bowl and whisk until they form soft peaks. Gradually whisk in the sugar. Fold in half of the sifted flour, then fold in the rest with the orange juice.

3 Spoon the mixture into the prepared tin, spreading evenly. Bake for 15–18 minutes, or until golden brown and firm to the touch.

4 ▲ Meanwhile, spread out a sheet of non-stick baking paper and sprinkle with caster sugar. Turn out the cake on to this and remove the lining paper. Roll up the sponge loosely from one short side, with the paper inside. Cool.

5 Unroll and remove the paper. Stir the strawberries into the fromage frais and spread over the sponge. Re-roll and serve decorated with strawberries.

SERVES 6

4 egg whites
4 oz (115 g) golden caster sugar
3 oz (75 g) plain flour, sifted
2 tablespoons (30 ml) orange juice
caster sugar, for sprinkling
4 oz (115 g) strawberries, chopped
5 oz (150 g) low-fat fromage frais
strawberries, to decorate

NUTRITION NOTES
Per portion

Energy	154Kcals/646kJ
Fat	0.24g
Saturated Fat	0.01g
Cholesterol	0.25mg
Fibre	0.61g

Peach Swiss Roll

A feather-light sponge enclosing peach jam – delicious at tea time.

SERVES 6–8

3 eggs	
4 oz (115 g) caster sugar, plus extra for sprinkling	
3 oz (75 g) plain flour, sifted	
1 tablespoon (15 ml) boiling water	
6 tablespoons (90 ml) peach jam	
icing sugar, for dusting (optional)	

~ COOK'S TIP ~

To decorate the Swiss roll with glacé icing, make the icing with 4 oz (115 g) icing sugar and enough warm water to make a thin glacé icing. Put in a piping bag fitted with a small writing nozzle and pipe lines over the top.

NUTRITION NOTES

Per portion

Energy	178Kcals/746kJ
Fat	2.54g
Saturated Fat	0.67g
Cholesterol	82.5mg
Fibre	0.33g

1 ▲ Preheat the oven to 200°C/ 400°F/Gas 6. Grease a 12 × 8 in (30 × 20 cm) Swiss roll tin and line with non-stick baking paper. Combine the eggs and sugar in a bowl. Beat with an electric whisk until thick and mousse-like (when the whisk is lifted, a trail should remain on the surface of the mixture for 15 seconds).

2 ▲ Carefully fold in the flour with a large metal spoon, then add the boiling water in the same way.

3 ▲ Spoon into the prepared tin, spread evenly to the edges and bake for about 10–12 minutes until the cake springs back when lightly pressed in the centre.

4 ▲ Spread a sheet of greaseproof paper on a flat surface, sprinkle it with caster sugar, then invert the cake on top. Peel off the paper.

5 ▲ Neatly trim the edges of the cake. Make a cut two-thirds of the way through the cake, about ½ in (1 cm) from the short edge nearest you.

6 ▲ Spread the cake with the peach jam and roll up quickly from the partially cut end. Hold in position for a minute, making sure the join is underneath. Cool on a wire rack. Decorate with piped glacé icing (see Cook's Tip) or dust with icing sugar before serving.

Chestnut and Orange Roulade

This moist cake is ideal to serve as a dessert.

SERVES 8

3 eggs, separated
4 oz (115 g) caster sugar
8 oz (225 g) canned unsweetened chestnut purée
grated rind and juice of 1 orange
icing sugar, for dusting
FOR THE FILLING
8 oz (225 g) low-fat soft cheese
1 tablespoon (15 ml) clear honey
1 orange

1 ▲ Preheat the oven to 180°C/350°/Gas 4. Grease a 12 × 8 in (30 × 20 cm) Swiss roll tin and line with baking paper. Whisk the egg yolks and sugar in a bowl until thick.

2 ▲ Put the chestnut purée in a separate bowl. Whisk in the orange rind and juice, then whisk the chestnut purée into the egg mixture.

3 ▲ Whisk the egg whites in a grease-free bowl until fairly stiff. Using a metal spoon, stir a generous spoonful of the whites into the chestnut mixture to lighten it, then fold in the rest. Spoon into the prepared tin and bake for 30 minutes until firm. Cool for 5 minutes, then cover with a clean damp tea towel until completely cold.

4 ▲ Meanwhile, make the filling. Mix the soft cheese with the honey. Add the orange rind, finely grated. Peel away all the pith from the orange, cut the fruit into segments, chop roughly and set aside. Add any juice to the cheese mixture, then beat until smooth. Mix in the orange.

5 ▲ Dust a sheet of greaseproof paper thickly with icing sugar. Carefully turn the roulade out on to the paper, then peel off the lining paper. Spread the filling over the roulade and roll up like a Swiss roll. Transfer to a plate and dust with some more icing sugar.

~ COOK'S TIP ~

Do not whisk the egg whites too stiffly or it will be difficult to fold them into the mixture and they will form lumps in the roulade.

NUTRITION NOTES

Per portion

Energy	185Kcals/775kJ
Fat	4.01g
Saturated Fat	1.47g
Cholesterol	76.25mg
Fibre	1.4g

Chocolate, Date and Walnut Pudding

Proper puddings are not totally taboo when you're cutting calories or fat – this one stays within the rules! Serve hot, with yogurt or skimmed-milk custard.

SERVES 4

1 oz (25 g) chopped walnuts
1 oz (25 g) chopped dates
2 eggs
1 teaspoon (5 ml) vanilla essence
2 tablespoons (30 ml) golden caster sugar
3 tablespoons (45 ml) plain flour
1 tablespoon (15 ml) cocoa powder
2 tablespoons (30 ml) skimmed milk

NUTRITION NOTES

Per portion
Energy	169Kcals/708kJ
Fat	8.1g
Saturated Fat	1.7g
Cholesterol	96mg
Fibre	1.8g

1 ▲ Preheat the oven to 180°C/ 350°F/Gas 4. Grease a 2 pint (1.2 litre) pudding basin and place a small circle of greaseproof or non-stick baking paper in the base. Spoon in the walnuts and dates.

2 ▲ Separate the eggs and place the yolks in a bowl with the vanilla essence and sugar. Place the bowl over a pan of hot water and whisk until the mixture is thick and pale.

3 ▲ Sift the flour and cocoa into the mixture and fold them in with a metal spoon. Stir in the milk, to soften the mixture slightly. Whisk the egg whites until they hold soft peaks and fold them in.

4 ▲ Spoon the mixture into the basin and bake for 40–45 minutes, or until the pudding is well risen and firm to the touch. Run a knife around the pudding, turn it out and serve.

Feather-light Peach Pudding

On chilly days, try this hot fruit pudding with its tantalizing sponge topping.

1 ▲ Preheat the oven to 180°C/ 350°F/Gas 4. Drain the peaches and put into a 1¾ pint (1 litre) dish with 2 tablespoons (30 ml) of the juice.

2 ▲ Put all the remaining ingredients, except the icing sugar into a mixing bowl. Beat for 3–4 minutes, until thoroughly combined.

3 ▲ Spoon the sponge mixture over the peaches and level the top evenly. Cook in the oven for 35–40 minutes, or until springy to the touch.

4 ▲ Lightly dust the top with icing sugar before serving hot with custard.

~ COOK'S TIP ~

For a simple sauce, blend 1 teaspoon (5 ml) arrowroot with 1 tablespoon (15 ml) peach juice in a small saucepan. Stir in the remaining peach juice from the can and simmer for 1 minute.

SERVES 4

14 oz (400 g) canned peach slices
2 oz (50 g) low-fat spread
1½ oz (40 g) soft light brown sugar
1 egg, beaten
2 oz (50 g) plain wholemeal flour
2 oz (50 g) plain flour
1 teaspoon (5 ml) baking powder
½ teaspoon (2.5 ml) ground cinnamon
4 tablespoons (60 ml) skimmed milk
½ teaspoon (2.5 ml) vanilla essence
2 teaspoons (10 ml) icing sugar
low-fat ready-to-serve custard

NUTRITION NOTES
Per portion
Energy	255Kcals/1071kJ
Fat	6.78g
Saturated Fat	1.57g
Cholesterol	0
Fibre	2.65g

Snowballs

A variation on the basic meringue recipe, these snowballs are made with cornflour. They make an excellent accompaniment to ice cream.

MAKES ABOUT 20

2 egg whites

4 oz (115 g) caster sugar

1 tablespoon (15 ml) cornflour, sifted

1 teaspoon (5 ml) white wine vinegar

¼ teaspoon (1.5 ml) vanilla essence

NUTRITION NOTES

Per portion	
Energy	29Kcal/124kJ
Fat	0.01g
Saturated Fat	0
Cholesterol	0
Fibre	0

1 ▲ Preheat the oven to 150°C/300°F/Gas 2. Line two baking sheets with non-stick baking paper. Whisk the egg whites in a large grease-free bowl until stiff, using an electric whisk.

2 ▲ Add the sugar, whisking until the meringue is very stiff. Whisk in the cornflour, vinegar and vanilla.

3 ▲ Drop teaspoonfuls of the mixture on to the baking sheets, shaping them into mounds, and bake for 30 minutes until crisp.

4 ▲ Remove from the oven and leave to cool on the baking sheet. When the snowballs are cold, remove them from the baking paper with a palette knife.

Muscovado Meringues

These light brown meringues are extremely low in fat and are delicious served sandwiched together with a fresh fruit soft cheese filling.

1 ▲ Preheat the oven to 160°C/ 325°F/Gas 3. Line two baking sheets with non-stick baking paper. Press the sugar through a metal sieve.

2 ▲ Whisk the egg whites in a clean, dry bowl, until very stiff and dry, then whisk in the sugar, about 1 tablespoon (15 ml) at a time, until the meringue is very thick and glossy.

3 ▲ Spoon small mounds of the meringue mixture on to the prepared baking sheets.

4 ▲ Sprinkle the meringues with the chopped walnuts. Bake for 30 minutes. Cool for 5 minutes on the baking sheets, then leave on a wire rack.

MAKES ABOUT 20

4 oz (115 g) light muscovado sugar	
2 egg whites	
1 teaspoon (5 ml) finely chopped walnuts	

NUTRITION NOTES
Per portion

Energy	197Kcals/826kJ
Fat	6.8g
Saturated Fat	1.4g
Cholesterol	25mg
Fibre	0.7g

Coffee Sponge Drops

These are delicious on their own, but taste even better with a filling made by mixing low-fat soft cheese with drained and chopped stem ginger.

MAKES 12

2 oz (50 g) plain flour
1 tablespoon (15 ml) instant coffee powder
2 eggs
3 oz (75 g) caster sugar
FOR THE FILLING
4 oz (115 g) low-fat soft cheese
1½ oz (40 g) chopped stem ginger

1 ▲ Preheat the oven to 190°C/ 375°F/Gas 5. Line two baking sheets with non-stick baking paper. Beat the soft cheese and stem ginger together. Chill until required. Sift the flour and coffee powder together.

3 ▲ Carefully add the sifted flour and coffee mixture and gently fold in with a metal spoon, being careful not to knock out any air.

2 ▲ Combine the eggs and caster sugar in a bowl. Beat with a hand-held electric whisk until thick and mousse-like. (When the whisk is lifted, a trail should remain on the surface of the mixture for at least 15 seconds.)

4 ▲ Spoon the mixture into a piping bag fitted with a ½ in (1 cm) plain nozzle. Pipe 1½ in (4 cm) rounds on the baking sheets. Bake for 12 minutes. Cool on a wire rack, then sandwich together with the filling.

~ COOK'S TIP ~
As an alternative to stem ginger in the filling, try walnuts.

NUTRITION NOTES
Per portion
Energy	69Kcals/290kJ
Fat	1.36g
Saturated Fat	0.5g
Cholesterol	33.33mg
Fibre	0.29g

Raspberry Vacherin

Meringue rounds filled with orange-flavoured fromage frais and fresh raspberries make a perfect dinner-party dessert.

SERVES 6

3 egg whites

6 oz (175 g) caster sugar

1 teaspoon (5 ml) chopped almonds

icing sugar, for dusting

raspberry leaves, to
    decorate (optional)

FOR THE FILLING

6 oz (175 g) low-fat soft cheese

1–2 tablespoons (15–30 ml)
    clear honey

1 tablespoon (15 ml) Cointreau

4 fl oz (120 ml) low-fat
    fromage frais

8 oz (225 g) raspberries

~ COOK'S TIP ~

When making the meringue,
whisk the egg whites until they
are so stiff that you can turn
the bowl upside down without
them falling out.

NUTRITION NOTES

Per portion

Energy	248Kcals/1041kJ
Fat	2.22g
Saturated Fat	0.82g
Cholesterol	4mg
Fibre	1.06g

1 ▲ Preheat the oven to 140°C/ 275°F/Gas 1. Draw an 8 in (20 cm) circle on two pieces of non-stick baking paper. Turn the paper over so the marking is on the underside and use it to line two heavy baking sheets.

2 ▲ Whisk the egg whites in a grease-free bowl until very stiff, then gradually whisk in the caster sugar to make a stiff meringue mixture.

3 ▲ Spoon the mixture on to the circles on the prepared baking sheets, spreading the meringue evenly to the edges. Sprinkle one meringue round with the chopped almonds.

4 ▲ Bake for 1½–2 hours, then carefully lift the meringue rounds off the baking sheets, peel away the paper and cool on a wire rack.

5 ▲ To make the filling, cream the soft cheese with the honey and liqueur in a bowl. Fold in the fromage frais and raspberries, reserving three for decoration.

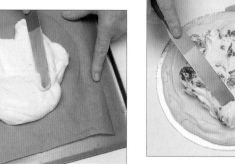

6 ▲ Place the plain meringue round on a board, spread with the filling and top with the nut-covered round. Dust with icing sugar, transfer to a serving plate and decorate with the reserved raspberries, and a sprig of raspberry leaves, if liked.

Baked Blackberry Cheesecake

This light, low-fat cheesecake is best made with wild blackberries, but cultivated ones will do; or substitute other soft fruit, such as loganberries, raspberries or blueberries.

SERVES 5

6 oz (175 g) low-fat cottage cheese
5 oz (150 g) low-fat natural yogurt
1 tablespoon (15 ml) plain wholemeal flour
1 oz (25 g) golden caster sugar
1 egg
1 egg white
finely grated rind and juice of ½ lemon
7 oz (200 g) fresh or frozen and thawed blackberries

~ COOK'S TIP ~

If you prefer to use canned blackberries, choose those canned in natural juice and drain the fruit well before adding it to the cheesecake mixture. The juice can be served with the cheesecake, but this will increase the total calories.

NUTRITION NOTES

Per portion

Energy	103Kcals/437kJ
Fat	2g
Saturated Fat	0.8g
Cholesterol	41mg
Fibre	1.6g

1 ▲ Preheat the oven to 180°C/350°F/Gas 4. Lightly grease and line base of a 7 in (18 cm) sandwich tin.

2 ▲ Place the cottage cheese in a food processor and process until smooth. Alternatively, rub it through a sieve, to obtain a smooth mixture.

3 ▲ Add the yogurt, flour, sugar, egg and egg white and mix. Add the lemon rind, juice and blackberries, reserving a few for decoration.

4 ▲ Tip the mixture into the tin and bake for 30–35 minutes, or until it is just set. Turn off the oven and leave for a further 30 minutes.

5 ▲ Run a knife around the edge of the cheesecake, then turn it out. Remove the lining paper and place the cheesecake on a warm serving plate.

6 Decorate the cheesecake with the reserved blackberries and serve it warm.

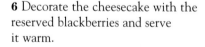

Mango and Amaretti Strudel

Fresh mango and crushed amaretti wrapped in wafer-thin filo pastry make a special treat that is equally delicious made with apricots or plums.

SERVES 4

1 large mango
grated rind of 1 lemon
2 amaretti biscuits
1 oz (25 g) demerara sugar
4 tablespoons (60 ml) wholemeal breadcrumbs
2 sheets filo pastry, each 19 x 11 in (48 x 28 cm)
¾ oz (20 g) soft margarine, melted
1 tablespoon (15 ml) chopped almonds
icing sugar, for dusting

```
~ COOK'S TIP ~

The easiest way to prepare a
mango is to cut horizontally
through the fruit, keeping the
knife blade close to the stone.
Repeat on the other side of the
stone and peel off the skin.
Remove the remaining skin
and flesh from around the stone.
```

NUTRITION NOTES
Per portion
Energy   239Kcals/1006kJ
Fat   8.45g
Saturated Fat   4.43g
Cholesterol   17.25mg
Fibre   3.3g

1 ▲ Preheat the oven to 190°C/ 375°F/Gas 5. Lightly grease a large baking sheet. Halve, stone and peel the mango. Cut the flesh into cubes, then place them in a bowl, and sprinkle with grated lemon rind.

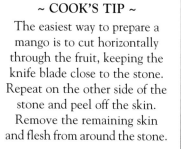

2 ▲ Crush the amaretti biscuits and mix them with the demerara sugar and the wholemeal breadcrumbs.

3 ▲ Lay one sheet of filo on a flat surface and brush with a quarter of the margarine. Top with the second sheet, brush with one-third of the remaining margarine, then fold both sheets over to make a rectangle 11 × 9 in (28 × 23 cm). Brush with half the remaining margarine.

4 ▲ Sprinkle the filo with the amaretti mixture, leaving a 2 in (5 cm) border on each long side. Arrange the mango cubes over the top.

5 ▲ Roll up the filo from one of the long sides. Lift the strudel on to the baking sheet with the join underneath. Brush with the remaining melted margarine and sprinkle with the chopped almonds.

6 ▲ Bake for 20–25 minutes until golden brown, then transfer to a board. Dust with the icing sugar, slice diagonally and serve warm.

Blueberry and Orange Crêpe Baskets

Impress your guests with these pretty, fruit-filled crêpes. When blueberries are out of season, replace them with other soft fruit, such as raspberries.

SERVES 6

FOR THE PANCAKES

5 oz (150 g) plain flour

pinch of salt

2 egg whites

7 fl oz (200 ml) skimmed milk

¼ pint (150 ml) orange juice

FOR THE FILLING

4 medium-size oranges

8 oz (225 g) blueberries

1 ▲ Preheat the oven to 200°C/ 400°F/Gas 6. To make the pancakes, sift the flour and salt into a bowl. Make a well in the centre of the flour and add the egg whites, milk and orange juice. Whisk hard, until all the liquid has been incorporated and the batter is smooth and bubbly.

2 ▲ Lightly grease a heavy or non-stick pancake pan and heat until it is very hot. Pour in just enough batter to cover the base of the pan, swirling it to cover the pan evenly.

3 ▲ Cook until the pancake has set and is golden, and then turn it to cook the other side. Remove the pancake to a sheet of absorbent kitchen paper, and then cook the remaining batter, to make a total of 6–8 pancakes.

4 ▲ Place six small ovenproof bowls or moulds on a baking sheet and arrange the pancakes over these. Bake the pancakes in the oven for about 10 minutes, until they are crisp and set into the shape of the moulds. Lift the "baskets" off the moulds.

5 ▲ For the filling, pare a thin piece of orange rind from one orange and cut it in fine strips. Blanch the strips in boiling water for 30 seconds, rinse in cold water and set aside. Cut the peel and white pith from the oranges.

6 ▲ Divide the oranges into segments, catching the juice, combine with the blueberries and warm them gently. Spoon the fruit into the baskets and scatter the shreds of rind over the top. Serve with yogurt or light crème fraîche.

~ COOK'S TIP ~

Don't fill the pancake baskets until you're ready to serve them because they will absorb the fruit juice and begin to soften.

NUTRITION NOTES

Per portion	
Energy	159Kcals/673kJ
Fat	0.5g
Saturated Fat	0.1g
Cholesterol	1mg
Fibre	3.3g

Filo and Apricot Purses

Filo pastry is very easy to use and is low in fat. Keep a packet in the freezer ready for rustling up a speedy tea-time treat.

MAKES 12

4 oz (115 g) dried apricots

3 tablespoons (45 ml) apricot compote or conserve

3 amaretti biscuits, crushed

3 sheets filo pastry

4 teaspoons (20 ml) soft margarine, melted

icing sugar, for dusting

NUTRITION NOTES

Per portion

Energy	58Kcals/245kJ
Fat	1.85g
Saturated Fat	0.4g
Cholesterol	0.12mg
Fibre	0.74g

1 ▲ Preheat the oven to 180°C/ 350°F/Gas 4. Grease two baking sheets. Chop the apricots, put them in a bowl and stir in the apricot compote. Add the crushed amaretti biscuits and mix well.

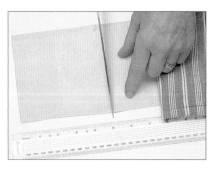

2 ▲ Cut the filo pastry into 24 5 in (13 cm) squares, pile the squares on top of each other and cover with a clean tea towel to prevent the pastry from drying and becoming brittle.

3 ▲ Lay one pastry square on a flat surface, brush lightly with melted margarine and lay another square diagonally on top. Brush the top square with melted margarine. Spoon a small mound of apricot mixture in the centre of the pastry, bring up the edges and pinch together in a money-bag shape. Repeat with the remaining squares to make 12 purses.

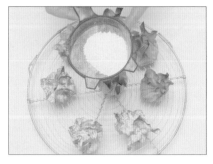

4 ▲ Arrange the purses on the prepared baking sheets and bake for 5–8 minutes until golden brown. Dust with icing sugar and serve warm.

Filo Scrunchies

Quick and easy to make, these pastries are ideal to serve at tea time. Eat them warm or they will lose their crispness.

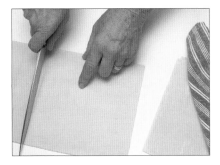

1 ▲ Preheat the oven to 190°C/ 375°F/Gas 5. Halve the apricots or plums, remove the stones and slice the fruit. Cut the filo pastry into 12 7 in (18 cm) squares. Pile the squares on top of each other and cover with a clean tea towel.

4 ▲ Place the scrunchies on a baking sheet. Bake for 8–10 minutes until golden brown, then loosen the scrunchies from the baking sheet with a palette knife and transfer to a wire rack. Dust with icing sugar and serve at once.

MAKES 6

5 apricots or plums
4 sheets filo pastry
4 tbsp (20 ml) soft margarine, melted
2 oz (50 g) demerara sugar
2 tbsp (30 ml) flaked almonds
icing sugar, for dusting

NUTRITION NOTES
Per portion
Energy	132Kcals/555kJ
Fat	4.19g
Saturated Fat	0.63g
Cholesterol	0
Fibre	0.67g

2 ▲ Remove one square of filo and brush it with melted margarine. Lay a second filo square on top, then, using your fingers, mould the pastry into folds. Make five more scrunchies in the same way, working quickly so that the pastry does not dry out.

3 ▲ Arrange a few slices of fruit in the folds of each scrunchie, then sprinkle generously with the demerara sugar and flaked almonds.

Plum Filo Pockets

These attractive party parcels are high in fibre as well as being a tasty treat.

SERVES 4

4 oz (115 g) skimmed milk soft cheese

1 tablespoon (15 ml) light
   muscovado sugar

½ teaspoon (2.5 ml) ground cloves

8 large plums, halved and stoned

8 sheets filo pastry

sunflower oil, for brushing

icing sugar, to sprinkle

NUTRITION NOTES

Per portion	
Energy	188Kcals/790kJ
Fat	1.87g
Saturated Fat	0.27g
Cholesterol	0.29mg
Fibre	2.55g

1 ▲ Preheat the oven to 220°C/
425°F/Gas 7. Mix together the
cheese, sugar and cloves.

2 ▲ Sandwich the plum halves back
together with a spoonful of the
cheese mixture in each plum.

3 Spread out the pastry and cut into
16 pieces, about 9 in (23 cm) square.
Brush one lightly with oil and place
a second at a diagonal on top. Repeat
with the remaining squares.

4 ▲ Place a plum on each pastry
square, and gather the corners
together. Place on a baking sheet.
Bake for 15–18 minutes, until
golden, then dust with icing sugar.

Glazed Apricot Sponge

Puddings can be very high in saturated fat, but this one uses the minimum of oil and no eggs.

1 ▲ Preheat the oven to 180°C/350°F/ Gas 4. Lightly oil a 1½ pint (900 ml) pudding basin. Spoon in the syrup.

2 ▲ Drain the apricots and reserve the juice. Arrange about eight halves in the basin. Purée the rest of the apricots with the juice and set aside.

3 ▲ Mix the flour, breadcrumbs, sugar and cinnamon, then beat in the oil and milk. Spoon into the basin and bake for 50–55 minutes, or until firm and golden. Turn out and serve with the puréed fruit as a sauce.

SERVES 4

2 teaspoons (10 ml) golden syrup
14½ oz (411 g) can apricot halves in fruit juice
5 oz (150 g) self-raising flour
3 oz (75 g) fresh breadcrumbs
3½ oz (90 g) light muscovado sugar
1 teaspoon (5 ml) ground cinnamon
2 tablespoons (30 ml) sunflower oil
6 fl oz (175 ml) skimmed milk

NUTRITION NOTES
Per portion

Energy	364Kcals/1530kJ
Fat	6.47g
Saturated Fat	0.89g
Cholesterol	0.88mg
Fibre	2.37g

Latticed Peaches

An elegant dessert; it certainly doesn't look low in fat, but it really is. Use canned peach halves when fresh peaches are out of season, or if you're short of time.

Serves 6

For the pastry

4 oz (115 g) plain flour

3 tablespoons (45 ml) butter or sunflower margarine

3 tablespoons (45 ml) low-fat natural yogurt

2 tablespoons (30 ml) orange juice

skimmed milk, for glaze

For the filling

3 ripe peaches or nectarines

3 tablespoons (45 ml) ground almonds

2 tablespoons (30 ml) low-fat natural yogurt

finely grated rind of 1 small orange

½ teaspoon (1.5 ml) natural almond essence

For the sauce

1 ripe peach or nectarine

3 tablespoons (45 ml) orange juice

~ COOK'S TIP ~

This dessert is best eaten fairly fresh from the oven, as the pastry can toughen slightly if left to stand. So assemble the peaches in their pastry on a baking sheet, chill in the fridge, and bake just before serving.

NUTRITION NOTES

Per portion	
Energy	219Kcal/916kJ
Fat	10.8g
Saturated Fat	1.6g
Cholesterol	1mg
Fibre	2.4g

1 ▲ For the pastry, sift the flour into a bowl and, using your fingertips, rub in the butter or margarine evenly. Stir in the yogurt and orange juice to bind the mixture into a firm dough.

2 ▲ Roll out about half the pastry thinly and use a biscuit cutter to stamp out rounds about 3 in (7.5 cm) in diameter, slightly larger than the circumference of the peaches. Place on a lightly greased baking sheet.

3 ▲ Skin the peaches or nectarines, halve and remove the stones. Mix together the almonds, yogurt, orange rind and almond essence. Spoon into each peach half and place, cut-side down, on to the pastry rounds.

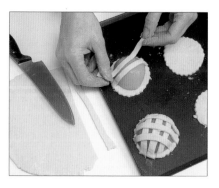

4 ▲ Roll out the remaining pastry thinly and cut into thin strips. Arrange the strips over the peaches to form a lattice, brushing with milk to secure firmly. Trim off the ends.

5 ▲ Chill in the fridge for 30 minutes. Preheat the oven to 200°C/400°F/ Gas 6. Brush with milk and bake for 15–18 minutes, until golden brown.

6 ▲ For the sauce, skin the peach or nectarine and halve it to remove the stone. Place the flesh in a food processor, with the orange juice, and purée it until smooth. Serve the peaches hot, with the peach sauce spooned around.

EVERYDAY BREADS

THOUGH THE PACE OF TODAY'S LIFE
LEAVES LITTLE TIME FOR BAKING,
BREADMAKING CAN BE VERY
THERAPEUTIC. THE PROCESS IS
SIMPLE YET INFINITELY VARIABLE,
AS THE LOAVES THAT FOLLOW
PROVE. ROLL UP YOUR SLEEVES AND
CREATE A TRADITION.

White Bread

MAKES 2 LOAVES

2 fl oz (65 ml) lukewarm water
1 tablespoon active dried yeast
2 tablespoons sugar
16 fl oz (450 ml) lukewarm milk
1 oz (30 g) butter or margarine, at room temperature
2 teaspoons salt
1 lb 14 oz–2 lbs (850–900 g) strong flour

1 Combine the water, dried yeast and 1 tablespoon of sugar in a measuring jug and leave to stand for 15 minutes until the mixture is frothy.

2 ▼ Pour the milk into a large bowl. Add the remaining sugar, the butter or margarine, and salt. Stir in the yeast mixture.

3 Stir in the flour, 5 oz (140 g) at a time, until a stiff dough is obtained. Alternatively, use a food processor.

4 ▲ Transfer the dough to a floured surface. To knead, push the dough away from you with the palm of your hand, then fold it towards you, and push it away again. Repeat until the dough is smooth and elastic.

5 Place the dough in a large greased bowl, cover with a plastic bag, and leave to rise in a warm place until doubled in volume, 2–3 hours.

6 Grease 2 9 × 5 in (23 × 13 cm) tins.

7 ▲ Punch down the risen dough with your fist and divide in half. Form into a loaf shape and place in the tins, seam-side down. Cover and let rise in a warm place until almost doubled in volume, about 45 minutes.

8 Preheat a 375°F/190°C/Gas 5 oven.

9 Bake until firm and brown, 45–50 minutes. Turn out and tap the bottom of a loaf: if it sounds hollow the loaf is done. If necessary, return to the oven and bake a few minutes more. Let cool on a rack.

Country Bread

MAKES 2 LOAVES

| 12 oz (350 g) wholewheat flour |
| 12 oz (350 g) plain flour |
| 5 oz (140 g) strong plain flour |
| 4 tsp salt |
| 2 oz (55 g) butter, at room temperature |
| 16 fl oz (450 ml) lukewarm milk |
| FOR THE STARTER |
| 1 tbsp active dry yeast |
| 8 fl oz (250 ml) lukewarm water |
| 5 oz (140 g) plain flour |
| 1/4 tsp caster sugar |

1 ▲ For the starter, combine the yeast, water, flour and sugar in a bowl and stir with a fork. Cover and leave in a warm place for 2–3 hours, or leave overnight in a cool place.

2 Place the flours, salt and butter in a food processor and process just until blended, 1–2 minutes.

3 Stir together the milk and starter, then slowly pour into the processor, with the motor running, until the mixture forms a dough. If necessary, add more water. Alternatively, the dough can be mixed by hand. Transfer to a floured surface and knead until smooth and elastic.

4 Place in an ungreased bowl, cover with a plastic bag, and leave to rise in a warm place until doubled in volume, about 1 1/2 hours.

5 Transfer to a floured surface and knead briefly. Return to the bowl and leave to rise until tripled in volume, about 1 1/2 hours.

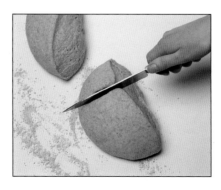

6 ▲ Divide the dough in half. Cut off one-third of the dough from each half and shape into balls. Shape the larger remaining portion of each half into balls. Grease a baking sheet.

7 ▲ For each loaf, top the large ball with the small ball and press the centre with the handle of a wooden spoon to secure. Cover with a plastic bag, slash the top, and leave to rise.

8 Preheat a 400°F/200°C/Gas 6 oven. Dust the dough with flour and bake until the top is browned and the bottom sounds hollow when tapped, 45–50 minutes. Cool on a rack.

Split Tin

MAKES 1 LOAF

1¼ lb (500 g) unbleached white bread flour, plus extra for dusting
2 teaspoons (10 ml) salt
½ oz (15 g) fresh yeast
½ pint (300 ml) lukewarm water
4 tablespoons (60 ml) lukewarm milk

As its name suggests, this homely loaf is so called because of the centre split. Some bakers mould the dough in two loaves – they join together whilst proving but retain the characteristic crack after baking.

1 Lightly grease a 2 lb (900 g) loaf tin 7¼ × 4½ in (18.5 × 12 cm). Sift the flour and salt together and make a well in the centre. Mix the yeast with half the lukewarm water in a jug, then stir in the remaining water.

2 Pour the yeast mixture into the centre of the flour and using your fingers, mix in a little flour. Gradually mix in more of the flour from around the edge of the bowl to form a batter.

3 Sprinkle a little more flour from around the edge over the batter and leave in a warm place to "sponge". Bubbles will appear in the batter after about 20 minutes. Add the milk and remaining flour; mix to a firm dough.

4 ▲ Place on a lightly floured surface and knead for about 10 minutes until smooth and elastic. Place in a lightly oiled bowl, cover with lightly oiled clear film and leave to rise, in a warm place, for 1–1¼ hours, or until nearly doubled in bulk.

5 Knock back the dough and turn out on to a lightly floured surface. Shape it into a rectangle. Roll up lengthways, tuck the ends under and place seam side down in the tin. Cover and leave to rise for about 20–30 minutes, or until nearly doubled in bulk.

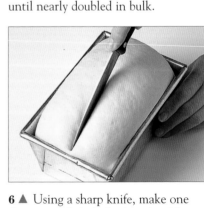

6 ▲ Using a sharp knife, make one deep central slash the length of the bread; dust with flour. Leave for 10–15 minutes.

7 Meanwhile, preheat the oven to 230°C/450°F/Gas 8. Bake for 15 minutes, then reduce the oven temperature to 200°C/400°F/Gas 6. Bake for 20–25 minutes more, or until the bread is golden.

Plaited Loaf

MAKES 1 LOAF

1 tablespoon active dried yeast
1 teaspoon honey
8 fl oz (250 ml) lukewarm milk
2 oz (55 g) butter, melted
15 oz (420 g) strong flour
1 teaspoon salt
1 egg, lightly beaten
1 egg yolk beaten with 1 teaspoon milk, for glazing

1 ▼ Combine the yeast, honey, milk and butter. Stir and leave for 15 minutes to dissolve.

2 In a large bowl, mix together the flour and salt. Make a well in the centre and add the yeast mixture and egg. With a wooden spoon, stir from the centre, incorporating flour with each turn, to obtain a rough dough.

3 Transfer to a floured surface and knead until smooth and elastic. Place in a clean bowl, cover and leave to rise in a warm place until doubled in volume, about 1½ hours.

4 Grease a baking sheet. Punch down the dough and divide into three equal pieces. Roll to shape each piece into a long thin strip.

5 ▲ Begin plaiting with the centre strip, tucking in the ends. Cover loosely and leave to rise in a warm place for 30 minutes.

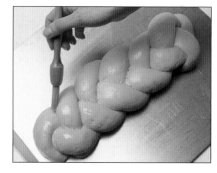

6 ▲ Preheat the oven to 375°F/ 190°C/Gas 5 oven. Place the bread in a cool place while the oven heats. Brush with the glaze and bake until golden, for 40–45 minutes. Turn out onto a rack to cool.

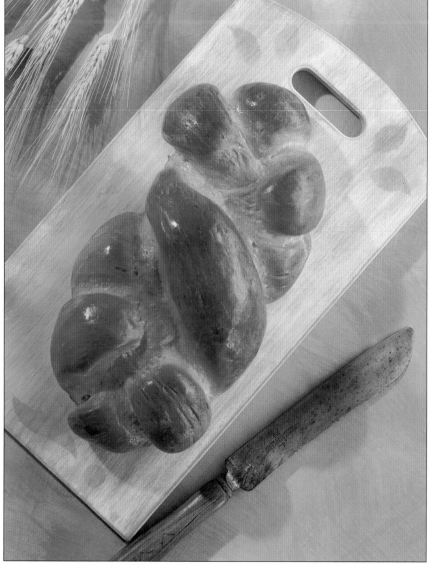

Sourdough Bread

MAKES 1 LOAF

12 oz (350 g) flour
1 tablespoon salt
8 fl oz (250 ml) Sourdough Starter
4 fl oz (120 ml) lukewarm water

1 ▲ Combine the flour and salt in a large bowl. Make a well in the centre and add the starter and water. With a wooden spoon, stir from the centre, incorporating more flour with each turn, to obtain a rough dough.

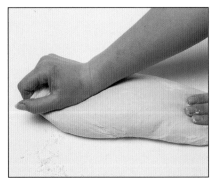

2 ▲ Transfer the dough to a floured surface. To knead, push the dough away from you with the palm of your hand, then fold it towards you, and push it away again. Repeat the process until the dough has become smooth and elastic.

3 Place in a clean bowl, cover, and leave to rise in a warm place until doubled in volume, about 2 hours.

4 Lightly grease an 8 × 4 in (20 × 10 cm) bread tin.

5 ▼ Punch down the dough with your fist. Knead briefly, then form into a loaf shape and place in the tin, seam-side down. Cover with a plastic bag, and leave to rise in a warm place, for about 1½ hours.

6 Preheat the oven to 425°F/220°C/Gas 7. Dust the top of the loaf with flour, then score lengthways. Bake for 15 minutes. Lower the heat to 375°F/190°C/Gas 5 and bake for about 30 minutes more, or until the bottom sounds hollow when tapped.

Sourdough Starter

MAKES 1¼ PINTS (750 ML)

1 teaspoon active dried yeast
6 fl oz (175 ml) lukewarm water
2 oz (50 g) flour

~ COOK'S TIP ~

After using, feed the starter with a handful of flour and enough water to restore it to a thick batter. The starter can be refrigerated for up to 1 week, but must be brought back to room temperature before using.

1 ▲ For the starter, combine the yeast and water, stir and leave for 15 minutes to dissolve.

2 ▼ Sprinkle over the flour and whisk until it forms a batter. Cover and leave to rise in a warm place for at least 24 hours or preferably 2–4 days, before using.

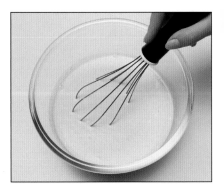

Rye Bread

Rye bread is popular in northern Europe and makes an excellent base for open sandwiches.

MAKES 2 LOAVES

12 oz (350 g) wholemeal flour
8 oz (225 g) rye flour
4 oz (115 g) strong white flour
1½ teaspoons (7.5ml) salt
2 tablespoons (30 ml) caraway seeds
16 fl oz (475 ml) warm water
2 teaspoons (10 ml) dried yeast
pinch of sugar
2 tablespoons (30 ml) molasses

2 ▲ Put half the water in a jug. Sprinkle the yeast on top. Add the sugar, mix and leave for 10 minutes.

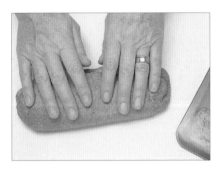

5 ▲ Turn the dough on to a floured surface and knead for 2 minutes. Divide the dough in half, then shape into two 9 in (23 cm) long oval loaves. Flatten the loaves slightly and place them on the baking sheet.

1 ▲ Put the flours and salt in a bowl. Set aside 1 tsp (5 ml) of the caraway seeds and add the rest to the bowl.

3 ▲ Make a well in the flour mixture, then add the yeast mixture with the molasses and the remaining water. Gradually incorporate the flour and mix to a soft dough, adding a little extra water, if necessary.

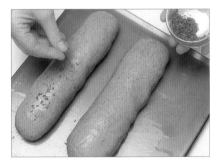

6 ▲ Brush with water and sprinkle with the remaining caraway seeds. Cover and leave in a warm place for about 40 minutes, until well risen. Preheat the oven to 200°C/400°F/ Gas 6. Bake the loaves for 30 minutes or until they sound hollow when tapped underneath. Cool on a wire rack.

~ COOK'S TIP ~

To make caraway-seed bread rolls, divide each of the two flattened loaves into eight equal portions. Place them on the baking sheet, brush with water and sprinkle with caraway seeds. Vary the topping by using poppy seeds, if you prefer.

4 ▲ Transfer to a floured surface and knead for 5 minutes until smooth and elastic. Return to the clean bowl, cover and leave in a warm place for about 2 hours until doubled in bulk. Grease a baking sheet.

Pecan Rye Bread

MAKES 2 LOAVES

1¹/₂ tablespoons active dried yeast
24 fl oz (700 ml) lukewarm water
1 lb 8 oz (700 g) strong flour
1 lb 2 oz (500 g) rye flour
2 tablespoons salt
1 tablespoon honey
2 teaspoons caraway seeds, (optional)
4 oz (115 g) butter, at room temperature
8 oz (225 g) pecans, chopped

1 Combine the yeast and 4 fl oz (125 ml) of the water. Stir and leave for 15 minutes to dissolve.

2 In the bowl of an electric mixer, combine the flours, salt, honey, caraway seeds and butter. With the dough hook, mix on low speed until well blended.

3 Add the yeast mixture and the remaining water and mix on medium speed until the dough forms a ball.

4 ▲ Transfer to a floured surface and knead in the pecans.

5 Return the dough to a bowl, cover with a plastic bag and leave in a warm place until doubled, about 2 hours.

6 Grease 2 8¹/₂ × 4¹/₂ in (21.5 × 11.5 cm) bread tins.

7 ▲ Punch down the risen dough.

8 Divide the dough in half and form into loaves. Place in the tins, seam side down. Dust the tops with flour.

9 Cover with plastic bags and leave to rise in a warm place until doubled in volume, about 1 hour.

10 Preheat a 375°F/190°C/Gas 5 oven.

11 ▼ Bake until the bottoms sound hollow when tapped, 45–50 minutes. Cool on racks.

Sourdough Rye Bread

MAKES 2 LOAVES

2 teaspoons active dried yeast
4 fl oz (125 ml) lukewarm water
1 oz (30 g) butter, melted
1 tablespoon salt
4 oz (115 g) wholemeal flour
14–16 oz (400–450 g) plain flour
1 egg mixed with 1 tablespoon water, for glazing
FOR THE STARTER
1 tablespoon active dried yeast
12 fl oz (350 ml) lukewarm water
3 tablespoons black treacle
2 tablespoons caraway seeds
9 oz (250 g) rye flour

1   For the starter, combine the dried yeast and water, stir and leave for 15 minutes to dissolve.

2 ▲   Stir in the black treacle, caraway seeds and rye flour. Cover and leave in a warm place for 2–3 days.

3   In a large bowl, combine the dried yeast and water, stir and leave for 10 minutes. Stir in the melted butter, salt, wholemeal flour and 14 oz (400 g) of the plain flour.

4 ▲   Make a well in the centre and pour in the starter.

5   Stir to obtain a rough dough, then transfer to a floured surface and knead until smooth and elastic. Return to the bowl, cover and leave to rise in a warm place until doubled in volume, about 2 hours.

6   Grease a large baking sheet. Knock back the dough and knead briefly. Cut the dough in half and form each half into log-shaped loaves.

7 ▼   Place the loaves on the baking sheet and score the tops with a sharp knife. Cover and leave to rise in a warm place until almost doubled, about 50 minutes.

8   Preheat the oven to 375°F/190°C/ Gas 5. Brush the loaves with the egg wash to glaze them, then bake until the bottoms sound hollow when tapped, about 50–55 minutes. If the tops brown too quickly, place a sheet of foil over the tops to protect them. Cool on a wire rack.

Buttermilk Graham Bread

SERVES 8

2 teaspoons active dried yeast

4 fl oz (120 ml) lukewarm water

8 oz (225 g) graham or wholewheat flour

12 oz (350 g) plain flour

4½ oz (130 g) cornmeal

2 teaspoons salt

2 tablespoons sugar

4 tablespoons butter, at room temperature

16 fl oz (475 ml) lukewarm buttermilk

1 beaten egg, for glazing

sesame seeds, for sprinkling

1 Combine the yeast and water, stir, and leave for 15 minutes to dissolve.

2 ▲ Mix together the two flours, cornmeal, salt and sugar in a large bowl. Make a well in the centre and pour in the yeast mixture, then add the butter and the buttermilk.

3 ▲ Stir from the centre, mixing in the flour until a rough dough is formed. If too stiff, use your hands.

4 ▲ Transfer to a floured surface and knead until smooth. Place in a clean bowl, cover, and leave in a warm place for 2–3 hours.

5 ▲ Grease 2 8 in (20 cm) square baking tins. Punch down the dough. Divide into eight pieces and roll them into balls. Place four in each tin. Cover and leave in a warm place for about 1 hour.

6 Preheat the oven to 375°F/190°C/ Gas 5. Brush with the glaze, then sprinkle over the sesame seeds. Bake for about 50 minutes, or until the bottoms sound hollow when tapped. Cool on a wire rack.

Bread Stick

A bread stick is perfect for garlic bread or sandwiches.

1 Combine the yeast and water, stir, and leave for 15 minutes to dissolve. Stir in the salt.

2 Add the flour, 4 oz (115 g) at a time. Beat in with a wooden spoon, adding just enough flour to obtain a dough. Alternatively, use an electric mixer with a dough hook attachment.

3 Transfer to a floured surface and knead until smooth and elastic.

4 Shape into a ball, place in a greased bowl, and cover with a plastic bag. Leave to rise in a warm place until doubled in volume, for 2–4 hours.

5 ▲ Transfer to a lightly floured board, halve the dough and shape into two long loaves. Place on a baking sheet sprinkled with cornmeal, and leave to rise for 5 minutes.

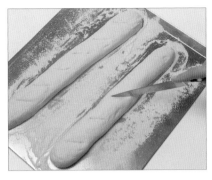

6 ▲ Score the tops in several places with a very sharp knife. Brush with water and place in a cold oven. Set a pan of boiling water on the bottom of the oven and set the oven to 200°C/400°F/Gas 6. Bake for about 40 minutes. Cool on a rack.

MAKES 2 LOAVES

2 teaspoons (10 ml) active dry yeast
16 fl oz (475 ml) lukewarm water
1 teaspoon (5 ml) salt
1½–2 lb (675–900 g) plain flour
cornmeal, for sprinkling

Three Grain Bread

A mixture of grains gives this close-textured bread a delightful nutty flavour. Make two smaller twists, if preferred.

MAKES 1 LOAF

16 fl oz (475 ml) warm water
2 teaspoons (10 ml) dried yeast
pinch of sugar
8 oz (225 g) strong white flour
1½ teaspoons (7.5 ml) salt
8 oz (225 g) malted brown flour
8 oz (225 g) rye flour
2 tablespoons (30 ml) linseed
3 oz (75 g) medium oatmeal
3 tablespoons (45 ml) sunflower seeds
2 tablespoons (30 ml) malt extract

1 ▲ Put half the water in a jug. Sprinkle the yeast on top. Add the sugar, mix and leave for 10 minutes.

2 ▲ Sift the white flour and salt into a bowl and add the other flours. Set aside 1 teaspoon (5 ml) of the linseed and add the rest to the flour mixture with the oatmeal and sunflower seeds. Add the yeast mixture to the bowl with the malt extract and the remaining water.

3 Gradually incorporate the flour.

4 ▲ Mix to a soft dough, adding extra water if necessary. Turn out on to a floured surface and knead for 5 minutes until smooth and elastic. Return to the clean bowl, cover with a damp dish towel and leave to rise for about 2 hours until doubled in bulk.

5 ▲ Grease a baking sheet. Turn the dough on to a floured surface, knead for 2 minutes, then divide in half. Roll each half into a 12 in (30 cm) sausage.

6 ▲ Twist the two sausages together, dampen the ends and press to seal. Lift the twist on to the prepared baking sheet. Brush the plait with water, sprinkle with the remaining linseed and cover loosely with a large plastic bag. Leave in a warm place until well risen. Preheat the oven to 220°C/425°F/Gas 7.

7 ▲ Bake the loaf for 10 minutes, then lower the oven temperature to 200°C/400°F/Gas 6 and cook for 20 minutes more, or until the loaf sounds hollow when it is tapped underneath. Transfer to a wire rack to cool.

Multi-Grain Bread

MAKES 2 LOAVES

1 tablespoon active dried yeast
2 fl oz (65 ml) lukewarm water
2¹/₂ oz (70 g) rolled oats (not quick cooking)
16 fl oz (450 ml) milk
2 teaspoons salt
2 fl oz (65 ml) oil
2 oz (55 g) light brown sugar
2 tablespoons honey
2 eggs, lightly beaten
1 oz (30 g) wheat germ
6 oz (170 g) soya flour
12 oz (350 g) wholemeal flour
15 oz–1 lb 1¹/₂ oz (420–490 g) strong flour

1 Combine the yeast and water, stir, and leave for 15 minutes to dissolve.

2 ▲ Place the oats in a large bowl. Scald the milk, then pour over the rolled oats.

3 Stir in the salt, oil, sugar and honey. Leave until lukewarm.

~ **VARIATION** ~

Different flours may be used in this recipe, such as rye, barley, buckwheat or cornmeal. Try replacing the wheat germ and the soya flour with one or two of these, using the same total amount.

4 ▲ Stir in the yeast mixture, eggs, wheat germ, soya and wholemeal flours. Gradually stir in enough strong flour to obtain a rough dough.

5 Transfer the dough to a floured surface and knead, adding flour if necessary, until smooth and elastic. Return to a clean bowl, cover and leave to rise in a warm place until doubled in volume, about 2¹/₂ hours.

6 Grease 2 8¹/₂ × 4¹/₂ in (21.5 × 11.5 cm) bread tins. Punch down the risen dough and knead briefly.

7 Divide the dough into quarters. Roll each quarter into a cylinder 1¹/₂ in (3 cm) thick. Twist together 2 cylinders and place in a tin; repeat for remaining cylinders.

8 Cover and leave to rise until doubled in size, about 1 hour.

9 Preheat a 375°F/190°C/Gas 5 oven.

10 ▲ Bake for 45–50 minutes, until the bottoms sound hollow when tapped lightly. Cool on a rack.

Sesame Seed Bread

MAKES 1 LOAF

2 tsp active dry yeast
10 fl oz (300 ml) lukewarm water
7 oz (200 g) plain flour
7 oz (200 g) wholewheat flour
2 tsp salt
2½ oz (70 g) toasted sesame seeds
milk, for glazing
2 tbsp sesame seeds, for sprinkling

1   Combine the yeast and 5 tbsp of the water and leave to dissolve. Mix the flours and salt in a large bowl. Make a well in the centre and pour in the yeast and water.

2 ▲   With a wooden spoon, stir from the centre, incorporating flour with each turn, to obtain a rough dough.

3 ▲   Transfer to a lightly floured surface. To knead, push the dough away from you with the palm of your hand, then fold it towards you and push away again. Repeat until smooth and elastic, then return to the bowl and cover with a plastic bag. Leave the dough in a warm place for about 1½–2 hours, until doubled in volume.

4 ▲   Grease a 9 in (23 cm) cake tin. Punch down the dough and knead in the sesame seeds. Divide the dough into 16 balls and place in the pan. Cover with a plastic bag and leave in a warm place until risen above the rim of the tin.

5 ▼   Preheat a 425°F/220°C/Gas 7 oven. Brush the loaf with milk and sprinkle with the sesame seeds. Bake for 15 minutes. Lower the heat to 375°F/190°C/Gas 5 and bake until the bottom sounds hollow when tapped, about 30 minutes more. Cool on a rack.

Granary Cob

MAKES 1 LOAF

1 lb (450 g) granary or malthouse flour
2 teaspoons (10 ml) salt
½ oz (15 g) fresh yeast
½ pint (300 ml) lukewarm water or milk and water mixed
FOR THE TOPPING
2 tablespoons (30 ml) water
½ teaspoon (2.5ml) salt
wheat flakes or cracked wheat, to sprinkle

Cob is an old word meaning "head". If you make a slash across the top of the dough, the finished loaf, known as a Danish cob, will look like a large roll. A Coburg cob has a cross cut in the top before baking.

1 Lightly flour a baking sheet. Sift the flour and salt together in a large bowl and make a well in the centre. Place in a very low oven for 5 minutes.

2 ▲ Mix the yeast with a little of the water or milk mixture then blend in the rest. Add the yeast mixture to the centre of the flour and mix to a dough.

3 Turn out on to a floured surface and knead for about 10 minutes. Place in a lightly oiled bowl, cover with lightly oiled clear film and leave to rise, in a warm place, for 1¼ hours, or until doubled in bulk.

4 ▲ Turn the dough out on to a lightly floured surface and knock back. Knead for 2–3 minutes, then roll into a plump, round ball. Place in the centre of the prepared baking sheet. Cover with an inverted bowl and leave to rise, in a warm place, for 30–45 minutes.

5 Mix the water and salt and brush over the bread. Sprinkle with wheat flakes or cracked wheat.

6 Meanwhile, preheat the oven to 230°C/450°F/Gas 8. Bake for 15 minutes, then reduce the oven temperature to 200°C/400°F/Gas 6 and bake for a further 20 minutes, or until the loaf is firm to the touch and sounds hollow when tapped on the base.

Oatmeal Bread

MAKES 2 LOAVES

16 fl oz (450 ml) milk
1 oz (30 g) butter
2 oz (55 g) dark brown sugar
2 teaspoons salt
1 tablespoon active dried yeast
2 fl oz (65 ml) lukewarm water
13³/₄ oz (390 g) rolled oats (not quick-cooking)
1 lb 8 oz–1 lb 14 oz (700–850 g) strong flour

1 ▲ Scald the milk. Remove from the heat and stir in the butter, brown sugar and salt. Leave until lukewarm.

2 Combine the yeast and warm water in a large bowl and leave until the yeast is dissolved and the mixture is frothy. Stir in the milk mixture.

3 ▲ Add 10 oz (285 g) of the oats and enough flour to obtain a soft dough.

4 Transfer to a floured surface and knead until smooth and elastic.

5 ▲ Place in a greased bowl, cover with a plastic bag, and leave until doubled in volume, 2–3 hours.

6 Grease a large baking sheet. Transfer the dough to a lightly floured surface and divide in half.

7 ▼ Shape into rounds. Place on the baking sheet, cover with a tea towel and leave to rise until doubled in volume, about 1 hour.

8 Preheat a 400°F/200°C/Gas 6 oven. Score the tops and sprinkle with the remaining oats. Bake until the bottoms sound hollow when tapped, 45–50 minutes. Cool on racks.

Granary Baps

These make excellent picnic fare, filled with cottage cheese, tuna, salad and mayonnaise. They are also very good served warm with soup.

MAKES 8

½ pint (300 ml) warm water
1 teaspoon (5 ml) dried yeast
pinch of sugar
1 lb (450 g) malted brown flour
1 teaspoon (5 ml) salt
1 tablespoon (15 ml) malt extract
1 tablespoon (15 ml) rolled oats

1 ▲ Put half the warm water in a jug. Sprinkle in the yeast. Add the sugar, mix and leave for 10 minutes.

2 ▲ Put the malted brown flour and salt in a mixing bowl and make a well in the centre. Add the yeast mixture with the malt extract and the remaining water. Gradually mix in the flour to make a soft dough.

3 ▲ Turn the dough on to a floured surface and knead for 5 minutes until smooth and elastic. Return to the clean bowl, cover with a damp dish towel and leave in a warm place to rise for about 2 hours until doubled in bulk.

4 ▲ Lightly grease two large baking sheets. Turn the dough on to a floured surface, knead for 2 minutes, then divide into eight pieces. Shape the pieces into balls and flatten them to make neat 4 in (10 cm) rounds.

5 ▲ Place the rounds on the baking sheets, cover loosely with a large plastic bag, and leave to stand in a warm place until well risen. Preheat the oven to 220°C/425°F/Gas 7.

6 ▲ Brush the baps with water, sprinkle with the oats and bake for about 20–25 minutes or until they sound hollow when tapped underneath. Cool on a wire rack, then serve with the filling of your choice.

~ COOK'S TIP ~

To make a large loaf, shape the dough into a round, flatten it slightly and bake for 30–40 minutes. Test by tapping the base of the loaf – if it sounds hollow, it is cooked.

Brown Soda Bread

This is very easy to make – simply mix and bake. Instead of yeast, bicarbonate of soda and cream of tartar are the raising agents. This is a great recipe for those new to bread making.

MAKES 1 LOAF

1 lb (450 g) plain flour
1 lb (450 g) wholemeal flour
2 teaspoons (10 ml) salt
1 tablespoon (15 ml) bicarbonate of soda
4 teaspoons (20 ml) cream of tartar
2 teaspoons (10 ml) caster sugar
2 oz (50 g) butter
up to 1½ pints (900 ml) buttermilk or skimmed milk
extra wholemeal flour, to sprinkle

1 Lightly grease a baking sheet. Preheat the oven to 190°C/375°F/Gas 5.

2 ▲ Sift all the dry ingredients into a large bowl, tipping any bran from the flour back into the bowl.

3 ▲ Rub the butter into the flour mixture, then add enough buttermilk or milk to make a soft dough. You may not need it all, so add cautiously.

4 ▲ Knead the dough lightly until smooth, then transfer to the baking sheet and shape to a large round about 2 in (5 cm) thick.

5 ▲ Using the floured handle of a wooden spoon, make a large cross on top of the dough. Sprinkle over a little extra wholemeal flour. Bake for 40–50 minutes until risen and firm. Leave to cool for 5 minutes before transferring to a wire rack.

Sage Soda Bread

This wonderful loaf, quite unlike bread made with yeast, has a velvety texture and a p̶
sage aroma.

1 ▲ Preheat the oven to 220°C/ 425°F/Gas 7. Sift the dry ingredients into a mixing bowl.

2 ▲ Stir in the sage and add enough buttermilk to make a soft dough.

3 ▲ Shape the dough into a round loaf with your hands and place on a lightly oiled baking sheet.

~ COOK'S TIP ~
As an alternative to the sage, try using either finely chopped rosemary or thyme.

4 ▲ Cut a deep cross in the top. Bake in the oven for about 40 minutes until the loaf is well risen and sounds hollow when tapped on the bottom. Leave to cool on a wire rack.

MAKES 1 LOAF

6 oz (175 g) wholemeal flour
4 oz (115 g) strong white flour
½ teaspoon (2.5 ml) salt
1 teaspoon (5 ml) bicarbonate of soda
2 tablespoons (30 ml) shredded fresh sage or 2 teaspoons (10 ml) dried sage
½–¾ pint (300–450 ml) cups buttermilk

Rosemary Bread

Sliced thinly, this herb bread is delicious with soup for a light meal.

MAKES 1 LOAF

¼ oz (10 g) dried fast-action yeast
6 oz (175 g) wholemeal flour
6 oz (175 g) self-raising flour
2 teaspoons (10 ml) butter, melted, plus extra to grease bowl and tin
2 fl oz (50 ml) warm water
8 fl oz (250 ml) skimmed milk, at room temperature
1 tablespoon (15 ml) sugar
1 teaspoon (5 ml) salt
1 tablespoon (15 ml) sesame seeds
1 tablespoon (15 ml) dried chopped onion
1 tablespoon (15 ml) fresh rosemary leaves, plus extra to decorate
4 oz (115 g) cubed Cheddar cheese
coarse salt, to decorate

1 ▲ Mix the fast-action yeast with the flours in a large mixing bowl. Add the melted butter. Stir in the warm water, milk, sugar, salt, sesame seeds, onion and rosemary. Knead thoroughly until quite smooth.

2 ▲ Flatten the dough, then add the cheese cubes. Quickly knead them in until they are well combined.

3 Place the dough in a large clean bowl greased with a little butter, turning it so that it becomes lightly greased on all sides. Cover with a clean, dry cloth. Put the greased bowl and dough in a warm place for about 1½ hours, or until the dough has risen and doubled in size.

4 Grease a 9 × 5 in (23 × 13 cm) loaf tin with the remaining butter. Knock down the dough to remove some of the air, and shape it into a loaf. Put the loaf into the tin, cover with the clean cloth used earlier and leave for about 1 hour until it has doubled in size once again. Preheat the oven to 190°C/375°F/Gas 5.

5 Bake for 30 minutes. During the last 5–10 minutes of baking, cover the loaf with foil to prevent it becoming too dark in colour. Remove from the loaf tin and leave to cool on a wire rack. Decorate with rosemary leaves and coarse salt scattered on top.

Spiral Herb Bread

MAKES 2 LOAVES

2 tablespoons active dried yeast
1 pt (600 ml) lukewarm water
15 oz (420 g) strong flour
1 lb 2 oz (505 g) wholemeal flour
3 teaspoons salt
1 oz (30 g) butter
1 large bunch of parsley, finely chopped
1 bunch of spring onions, chopped
1 garlic clove, finely chopped
salt and freshly ground black pepper
1 egg, lightly beaten
milk, for glazing

1   Combine the yeast and 2 fl oz (65 ml) of the water, stir and leave for 15 minutes to dissolve.

2   Combine the flours and salt in a large bowl. Make a well in the centre and pour in the yeast mixture and the remaining water. With a wooden spoon, stir from the centre, working outwards to obtain a rough dough.

3   Transfer the dough to a floured surface and knead until smooth and elastic. Return to the bowl, cover with a plastic bag, and leave until doubled in volume, about 2 hours.

4 ▲   Meanwhile, combine the butter, parsley, spring onions and garlic in a large frying pan. Cook over low heat, stirring, until softened. Season and set aside.

5   Grease 2 9 × 5 in (23 × 13 cm) tins. When the dough has risen, cut in half and roll each half into a rectangle about 14 × 9 in (35 × 23 cm).

6 ▼   Brush both with the beaten egg. Divide the herb mixture between the two, spreading just up to the edges.

7 ▲   Roll up to enclose the filling and pinch the short ends to seal. Place in the tins, seam-side down. Cover, and leave in a warm place until the dough rises above the rim of the tins.

8   Preheat a 375°F/190°C/Gas 5 oven. Brush with milk and bake until the bottoms sound hollow when tapped, about 55 minutes. Cool on a rack.

Dill Bread

4 teaspoons active dried yeast
16 fl oz (450 ml) lukewarm water
2 tablespoons sugar
2 lb 5½ oz (1.05 kg) strong flour
½ onion, chopped
4 tablespoons oil
1 large bunch of dill, finely chopped
2 eggs, lightly beaten
5½ oz (150 g) cottage cheese
4 teaspoons salt
milk, for glazing

1   Mix together the yeast, water and sugar in a large bowl and leave for 15 minutes to dissolve.

2   ▼   Stir in about half of the flour. Cover and leave to rise in a warm place for 45 minutes.

3   ▲   In a frying pan, cook the onion in 1 tablespoon of the oil until soft. Set aside to cool, then stir into the yeast mixture. Stir the dill, eggs, cottage cheese, salt and remaining oil into the yeast. Gradually add the remaining flour until the mixture is too stiff to stir.

4   ▲   Transfer to a floured surface and knead until smooth and elastic. Place in a bowl, cover and leave to rise until doubled in volume, 1–1½ hours.

5   ▲   Grease a large baking sheet. Cut the dough in half and shape into 2 rounds. Leave to rise in a warm place for 30 minutes.

6   Preheat a 375°F/190°C/Gas 5 oven. Score the tops, brush with the milk and bake until browned, for about 50 minutes. Cool on a rack.

Cheese Bread

MAKES 1 LOAF

1 tablespoon active dried yeast
8 fl oz (250 ml) lukewarm milk
1 oz (30 g) butter
15 oz (420 g) strong flour
2 teaspoons salt
3½ oz (100 g) mature cheddar cheese, grated

1 Combine the yeast and milk. Stir and leave for 15 minutes to dissolve.

2 Melt the butter, let cool, and add to the yeast mixture.

3 Mix the flour and salt together in a large bowl. Make a well in the centre and pour in the yeast mixture.

4 With a wooden spoon, stir from the centre, incorporating flour with each turn, to obtain a rough dough. If the dough seems too dry, add 2–3 tablespoons water.

5 Transfer to a floured surface and knead until smooth and elastic. Return to the bowl, cover and leave to rise in a warm place until doubled in volume, 2–3 hours.

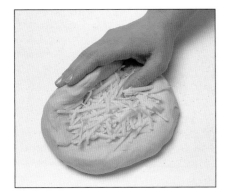

6 ▲ Grease a 9 × 5 in (23 × 13 cm) bread tin. Punch down the dough with your fist. Knead in the cheese, distributing it as evenly as possible.

7 ▼ Twist the dough, form into a loaf shape and place in the tin, tucking the ends under. Leave in a warm place until the dough rises above the rim of the tin.

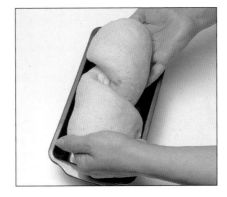

8 ▲ Preheat a 400°F/200°C/Gas 6 oven. Bake for 15 minutes, then lower to 375°F/190°C/Gas 5 and bake until the bottom sounds hollow when tapped, about 30 minutes more.

Sun-Dried Tomato Plait

This is a marvellous Mediterranean-flavoured bread to serve at a summer buffet or barbecue.

MAKES 1 LOAF

½ pint (300 ml) warm water
1 teaspoon (5 ml) dried yeast
pinch of sugar
8 oz (225 g) wholemeal flour
8 oz (225 g) strong white flour
1 teaspoon (5 ml) salt
¼ teaspoon (1.5 ml) freshly ground black pepper
4 oz (115 g) drained sun-dried tomatoes in oil, chopped, plus 1 tablespoon (15 ml) oil from the jar
1 oz (25 g) freshly grated Parmesan cheese
2 tablespoons (30 ml) red pesto
1 teaspoon (5 ml) coarse sea salt

1 ▲ Put half the warm water in a jug. Sprinkle the yeast on top. Add the sugar, mix and leave for 10 minutes.

2 ▲ Put the wholemeal flour in a mixing bowl. Sift in the white flour, salt and pepper. Add the yeast mixture, sun-dried tomatoes, oil, Parmesan, pesto and the remaining water. Gradually incorporate the flour and mix to a soft dough, adding a little extra water if necessary.

3 ▲ Transfer the dough to a floured surface and knead for 5 minutes until smooth and elastic. Return to the clean bowl, cover with a damp dish towel and leave in a warm place for about 2 hours until doubled in bulk. Lightly grease a baking sheet.

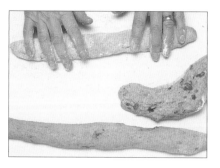

4 ▲ Transfer the dough on to a lightly floured surface and knead for a few minutes. Divide the dough into three equal pieces and shape each into a 12 in (30 cm) long sausage.

5 ▲ Dampen the ends of the three sausages. Press them together at one end, plait them loosely, then press them together at the other end. Place on the baking sheet, cover and leave in a warm place for 30 minutes until well risen. Preheat the oven to 220°C/425°F/Gas 7.

6 ▲ Sprinkle the plait with the coarse sea salt. Bake for 10 minutes, then lower the temperature to 200°C/400°F/Gas 6 and bake for a further 15–20 minutes, or until the loaf sounds hollow when tapped underneath. Cool on a wire rack.

~ COOK'S TIP ~

If you are unable to locate red pesto, use 2 tablespoons (30 ml) chopped fresh basil mixed with 1 tablespoon (15 ml) sun-dried tomato paste.

Parma Ham and Parmesan Bread

This nourishing bread is almost a meal in itself.

MAKES 1 LOAF

8 oz (225 g) self-raising wholemeal flour

8 oz (225 g) self-raising white flour

1 teaspoon (5 ml) baking powder

1 teaspoon (5 ml) salt

1 teaspoon (5 ml) black pepper

3 oz (75 g) Parma ham

1 oz (25 g) freshly grated Parmesan cheese

2 tablespoons (30 ml) chopped fresh parsley

3 tablespoons (45 ml) Meaux mustard

12 fl oz (350 ml) buttermilk

skimmed milk, to glaze

1 ▲ Preheat the oven to 200°C/ 400°F/Gas 6. Flour a baking sheet. Place the wholemeal flour in a bowl and sift in the white flour, baking powder and salt. Add the pepper and the ham. Set aside about 1 tablespoon (15 ml) of the grated Parmesan and stir the rest into the flour mixture with the parsley. Make a well in the centre.

2 ▲ Mix the mustard and buttermilk, pour into the flour and quickly mix to a soft dough.

3 ▲ Transfer the dough to a floured surface and knead briefly. Shape into an oval loaf, brush with milk and sprinkle with the reserved Parmesan. Place on the prepared baking sheet.

4 ▲ Bake the loaf for 25–30 minutes, or until it sounds hollow when tapped underneath. Allow to cool before serving.

Courgette Yeast Bread

The grated courgettes give extra moisture to this tasty loaf.

MAKES 1 LOAF

1 lb (450 g) courgettes, grated
2 tablespoons (30 ml) salt
2 teaspoons (10 ml) active dry yeast
½ pint (300 ml) lukewarm water
14 oz (400 g) plain flour
olive oil, for brushing

1 ▲ In a colander, alternate layers of grated courgettes and salt. Leave for 30 minutes, then squeeze out the moisture with your hands.

2 Combine the yeast with 2 fl oz (50 ml) of the lukewarm water, stir and leave for 15 minutes to dissolve the yeast.

3 ▲ Place the courgettes, yeast and flour in a bowl. Stir together and add just enough of the remaining water to obtain a rough dough.

4 Transfer to a floured surface and knead until smooth and elastic. Return the dough to the bowl, cover with a plastic bag, and leave to rise in a warm place until doubled in volume, for about 1½ hours.

5 Grease a baking sheet. Punch down the risen dough with your fist and knead into a tapered cylinder. Place on the baking sheet, cover and leave to rise in a warm place until doubled in volume, for about 45 minutes.

6 ▲ Preheat the oven to 220°C/ 425°F/Gas 7. Brush the bread with olive oil and bake for about 40–45 minutes, or until the loaf is a golden colour. Cool on a rack before serving.

Spinach and Bacon Bread

This bread is so tasty that it is a good idea to make double the quantity and freeze one of the loaves. Use smoked lean back bacon for the best possible flavour with the minimum of fat.

MAKES 2 LOAVES

¾ pint (450 ml) warm water
2 teaspoons (10 ml) dried yeast
pinch of sugar
1 tablespoon (15 ml) olive oil
1 onion, chopped
4 oz (115 g) rindless smoked bacon rashers, chopped
8 oz (225 g) chopped spinach, thawed if frozen
1½ lb (675 g) strong plain flour
1½ teaspoons (7.5 ml) salt
1½ teaspoons (7.5 ml) grated nutmeg
1 oz (25 g) grated reduced-fat Cheddar cheese

1 ▲ Put the water in a bowl. Sprinkle the yeast on top and add the sugar. Mix, and leave for 10 minutes. Grease two 9 in (23 cm) cake tins.

2 ▲ Heat the oil in a frying pan and fry the onion and bacon for 10 minutes until golden brown. If using frozen spinach, drain it thoroughly.

3 ▲ Sift the flour, salt and nutmeg into a mixing bowl and make a well in the centre. Add the yeast mixture. Tip in the fried bacon and onion (with the oil), then add the spinach. Gradually incorporate the flour mixture and mix to a soft dough.

4 ▲ Transfer the dough to a floured surface and knead for 5 minutes. Return to the clean bowl, cover with a damp dish towel and leave in a warm place to rise for about 2 hours, until doubled in bulk.

5 ▲ Transfer the dough to a floured surface, knead briefly, then divide it in half. Shape each half into a ball, flatten slightly and place in a tin, pressing the dough to the edges. Mark each loaf into eight wedges and sprinkle with the cheese. Cover loosely with a plastic bag and leave in a warm place until well risen. Preheat the oven to 200°C/400°F/Gas 6.

6 ▲ Bake the loaves for 25–30 minutes, or until they sound hollow when they are tapped underneath. Transfer to a wire rack to cool.

~ COOK'S TIP ~

If using frozen spinach, be sure to squeeze out any excess liquid or the resulting dough will be too sticky.

Walnut Bread

MAKES 1 LOAF

15 oz (420 g) wholemeal flour
5 oz (140 g) strong flour
2¹/₂ teaspoons salt
18 fl oz (525 ml) lukewarm water
1 tablespoon honey
1 tablespoon active dried yeast
5 oz (140 g) walnut pieces, plus more for decorating
1 beaten egg, for glazing

1 Combine the flours and salt in a large bowl. Make a well in the centre and add 8 fl oz (250 ml) of the water, the honey and the yeast.

2 Set aside until the yeast dissolves and the mixture is frothy.

3 Add the remaining water. With a wooden spoon, stir from the centre, incorporating flour with each turn, to obtain a smooth dough. Add more flour if the dough is too sticky and use your hands if the dough becomes too stiff to stir.

4 Transfer to a floured board and knead, adding flour if necessary, until the dough is smooth and elastic. Place in a greased bowl and roll the dough around in the bowl to coat thoroughly on all sides.

5 ▲ Cover with a plastic bag and leave in a warm place until doubled in volume, about 1¹/₂ hours.

6 ▲ Punch down the dough and knead in the walnuts evenly.

7 Grease a baking sheet. Shape into a round loaf and place on the baking sheet. Press in walnut pieces to decorate the top. Cover loosely with a damp cloth and leave to rise in a warm place until doubled, 25–30 minutes.

8 Preheat a 425°F/220°C/Gas 7 oven.

9 ▲ With a sharp knife, score the top. Brush with the glaze. Bake for 15 minutes. Lower the heat to 375°F/190°C/Gas 5 and bake until the bottom sounds hollow when tapped, about 40 minutes. Cool on a rack.

Courgette and Walnut Loaf

A moist and crunchy loaf – a real treat.

1 ▲ Preheat the oven to 180°C/ 350°F/Gas 4. Grease the base and sides of a 2 lb (900 g) loaf tin and line with greaseproof paper.

2 Beat the eggs and sugar together and gradually add the oil.

3 ▲ Sift the flour together with the baking powder, bicarbonate of soda, cinnamon and allspice.

4 ▲ Mix into the egg mixture with the rest of the ingredients, reserving 1 tablespoon (15 ml) of the seeds.

5 Spoon into the loaf tin, level off the top, and sprinkle with the reserved sunflower seeds.

6 ▲ Bake for about 1 hour or until a skewer inserted in the centre of the loaf comes out clean. Leave to cool slightly, then turn out on to a wire cooling rack.

MAKES 1 LOAF
3 eggs
3 oz (75 g) light brown sugar
2 fl oz (50 ml) sunflower oil
8 oz (225 g) wholemeal flour
1 teaspoon (5 ml) baking powder
1 teaspoon (5 ml) bicarbonate of soda
1 teaspoon (5 ml) ground cinnamon
½ teaspoon (2.5 ml) ground allspice
½ tablespoon (7.5 ml) green cardamoms, seeds removed and crushed
5 oz (150 g) coarsely grated courgette
2 oz (50 g) walnuts, chopped
2 oz (50 g) sunflower seeds

Prune Bread

MAKES 1 LOAF

8 oz (225 g) dried prunes
1 tablespoon active dried yeast
3 oz (85 g) wholemeal flour
13½–15 oz (385–420 g) strong flour
½ teaspoon bicarbonate of soda
1 teaspoon salt
1 teaspoon pepper
1 oz (30 g) butter, at room temperature
6 fl oz (175 ml) buttermilk
2 oz (55 g) walnuts, chopped
milk, for glazing

1 Simmer the prunes in water to cover until soft, or soak overnight. Drain, reserving 2 fl oz (65 ml) of the soaking liquid. Stone and chop the prunes.

2 Combine the yeast and the reserved prune liquid, stir and leave for 15 minutes to dissolve.

3 In a large bowl, stir together the flours, bicarbonate of soda, salt and pepper. Make a well in the centre.

4 ▲ Add the chopped prunes, butter, and buttermilk. Pour in the yeast mixture. With a wooden spoon, stir from the centre, incorporating more flour with each turn, to obtain a rough dough.

5 Transfer to a floured surface and knead until smooth and elastic. Return to the bowl, cover with a plastic bag and leave to rise in a warm place until doubled in volume, about 1½ hours.

6 Grease a baking sheet.

7 ▲ Punch down the dough with your fist, then knead in the walnuts.

8 Shape the dough into a long, cylindrical loaf. Place on the baking sheet, cover loosely, and leave to rise in a warm place for 45 minutes.

9 Preheat a 425°F/220°C/Gas 7 oven.

10 ▼ With a sharp knife, score the top deeply. Brush with milk and bake for 15 minutes. Lower to 375°F/190°C/Gas 5 and bake until the bottom sounds hollow when tapped, about 35 minutes more. Cool.

Orange Wheat Loaf

Perfect just with butter as a breakfast bread or tea bread and lovely for banana sandwiches.

MAKES 1 LOAF

10 oz (275 g) wholemeal plain flour
½ teaspoon (2.5 ml) salt
2 oz (50 g) butter
1 oz (25 g) soft light brown sugar
½ sachet easy-blend dried yeast
grated rind and juice of ½ orange

1 ▲ Sift the flour into a large bowl and add any wheat flakes from the sieve. Add the salt and rub in the butter lightly with your fingertips.

5 ▲ Bake the bread for 30–35 minutes, or until it sounds hollow when you tap the bottom. Tip out of the tin and leave to cool on a wire rack.

2 ▲ Stir in the sugar, yeast and orange rind. Pour the orange juice into a measuring jug and make up to 7 fl oz (200 ml) with hot water (not more than hand hot).

3 ▲ Stir the liquid into the flour and mix to a ball of dough. Knead the dough on a floured surface until smooth.

4 Place the dough in a greased 1 lb (450 g) loaf tin and leave in a warm place until doubled in size. Preheat the oven to 220°C/425°F/Gas 7.

Corn Bread

MAKES 1 LOAF

4 oz (115 g) plain flour
2¹/₂ oz (75 g) caster sugar
1 tsp salt
1 tbsp baking powder
6 oz (170 g) cornmeal, or polenta
12 fl oz (350 ml) milk
2 eggs
3 oz (85 g) butter, melted
4 oz (115 g) margarine, melted

1 Preheat a 400°F/200°C/Gas 6 oven. Line a 9 × 5 in (23 × 13 cm) loaf tin with greaseproof paper and grease.

2 Sift the flour, sugar, salt and baking powder into a mixing bowl.

3 ▼ Add the cornmeal and stir to blend. Make a well in the centre.

4 ▲ Whisk together the milk, eggs, butter and margarine. Pour the mixture into the well. Stir until just blended; do not overmix.

5 Pour into the tin and bake until a skewer inserted in the centre comes out clean, about 45 minutes. Serve hot or at room temperature.

Spicy Sweetcorn Bread

MAKES 9 SQUARES

3–4 whole canned chilli peppers, drained
2 eggs
16 fl oz (450 ml) buttermilk
2 oz (55 g) butter, melted
2 oz (55 g) plain flour
1 tsp bicarbonate of soda
2 tsp salt
6 oz (170 g) cornmeal, or polenta
12 oz (350 g) canned sweetcorn or frozen sweetcorn, thawed

1 Preheat a 400°F/200°C/Gas 6 oven. Line the bottom and sides of a 9 in (23 cm) square cake tin with greaseproof paper and grease lightly.

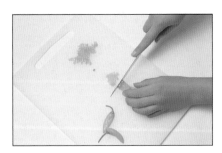

2 ▲ With a sharp knife, finely chop the chillis and set aside.

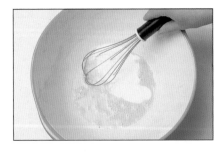

3 ▲ In a large bowl, whisk the eggs until frothy, then whisk in the buttermilk. Add the melted butter.

4 In another large bowl, sift together the flour, bicarbonate of soda and salt. Fold into the buttermilk mixture in 3 batches, then fold in the cornmeal in 3 batches.

5 ▲ Fold in the chillis and sweetcorn.

6 Pour the mixture into the prepared tin and bake until a skewer inserted in the middle comes out clean, 25–30 minutes. Let stand for 2–3 minutes before unmoulding. Cut into squares and serve warm.

Corn Bread (top), Spicy Sweetcorn Bread

Onion Focaccia

This pizza-like flat bread is characterized by its soft dimpled surface.

MAKES 2 ROUND LOAVES

1½ lb (675 g) strong plain flour
½ teaspoon (2.5 ml) salt
½ teaspoon (2.5 ml) caster sugar
1 tablespoon (15 ml) easy-blend dried yeast
4 tablespoons (60 ml) extra virgin olive oil
¾ pint (450 ml) hand-hot water
TO FINISH
2 red onions, thinly sliced
3 tablespoons (45 ml) extra virgin olive oil
1 tablespoon (15 ml) coarse salt

1 Sift the flour, salt and sugar into a large bowl. Stir in the yeast, oil and water and mix to a dough using a round-bladed knife. (Add a little extra water if the dough is dry.)

2 ▲ Turn out on to a lightly floured surface and knead for 10 minutes until smooth and elastic. Put the dough in a clean, lightly oiled bowl and cover with clear film. Leave to rise in a warm place until doubled in bulk.

3 ▲ Place two 10 in (25 cm) metal flan rings on baking sheets. Oil the sides of the rings and the baking sheets.

4 ▲ Preheat the oven to 200°C/ 400°F/Gas 6. Halve the dough and roll each piece to a 10 in (25 cm) round. Press into the rings, cover with a dampened dish towel and leave for 30 minutes to rise.

5 ▲ Make deep holes, about 1 in (2.5 cm) apart, in the dough. Cover and leave for a further 20 minutes.

6 ▲ Scatter with the onions and drizzle over the oil. Sprinkle with the salt, then a little cold water, to stop a crust from forming.

7 ▲ Bake for about 25 minutes, sprinkling with water again during cooking. Cool on a wire rack.

Saffron Focaccia

A dazzling yellow bread with a distinctive flavour.

MAKES 1 ROUND LOAF

pinch of saffron threads
¼ pint (150 ml) boiling water
8 oz (225 g) plain flour
½ teaspoon (2.5 ml) salt
1 teaspoon (5 ml) easy-blend dried yeast
1 tablespoon (15 ml) olive oil
FOR THE TOPPING
2 garlic cloves, sliced
1 red onion, cut into thin wedges
rosemary sprigs
12 black olives, stoned and coarsely chopped
1 tablespoon (15 ml) olive oil

1 ▲ Infuse the saffron in the boiling water. Leave until cooled to lukewarm.

2 ▲ Place the flour, salt, yeast and olive oil in a food processor. Turn on and gradually add the saffron and its liquid until the dough forms a ball.

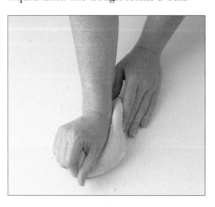

3 ▲ Transfer to a floured board and knead for 10–15 minutes. Place in a bowl, cover and leave to rise for about 30–40 minutes, until doubled in size.

4 ▲ Punch down the risen dough on a lightly floured surface and roll out into an oval shape, ½ in (1 cm) thick. Place on a lightly greased baking sheet and leave to rise for 20–30 minutes.

5 Preheat the oven to 200°C/400°F/ Gas 6. Press indentations in the dough.

6 ▲ Cover with the topping ingredients, brush lightly with olive oil, and bake for about 25 minutes or until the loaf sounds hollow when tapped on the bottom. Leave to cool.

Cheese and Onion Sticks

An extremely tasty bread which is very good with soups or salads. Use an extra-strong cheese to give plenty of flavour without piling on the fat.

Makes 2 Sticks

½ pint (300 ml) warm water

1 teaspoon (5 ml) dried yeast

pinch of sugar

1 tablespoon (15 ml) sunflower oil

1 red onion, finely chopped

1 lb (450 g) strong white flour

1 teaspoon (5 ml) salt

1 teaspoon (5 ml) dry mustard

3 tablespoons (45 ml) chopped fresh herbs, such as thyme, parsley, marjoram or sage

3 oz (75 g) grated reduced-fat Cheddar cheese

1 ▲ Put the water in a jug. Sprinkle the yeast on top. Add the sugar, mix well and leave for 10 minutes.

2 ▲ Heat the oil in a frying pan and fry the onion until it is well coloured.

3 ▲ Stir the flour, salt and mustard into a mixing bowl, then add the chopped herbs. Set aside 2 tablespoons (30 ml) of the cheese. Stir the rest into the flour mixture and make a well in the centre. Add the yeast mixture with the fried onions and oil, then gradually incorporate the flour and mix to a soft dough, adding extra water if necessary.

4 ▲ Transfer the dough to a floured surface and knead for 5 minutes until smooth and elastic. Return to the clean bowl, cover with a damp dish towel and leave in a warm place to rise for 2 hours, until doubled in bulk. Lightly grease two baking sheets.

5 ▲ Transfer the dough on to a floured surface, knead briefly, then divide the mixture in half and roll each piece into a 12 in (30 cm) long stick. Place on a baking sheet and make diagonal cuts along the top.

6 ▲ Sprinkle the sticks with the reserved cheese. Cover and leave for 30 minutes until well risen. Preheat the oven to 220°C/425°F/Gas 7. Bake the sticks for 25 minutes or until they sound hollow when tapped underneath.

~ COOK'S TIP ~

To make Onion and Coriander Sticks, omit the cheese, herbs and mustard. Add 1 tablespoon (15 ml) ground coriander and 3 tablespoons (45 ml) chopped fresh coriander instead.

Saffron and Basil Breadsticks

Saffron lends its delicate flavour, as well as rich yellow colour, to these tasty breadsticks.

MAKES 32 STICKS

generous pinch of saffron strands
2 tablespoons (30 ml) hot water
1 lb (450 g) strong white flour
1 teaspoon (5 ml) salt
2 teaspoons (10 ml) easy-blend dried yeast
½ pint (300 ml) lukewarm water
3 tablespoons (45 ml) olive oil
3 tablespoons (45 ml) chopped fresh basil

1 ▲ Infuse the saffron strands in the hot water for 10 minutes.

2 ▲ Sift the flour and salt into a large mixing bowl. Stir in the yeast, then make a well in the centre of the dry ingredients. Pour in the lukewarm water and saffron liquid.

3 ▲ Add the oil and basil and mix to a soft dough.

4 ▲ Turn out and knead the dough on a lightly floured surface for about 10 minutes until smooth and elastic. Place in a greased bowl, cover with clear film and leave for about 1 hour until it has doubled in size.

5 ▲ Knock back and knead the dough on a lightly floured surface for 2–3 minutes.

6 ▲ Preheat the oven to 220°C/425°F/Gas 7. Divide the dough into 32 pieces and shape into long sticks. Place well apart on greased baking sheets, then leave for a further 15–20 minutes until they become puffy. Bake for about 15 minutes until crisp and golden. Serve warm.

~ COOK'S TIP ~

Use powdered saffron if saffron strands are not available. Turmeric is an inexpensive alternative: it imparts a lovely gold colour, but its flavour is not as delicate.

Flat Bread with Sage

This bread is perfect served hot to accompany a pasta supper.

MAKES 1 ROUND LOAF

2 teaspoons (10 ml) active dry yeast

8 fl oz (250 ml) lukewarm water

12 oz (375 g) plain flour

2 teaspoons (10 ml) salt

5 tablespoons (75 ml) extra virgin olive oil

12 fresh sage leaves, chopped

1 Combine the yeast and water, stir and leave for 15 minutes to dissolve.

2 Mix the flour and salt in a large bowl, and make a well in the centre.

3 Stir in the yeast mixture and 4 tablespoons (60 ml) of the oil. Stir gently from the centre, incorporating flour with each turn, to obtain a rough dough.

4 ▲ Transfer to a floured surface and knead until smooth and elastic. Place in a lightly oiled bowl. Cover and leave to rise in a warm place until doubled in volume, for about 2 hours.

5 ▲ Preheat the oven to 200°C/ 400°F/Gas 6 and place a baking sheet in the centre of the oven.

6 ▲ Punch down the dough. Knead in the sage, then roll into a 12 in (30 cm) round. Leave to rise slightly.

7 ▲ Dimple the surface all over with your finger. Drizzle the remaining oil on top. Slide a floured board under the bread, carry to the oven, and slide off on to the hot baking sheet. Bake for about 35 minutes or until golden brown. Cool on a rack.

Sweet Sesame Loaf

MAKES 1 OR 2 LOAVES

3 oz (85 g) sesame seeds
10 oz (285 g) plain flour
2¹/₂ teaspoons baking powder
1 teaspoon salt
2 oz (55 g) butter or margarine, at room temperature
4¹/₂ oz (125 g) sugar
2 eggs, at room temperature
grated rind of 1 lemon
12 fl oz (350 ml) milk

1   Preheat a 350°F/180°C/Gas 4 oven. Line a 9 × 5 in (23 × 13 cm) loaf tin with greaseproof paper and grease.

2 ▲   Reserve 2 tablespoons of the sesame seeds. Spread the rest on a baking sheet and bake until lightly toasted, about 10 minutes.

3   Sift the flour, salt and baking powder into a bowl.

4 ▲   Stir in the toasted sesame seeds and set aside.

5   With an electric mixer, cream the butter or margarine and sugar together until light and fluffy. Beat in the eggs, then stir in the lemon rind and milk.

6 ▼   Pour the milk mixture over the dry ingredients and fold in with a large metal spoon until just blended.

7 ▲   Pour into the tin and sprinkle over the reserved sesame seeds.

8   Bake until a skewer inserted in the centre comes out clean, about 1 hour. Let cool in the tin for about 10 minutes. Turn out onto a wire rack to cool completely.

Apricot Nut Loaf

MAKES 1 LOAF

4 oz (115 g) dried apricots
1 large orange
3 oz (85 g) raisins
5 oz (140 g) caster sugar
3 fl oz (85 ml) oil
2 eggs, lightly beaten
9 oz (250 g) plain flour
2 tsp baking powder
¹/₂ tsp salt
1 tsp bicarbonate of soda
2 oz (55 g) chopped walnuts

1   Preheat a 350°F/180°C/Gas 4 oven. Line a 9 × 5 in (23 × 13 cm) loaf tin with greaseproof paper and grease.

2   Place the apricots in a bowl, cover with lukewarm water and leave to stand for 30 minutes.

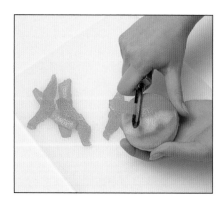

3 ▲   With a vegetable peeler, remove the orange rind, leaving the pith.

4   With a sharp knife, finely chop the orange rind strips.

5   Drain the apricots and chop coarsely. Place in a bowl with the orange rind and raisins. Set aside.

6   Squeeze the peeled orange. Measure the juice and add enough hot water to obtain 6 fl oz (175 ml) liquid.

7 ▼   Pour the orange juice mixture over the apricot mixture. Stir in the sugar, oil and eggs. Set aside.

8   In another bowl, sift together the flour, baking powder, salt and bicarbonate of soda. Fold the flour mixture into the apricot mixture in 3 batches.

9 ▲   Stir in the walnuts.

10   Spoon the mixture into the prepared tin and bake until a skewer inserted in the centre comes out clean, 55–60 minutes. If the loaf browns too quickly, protect the top with a sheet of foil. Let cool in the pan for 10 minutes before transferring to a rack to cool completely.

Apple-sauce Bread

Apples and spices such as cinnamon and nutmeg are a match made in heaven.

1 Preheat the oven to 180°C/350°F/Gas 4. Grease and line a 9 × 5 in (23 × 13 cm) loaf tin with greaseproof paper.

2 ▲ Break the egg into a bowl and beat lightly. Stir in the apple sauce, butter or margarine, and both sugars.

3 In another bowl, sift together the flour, baking powder, bicarbonate of soda, salt, cinnamon and nutmeg. Fold the dry ingredients into the apple-sauce mixture in three batches.

4 ▲ Stir in the currants or raisins and chopped pecans.

5 Pour into the prepared tin and bake for about 1 hour, or until a skewer inserted in the centre comes out clean. Allow to stand for 10 minutes before transferring to a cooling rack.

MAKES 1 LOAF
1 egg
8 fl oz (250 ml) apple sauce
4 tablespoons (60 ml) butter or margarine, melted
3 oz (75 g) dark brown sugar, firmly packed
2 oz (50 g) granulated sugar
8 oz (225 g) flour
2 teaspoons (10 ml) baking powder
½ teaspoon (2.5 ml) bicarbonate of soda
½ teaspoon (2.5 ml) salt
1 teaspoon (5 ml) ground cinnamon
½ teaspoon (2.5 ml) grated nutmeg
3 oz (75 g) currants or raisins
6 oz (175 g) pecans, chopped

Banana and Cardamom Bread

The combination of banana and cardamom is delicious in this soft-textured moist loaf. It is perfect for tea time, served with butter and jam.

MAKES 1 LOAF

¼ pint (150 ml) warm water
1 teaspoon (5 ml) dried yeast
pinch of sugar
10 cardamom pods
14 oz (400 g) strong white flour
1 teaspoon (5 ml) salt
2 tablespoons (30 ml) malt extract
2 ripe bananas, mashed
1 teaspoon (5 ml) sesame seeds

1 ▲ Put the warm water in a bowl. Sprinkle the yeast on top. Add the sugar, mix and leave for 10 minutes.

2 ▲ Split the cardamom pods. Remove the seeds and chop finely.

3 ▲ Sift the flour and salt into a mixing bowl and make a well in the centre. Add the yeast mixture with the malt extract, chopped cardamom seeds and bananas.

4 ▲ Gradually incorporate the flour and mix to a soft dough, adding extra water if necessary. Turn the dough on to a floured surface and knead for about 5 minutes. Return to the clean bowl, cover with a damp dish towel and leave to rise for 2 hours, until doubled in bulk.

5 ▲ Grease a baking sheet. Turn the dough on to a floured surface, knead briefly, then divide into three and shape into a plait. Place the plait on the baking sheet and cover loosely with a plastic bag. Leave until well risen. Preheat the oven to 220°C/425°F/Gas 7.

6 ▲ Brush the plait lightly with water and sprinkle with the sesame seeds. Bake for 10 minutes, then lower the oven temperature to 200°C/400°F/Gas 6. Cook for 15 minutes more, or until the loaf sounds hollow when tapped.

~ COOK'S TIP ~

Make sure the bananas are really ripe so that they impart maximum flavour to the bread. If you prefer, place the dough in one piece in a 1 lb (450 g) loaf tin and bake for an extra 5 minutes. As well as being low in fat, bananas are a good source of potassium, therefore making an ideal nutritious, low-fat snack.

Wholewheat Banana Nut Loaf

MAKES 1 LOAF

4 oz (115 g) butter, at room temperature
4 oz (115 g) caster sugar
2 eggs, at room temperature
4 oz (115 g) plain flour
1 tsp bicarbonate of soda
$^1/_4$ tsp salt
1 tsp ground cinnamon
2 oz (55 g) wholewheat flour
3 large ripe bananas
1 tsp vanilla essence
2 oz (55 g) chopped walnuts

1 Preheat a 350°F/180°C/Gas 4 oven. Line the bottom and sides of a 9 × 5 in (23 × 13 cm) loaf tin with greaseproof paper and grease the paper.

2 With an electric mixer, cream the butter and sugar together until light and fluffy.

3 ▲ Add the eggs, 1 at a time, beating well after each addition.

4 Sift the plain flour, bicarbonate of soda, salt and cinnamon over the butter mixture and stir to blend.

5 ▲ Stir in the wholewheat flour.

6 ▲ With a fork, mash the bananas to a purée, then stir into the mixture. Stir in the vanilla and nuts.

7 ▲ Pour the mixture into the prepared tin and spread level.

8 Bake for about 50–60 minutes, until a skewer inserted in the centre comes out clean. Let stand 10 minutes before transferring to a rack.

Date and Pecan Loaf

MAKES 1 LOAF

6 oz (170 g) stoned dates, chopped
6 fl oz (175 ml) boiling water
2 oz (55 g) unsalted butter, at room temperature
2 oz (55 g) dark brown sugar
2 oz (55 g) caster sugar
1 egg, at room temperature
2 tbsp brandy
5½ oz (165 g) plain flour
2 tsp baking powder
½ tsp salt
¾ tsp freshly grated nutmeg
3 oz (85 g) coarsely chopped pecans or walnuts

1 ▲ Place the dates in a bowl and pour over the boiling water. Set aside to cool.

2 Preheat a 350°F/180°C/Gas 4 oven. Line a 9 × 5 in (23 × 13 cm) loaf tin with greaseproof paper and grease.

3 ▲ With an electric mixer, cream the butter and sugars until light and fluffy. Beat in the egg and brandy, then set aside.

4 Sift the flour, baking powder, salt and nutmeg together, 3 times.

5 ▼ Fold the dry ingredients into the sugar mixture in 3 batches, alternating with the dates and water.

6 ▲ Fold in the nuts.

7 Pour the mixture into the prepared tin and bake for 45–50 minutes, until a skewer inserted in the centre comes out clean. Allow to cool in the tin for 10 minutes before transferring to a rack to cool completely.

Raisin Bread

MAKES 2 LOAVES

1 tablespoon active dried yeast
16 fl oz (450 ml) lukewarm milk
5 oz (140 g) raisins
2^1/$_2$ oz (70 g) currants
1 tablespoon sherry or brandy
^{1}/$_2$ teaspoon grated nutmeg
grated rind of 1 large orange
2^1/$_4$ oz (60 g) sugar
1 tablespoon salt
4 oz (115 g) butter, melted
1 lb 8 oz–1 lb 14 oz (700–850 g) strong flour
1 egg beaten with 1 tablespoon cream, for glazing

1   Stir together the yeast and 4 fl oz (125 ml) of the milk and let stand for 15 minutes to dissolve.

2 ▲   Mix the raisins, currants, sherry or brandy, nutmeg and orange rind together and set aside.

3   In another bowl, mix the remaining milk, sugar, salt and half the butter. Add the yeast mixture. With a wooden spoon, stir in half the flour, 5 oz (140 g) at a time, until blended. Add the remaining flour as needed for a stiff dough.

4   Transfer to a floured surface and knead until smooth and elastic. Place in a greased bowl, cover and leave to rise in a warm place until doubled in volume, about 2^1/$_2$ hours.

5   Punch down the dough, return to the bowl, cover and leave to rise in a warm place for 30 minutes.

6   Grease 2 8^1/$_2$ × 4^1/$_2$ in (21.5 × 11.5 cm) bread tins. Divide the dough in half and roll each half into a 20 × 7 in (50 × 18 cm) rectangle.

7 ▲   Brush the rectangles with the remaining melted butter. Sprinkle over the raisin mixture, then roll up tightly, tucking in the ends slightly as you roll. Place in the prepared tins, cover, and leave to rise until almost doubled in volume.

8 ▲   Preheat the oven to 400°F/ 200°C/Gas 6. Brush the loaves with the glaze. Bake for 20 minutes, then lower the temperature to350°F/ 180°C/ Gas 4 and bake until golden, for about 25–30 minutes more. Cool on racks.

Sweet Potato and Raisin Bread

The natural sweetness of sweet potato is used in this healthy loaf.

MAKES 1 LOAF

8–10 oz (225–275 g) plain flour
2 teaspoons (10 ml) baking powder
½ teaspoon (2.5 ml) salt
1 teaspoon (5 ml) ground cinnamon
½ teaspoon (2.5 ml) grated nutmeg
1 lb (450 g) mashed cooked sweet potatoes
3 oz (75 g) light brown sugar, firmly packed
4 oz (115 g) butter or margarine, melted and cooled
3 eggs, beaten
3 oz (75 g) raisins

1 ▲ Preheat the oven to 180°C/350°F/Gas 4. Grease a 9 × 5 in (23 × 13 cm) loaf tin.

2 Sift the flour, baking powder, salt, cinnamon and nutmeg into a small bowl. Set aside.

5 ▲ Transfer the batter to the prepared tin. Bake for 1–1¼ hours, or until a skewer inserted in the centre comes out clean.

6 Cool in the pan on a wire rack for 15 minutes, then turn the bread on to the wire rack and cool completely.

3 ▲ With an electric mixer, beat the mashed sweet potatoes with the brown sugar, butter or margarine and eggs until well mixed.

4 ▲ Add the flour mixture and the raisins. Stir with a wooden spoon until the flour is just mixed in.

Sultana Bread

A lightly sweetened fruit bread that is delicious served warm. It is also excellent toasted and topped with butter.

MAKES 1 LOAF

¼ pint (150 ml) warm water
1 teaspoon (5 ml) dried yeast
1 tablespoon (15 ml) clear honey
8 oz (225 g) wholemeal flour
8 oz (225 g) strong white flour
1 teaspoon (5 ml) salt
4 oz (115 g) sultanas
2 oz (50 g) walnuts, finely chopped
6 fl oz (175 ml) warm skimmed milk, plus extra for glazing

1 ▲ Put the water in a jug. Sprinkle the yeast on top. Add a few drops of the honey to activate the yeast, mix well and leave for 10 minutes.

2 ▲ Put the flours in a mixing bowl, with the salt and sultanas. Set aside 1 tablespoon (15 ml) of the walnuts and add the rest to the bowl. Mix lightly and make a well in the centre.

3 ▲ Add the yeast and honey mixture to the flour mixture with the milk and remaining honey. Gradually incorporate the flour, mixing to a soft dough; add a little extra water if the dough feels too dry to work with.

4 ▲ Turn the dough on to a floured surface and knead for 5 minutes until smooth and elastic. Return to the clean bowl, cover with a damp dish towel and leave in a warm place to rise for about 2 hours until doubled in bulk. Grease a baking sheet.

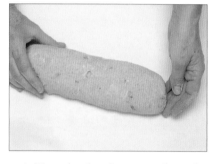

5 ▲ Turn the dough on to a floured surface and form into a 11 in (28 cm) long sausage shape. Place on the baking sheet. Make some diagonal cuts down the length of the loaf.

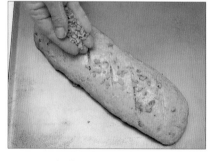

6 ▲ Brush the loaf with milk, sprinkle with the reserved walnuts and leave to rise for about 40 minutes. Preheat the oven to 220°C/425°F/Gas 7. Bake for 10 minutes. Lower the temperature to 200°C/400°F/Gas 6 and bake for about 20 minutes more, or until the loaf sounds hollow when tapped.

~ COOK'S TIP ~

To make Apple and Hazelnut Bread, replace the sultanas with two chopped eating apples and use chopped toasted hazelnuts instead of the walnuts. Add 1 teaspoon (5 ml) ground cinnamon with the flour.

Plaited Prune Bread

MAKES 1 LOAF

1 tbsp active dry yeast
2 fl oz (65 ml) lukewarm water
2 fl oz (65 ml) lukewarm milk
2 oz (55 g) caster sugar
1/2 tsp salt
1 egg
2 oz (55 g) butter, at room temperature
15 oz–1 lb 2 oz (420–500 g) plain flour
1 egg beaten with 2 tsp water, for glazing
FOR THE FILLING
7 oz (200 g) cooked prunes
2 tsp grated lemon rind
1 tsp grated orange rind
1/4 tsp freshly grated nutmeg
1 1/2 oz (45 g) butter, melted
2 oz (55 g) very finely chopped walnuts
2 tbsp caster sugar

1 In a large bowl, combine the yeast and water, stir and leave for 15 minutes to dissolve.

2 Stir in the milk, sugar, salt, egg and butter. Gradually stir in 12 oz (350 g) of the flour to obtain a soft dough.

3 Transfer to a floured surface and knead in just enough flour to obtain a dough that is smooth and elastic. Put into a clean bowl, cover and leave to rise in a warm place until doubled in volume, about 1 1/2 hours.

~ **VARIATION** ~

For Plaited Apricot Bread, replace the prunes with the same amount of dried apricots. It is not necessary to cook them, but to soften, soak them in hot tea and discard the liquid before using.

4 ▲ Meanwhile, for the filling, combine the prunes, lemon and orange rinds, nutmeg, butter, walnuts and sugar and stir together to blend. Set aside.

5 Grease a large baking sheet. Punch down the dough and transfer to a lightly floured surface. Knead briefly, then roll out into a 15 × 10 in (38 × 25 cm) rectangle. Carefully transfer to the baking sheet.

6 ▲ Spread the filling in the centre.

7 ▲ With a sharp knife, cut 10 strips at an angle on either side of the filling, cutting just to the filling.

8 ▲ For a plaited pattern, fold up one end neatly, then fold over the strips from alternating sides until all the strips are folded over. Tuck excess dough underneath at the ends.

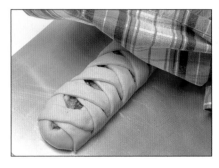

9 ▲ Cover loosely with a tea towel and leave to rise in a warm place until almost doubled in volume.

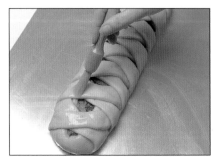

10 ▲ Preheat a 375°F/190°C/Gas 5 oven. Brush with the glaze. Bake until browned, about 30 minutes. Transfer to a rack to cool.

CLASSIC BREADS FROM AROUND THE WORLD

THIS COLLECTION FEATURES SAVOURY AND SWEET CLASSICS FROM AROUND THE WORLD, INCLUDING A GOOD SELECTION OF LESSER-KNOWN SPECIALITIES.

British Cottage Loaf

MAKES 1 LOAF

1½ lb (675 g) unbleached white bread flour
2 teaspoons (10 ml) salt
¾ oz (20 g) fresh yeast
14 fl oz (400 ml) lukewarm water

~ COOK'S TIPS ~

• To ensure a good-shaped cottage loaf the dough needs to be firm enough to support the weight of the top ball.
• Do not over-prove the dough on the second rising or the loaf may topple over.

Snipping the top and bottom sections of the dough at 2 in (5 cm) intervals not only looks good but also helps the loaf to expand in the oven.

1 Lightly grease 2 baking sheets. Sift the flour and salt into a large bowl and make a well in the centre.

2 Mix the yeast in ¼ pint (150 ml) of the water until dissolved. Pour into the flour with the remaining water and mix to a firm dough.

3 Knead on a lightly floured surface for 10 minutes until smooth and elastic. Place in a lightly oiled bowl, cover with lightly oiled clear film and leave to rise, in a warm place, for 1 hour, or until doubled in bulk.

4 ▲ Turn out on to a lightly floured surface and knock back. Knead for 2–3 minutes then divide the dough into two-thirds and one-third; shape each to a ball. Transfer to the prepared baking sheets. Cover with inverted bowls and leave to rise, in a warm place, for about 30 minutes (see Cook's Tips).

5 Gently flatten the top of the larger round of dough and cut a cross in the centre, about 1½ in (4 cm) across. Brush with a little water and place the smaller round on top.

6 ▲ Press a hole through the middle of the top ball, down into the lower part, using the thumb and first two fingers of one hand. Cover with oiled clear film and leave in a warm place for 10 minutes. Preheat the oven to 220°C/425°F/Gas 7 and place the bread on the lower shelf. It will finish expanding as the oven heats up. Bake for 35–40 minutes, or until it is golden brown and sounds hollow when tapped. Cool on a wire rack.

British Grant Loaves

This quick and easy recipe was created by Doris Grant and was included in her cookbook, published in the 1940s – the dough requires no kneading and takes only a minute to mix. The loaves should keep moist for several days.

MAKES 3 LOAVES

3 lb (1.5 kg) wholemeal bread flour
1 tablespoon (15 ml) salt
1 tablespoon (15 ml) easy-blend dried yeast
2 pints (1.2 litres) warm water
1 tablespoon (15 ml) muscovado sugar

1 Grease 3 loaf tins, 8½ × 4½ × 2½ in (21 × 12 × 6 cm) and set aside in a warm place. Sift the flour and salt in a large bowl and warm slightly to take off the chill.

2 Sprinkle the dried yeast over ¼ pint (150 ml) of the water. After a couple of minutes stir in the sugar. Leave for 10 minutes.

3 Make a well in the centre of the flour and stir in the yeast mixture and remaining water. The dough should be slippery. Mix for about 1 minute, working the sides into the middle.

4 ▲ Divide among the prepared tins, cover with oiled clear film and leave to rise, in a warm place, for 30 minutes, or until the dough has risen by about a third.

5 Meanwhile, preheat the oven to 200°C/400°F/Gas 6. Bake for 40 minutes, or until the loaves are crisp and sound hollow when tapped. Turn out on to a wire rack to cool.

British Poppy-Seeded Bloomer

MAKES 1 LOAF

1½ lb (675 g) unbleached white bread flour
2 teaspoons (10 ml) salt
½ oz (15 g) fresh yeast
15 fl oz (430 ml) water
FOR THE TOPPING
½ teaspoon (2.5 ml) salt
2 tablespoons (30 ml) water
poppy seeds, for sprinkling

This satisfying white bread, which is the British version of the chunky baton loaf found throughout Europe, is made by a slower rising method and with less yeast than usual. It produces a longer-keeping loaf with a fuller flavour. The dough takes about 8 hours to rise, so you'll need to start this bread early in the morning.

1 Lightly grease a baking sheet. Sift the flour and salt together into a large bowl and make a well in the centre.

2 ▲ Mix the yeast and ¼ pint (150 ml) of the water in a jug or bowl. Mix in the remaining water. Add to the centre of the flour. Mix, gradually incorporating the surrounding flour, until the mixture forms a firm dough.

~ COOK'S TIP ~

The traditional cracked, crusty appearance of this loaf is difficult to achieve in a domestic oven. However, you can get a similar result by spraying the oven with water before baking. If the underneath of the loaf is not very crusty at the end of baking, turn the loaf over on the baking sheet, switch off the heat and leave in the oven for a further 5–10 minutes.

3 ▲ Turn out on to a lightly floured surface and knead the dough very well, for at least 10 minutes, until smooth and elastic. Place the dough in a lightly oiled bowl, cover with lightly oiled clear film and leave to rise, at cool room temperature, about 15–18°C/60–65°F, for 5–6 hours, or until doubled in bulk.

4 Knock back the dough, turn out on to a lightly floured surface and knead it quite hard for about 5 minutes. Return the dough to the bowl, and re-cover. Leave to rise, at cool room temperature, for a further 2 hours.

5 ▲ Knock back again and repeat the thorough kneading. Leave to rest for 5 minutes, then roll out on a lightly floured surface into a rectangle 1 in (2.5 cm) thick. Roll the dough up from one long side and shape it into a square-ended thick baton shape about 13 × 5 in (33 × 13 cm).

6 ▲ Place it seam side up on a lightly floured baking sheet, cover and leave to rest for 15 minutes. Turn the loaf over and place on the greased baking sheet. Plump up by tucking the dough under the sides and ends, then cut 6 diagonal slashes on the top. Leave to rest, covered, in a warm place, for 10 minutes. Meanwhile preheat the oven to 230°C/450°F/Gas 8.

7 ▲ Mix the salt and water together and brush this glaze over the bread. Sprinkle with poppy seeds.

8 Spray the oven with water, bake the bread immediately for 20 minutes, then reduce the oven temperature to 200°C/400°F/Gas 6; bake for 25 minutes more, or until golden. Transfer to a wire rack to cool.

British Harvest Festival Sheaf

MAKES 1 LARGE LOAF

2 lb (900 g) unbleached white bread flour
1 tablespoon (15 ml) salt
½ oz (15 g) fresh yeast
5 tablespoons (75 ml) lukewarm milk
14 fl oz (400 ml) cold water
FOR THE GLAZE
1 egg
1 tablespoon (15 ml) milk

1 Lightly grease a large baking sheet, at least 15 × 13 in (38 × 33 cm). Sift the flour and salt together into a large bowl and make a well in the centre.

2 Cream the yeast with the milk in a jug. Add to the centre of the flour with the water and mix to a stiff dough. Turn out on to a lightly floured surface and knead for about 10–15 minutes until smooth and elastic.

3 Place in a lightly oiled bowl, cover with lightly oiled clear film and leave to rise, at room temperature, for about 2 hours, or until doubled in bulk.

4 Turn the dough out on to a lightly floured surface, knock back and knead for about 1 minute. Cover and leave to rest for 10 minutes.

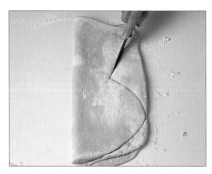

5 ▲ Divide the dough in two. Roll out one piece to a 14 × 10 in (35 × 25 cm) oblong. Fold loosely in half lengthways. Cut out a half mushroom shape for the sheaf (leave the folded edge uncut). Make the stalk "base" about 7 in (18 cm) long.

This is one of the most visually stunning breads. Celebratory loaves can be seen in various forms in churches and at some bakers throughout Britain around the September harvest.

6 Place the dough on the baking sheet and open out. Prick with a fork and brush with water to prevent a skin from forming. Reserve 3 oz (75 g) of the trimmings for the tie. Cover and set aside. Divide the remaining dough in two and mix the rest of the trimmings with one half. Cover and set aside. Beat together the egg and milk for the glaze.

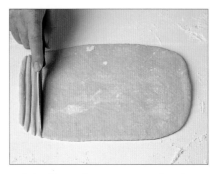

7 ▲ Roll out the remaining dough on a lightly floured surface to a rectangle, 11 × 7 in (28 × 18 cm), and cut into 30–35 thin strips 7 in (18 cm) long. Place side by side lengthways on the base, as close as possible, to represent wheat stalks. Brush with some glaze.

8 Take the larger piece of reserved dough and divide into four. Divide each piece into 25 and shape into oblong rolls to make 100 wheat ears. Make each roll pointed at one end.

9 ▲ Holding one roll at a time, snip along each side towards the centre, using scissors, to make wheat ears.

10 Preheat the oven to 220°C/425°F/ Gas 7. Arrange the ears around the outer edge of the top of the mushroom shape, overlapping on to the baking sheet. Make a second row lower down, placing it between the first ears. Repeat until they are all used. Brush with glaze as you work to stop the dough from drying out.

11 ▲ Divide the smaller piece of reserved dough into 6 pieces and roll each to a 17 in (43 cm) strip. Make 2 plaits each with 3 strips. Place across the wheat stalks to make a tied bow. Brush with some glaze. Prick between the wheat ears and stalks using a sharp knife and bake the sheaf for 15 minutes.

12 Reduce the oven temperature to 180°C/350°F/Gas 4. Brush the bread with the remaining glaze and bake for a further 30–35 minutes, or until golden and firm. Leave to cool on the baking sheet.

~ COOK'S TIP ~

Harvest loaves are often baked for display, rather than for eating. If you'd like to do this, then leave the baked loaf in the oven, reduce the temperature to very low, 120°C/250°F/Gas ½, for several hours until the dough dries out.

British Lardy Cake

MAKES 1 LOAF

1 lb (450 g) unbleached white bread flour
1 teaspoon (5 ml) salt
½ oz (15 g) lard
1 oz (25 g) caster sugar
¾ oz (20 g) fresh yeast
½ pint (300 ml) lukewarm water
FOR THE FILLING
3 oz (75 g) lard
3 oz (75 g) soft light brown sugar
4 oz (115 g) currants, slightly warmed
3 oz (75 g) sultanas, slightly warmed
1 oz (25 g) mixed chopped peel
1 teaspoon (5 ml) mixed spice
FOR THE GLAZE
2 teaspoons (10 ml) sunflower oil
1–2 tablespoons (15–30 ml) caster sugar

This special rich fruit bread was originally made throughout many counties of England for celebrating the harvest. Using lard rather than butter or margarine makes an authentic lardy cake.

1 Grease a 10 × 8 in (25 × 20 cm) shallow roasting tin. Sift the flour and salt into a bowl and rub in the lard. Add the sugar. Make a well in the centre.

2 Cream the yeast with half of the water, then blend in the rest. Add to the flour and mix to a smooth dough.

3 Turn out on to a lightly floured surface and knead for about 10 minutes until smooth and elastic. Place in a lightly oiled bowl, cover with lightly oiled clear film and leave to rise, in a warm place, for 1 hour, or until doubled in bulk.

4 Turn the dough out on to a lightly floured surface and knock back. Knead for 2–3 minutes. Roll into a rectangle about ¼ in (5 mm) thick.

5 ▲ Using half the lard for the filling, cover the top two-thirds of the dough with flakes of lard. Sprinkle over half the sugar, half the dried fruits and peel and half the mixed spice. Fold the bottom third up and the top third down, sealing the edges with the rolling pin.

6 Turn the dough by 90 degrees. Repeat the rolling and cover with the remaining lard, fruit and peel and mixed spice. Fold, seal and turn as before. Roll out to fit the prepared tin. Cover with oiled clear film and leave to rise, in a warm place, for 30–45 minutes, until doubled in size.

7 Meanwhile, preheat the oven to 200°C/400°F/Gas 6. Brush the cake with oil and sprinkle with caster sugar.

8 ▲ Score a criss-cross pattern on top using a sharp knife, then bake for 30–40 minutes until golden. Turn out on to a wire rack to cool slightly. Serve warm, cut into slices or squares.

British Malted Currant Bread

This spiced currant bread makes a good tea or breakfast bread, sliced and spread with a generous amount of butter. It also makes superb toast.

MAKES 2 LOAVES

2 oz (50 g) malt extract
2 tablespoons (30 ml) golden syrup
2 oz (50 g) butter
1 lb (450 g) unbleached white bread flour
1 teaspoon (5 ml) mixed spice
¾ oz (20 g) fresh yeast
6 fl oz (175 ml) lukewarm milk
6 oz (175 g) currants, slightly warmed
FOR THE GLAZE
2 tablespoons (30 ml) milk
2 tablespoons (30 ml) caster sugar

> ### ~ COOK'S TIP ~
> When making more than one loaf, the easiest way to prove them is to place the tins in an oiled large polythene bag.

4 Turn the dough out on to a floured surface, knock back, then knead in the currants. Divide the dough in two and shape into two loaves. Place in the prepared tins. Cover with oiled clear film and leave to rise, in a warm place, for 2–3 hours, or until the dough reaches the top of the tins.

5 ▲ Meanwhile, preheat the oven to 200°C/400°F/Gas 6. Bake for 35–40 minutes or until golden. While the loaves are baking, heat the milk and sugar for the glaze in a small pan. Turn out the loaves on to a wire rack, then invert them, so that they are the right way up. Brush the glaze evenly over the loaves and leave to cool.

1 ▲ Lightly grease two 1 lb (450 g) loaf tins. Place the malt extract, golden syrup and butter in a saucepan and heat gently until the butter has melted. Set aside to cool completely.

2 Sift the flour and mixed spice together into a large bowl and make a well in the centre. Cream the yeast with a little of the milk, then blend in the remaining milk. Add the yeast mixture and cooled malt mixture to the centre of the flour and blend together to form a dough.

3 Turn out the dough on to a lightly floured surface and knead for about 10 minutes until smooth and elastic. Place in a lightly oiled bowl, cover with lightly oiled clear film and leave to rise, in a warm place, for 1½–2 hours, or until doubled in bulk.

Welsh Bara Brith

MAKES 1 LOAF

¾ oz (20 g) fresh yeast
7 fl oz (210 ml) lukewarm milk
1 lb (450 g) unbleached white bread flour
3 oz (75 g) butter or lard
1 teaspoon (5 ml) mixed spice
½ teaspoon (2.5 ml) salt
2 oz (50 g) light brown sugar
1 egg, lightly beaten
4 oz (115 g) seedless raisins, slightly warmed
3 oz (75 g) currants, slightly warmed
1½ oz (40 g) mixed chopped peel
1–2 tablespoons (15–30 ml) clear honey, for glazing

This rich, fruity bread – the name literally means "speckled bread" – is a speciality from North Wales. The honey glaze makes a delicious topping.

1 Grease a baking sheet. In a jug, blend the yeast with a little of the milk, then stir in the remainder. Set aside for 10 minutes.

2 ▲ Sift the flour into a large bowl and rub in the butter or lard until the mixture resembles breadcrumbs. Stir in the mixed spice, salt and sugar and make a well in the centre.

3 Add the yeast mixture and beaten egg to the centre of the flour and mix to a rough dough.

4 Turn out the dough on to a lightly floured surface and knead for about 10 minutes until smooth and elastic. Place in a lightly oiled bowl, cover with lightly oiled clear film and leave to rise, in a warm place, for 1½ hours, or until doubled in bulk.

5 ▲ Turn out the dough on to a floured surface, knock back, and knead in the dried fruits and peel. Shape into a round and place on the baking sheet. Cover with oiled clear film and leave to rise, in a warm place, for 1 hour, or until doubled in size.

6 Meanwhile, preheat the oven to 200°C/400°F/Gas 6. Bake for 30 minutes or until the bread sounds hollow when tapped on the base. If the bread starts to over-brown, cover it loosely with foil for the last 10 minutes. Transfer the bread to a wire rack, brush with honey and leave to cool.

~ VARIATION ~

The bara brith can be baked in a 2½–3 pint (1.5–1.75 litre) loaf tin or deep round or square cake tin, if you prefer.

Welsh Clay Pot Loaves

These breads are flavoured with chives, sage, parsley and garlic. You can use any selection of your favourite herbs. For even more flavour, try adding a little grated raw onion and grated cheese to the dough.

MAKES 2 LOAVES

4 oz (115 g) wholemeal bread flour
12 oz (350 g) unbleached white bread flour
1½ teaspoons (7.5 ml) salt
½ oz (15 g) fresh yeast
¼ pint (150 ml) lukewarm milk
4 fl oz (120 ml) lukewarm water
2 oz (50 g) butter, melted
1 tablespoon (15 ml) chopped fresh chives
1 tablespoon (15 ml) chopped fresh parsley
1 teaspoon (5 ml) chopped fresh sage
1 garlic clove, crushed
beaten egg, for glazing
fennel seeds, for sprinkling (optional)

4 Turn the dough out on to a floured surface and knock back. Divide in two. Shape and fit into the flower pots. They should about half fill the pots. Cover with oiled clear film and leave to rise for 30–45 minutes, in a warm place, or until the dough is 1 in (2.5 cm) from the top of the pots.

1 ▲ Lightly grease 2 clean 5½ in (14 cm) diameter, 4½ in (12 cm) high clay flower pots. Sift the flours and salt into a bowl and make a well in the centre. Blend the yeast with a little of the milk until smooth, then stir in the remaining milk. Pour into the centre of the flour and sprinkle over a little of the flour from around the edge. Cover and leave in a warm place for 15 minutes.

2 ▲ Add the water, melted butter, herbs and garlic to the flour mixture and blend together to form a dough. Turn out on to a floured surface and knead for 10 minutes until the dough is smooth and elastic.

3 Place in a lightly oiled bowl, cover with lightly oiled clear film and leave to rise, in a warm place, for 1¼–1½ hours, or until doubled in bulk.

5 ▲ Meanwhile, preheat the oven to 200°C/400°F/Gas 6. Brush the tops with beaten egg and sprinkle with fennel seeds, if using. Bake for 35–40 minutes or until golden. Turn out on to a wire rack to cool.

Scottish Morning Rolls

MAKES 10 ROLLS

1 lb (450 g) unbleached plain white flour, plus extra for dusting
2 teaspoons (10 ml) salt
¾ oz (20 g) fresh yeast
¼ pint (150 ml) lukewarm milk
¼ pint (150 ml) lukewarm water
2 tablespoons (30 ml) milk

These rolls are best served warm, as soon as they are baked. In Scotland they are a firm favourite for breakfast with a fried egg and bacon.

1 Grease 2 baking sheets. Sift the flour and salt into a bowl and make a well in the centre. Mix the yeast with the milk, then mix in the water. Add to the centre of the flour and mix together to form a soft dough.

2 Knead the dough lightly in the bowl, then cover with lightly oiled clear film and leave to rise, in a warm place, for 1 hour, or until doubled in bulk. Turn the dough out on to a floured surface and knock back.

3 ▲ Divide the dough into 10 equal pieces. Knead lightly and, using a rolling pin, shape each piece to a flat oval 4 × 3 in (10 × 7.5 cm) or a flat round 3½ in (9 cm).

4 Place on the baking sheets and cover with oiled clear film. Leave to rise, in a warm place, for 30 minutes.

5 ▲ Meanwhile, preheat the oven to 200°C/400°F/Gas 6. Press each roll in the centre with the three middle fingers to equalise the air bubbles and to help prevent blistering. Brush with milk and dust with flour. Bake for 15–20 minutes or until lightly browned. Dust with more flour and cool slightly. Serve warm.

Cornish Saffron Breads

Often called saffron cake, this light, delicately spiced bread contains strands of saffron and is made in a loaf tin. Whatever the name, the flavour and texture are superb.

MAKES 2 LOAVES

½ pint (300 ml) milk
½ teaspoon (2.5 ml) saffron strands
14 oz (400 g) unbleached white bread flour
1 oz (25 g) fresh yeast
2 oz (50 g) ground almonds
½ teaspoon (2.5 ml) grated nutmeg
½ teaspoon (2.5 ml) ground cinnamon
2 oz (50 g) caster sugar
½ teaspoon (2.5 ml) salt
3 oz (75 g) butter, softened
2 oz (50 g) sultanas
2 oz (50 g) currants
extra milk and sugar, to glaze

7 ▲ Turn the dough out on to a lightly floured surface, knock back, and knead in the sultanas and currants. Divide in two and shape into two loaves. Place in the prepared tins. Cover with oiled clear film and leave to rise, in a warm place, for 1½ hours, or until the dough reaches the top of the tins.

8 Preheat the oven to 220°C/425°F/ Gas 7. Bake the loaves for 10 minutes, then reduce the oven temperature to 190°C/375°F/Gas 5 and bake for 15–20 minutes or until golden.

9 To make the glaze, heat milk and sugar together. When the loaves are cooked, brush them with the glaze, leave in the tins for 5 minutes, then turn out on to a wire rack to cool.

1 Grease two 2 lb (900 g) loaf tins. Heat half the milk until almost boiling.

2 ▲ Place the saffron strands in a small heatproof bowl and pour over the milk. Stir gently, then leave to infuse for 30 minutes.

3 Heat the remaining milk in the same pan until it is just lukewarm.

4 Place 2 oz (50 g) flour in a small bowl, crumble in the yeast and stir in the lukewarm milk. Mix well, then leave for about 15 minutes until the yeast starts to ferment.

5 Mix the remaining flour, ground almonds, spices, sugar and salt together in a large bowl and make a well in the centre. Add the saffron infusion, yeast mixture and softened butter to the centre of the flour and mix to a very soft dough.

6 Turn out on to a floured surface and knead the dough for 5 minutes until smooth and elastic. Place in a lightly oiled bowl, cover with oiled clear film and leave to rise, in a warm place, for 1½–2 hours, or until doubled in bulk.

French Kugelhopf

Makes 1 loaf

5 oz (150 g) unsalted butter, softened
12 walnut halves
1½ lb (675 g) unbleached white bread flour
1½ teaspoons (7.5 ml) salt
¾ oz (20 g) fresh yeast
10 fl oz (300 ml) milk
4 oz (115 g) smoked bacon, diced
1 onion, finely chopped
1 tablespoon (15 ml) vegetable oil
5 eggs, beaten
freshly ground black pepper

~ VARIATION ~

For a sweet kugelhopf, replace the walnuts with almonds and the bacon and onion with 4 oz (115 g) raisins and 2 oz (50 g) mixed peel. Add 2 oz (50 g) caster sugar in step 2 and omit the pepper.

This inviting, fluted ring-shaped bread originates from Alsace, although Germany, Hungary and Austria all have their own variations of this popular recipe. Kugelhopf can be sweet or savoury; this version is richly flavoured with nuts, onion and bacon.

1 ▲ Use 1 oz (25 g) of the butter to grease a 9 in (23 cm) kugelhopf mould. Place 8 walnut halves around the base and chop the remainder.

2 Sift the flour and salt into a bowl and season with pepper. Make a well in the centre. Cream the yeast with 3 tablespoons (45 ml) of the milk. Pour into the centre of the flour with the remaining milk. Mix in a little flour to make a thick batter. Sprinkle a little of the remaining flour over the top of the batter, cover with clear film and leave in a warm place for 20–30 minutes until the mixture bubbles.

3 ▲ Fry the bacon and onion in the oil until the onion is golden.

4 Add the eggs to the flour mixture and gradually beat in the flour, using your hand. Beat in the remaining butter to form a soft dough. Cover with oiled clear film and leave to rise, in a warm place, for 45–60 minutes, or until almost doubled in bulk. Preheat the oven to 200°C/400°F/Gas 6.

5 ▲ Knock back the dough and gently knead in the bacon, onion and nuts. Place in the mould, cover with oiled clear film and leave to rise, in a warm place, for about 1 hour.

6 Bake for 40–45 minutes, or until the loaf has browned and sounds hollow when tapped on the base. Cool in the mould for 5 minutes, then on a wire rack.

French Pain Polka

This attractive, deeply cut, crusty bread is made by using a little of the previous day's dough as a starter. However, if you do not have any you can make a starter dough, the details for which are given.

MAKES 1 LOAF

8 oz (225 g) 6–15-hours-old French baguette dough

OR FOR THE STARTER

¼ oz (10 g) fresh yeast
4 fl oz (120 ml) lukewarm water
4 oz (115 g) unbleached plain flour

FOR THE DOUGH

¼ oz (10 g) fresh yeast
scant ½ pint (300 ml) lukewarm water
1 lb (450 g) unbleached white bread flour, plus extra for dusting
1 tablespoon (15 ml) salt

> ### ~ COOK'S TIP ~
> The piece of previously made dough can be kept covered in the fridge for up to 2 days, or frozen for up to a month. Just let it come back to room temperature and allow it to rise for an hour before using.

1 ▲ Lightly flour a baking sheet. If you have French baguette dough, proceed to step 2. Make the starter. Mix the yeast with the water, then gradually stir in sufficient flour to form a batter. Beat vigorously, then gradually add the remaining flour and mix to a soft dough. Knead for 5 minutes. Place in a bowl, cover with oiled clear film, and leave at room temperature for 4–5 hours, or until well risen and starting to collapse.

2 In a bowl, mix the yeast for the dough with half of the water, then stir in the remainder. Add the previously made dough or starter (step 1) and knead to dissolve the dough. Gradually add the flour and salt and mix to a dough. Turn out on to a lightly floured surface and knead for 8–10 minutes until the dough is smooth and elastic.

3 Place the dough in a lightly oiled bowl, cover with lightly oiled clear film and leave to rise, in a warm place, for about 1½ hours, or until doubled in bulk.

4 Turn out the dough on to a lightly floured surface, knock back and shape into a round ball. Flatten slightly and place on the prepared baking sheet. Cover with oiled clear film and leave to rise, in a warm place, for 1 hour.

5 ▲ Dust the top of the loaf with flour and cut the top fairly deeply in a criss-cross pattern. Leave to rest for 10 minutes. Meanwhile, preheat the oven to 230°C/450°F/Gas 8.

6 Bake for 25–30 minutes, or until browned. Spray the inside of the oven with water as soon as the bread goes into the oven, and 3 times during the first 10 minutes of baking. Transfer to a wire rack to cool.

French Pain Bouillie

MAKES 2 LOAVES

¼ oz (10 g) fresh yeast
2 tablespoons (30 ml) lukewarm water
1 teaspoon (5 ml) caraway seeds, crushed
2 teaspoons (10 ml) salt
12 oz (350 g) unbleached white bread flour
olive oil, for brushing
FOR THE PORRIDGE
8 oz (225 g) rye flour
¾ pint (450 ml) boiling water
1 teaspoon (5 ml) clear honey

This is an old-fashioned style of rye bread, made before sourdough starters were used. Rye flour is mixed with boiling water like a porridge and left overnight to ferment. The finished bread has a rich earthy flavour, with just a hint of caraway.

1 ▲ Lightly grease a 9¼ × 5 in (23.5 × 13 cm) loaf tin. Place the rye flour for the porridge in a large bowl. Pour over the boiling water and leave to stand for 5 minutes. Stir in the honey. Cover with clear film and leave in a warm place for about 12 hours.

2 ▲ Make the dough. Put the yeast in a jug and blend in the water. Stir the mixture into the porridge with the crushed caraway seeds and salt. Add the white flour a little at a time, mixing first with a wooden spoon and then with your hands, until the mixture forms a firm dough.

3 Turn out on to a lightly floured surface and knead for 6–8 minutes until smooth and elastic. Return to the bowl, cover with oiled clear film and leave to rise, in a warm place, for 1½ hours, until doubled in bulk.

4 ▲ Turn out the dough on to a floured surface and knock back. Cut and roll into rectangles 15 × 4½ in (38 × 12 cm). Fold the bottom third up and the top third down and seal the edges. Turn over.

5 Brush one side of each piece of folded dough with olive oil and place side by side in the prepared tin, oiled edges next to each other. Cover with lightly oiled clear film and leave to rise, in a warm place, for 1 hour, or until the dough reaches the top of the tin.

6 Meanwhile, preheat the oven to 220°C/425°F/Gas 7. Brush the tops of the loaves with olive oil and, using a sharp knife, slash with one or two cuts. Bake for 30 minutes, then reduce the oven temperature to 190°C/375°F/Gas 5 and bake for a further 25–30 minutes. Turn out on to a wire rack to cool.

> **~ COOK'S TIP ~**
> Serve thickly sliced, with a little butter.

French Epi

This pretty, wheat-ear shaped crusty loaf makes a good presentation bread. The recipe uses a piece of fermented French baguette dough as a starter, which improves the flavour and texture of the finished bread.

MAKES 2 LOAVES

¼ oz (7 g) fresh yeast
9 fl oz (275 ml) lukewarm water
4 oz (115 g) 6–10-hours-old French baguette dough
8 oz (225 g) unbleached white bread flour
3 oz (75 g) fine French plain flour
1 teaspoon (5 ml) salt

~ COOK'S TIP ~

You can use any amount up to 10 per cent of previously made French baguette dough for this recipe. The épi can also be shaped into a circle.

1 ▲ Sprinkle a baking sheet with flour. Mix the yeast with the water in a jug. Place the French bread dough in a large bowl and break up. Add a little of the yeast water to soften the dough. Mix in a little of the bread flour, then alternate the additions of yeast water and both flours until incorporated. Sprinkle the salt over the dough and knead in. Turn out on to a floured surface and knead for 5 minutes until smooth and elastic.

2 Place in an oiled bowl, cover with oiled clear film and leave to rise, in a warm place, for about 1 hour, or until the dough has doubled in bulk.

3 ▲ Knock back the dough with your fist, then cover the bowl again with the oiled clear film and leave to rise, in a warm place, for about 1 hour.

4 Divide the dough in half, place on a lightly floured surface and stretch each piece into a baguette.

5 Let the dough rest between rolling for a few minutes, if necessary, to avoid tearing. Pleat a floured dish towel on a baking sheet to make 2 moulds for the loaves. Place them between the pleats of the towel, cover with lightly oiled clear film and leave to rise, in a warm place, for 30 minutes.

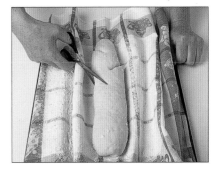

6 ▲ Preheat the oven to 230°C/450°F/ Gas 8. Using scissors, make diagonal cuts halfway through the dough about 2 in (5 cm) apart, alternating the cuts along the loaf. Gently pull the dough in the opposite direction.

7 Place on the baking sheet and bake for 20 minutes, until golden. Spray inside the oven with water 2–3 times during the first 5 minutes of baking. Transfer to a wire rack to cool.

French Pain de Campagne Rustique

MAKES 1 LOAF

FOR THE CHEF
2 oz (50 g) wholemeal bread flour
3 tablespoons (45 ml) warm water

FOR THE 1ST REFRESHMENT
4 tablespoons (60 ml) warm water
3 oz (75 g) wholemeal bread flour

FOR THE 2ND REFRESHMENT
4 fl oz (120 ml) lukewarm water
4 oz (115 g) unbleached white bread flour
1 oz (25 g) wholemeal bread flour

FOR THE DOUGH
5–6 fl oz (150–175 ml) lukewarm water
12 oz (350 g) unbleached white bread flour
2 teaspoons (10 ml) salt

~ COOK'S TIPS ~

• You will need to start making this bread about four days before you'd like to eat it.

• To make another loaf, keep the piece of starter dough (see step 6) in the fridge for up to 3 days. Use dough for the 2nd refreshment in place of the *levain* in step 3, gradually mix in the water, then the flours and leave to rise as described.

1 ▲ To make the *chef*, place the flour in a small bowl, add the water and knead for 3–4 minutes to form a dough. Cover with clear film and leave the *chef* in a warm place for 2 days.

This superb country bread is made using a natural French *chef* starter to produce a rustic flavour and texture. In France, breads like this are often made three or four times the size of this loaf.

2 Pull off the crust and discard, then remove 2 tablespoons (30 ml) of the moist centre. Place in a bowl and gradually mix in the water for the 1st refreshment. Mix in the flour and knead for 3–4 minutes to form a dough or *levain*, cover with clear film and leave in a warm place for a day.

3 ▲ Discard the crust from the *levain* and gradually mix in the water for the 2nd refreshment. Mix in the flours a little at a time, mixing well after each addition to form a firm dough. Cover with lightly oiled clear film and leave to rise, in a warm place, for about 10 hours, or until doubled in bulk.

4 Lightly flour a baking sheet. For the final stage in the preparation of the dough, gradually mix the water into the *levain* in the bowl, then gradually mix in the flour, then the salt. Turn out the dough on to a lightly floured surface and knead for about 5 minutes until smooth and elastic.

5 Place the dough in a large lightly oiled bowl, cover with lightly oiled clear film and leave to rise, in a warm place, for 1½–2 hours, or until the dough has almost doubled in bulk.

6 Knock back the dough and cut off 4 oz (115 g). Set aside for making the next loaf. Shape the remaining dough into a ball – you should have about 12 oz (350 g).

7 Line a 4 in (10 cm) high, 9 in (23 cm) round basket or large bowl with a dish towel and dust with flour.

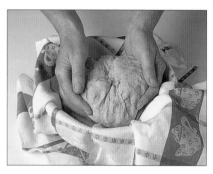

8 ▲ Place the dough ball seam side up in the prepared basket or bowl. Cover with lightly oiled clear film and leave to rise, in a warm place, for 2–3 hours, or until almost doubled in bulk.

9 Preheat the oven to 230°C/450°F/ Gas 8. Invert the loaf on to the baking sheet and sprinkle with flour.

10 ▲ Slash the top of the loaf, using a sharp knife, four times at right angles to each other, to form a square pattern.

11 Sprinkle with a little more flour, if you like, then bake for 30–35 minutes, or until the loaf has browned and sounds hollow when tapped on the base. Transfer to a wire rack to cool.

French Fougasse

MAKES 2 LOAVES

1 lb (450 g) unbleached white bread flour
1 teaspoon (5 ml) salt
¾ oz (20 g) fresh yeast
9 fl oz (280 ml) lukewarm water
1 tablespoon (15 ml) extra virgin olive oil

FOR THE FILLING

2 oz (50 g) Roquefort cheese, crumbled
1½ oz (40 g) walnut pieces, chopped
1 oz (25 g) drained, canned anchovy fillets, soaked in milk and drained again, chopped
olive oil, for brushing

A fougasse is a lattice-shaped, flattish loaf from the South of France. It can be cooked as a plain bread or flavoured with cheese, anchovies, herbs, nuts or olives. On Christmas Eve in Provence a fougasse flavoured with orange flower water is part of a table centrepiece of thirteen desserts, used to symbolize Christ and the Twelve Apostles.

2 Place the dough in an oiled bowl, cover with oiled clear film and leave to rise, in a warm place, for about 1 hour, or until doubled in bulk.

3 ▲ Turn out on to a floured surface and knock back. Divide in half and flatten one piece. Sprinkle over the cheese and walnuts and fold the dough over on itself 2–3 times to incorporate. Repeat with the other piece of dough, this time incorporating the anchovies. Shape each piece of flavoured dough into a ball.

4 Flatten each ball of dough and fold the bottom third up and the top third down, to make an oblong. Roll the cheese dough into a rectangle measuring about 11 × 6 in (28 × 15 cm). Make 4 diagonal cuts almost to the edge. Stretch the dough evenly, so that it resembles a ladder.

5 Shape the anchovy dough into an oval with a flat base, about 10 in (25 cm) long. Make 3 diagonal slits on each side towards the flat base, and pull to open the cuts. Transfer to the baking sheets, cover with oiled clear film and leave to rise, in a warm place, for about 30–45 minutes, or until nearly doubled in bulk.

6 Meanwhile, preheat the oven to 220°C/425°F/Gas 7. Brush both loaves with a little olive oil and bake for 25 minutes, or until golden. Transfer to a wire rack to cool.

~ VARIATION ~

To make a sweet fougasse, replace 1 tablespoon (15 ml) of the water with orange flower water. Include 2 oz (50 g) chopped candied orange peel and 1 oz (25 g) sugar.

1 ▲ Lightly grease 2 baking sheets. Sift the flour and salt together into a large bowl and make a well in the centre. In a measuring jug, cream the yeast with 4 tablespoons (60 ml) of the water. Pour the yeast mixture into the centre of the flour with the remaining water and the olive oil and mix to a soft dough. Turn out on to a floured surface and knead for 8–10 minutes until smooth and elastic.

French Pain aux Noix

This delicious butter- and milk-enriched wholemeal bread is filled with walnuts. It is the perfect companion for cheese.

MAKES 2 LOAVES

2 oz (50 g) butter
12 oz (350 g) wholemeal bread flour
4 oz (115 g) unbleached white bread flour
1 tablespoon (15 ml) light brown muscovado sugar
1½ teaspoons (7.5 ml) salt
¾ oz (20 g) fresh yeast
9 fl oz (275 ml) lukewarm milk
6 oz (175 g) walnut pieces

3 Knead on a lightly floured surface for 6–8 minutes. Place in a lightly oiled bowl, cover with oiled clear film and leave to rise, in a warm place, for 1 hour, or until doubled in bulk.

4 ▲ Turn out the dough on to a lightly floured surface and gently knock back. Press or roll out to flatten and then sprinkle over the nuts. Gently press the nuts into the dough, then roll it up. Return to the oiled bowl, re-cover and leave, in a warm place, for 30 minutes.

5 Turn out on to a floured surface, divide in half and shape each piece into a ball. Place on the baking sheets, cover with oiled clear film and leave to rise, in a warm place, for 45 minutes, until doubled in bulk.

6 Preheat the oven to 220°C/425°F/ Gas 7. Slash the top of each loaf 3 times. Bake for 35 minutes, or until they sound hollow when tapped. Transfer to a wire rack to cool.

1 ▲ Grease 2 baking sheets. Place the butter in a small pan and heat until melted and starting to brown, then set aside to cool. Mix the flours, sugar and salt in a bowl and make a well in the centre. Cream the yeast with half the milk. Add to the centre of the flour with the remaining milk.

2 ▲ Pour the cool melted butter through a fine strainer into the centre of the flour so that it joins the liquids already there. Using your hand, mix the liquids together in the bowl and gradually mix in small quantities of the flour to make a batter. Continue until the mixture forms a moist dough.

French Baguettes

Makes 3 loaves

1¼ lb (500 g) unbleached white bread flour
4 oz (115 g) fine French plain flour
2 teaspoons (10 ml) salt
½ oz (15 g) fresh yeast
18 fl oz (550 ml) lukewarm water

Baguettes are difficult to reproduce at home as they require a very hot oven and steam. However, by using less yeast and a triple fermentation you can produce a bread with a superior taste and far better texture than mass-produced baguettes. These are best eaten on the day of baking.

1 Sift the flours and salt into a bowl. Add the yeast to the water in another bowl and stir to dissolve. Gradually beat in half the flour mixture to form a batter. Cover with clear film and leave at room temperature for 3 hours, or until nearly trebled in size and starting to collapse.

2 Add the remaining flour a little at a time, beating with your hand. Turn out on to a floured surface and knead for 8–10 minutes to form a moist dough. Place in an oiled bowl, cover with oiled clear film and leave to rise, in a warm place, for 1 hour.

3 When the dough has almost doubled in bulk, knock it back, turn out on to a floured surface and divide into 3. Shape each into a rectangle 6 × 3 in (15 × 7.5 cm).

4 Fold the bottom third up lengthways and the top third down and press down to make sure the pieces of dough are in contact. Seal the edges. Repeat two or three more times until each loaf is an oblong. Leave to rest in between folding for a few minutes, if necessary, to avoid tearing the dough.

5 ▲ Gently stretch each piece of dough lengthways into a 13–14 in (33–35 cm) long loaf. Pleat a floured dish towel on a baking sheet to make 3 moulds for the loaves. Place the breads between the pleats of the towel to help hold their shape while rising. Cover with lightly oiled clear film and leave to rise, in a warm place, for about 45–60 minutes.

6 Preheat the oven to maximum, at least 230°C/450°F/Gas 8. Roll the loaves on to a baking sheet, spaced well apart. Slash the top of each loaf several times with long diagonal slits. Bake at the top of the oven for 20–25 minutes, or until golden. Spray inside the oven with water 2–3 times during the first 5 minutes of baking. Transfer to a wire rack to cool.

> **~ VARIATION ~**
>
> If you make baguettes regularly you may want to purchase baguette frames to hold and bake the breads in, or long *bannetons* in which to prove this wonderful bread.

French Brioche

Rich and buttery yet light and airy, this wonderful loaf captures the essence of the classic French bread.

1 Sift the flour and salt together into a large bowl and make a well in the centre. Put the yeast in a measuring jug and stir in the milk.

2 ▲ Add the yeast mixture to the centre of the flour with the eggs and mix together to form a soft dough.

3 ▲ Using your hand, beat the dough for 4–5 minutes until smooth and elastic. Cream the butter and sugar together. Gradually add the butter mixture to the dough, ensuring it is incorporated before adding more. Beat until smooth, shiny and elastic.

MAKES 1 LOAF

12 oz (350 g) unbleached white bread flour
½ teaspoon (2.5 ml) salt
½ oz (15 g) fresh yeast
4 tablespoons (60 ml) lukewarm milk
3 eggs
6 oz (175 g) butter, softened
1 oz (25 g) caster sugar
FOR THE GLAZE
1 egg yolk
1 tablespoon (15 ml) milk

4 Cover the bowl with lightly oiled clear film and leave the dough to rise, in a warm place, for 1–2 hours or until doubled in bulk.

5 Lightly knock back the dough, then re-cover and place in the fridge for 8–10 hours or overnight.

6 Lightly grease a 2¾ pint (1.6 litre) brioche mould. Turn the dough out on to a lightly floured surface. Cut off almost a quarter and set aside. Shape the rest into a ball and place in the prepared mould. Shape the reserved dough into an elongated egg shape. Using two or three fingers, make a hole in the centre of the large ball of dough. Gently press the narrow end of the egg-shaped dough into the hole.

7 Mix together the egg yolk and milk for the glaze, and brush a little over the brioche. Cover with lightly oiled clear film and leave to rise, in a warm place, for 1½–2 hours, or until the dough nearly reaches the top of the mould.

8 Meanwhile, preheat the oven to 230°C/450°F/Gas 8. Brush the brioche with the remaining glaze and bake for 10 minutes. Reduce the oven temperature to 190°C/375°F/Gas 5 and bake for a further 20–25 minutes, or until golden. Turn out on to a wire rack to cool.

French Croissants

MAKES 14 CROISSANTS

12 oz (350 g) unbleached white bread flour
4 oz (115 g) fine French plain flour
1 teaspoon (5 ml) salt
1 oz (25 g) caster sugar
½ oz (15 g) fresh yeast
scant 8 fl oz (225 ml) lukewarm milk
1 egg, lightly beaten
8 oz (225 g) butter
FOR THE GLAZE
1 egg yolk
1 tablespoon (15 ml) milk

Golden layers of flaky pastry, puffy, light and flavoured with butter is how the best croissants should be. Serve warm on the day of baking.

~ COOK'S TIP ~

Make sure that the block of butter and the dough are about the same temperature when combining, to ensure the best results.

1 ▲ Sift the flours and salt into a bowl. Stir in the sugar. Make a well in the centre. Cream the yeast with 3 tablespoons (45 ml) of the milk, then stir in the rest. Add the yeast mixture to the centre of the flour, then add the egg and gradually beat in the flour until it forms a dough.

2 Turn out on to a floured surface and knead for 3–4 minutes. Place in an oiled bowl, cover with oiled clear film and leave to rise, in a warm place, for about 45 minutes–1 hour, or until doubled in bulk.

3 Knock back, re-cover and chill in the fridge for 1 hour. Flatten the butter into a block about ¾ in (2 cm) thick. Knock back the dough and turn out on to a floured surface. Roll out into a rough 10 in (25 cm) square, with edges thinner than the centre.

4 ▲ Place the block of butter diagonally in the centre and fold the corners of the dough over the butter like an envelope, tucking in the edges to completely enclose the butter.

5 ▲ Roll the dough into a rectangle about ¾ in (2 cm) thick, twice as long as it is wide. Fold the bottom third up and the top third down and seal the edges. Chill for 20 minutes.

6 Repeat the rolling, folding and chilling twice more, turning the dough by 90 degrees each time. Roll out on a floured surface into a 25 × 13 in (62 × 33 cm) rectangle; trim to leave a 24 × 12 in (60 × 30 cm) rectangle. Cut in half lengthways. Cut crossways into 14 equal triangles with 6 in (15 cm) bases.

7 Place the dough triangles on 2 baking sheets, cover with clear film and chill for 10 minutes.

8 ▲ To shape the croissants, place each one with the wide end at the top, hold each side and pull gently to stretch the top of the triangle a little, then roll towards the point, finishing with the pointed end tucked underneath. Curve the ends towards the pointed end to make a crescent. Place on two baking sheets, spaced well apart.

9 Mix together the egg yolk and milk for the glaze. Lightly brush a little glaze over the croissants, avoiding the cut edges of the dough. Cover the croissants loosely with lightly oiled clear film and leave to rise, in a warm place, for about 30 minutes, or until they are nearly doubled in size.

10 Meanwhile, preheat the oven to 220°C/425°F/Gas 7. Brush the croissants with the remaining glaze and bake for 15–20 minutes, or until crisp and golden. Transfer to a wire rack to cool slightly. Serve warm.

~ VARIATION ~

To make chocolate-filled croissants, place a small square of chocolate at the wide end of each triangle before rolling up as in step 8.

French Petits Pains au Lait

MAKES 12 ROLLS

1 lb (450 g) unbleached white bread flour
2 teaspoons (10 ml) salt
1 tablespoon (15 ml) caster sugar
2 oz (50 g) butter, softened
½ oz (15 g) fresh yeast
9 fl oz (275 ml) lukewarm milk, plus 1 tablespoon (15 ml) extra milk, for glazing

---

~ VARIATION ~

These can also be made into long rolls. To shape, flatten each ball of dough and fold in half. Roll back and forth, using your hand to form a 5 in (13 cm) long roll, tapered at either end.

These classic French round milk rolls have a soft crust and a light, slightly sweet crumb. They won't last long!

1 Lightly grease 2 baking sheets. Sift the flour and salt together into a large bowl. Stir in the sugar. Rub the softened butter into the flour.

2 Cream the yeast with 4 tablespoons (60 ml) of the milk. Stir in the remaining milk. Pour into the flour mixture and mix to a soft dough.

3 Turn out on to a floured surface and knead for 8–10 minutes until smooth and elastic. Place in an oiled bowl, cover with oiled clear film and leave to rise, in a warm place, for 1 hour, or until doubled in bulk.

4 Turn out the dough on to a floured surface and gently knock back. Divide into 12, shape into balls and space well apart on the baking sheets.

5 ▲ Using a sharp knife, cut a cross in the top of each roll. Cover with lightly oiled clear film and leave to rise, in a warm place, for about 20 minutes, or until doubled in size.

6 Preheat the oven to 200°C/400°F/ Gas 6. Brush the rolls with milk and bake for 20–25 minutes, or until golden. Transfer to a wire rack to cool.

French Dimpled Rolls

MAKES 10 ROLLS

14 oz (400 g) unbleached white bread flour
1½ teaspoons (7.5 ml) salt
1 tablespoon (5 ml) caster sugar
½ oz (15 g) fresh yeast
4 fl oz (120 ml) lukewarm milk
6 fl oz (175 ml) lukewarm water

A French and Belgian speciality, these attractive rolls are distinguished by the split down the centre. They have a crusty finish while remaining soft and light inside – they taste lovely, too.

1 Lightly grease 2 baking sheets. Sift the flour and salt into a large bowl. Stir in the sugar and make a well in the centre.

2 Cream the yeast with the milk until dissolved, then pour into the centre of the flour mixture. Sprinkle over a little of the flour from around the edge. Leave at room temperature for 15–20 minutes, or until the mixture starts to bubble.

3 Add the water and gradually mix in the flour to form a fairly moist, soft dough. Turn out on to a lightly floured surface and knead for 8–10 minutes until smooth and elastic. Place in a lightly oiled bowl, cover with lightly oiled clear film and leave to rise, at room temperature, for about 1½ hours, or until doubled in bulk.

4 Turn out on to a floured surface and knock back. Re-cover and leave to rest for 5 minutes. Divide the dough into 10 pieces. Shape into balls by rolling under your hand, then roll until oval. Lightly flour the tops. Place spaced well apart on the baking sheets, cover with oiled clear film and leave to rise, at room temperature, for about 30 minutes, until almost doubled in size.

5 ▲ Oil the side of your hand and press the centre of each roll to make a deep split. Re-cover and leave to rest for 15 minutes. Place a roasting tin in the bottom of the oven and preheat the oven to 230°C/450°F/Gas 8. Pour 8 fl oz (250 ml) water into the tin and bake the rolls on a higher shelf for 15 minutes or until golden. Let cool.

Swiss Braid

MAKES 1 LOAF

12 oz (375 g) unbleached white bread flour
1 teaspoon (5 ml) salt
¾ oz (20 g) fresh yeast
2 tablespoons (30 ml) lukewarm water
¼ pint (150 ml) soured cream
1 egg, lightly beaten
2 oz (50 g) butter, softened
FOR THE GLAZE
1 egg yolk
1 tablespoon (15 ml) water

This plaited, attractively tapered loaf is known as zupfe in Switzerland. Often eaten at the weekend, it is has a glossy crust and a wonderfully light crumb.

1 Lightly grease a baking sheet. Sift the flour and salt together into a large bowl and make a well in the centre. Mix the yeast with the water in a jug.

2 ▲ Gently warm the soured cream in a small pan until it reaches blood heat (35–38°C). Add to the yeast mixture and mix together.

3 Add the yeast mixture and egg to the centre of the flour and mix to a dough. Beat in the softened butter.

4 ▲ Turn out on to a floured surface and knead for 5 minutes until smooth and elastic. Place in a lightly oiled bowl, cover with oiled clear film and leave to rise, in a warm place, for 1½ hours, or until doubled in size.

5 Turn out on to a floured surface and knock back. Cut in half and shape each piece of dough into a long rope about 14 in (35 cm) in length.

6 To make the braid, place the two pieces of dough on top of each other to form a cross. Starting with the bottom rope, fold the top end over and place between the two bottom ropes. Fold the remaining top rope over so that all four ropes are pointing down. Starting on the left, plait the first rope over the second, and the third over the fourth.

7 Continue plaiting to form a tapered bread. Tuck under the ends and place on the baking sheet. Cover with oiled clear film and leave to rise, in a warm place, for about 40 minutes.

8 Meanwhile, preheat the oven to 190°C/ 375°F/Gas 5. Mix the egg yolk and water for the glaze, and brush over the loaf. Bake the bread for 30–35 minutes, or until golden. Cool on a wire rack.

German Sourdough Bread

This bread includes rye, wholemeal and plain flours for a superb depth of flavour. Serve it cut in thick slices, with creamy butter or a sharp cheese.

MAKES 1 LOAF

FOR THE SOURDOUGH STARTER
3 oz (75 g) rye flour
3 fl oz (80 ml) warm water
pinch caraway seeds
FOR THE DOUGH
½ oz (15 g) fresh yeast
11 fl oz (315 ml) lukewarm water
10 oz (275 g) rye flour
5 oz (150 g) wholemeal bread flour
5 oz (150 g) unbleached white bread flour
2 teaspoons (10 ml) salt

1 ▲ Mix the rye flour, warm water and caraway for the starter together in a large bowl with your fingertips, to make a soft paste. Cover with a damp dish towel and leave in a warm place for about 36 hours. Stir after 24 hours.

2 Lightly grease a baking sheet. In a measuring jug, blend the yeast for the dough with the lukewarm water. Add to the starter and mix thoroughly.

3 ▲ Mix the rye flour, wholemeal bread flour and unbleached white bread flour for the dough with the salt in a large bowl; make a well in the centre. Pour in the yeast liquid and gradually incorporate the surrounding flour to make a smooth dough.

4 Turn out the dough on to a lightly floured surface and knead for 8–10 minutes until smooth and elastic. Place in a lightly oiled bowl, cover with lightly oiled clear film and leave to rise, in a warm place, for 1½ hours, or until nearly doubled in bulk.

5 ▲ Turn out on to a lightly floured surface, knock back and knead gently. Shape into a round and place in a floured basket or *couronne*, with the seam side up. Cover with lightly oiled clear film and leave to rise, in a warm place, for 2–3 hours.

6 Meanwhile, preheat the oven to 200°C/400°F/Gas 6. Turn out the loaf on to the baking sheet and bake for 35–40 minutes. Cool on a wire rack.

~ COOK'S TIP ~

Proving the dough in a floured basket or *couronne* gives it its characteristic patterned crust, but is not essential. Make sure that you flour the basket well, otherwise the dough may stick.

German Stollen

MAKES 1 LOAF

3 oz (75 g) sultanas
2 oz (50 g) currants
3 tablespoons (45 ml) rum
13 oz (375 g) unbleached white bread flour
½ teaspoon (2.5 ml) salt
2 oz (50 g) caster sugar
¼ teaspoon (1.5 ml) ground cardamom
½ teaspoon (2.5 ml) ground cinnamon
1½ oz (40 g) fresh yeast
4 fl oz (120 ml) lukewarm milk
2 oz (50 g) butter, melted
1 egg, lightly beaten
2 oz (50 g) mixed chopped peel
2 oz (50 g) blanched whole almonds, chopped
melted butter, for brushing
icing sugar, for dusting
FOR THE ALMOND FILLING
4 oz (115 g) ground almonds
2 oz (50 g) caster sugar
2 oz (50 g) icing sugar
½ teaspoon (2.5 ml) lemon juice
½ egg, lightly beaten

This German speciality bread, made for the Christmas season, is rich with rum-soaked fruits and is wrapped around a moist almond filling. The folded shape of the dough over the filling represents the baby Jesus wrapped in swaddling clothes.

3 ▲ Mix the yeast with the milk until creamy. Pour into the flour and mix in a little of the flour from around the edge to make a thick batter. Sprinkle some of the remaining flour over the top of the batter, then cover with clear film and leave in a warm place for 30 minutes.

4 Add the melted butter and egg and mix to a soft dough. Turn out the dough on to a floured surface and knead for 8–10 minutes until smooth and elastic. Place in an oiled bowl, cover with lightly oiled clear film and leave to rise, in a warm place, for 2–3 hours, until doubled in bulk.

1 ▲ Grease a baking sheet. Preheat the oven to 180°C/350°F/Gas 4. Put the sultanas and currants in a heatproof bowl and warm for 3–4 minutes. Pour over the rum and set aside.

2 Sift the flour and salt into a large bowl. Stir in the sugar and spices.

5 ▲ Mix the ground almonds and sugars for the filling. Add the lemon juice and enough egg to make a smooth paste. Shape into a 8 in (20 cm) sausage, cover and set aside.

6 Turn out the dough on to a lightly floured surface and knock back.

7 Pat out the dough into a rectangle about 1 in (2.5 cm) thick and sprinkle over the sultanas, currants, peel and almonds. Fold and knead to incorporate the fruit and nuts.

8 ▲ Roll out the dough into an oval about 12 × 9 in (30 × 23 cm). Roll the centre slightly thinner than the edges. Place the almond paste filling along the centre and fold over the dough to enclose it, making sure that the top of the dough doesn't completely cover the base. The top edge should be slightly in from the bottom edge. Press down to seal.

9 Place the loaf on the prepared baking sheet, cover with lightly oiled clear film and leave to rise, in a warm place, for 45–60 minutes, or until doubled in size.

10 Meanwhile, preheat the oven to 200°C/400°F/Gas 6. Bake the loaf for about 30 minutes, or until it sounds hollow when tapped on the base. Brush the top with melted butter and transfer to a wire rack to cool. Dust with icing sugar just before serving.

> **~ COOK'S TIP ~**
> You can dust the cooled stollen with icing sugar and cinnamon, or drizzle over a thin glacé icing.

German Pumpernickel

MAKES 2 LOAVES

1 lb (450 g) rye flour
8 oz (225 g) wholemeal flour
4 oz (115 g) bulgur wheat
2 teaspoons (10 ml) salt
2 tablespoons (30 ml) molasses
1½ pints (850 ml) warm water
1 tablespoon (15 ml) vegetable oil

~ COOK'S TIP ~

This bread improves on keeping for at least 24 hours, double-wrapped.

This famous German bread is extremely dense and dark, with an intense flavour. It is baked very slowly and although cooked in the oven, it is more like a steamed bread than a baked one.

1 Lightly grease two 7 × 3½ in (18 × 9 cm) loaf tins. Mix the rye flour, wholemeal flour, bulgur wheat and salt together in a large bowl.

2 Mix the molasses with the warm water and add to the flours with the oil. Mix to form a dense mass.

3 ▲ Place in the prepared tins, pressing well into the corners. Cover with lightly oiled clear film and leave in a warm place for 18–24 hours.

4 Preheat the oven to 110°C/225°F/Gas ¼. Cover the tins tightly with foil. Fill a roasting tin with boiling water and place a rack on top.

5 Place the tins on top of the rack and transfer very carefully to the oven. Bake the loaves for 4 hours. Increase the oven temperature to 160°C/325°F/Gas 3. Top up the water in the roasting tin if necessary, uncover the loaves and bake for a further 30–45 minutes, or until the loaves feel firm and the tops are crusty.

6 Leave to cool in the tins for 5 minutes, then turn out on to a wire rack. Serve cold, very thinly sliced.

Swedish Vört Limpa

This festive Swedish bread is flavoured with warm spices and fresh orange. The beer and port work nicely to soften the rye taste. The added sugars also give the yeast a little extra to feed on and so help aerate and lighten the bread. It is traditionally served with cheese.

MAKES 1 LOAF

12 oz (350 g) rye flour
12 oz (350 g) unbleached white bread flour
½ teaspoon (2.5 ml) salt
1 oz (25 g) caster sugar
1 teaspoon (5 ml) grated nutmeg
1 teaspoon (5 ml) ground cloves
1 teaspoon (5 ml) ground ginger
1½ oz (40 g) fresh yeast
½ pint (300 ml) light ale
4 fl oz (120 ml) port
1 tablespoon (15 ml) molasses
1 oz (25 g) butter, melted
1 tablespoon (15 ml) grated orange rind
3 oz (75 g) raisins
1 tablespoon (15 ml) malt extract, for glazing

1 Lightly grease a 12 × 4 in (30 × 10 cm) loaf tin. Mix together the rye and white flours, salt, sugar, nutmeg, cloves and ginger in a large bowl.

2 In another large bowl, using a wooden spoon, blend the yeast into the ale until dissolved, then stir in the port, molasses and melted butter.

3 Gradually add the flour mixture to the yeast liquid, beating to make a smooth batter. Continue adding the flour a little at a time and mixing until the mixture forms a soft dough.

4 ▲ Turn out on to a floured surface and knead for 8–10 minutes until smooth and elastic. Place in an oiled bowl, cover with oiled clear film and leave to rise, in a warm place, for 1 hour, or until doubled in size.

5 Turn out the dough on to a floured surface and knock back. Gently knead in the orange rind and raisins. Roll into a 12 in (30 cm) square.

6 ▲ Fold the bottom third of the dough up and the top third down, sealing the edges. Place in the loaf tin, cover with oiled clear film and leave to rise, in a warm place, for 1 hour, or until it reaches the top of the tin.

7 Meanwhile, preheat the oven to 190°C/375°F/Gas 5. Bake for 35–40 minutes, or until browned. Turn out on to a wire rack, brush with malt extract and leave to cool.

Swedish Knackerbröd

MAKES 8 CRISPBREADS

1 lb (450 g) rye flour
1 teaspoon (5 ml) salt
2 oz (50 g) butter
¾ oz (20 g) fresh yeast
9 fl oz (275 ml) lukewarm water
3 oz (75 g) wheat bran

A very traditional Swedish crispbread with a lovely rye flavour.

1 ▲ Lightly grease 2 baking sheets. Preheat the oven to 230°C/450°F/Gas 8. Mix the rye flour and salt in a large bowl. Rub in the butter, then make a well in the centre.

2 Cream the yeast with a little water, then stir in the remainder. Pour into the centre of the flour, mix to a dough, then mix in the bran. Knead on a lightly floured surface for 5 minutes until smooth and elastic.

3 Divide the dough into 8 pieces and roll each one out on a floured surface, to a 8 in (20 cm) round.

4 ▲ Place 2 rounds on the prepared baking sheets and prick all over with a fork. Cut a hole in the centre of each round, using a 1½ in (4 cm) cutter.

5 Bake for 15–20 minutes, or until golden and crisp. Transfer to a wire rack to cool. Repeat with the remaining crispbreads.

~ COOK'S TIP ~

The hole in the centre of these crispbreads is a reminder of the days when breads were strung on a pole, which was hung across the rafters to dry. Make smaller crispbreads, if you like, and tie them together with bright red ribbon for an unusual Christmas gift.

Finnish Barley Bread

MAKES 1 LOAF

8 oz (225 g) barley flour
1 teaspoon (5 ml) salt
2 tablespoons (10 ml) baking powder
1 oz (25 g) butter, melted
4 fl oz (120 ml) single cream
4 tablespoons (60 ml) milk

In Northern Europe breads are often made using cereals such as barley and rye, which produce very satisfying, tasty breads. This quick-to-prepare flat bread is best served warm with lashings of butter.

1 ▲ Grease a baking sheet. Preheat the oven to 200°C/400°F/Gas 6. Sift the dry ingredients into a bowl. Add the wet ingredients. Mix to a dough.

2 Turn out the dough on to a lightly floured surface and shape into a flat round about ½ in (1 cm) thick.

3 ▲ Transfer to the prepared baking sheet and, using a sharp knife, lightly mark the top into 6 sections.

4 Prick the surface of the round evenly with a fork. Bake for about 15–18 minutes, or until pale golden. Cut into wedges and serve warm.

~ COOK'S TIPS ~

• This flat bread tastes very good with cottage cheese, especially cottage cheese with chives.
• For a citrusy tang, add 2–3 teaspoons (10–15 ml) finely grated lemon, lime or orange rind to the flour mixture in step 1.

Swedish Lusse Bröd

MAKES 12 BUNS

4 fl oz (120 ml) milk
pinch of saffron threads
14 oz (400 g) unbleached white bread flour
2 oz (50 g) ground almonds
½ teaspoon (2.5 ml) salt
3 oz (75 g) caster sugar
1 oz (25 g) fresh yeast
4 fl oz (120 ml) lukewarm water
few drops of almond essence
2 oz (50 g) butter, softened
FOR THE GLAZE
1 egg, beaten with 1 tablespoon (15 ml) water

Saint Lucia Day, the 12th of December, marks the beginning of Christmas in Sweden. As part of the celebrations, young girls dressed in white robes wear headbands topped with lighted candles and walk through the village streets offering saffron buns to the townspeople.

1 ▲ Lightly grease 2 baking sheets. Place the milk in a small saucepan and bring to the boil. Add the saffron, remove from the heat and leave to infuse for about 15 minutes. Meanwhile, mix the flour, ground almonds, salt and sugar in a bowl.

2 Cream the yeast with the water. Add the saffron liquid, yeast mixture and almond essence to the flour mixture and mix to a dough. Gradually beat in the softened butter.

3 Turn out on to a lightly floured surface and knead for 5 minutes until smooth and elastic. Place in an oiled bowl, cover with oiled clear film and leave to rise, in a warm place, for about 1 hour, or until doubled in bulk.

4 ▲ Turn out on to a lightly floured surface and knock back. Divide into 12 equal pieces and make into different shapes: roll into a long rope and shape into an "S" shape; to make a star, cut a dough piece in half and roll into two ropes, cross one over the other and coil the ends; make an upturned "U" shape and coil the ends to represent curled hair; divide a dough piece in half, roll into two thin ropes and twist together.

5 Place on the baking sheets, spaced well apart, cover with oiled clear film and leave to rise, in a warm place, for about 30 minutes.

6 Preheat the oven to 200°C/400°F/ Gas 6. Brush the glaze over the rolls. Bake for 15 minutes, or until golden. Transfer to a wire rack to cool. Serve warm or cold.

Savoury Danish Crown

Filled with golden onions and cheese, this butter-rich bread ring is quite irresistible and needs no accompaniment.

1 Lightly grease a baking sheet. Sift the flour and salt together into a large bowl. Rub in 1½ oz (40 g) of the butter. Mix the yeast with the milk and water. Add to the flour with the egg and mix to a soft dough.

2 Turn out on to a floured surface and knead for 10 minutes until smooth and elastic. Place in an oiled bowl, cover with oiled clear film or slide into an oiled polythene bag and leave to rise, in a warm place, for about 1 hour, or until doubled in bulk.

3 Knock back and turn out on to a lightly floured surface. Roll out into an oblong about ½ in (1 cm) thick.

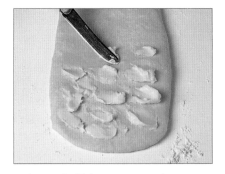

4 ▲ Dot half the remaining butter over the top two-thirds of the dough. Fold the bottom third up and the top third down and seal the edges. Turn by 90 degrees and repeat with the remaining butter. Fold and seal as before. Cover with oiled clear film and leave to rest for 15 minutes.

5 Turn by a further 90 degrees. Roll and fold again without any butter. Repeat once more. Wrap in lightly oiled clear film and leave to rest in the fridge for 30 minutes.

6 Meanwhile, heat the oil for the filling. Add the onions and cook for 10 minutes until golden. Remove from the heat and add the breadcrumbs, almonds, Parmesan and seasoning.

7 Mix half the beaten egg into the breadcrumb mixture.

8 Roll out the dough on a floured surface into a rectangle 22 × 9 in (56 × 23 cm). Spread with the filling to within ¾ in (2 cm) of the edges, then roll up like a Swiss roll from one long side. Cut in half lengthways. Plait together with the cut sides up and shape into a ring. Place on the baking sheet, cover with oiled clear film and leave to rise, in a warm place, for 30 minutes.

9 Meanwhile, preheat the oven to 200°C/400°F/Gas 6. Brush the remaining beaten egg over the dough. Sprinkle with sesame seeds and Parmesan cheese and bake for 40–50 minutes, or until golden. Transfer to a wire rack to cool. Serve warm or cold, cut into slices.

MAKES 1 LOAF
12 oz (350 g) unbleached white bread flour
1 teaspoon (5 ml) salt
6½ oz (185 g) butter, softened
¾ oz (20 g) fresh yeast
7 fl oz (200 ml) mixed lukewarm milk and water
1 egg, lightly beaten
FOR THE FILLING
2 tablespoons (30 ml) sunflower oil
2 onions, finely chopped
1½ oz (40 g) fresh breadcrumbs
1 oz (25 g) ground almonds
2 oz (50 g) freshly grated Parmesan cheese
1 egg, lightly beaten
salt and freshly ground black pepper
FOR THE TOPPING
1 tablespoon (15 ml) sesame seeds
1 tablespoon (15 ml) freshly grated Parmesan cheese

Danish Julekage

MAKES 1 LOAF

1 oz (25 g) fresh yeast
5 tablespoons (75 ml) lukewarm milk
1 lb (450 g) unbleached white bread flour
2 teaspoons (10 ml) salt
3 oz (75 g) butter
15 cardamom pods
½ teaspoon (2.5 ml) vanilla essence
2 oz (50 g) light brown soft sugar
grated rind of ½ lemon
2 eggs, lightly beaten
2 oz (50 g) ready-to-eat dried apricots, chopped
2 oz (50 g) glacé pineapple pieces, chopped
2 oz (50 g) red and green glacé cherries, chopped
1 oz (25 g) dried dates, chopped
1 oz (25 g) crystallized stem ginger, chopped
FOR THE GLAZE
1 egg white
2 teaspoons (10 ml) water
FOR THE DECORATION
1 tablespoon (15 ml) caster sugar
½ teaspoon (2.5 ml) ground cinnamon
8 pecan nuts or whole blanched almonds

In Scandinavia special slightly sweet holiday breads containing fragrant cardamom seeds are common. This exotic bread, enriched with butter and a selection of glacé and dried fruits or "jewels", is traditionally served over the Christmas period with hot spiced punch.

1 Lightly grease a 9 × 5 in (23 × 13 cm) loaf tin. In a measuring jug, cream the yeast with the milk.

2 ▲ Sift the flour and salt together into a large bowl. Add the butter and rub in. Make a well in the centre. Add the yeast mixture to the centre of the flour and butter mixture and stir in sufficient flour to form a thick batter. Sprinkle over a little of the remaining flour and set aside in a warm place for 15 minutes.

3 Remove the seeds from the cardamom pods. Put them in a mortar and crush with a pestle. Add the crushed seeds to the flour with the vanilla essence, sugar, lemon rind and eggs, then mix to a soft dough.

4 ▲ Turn out on to a floured surface and knead for 8–10 minutes until smooth and elastic. Place in an oiled bowl, cover with oiled clear film and leave to rise, in a warm place, for 1–1½ hours, or until doubled in bulk.

5 Knock back the dough and turn it out on to a lightly floured surface. Flatten into a rectangle and sprinkle over half of the apricots, pineapple, cherries, dates and ginger. Fold the sides into the centre and then fold in half to contain the fruit. Flatten into a rectangle again and sprinkle over the remaining fruit. Fold and knead gently to distribute the fruit. Cover the fruited dough with lightly oiled clear film and leave to rest for 10 minutes.

6 Roll the fruited dough into a rectangle 15 × 10 in (38 × 25 cm). With a short side facing you, fold the bottom third up lengthways and the top third down, tucking in the sides, to form a 9 × 5 in (23 × 13 cm) loaf. Place in the prepared tin, seam side down. Cover with lightly oiled clear film and leave to rise, in a warm place, for 1 hour, or until the dough has reached the top of the tin.

7 Meanwhile, preheat the oven to 180°C/350°F/Gas 4. Using a sharp knife, slash the top of the loaf lengthways and then make diagonal slits on either side.

8 Mix together the egg white and water for the glaze, and brush over the top. Mix the sugar and cinnamon in a bowl, then sprinkle over the top. Decorate with pecan nuts or almonds. Bake for 45–50 minutes, or until risen and browned. Transfer to a wire rack to cool.

~ VARIATIONS ~

• You can vary the fruits for this loaf. Try glacé peaches, yellow glacé cherries, sultanas, raisins, candied angelica, dried mango or dried pears and use in place of some or all of the fruits in the recipe. Use a mixture of colours and make sure that the total weight is the same as above.
• Use walnuts in place of the pecan nuts or almonds.

~ COOK'S TIP ~

If the top of the loaf starts to brown too quickly during cooking, cover loosely with foil.

Scandinavian Sunshine Loaf

MAKES 1 LARGE LOAF

FOR THE STARTER

4 tablespoons (60 ml) lukewarm milk

4 tablespoons (60 ml) lukewarm water

¼ oz (7 g) fresh yeast

3¾ oz (100 g) unbleached white bread flour

FOR THE DOUGH

½ oz (15 g) fresh yeast

17 fl oz (500 ml) lukewarm water

1 lb (450 g) rye flour

8 oz (225 g) unbleached white bread flour

1 tablespoon (15 ml) salt

milk, for glazing

caraway seeds, for sprinkling

Scandinavia, Land of the Midnight Sun, has numerous breads based on rye. This splendid table centrepiece is made with a blend of rye and white flours, the latter helping to lighten the bread.

1 ▲ Combine the milk and water for the starter in a bowl. Mix in the yeast until dissolved. Gradually stir the flour with a metal spoon.

2 Cover the bowl with clear film and leave the mixture in a warm place for 3–4 hours, or until well risen, bubbly and starting to collapse.

3 Mix the yeast for the dough with 4 tablespoons (60 ml) of the water until creamy, then stir in the remaining water. Gradually mix into the starter to dilute it. Gradually mix in the rye flour to form a smooth batter. Cover with lightly oiled clear film and leave in a warm place, for 3–4 hours, or until well risen.

4 Stir the bread flour and salt into the batter to form a dough. Turn on to a floured surface and knead for 5 minutes until smooth and elastic. Place in an oiled bowl, cover with oiled clear film and leave to rise, in a warm place, for 1 hour, until doubled in bulk.

5 ▲ Knock back on a floured surface. Cut the dough into 5 pieces. Roll one piece into a 20 in (50 cm) "sausage" and roll up into a spiral shape.

6 Cut the remaining pieces in half and shape each one into a 8 in (20 cm) rope. Place in a circle on a baking sheet, spaced equally apart, like rays of the sun, and curl the ends round, leaving a small gap in the centre. Place the spiral shape on top. Cover with oiled clear film and leave to rise, in a warm place, for 30 minutes.

7 Preheat the oven to 230°C/450°F/ Gas 8. Brush the bread with milk, sprinkle with caraway seeds and bake for 30 minutes, or until lightly browned. Cool on a wire rack.

Spanish Pan de Cebada

This Spanish country bread has a close, heavy texture and is quite satisfying. It is richly flavoured, incorporating barley and maize flours.

MAKES 1 LOAF

FOR THE SOURDOUGH STARTER
6 oz (175 g) maize meal
scant 1 pint (560 ml) water
8 oz (225 g) wholemeal bread flour
3 oz (75 g) barley flour

FOR THE DOUGH
¾ oz (20 g) fresh yeast
3 tablespoons (45 ml) lukewarm water
8 oz (225 g) wholemeal bread flour
1 tablespoon (15 ml) salt
maize meal, for dusting

1 ▲ In a saucepan, mix the maize meal for the sourdough starter with half the water, then blend in the remainder. Cook over a gentle heat, stirring until thickened. Transfer to a large bowl and set aside to cool.

2 Mix in the wholemeal flour and barley flour. Turn out on to a floured surface and knead for 5 minutes. Return to the bowl, cover with oiled clear film and leave the starter in a warm place for 36 hours.

3 ▲ Dust a baking sheet with maize meal. In a small bowl, cream the yeast with the water for the dough. Mix the yeast mixture into the starter with the wholemeal flour and salt and work to a dough. Turn out on to a lightly floured surface and knead for 4–5 minutes until smooth and elastic.

4 Transfer the dough to a lightly oiled bowl, cover with oiled clear film or an oiled polythene bag and leave, in a warm place, for 1½–2 hours to rise, or until nearly doubled in bulk.

5 ▲ Knock back the dough and turn out on to a lightly floured surface. Shape into a plump round. Sprinkle with a little maize meal.

6 Place the shaped bread on the baking sheet. Cover with an upturned bowl. Leave to rise, in a warm place, for about 1 hour, or until nearly doubled in bulk. Place a roasting tin in the bottom of the oven. Preheat the oven to 220°C/425°F/Gas 7.

7 Pour ½ pint (300 ml) cold water into the roasting tin. Remove the bowl and immediately place the risen loaf in the oven. Bake the bread for 10 minutes. Remove the tin of water, reduce the oven temperature to 190°C/375°F/Gas 5 and bake for about 20 minutes. Cool on a wire rack.

Spanish Twelfth Night Bread

MAKES 1 LOAF

1 lb (450 g) unbleached white bread flour
½ teaspoon (2.5 ml) salt
1 oz (25 g) yeast
scant ¼ pint (140 ml) mixed lukewarm milk and water
3 oz (75 g) butter
3 oz (75 g) caster sugar
2 teaspoons (10 ml) finely grated lemon rind
2 teaspoons (10 ml) finely grated orange rind
2 eggs
1 tablespoon (15 ml) brandy
1 tablespoon (15 ml) orange flower water
silver coin or dried bean (optional)
1 egg white, lightly beaten, for glazing

FOR THE DECORATION

a mixture of candied and glacé fruit slices
flaked almonds

January 6th, Epiphany or the Day of the Three Kings, is celebrated in Spain as a time to exchange Christmas presents. Historically this date was when the Three Wise Men arrived bearing gifts. An ornamental bread ring is specially baked for the occasion. The traditional version contains a silver coin, china figure or dried bean hidden inside – the lucky recipient is declared King of the festival!

2 In a bowl, mix the yeast with the milk and water until the yeast has dissolved. Pour the yeast mixture into the centre of the flour and stir in enough of the flour from around the sides of the bowl to make a thick batter.

3 Sprinkle a little of the remaining flour over the top of the batter and leave to "sponge", in a warm place, for about 15 minutes or until frothy.

4 Using an electric whisk or a wooden spoon, beat the butter and sugar together in a bowl until soft and creamy, then set aside.

5 Add the citrus rinds, eggs, brandy and orange flower water to the flour mixture and mix to a sticky dough.

~ COOK'S TIP ~

If you like, this bread can be baked in a 9½ in (24 cm) ring-shaped cake tin.

1 ▲ Lightly grease a large baking sheet. Sift the flour and salt together into a large bowl. Make a well in the centre.

6 ▲ Using one hand, beat the mixture until it forms a smooth dough. Gradually beat in the reserved butter mixture and beat for a few minutes until the dough is smooth and elastic. Cover with oiled clear film and leave to rise, in a warm place, for 1½ hours, or until doubled in bulk.

7 Knock back the dough and turn out on to a floured surface. Gently knead for 2 or 3 minutes, incorporating the lucky coin or bean, if using.

8 Using a rolling pin, roll out the dough into a long strip measuring about 26 × 5 in (65 × 13 cm).

9 ▲ Roll up the dough from one long side like a Swiss roll to make a long sausage shape. Place seam side down on the baking sheet and seal the ends. Cover with oiled clear film and leave to rise, in a warm place, for 1–1½ hours, or until doubled in size.

10 ▲ Meanwhile, preheat the oven to 180°C/350°F/Gas 4. Brush the dough ring with lightly beaten egg white and decorate with candied and glacé fruit slices, pushing them slightly into the dough. Sprinkle with almond flakes and bake for 30–35 minutes, or until risen and golden. Turn out on to a wire rack to cool.

Pan Gallego

MAKES 1 LOAF

| 12 oz (350 g) unbleached white bread flour |
| 4 oz (115 g) wholemeal bread flour |
| 2 teaspoons (10 ml) salt |
| ¾ oz (20 g) fresh yeast |
| 9 fl oz (275 ml) lukewarm water |
| 2 tablespoons (30 ml) olive oil or melted lard |
| 2 tablespoons (30 ml) pumpkin seeds |
| 2 tablespoons (30 ml) sunflower seeds |
| 1 tablespoon (15 ml) millet |
| maize meal, for dusting |

This is a typical round bread with a twisted top from Galicia. The olive oil gives a soft crumb and the millet, pumpkin and sunflower seeds scattered through the loaf provide an interesting mix of textures.

1 Sprinkle a baking sheet with maize meal. Mix the flours and salt together in a large bowl.

2 ▲ In a bowl, mix the yeast with the water. Add to the centre of the flours with the olive oil or melted lard and mix to a firm dough. Turn out on to a lightly floured surface and knead for about 10 minutes until smooth and elastic. Place in an oiled bowl, cover with oiled clear film and leave to rise, in a warm place, for 1½–2 hours, or until doubled in bulk.

3 ▲ Knock back the dough and turn out on to a lightly floured surface. Gently knead in the pumpkin seeds, sunflower seeds and millet. Re-cover and leave to rest for 5 minutes.

4 ▲ Shape into a ball; twist the centre to make a cap. Transfer to the baking sheet and dust with maize meal. Cover with an upturned bowl and leave to rise, in a warm place, for 45 minutes, or until doubled in bulk.

5 Place a roasting tin in the bottom of the oven. Preheat the oven to 220°C/ 425°F/Gas 7. Pour about ½ pint (300 ml) cold water into the roasting tin. Remove the bowl and place the risen loaf in the oven, above the roasting tin. Bake the bread for 10 minutes.

6 Remove the tin of water and bake the bread for a further 25–30 minutes, or until well browned and sounding hollow when tapped on the base. Transfer to a wire rack to cool.

Portuguese Corn Bread

While the Spanish make a corn bread with barley flour, the Portuguese use white bread flour and maize meal. This tempting version has a hard crust with a moist, mouthwatering crumb. It slices beautifully and tastes wonderful served simply with butter or olive oil, or with cheese.

MAKES 1 LOAF
¾ oz (20 g) fresh yeast
8 fl oz (250 ml) lukewarm water
8 oz (225 g) maize meal
1 lb (450 g) unbleached white bread flour
¼ pint (150 ml) lukewarm milk
2 tablespoons (30 ml) olive oil
1½ teaspoons (7.5 ml) salt
polenta, for dusting

1 ▲ Dust a baking sheet with a little maize meal. Put the yeast in a bowl and gradually mix in the water until smooth. Stir in half the maize meal and 2 oz (50 g) of the flour and mix to a batter, with a wooden spoon.

2 ▲ Cover the bowl with lightly oiled clear film and leave the batter undisturbed in a warm place for about 30 minutes, or until bubbles start to appear on the surface. Remove the clear film.

3 Stir the milk into the batter, then stir in the olive oil. Gradually mix in the remaining maize meal, flour and salt to form a pliable dough.

4 Turn out the dough on to a lightly floured surface and knead for about 10 minutes until smooth and elastic. Place in a lightly oiled bowl, cover with lightly oiled clear film and leave to rise for 1½–2 hours, or until doubled in bulk.

5 ▲ Turn out the dough on to a floured surface and knock back. Shape into a ball, flatten slightly and place on the prepared baking sheet. Dust with polenta, cover with a large upturned bowl and leave to rise, in a warm place, for 1 hour, or until doubled in size. Preheat the oven to 230°C/450°F/Gas 8.

6 Bake for 10 minutes, spraying the inside of the oven with water 2–3 times. Reduce the oven temperature to 190°C/375°F/Gas 5 and bake for a further 20–25 minutes, or until golden and hollow sounding when tapped. Cool on a wire rack.

Mallorcan Ensaimadas

Makes 16 rolls

8 oz (225 g) unbleached white bread flour
½ teaspoon (2.5 ml) salt
2 oz (50 g) caster sugar
½ oz (15 g) fresh yeast
5 tablespoons (75 ml) lukewarm milk
1 egg
2 tablespoons (30 ml) sunflower oil
2 oz (50 g) butter, melted
icing sugar, for dusting

1 Grease 2 baking sheets. Sift the flour and salt into a bowl. Stir in the sugar and make a well in the centre.

2 Cream the yeast with the milk, pour into the centre of the flour mixture, then sprinkle a little of the flour mixture evenly over the top of the liquid. Leave in a warm place for about 15 minutes, or until frothy.

3 In a small bowl, beat the egg with the oil. Add to the flour mixture and mix to a smooth dough.

These spiral- or snail-shaped rolls are a popular Spanish breakfast treat. Traditionally, lard or *saim* was used to brush over the strips of sweetened dough, but nowadays mainly butter is used to add a delicious richness.

4 Turn out on to a floured surface and knead for 8–10 minutes until smooth and elastic. Place in an oiled bowl, cover with oiled clear film and leave to rise, in a warm place, for 1 hour, or until doubled in bulk.

5 ▲ Turn out the dough on to a lightly floured surface. Knock back and divide the dough into 16 equal pieces. Shape each piece into a thin rope about 15 in (38 cm) long. Pour the melted butter on to a plate and dip the ropes into the butter to coat.

6 ▲ On the baking sheets, curl each rope into a loose spiral, spacing well apart. Tuck the ends under to seal. Cover with oiled clear film and leave to rise, in a warm place, for about 45 minutes, or until doubled in size.

7 Preheat the oven to 190°C/375°F/ Gas 5. Brush the rolls with water and dust with icing sugar. Bake for 10 minutes, or until light golden brown. Cool on a wire rack. Dust again with icing sugar and serve warm.

Italian Olive Bread

Black and green olives and good-quality fruity olive oil combine to make this strongly flavoured and irresistible Italian bread.

1 Lightly grease a baking sheet. Mix the flours, yeast and salt in a large bowl and make a well in the centre.

2 ▲ Add the water and oil to the centre of the flour and mix to a soft dough. Knead the dough on a lightly floured surface for 8–10 minutes until smooth and elastic. Place in a lightly oiled bowl, cover with oiled clear film and leave to rise, in a warm place, for 1 hour, or until doubled in bulk.

3 Turn out on to a floured surface and knock back. Flatten out and sprinkle over the olives. Knead to distribute the olives. Leave to rest for 5 minutes, then shape into an oval loaf. Place on the baking sheet.

4 ▲ Make 6 deep cuts in the top, and gently push the sections over. Cover with oiled clear film and leave to rise, in a warm place, for 30–45 minutes, or until doubled in size.

MAKES 1 LOAF

10 oz (275 g) unbleached white bread flour
2 oz (50 g) wholemeal bread flour
¼ oz (10 g) sachet easy-blend dried yeast
½ teaspoon (2.5 ml) salt
7½ fl oz (210 ml) lukewarm water
1 tablespoon (15 ml) extra virgin olive oil, plus extra, for brushing
4 oz (115 g) pitted black and green olives, coarsely chopped

~ VARIATION ~

For a nutty flavour, add some hazelnuts or pine nuts.

5 Meanwhile, preheat the oven to 200°C/400°F/Gas 6. Brush the bread with olive oil and bake for 35 minutes. Transfer to a wire rack to cool.

Italian Polenta Bread

Makes 1 loaf

2 oz (50 g) polenta
½ pint (300 ml) lukewarm water
½ oz (15 g) fresh yeast
½ teaspoon (2.5 ml) clear honey
8 oz (225 g) unbleached white bread flour
1 oz (25 g) butter
3 tablespoons (45 ml) pine nuts
1½ teaspoons (7.5 ml) salt

For the topping

1 egg yolk
1 tablespoon (15 ml) water
pine nuts, for sprinkling

Polenta is widely used in Italian cooking. Here it is combined with pine nuts to make a truly Italian bread with a fantastic flavour.

1 ▲ Lightly grease a baking sheet. Mix the polenta and 8 fl oz (250 ml) of the water together in a saucepan and slowly bring to the boil, stirring continuously with a large wooden spoon. Reduce the heat and simmer for 2–3 minutes, stirring occasionally. Set aside to cool for 10 minutes, or until just warm.

2 In a small bowl, mix the yeast with the remaining water and honey until creamy. Sift 4 oz (115 g) of the flour into a large bowl. Gradually beat in the yeast mixture, then gradually stir in the polenta mixture to combine. Turn out on to a lightly floured surface and knead for 5 minutes until smooth and elastic.

3 Cover the bowl with lightly oiled clear film. Leave the dough to rise, in a warm place, for about 2 hours, or until it has doubled in bulk.

4 ▲ Meanwhile, melt the butter in a small pan, add the pine nuts and cook over a medium heat, stirring, until pale golden. Set aside to cool.

5 Add the remaining flour and the salt to the polenta dough and mix to a soft dough. Knead in the pine nuts. Turn out on to a lightly floured surface and knead for 5 minutes until smooth and elastic.

6 Place in an oiled bowl, cover with clear film and leave to rise, in a warm place, for 1 hour, until doubled in bulk.

7 ▲ Knock back the dough and turn it out on to a floured surface. Cut the dough into 2 equal pieces and roll each piece into a fat sausage about 15 in (38 cm) long. Plait together and place on the baking sheet. Cover with lightly oiled clear film and leave to rise, in a warm place, for 45 minutes. Preheat the oven to 200°C/400°F/Gas 6.

8 Mix the egg yolk and water and brush over the loaf. Sprinkle with pine nuts and bake for 30 minutes, or until golden and sounding hollow when tapped. Cool on a wire rack.

Italian Prosciutto Loaf

This savoury Italian bread from Parma is spiked with the local dried ham. Just a small amount fills the loaf with marvellous flavour.

MAKES 1 LOAF

12 oz (350 g) unbleached white bread flour
1½ teaspoons (7.5 ml) salt
½ oz (15 g) fresh yeast
8 fl oz (250 ml) lukewarm water
1½ oz (40 g) prosciutto, torn into small pieces
1 teaspoon (5 ml) freshly ground black pepper

1 Grease a baking sheet. Sift the flour and salt into a bowl and make a well in the centre. Cream the yeast with 2 tablespoons (30 ml) of the water, then gradually mix in the rest. Pour into the centre of the flour.

2 ▲ Gradually beat in most of the flour with a wooden spoon to make a batter. Beat gently to begin with and then more vigorously as the batter thickens. When most of the flour is incorporated, mix in the rest with your hand to form a moist dough.

3 Turn out on to a lightly floured surface and knead for 5 minutes until smooth and elastic. Place in an oiled bowl, cover with lightly oiled clear film and leave to rise, in a warm place, for 1½ hours, or until doubled in bulk.

4 ▲ Turn out the dough on to a floured surface, knock back and knead for 1 minute. Flatten to a round, then sprinkle with half the prosciutto and pepper. Fold in half and repeat with the remaining ham and pepper. Roll up, tucking in the sides.

~ VARIATION ~

To make pesto bread, spread 3 tablespoons (45 ml) pesto over the flattened dough in step 4.

5 Place on the baking sheet, cover with oiled clear film and leave to rise, in a warm place, for about 30 minutes. On a floured surface, roll into an oval, fold in half and seal the edges. Flatten and fold again. Seal and fold again to make a long loaf.

6 Roll into a stubby long loaf. Draw out the edges by rolling the dough under the palms of your hands. Place on the baking sheet, cover with oiled clear film and leave to rise, in a warm place, for 45 minutes, or until the loaf has doubled in size. Preheat the oven to 200°C/400°F/Gas 6.

7 ▲ Slash the top of the loaf diagonally three or four times, using a sharp knife, and bake for 30 minutes, or until golden. Cool on a wire rack.

Italian Focaccia

Makes 2 loaves

¾ oz (20 g) fresh yeast

11–12 fl oz (315–350 ml) lukewarm water

3 tablespoons (45 ml) extra virgin olive oil

1¼ lb (500 g) unbleached white bread flour

2 teaspoons (10 ml) salt

1 tablespoon (15 ml) chopped fresh sage

For the topping

4 tablespoons (60 ml) extra virgin olive oil

4 garlic cloves, chopped

12 fresh sage leaves

This simple dimple-topped Italian flat bread is punctuated with olive oil and the aromatic flavours of sage and garlic to produce a truly succulent loaf.

4 ▲ Knock back the dough and turn out on to a floured surface. Gently knead in the chopped sage. Divide the dough into 2 equal pieces. Shape each into a ball, roll out into 10 in (25 cm) circles and place in the tins.

1 ▲ Lightly oil 2 10 in (25 cm) shallow round cake tins or pizza pans. Cream the yeast with 4 tablespoons (60 ml) of the water, then stir in the remaining water. Stir in the oil.

2 Sift the flour and salt together into a large bowl and make a well in the centre. Pour the yeast mixture into the well and incorporate the flour to make a soft dough.

3 Turn out the dough on to a lightly floured surface and knead for 8–10 minutes until smooth and elastic. Place in a lightly oiled bowl, cover with lightly oiled clear film, and leave to rise, in a warm place, for about 1–1½ hours, or until the dough has doubled in bulk.

5 ▲ Cover with lightly oiled clear film and leave to rise in a warm place for about 30 minutes. Uncover, and using your fingertips, poke the dough to make deep dimples over the entire surface. Replace the clear film cover and leave to rise until doubled in bulk.

6 Meanwhile, preheat the oven to 200°C/400°F/Gas 6. Sprinkle the loaves with olive oil and garlic for the topping and dot with sage leaves. Bake for 25–30 minutes, or until both loaves are golden. Immediately remove the focaccia from the tins and transfer them to a wire rack to cool slightly. These loaves are best served warm.

Italian Panini all'Olio

MAKES 16 ROLLS

1 lb (450 g) unbleached white bread flour
2 teaspoons (10 ml) salt
½ oz (15 g) fresh yeast
8 fl oz (250 ml) lukewarm water
4 tablespoons (60 ml) extra virgin olive oil, plus extra for brushing

The Italians adore interesting and elaborately shaped rolls. This distinctively flavoured bread dough, enriched with olive oil, can be used for making rolls or shaped as one large loaf.

1 Lightly oil 3 baking sheets. Sift the flour and salt together in a large bowl and make a well in the centre.

2 In a jug, cream the yeast with half of the water, then stir in the remainder. Add to the centre of the flour with the oil and mix to a dough.

3 Turn the dough out on to a lightly floured surface and knead for 8–10 minutes until smooth and elastic. Place in an oiled bowl, cover with oiled clear film and leave to rise, in a warm place, for 1 hour, or until the dough has nearly doubled in bulk.

4 Turn on to a lightly floured surface and knock back. Divide into 12 equal pieces of dough and shape into rolls as described in steps 5, 6 and 7.

5 ▲ For *tavalli* (twisted spiral rolls): roll each piece of dough into a strip about 12 in (30 cm) long and 1½ in (4 cm) wide. Twist into a loose spiral and join the ends together to make a circle. Place on the baking sheets, well spaced. Brush the *tavalli* with olive oil, cover with oiled clear film and leave to rise, in a warm place, for 20–30 minutes.

6 ▲ For *filoncini* (finger-shaped rolls): flatten each piece of dough into an oval and roll to about 9 in (23 cm) in length without changing the basic shape. Make it 2 in (5 cm) wide at one end and 4 in (10 cm) wide at the other. Roll up, starting from the wider end. Gently stretch the roll to 8–9 in (20–23 cm) long. Cut in half. Place on the baking sheets, well spaced. Brush with olive oil, cover with oiled clear film and leave to rise, in a warm place, for 20–30 minutes.

7 ▲ For *carciofi* (artichoke-shaped rolls): shape each piece of dough into a ball and space well apart on the baking sheets. Brush with olive oil, cover with oiled clear film and leave to rise, in a warm place, for about 20–30 minutes. Preheat the oven to 200°C/400°F/Gas 6. Using scissors, snip 4–5 ¼ in (5 mm) deep cuts in a circle on the top of each *carciofi*, then make 5 larger horizontal cuts around the sides. Bake for 15 minutes. Transfer to a wire rack to cool.

Italian Ciabatta

This irregular-shaped Italian bread is so called because it looks like an old shoe or slipper. It is made with a very wet dough flavoured with olive oil; cooking produces a bread with holes and a wonderfully chewy crust.

1 Cream the yeast for the *biga* starter with a little of the water. Sift the flour into a bowl. Gradually mix in the yeast mixture and enough of the remaining water to form a firm dough.

2 Turn out the *biga* starter dough on to a lightly floured surface and knead for about 5 minutes until smooth and elastic. Return the dough to the bowl, cover with lightly oiled clear film and leave in a warm place for 12–15 hours, or until the dough has risen and is starting to collapse.

3 Sprinkle 3 baking sheets with flour. Mix the yeast for the dough with a little of the water until creamy, then mix in the remainder. Add the yeast mixture to the *biga* and mix in.

4 Mix in the milk, beating thoroughly with a wooden spoon. Using your hand, gradually mix in the flour, lifting the dough as you mix. Mixing the dough will take 15 minutes or more and form a very wet mix, impossible to knead on a work surface.

5 Beat in the salt and olive oil. Cover with lightly oiled clear film and leave to rise, in a warm place, for 1½–2 hours, or until doubled in bulk.

6 ▲ Using a spoon, tip one-third of the dough at a time on to the baking sheets, trying to avoid knocking back the dough in the process.

7 ▲ Using floured hands, shape into oblong loaf shapes, about 1 in (2.5 cm) thick. Flatten slightly. Sprinkle with flour and leave to rise in a warm place for 30 minutes.

8 Meanwhile, preheat the oven to 220°C/425°F/Gas 7. Bake for 25–30 minutes, or until golden brown and sounding hollow when tapped on the base. Transfer to a wire rack to cool.

MAKES 3 LOAVES

FOR THE BIGA STARTER
¼ oz (10 g) fresh yeast
6–7 fl oz (175–200 ml) lukewarm water
12 oz (350 g) unbleached plain flour, plus extra for dusting

FOR THE DOUGH
½ oz (15 g) fresh yeast
14 fl oz (400 ml) lukewarm water
4 tablespoons (60 ml) lukewarm milk
1¼ lb (500 g) unbleached white bread flour
2 teaspoons (10 ml) salt
3 tablespoons (45 ml) extra virgin olive oil

~ VARIATION ~

Add 4 oz (115 g) chopped, drained sun-dried tomatoes in olive oil in step 5.

Italian Panettone

MAKES 1 LOAF

14 oz (400 g) unbleached white bread flour
½ teaspoon (2.5 ml) salt
½ oz (15 g) fresh yeast
4 fl oz (120 ml) lukewarm milk
2 eggs
2 egg yolks
3 oz (75 g) caster sugar
5 oz (150 g) butter, softened
4 oz (115 g) mixed chopped peel
3 oz (75 g) raisins
melted butter, for brushing

This classic Italian bread can be found throughout Italy around Christmas. It is a surprisingly light bread even though it is rich with butter and dried fruit.

2 Sift the flour and salt into a bowl. Cream the yeast with 4 tablespoons (60 ml) of the milk, then mix in the remainder.

3 ▲ Pour the yeast mixture into the centre of the flour, add the whole eggs and mix in sufficient flour to make a thick batter. Sprinkle a little flour over the top and leave to "sponge", in a warm place, for 30 minutes.

1 Using a double layer of greaseproof paper, line and butter a 6 in (15 cm) deep cake tin. Finish the paper 3 in (7.5 cm) above the top of the tin.

4 Add the egg yolks and sugar and mix to a soft dough. Work in the softened butter, then turn out on to a lightly floured surface and knead for 5 minutes until smooth and elastic. Place in a lightly oiled bowl, cover with lightly oiled clear film and leave to rise, in a slightly warm place, for 1½–2 hours, or until doubled in bulk.

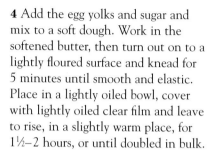

5 ▲ Knock back the dough and turn out on to a floured surface. Gently knead in the peel and raisins. Shape into a ball and place in the tin. Cover with oiled clear film and leave to rise, in a slightly warm place, for about 1 hour, or until doubled.

6 ▲ Meanwhile, preheat the oven to 190°C/375°F/Gas 5. Brush the loaf with melted butter and cut a cross in the top. Bake for 20 minutes, then reduce the oven temperature to 180°C/350°F/Gas 4. Brush the top with butter again and bake for 25–30 minutes more, or until golden. Cool in the tin for 5–10 minutes, then turn out on to a wire rack to cool.

Italian Pane al Cioccolato

This slightly sweet chocolate bread from Italy is often served with creamy mascarpone cheese as a dessert or snack. The dark chocolate pieces add texture to this light loaf.

MAKES 1 LOAF

12 oz (350 g) unbleached white bread flour
1½ tablespoons (25 ml) cocoa powder
½ teaspoon (2.5 ml) salt
1 oz (25 g) caster sugar
½ oz (15 g) fresh yeast
8 fl oz (250 ml) lukewarm water
1 oz (25 g) butter, softened
3 oz (75 g) plain continental chocolate, coarsely chopped
melted butter, for brushing

1 ▲ Lightly grease a 6 in (15 cm) round deep cake tin. Sift the flour, cocoa powder and salt together into a large bowl. Stir in the sugar. Make a well in the centre.

2 Cream the yeast with 4 tablespoons (60 ml) of the water, then stir in the rest. Add to the centre of the flour mixture and gradually mix to a dough.

3 Knead in the butter, then knead on a surface until smooth and elastic. Place in an oiled bowl, cover with clear film and leave to rise, in a warm place, for 1 hour, or until doubled.

4 ▲ Turn out on to a floured surface and knock back. Knead in the chocolate, then cover with oiled clear film; leave to rest for 5 minutes.

5 Shape the dough into a round and place in the tin. Cover with lightly oiled clear film and leave to rise, in a warm place, for 45 minutes, or until doubled.

6 ▲ Preheat the oven to 220°C/425°F/Gas 7. Bake for 10 minutes, then reduce the temperature to 190°C/375°F/Gas 5 and bake for 25–30 minutes more. Brush with melted butter and cool on a wire rack.

~ VARIATION ~

You can also bake this bread in one large or two small rounds on a baking sheet.

Sicilian Scroll

MAKES 1 LOAF

1 lb (450 g) finely ground semolina
4 oz (115 g) unbleached white bread flour
2 teaspoons (10 ml) salt
¾ oz (20 g) fresh yeast
12½ fl oz (360 ml) lukewarm water
2 tablespoons (30 ml) extra virgin olive oil
sesame seeds, for sprinkling

A wonderful pale yellow, crusty-topped loaf, enhanced with a nutty flavour from the sesame seeds. It's perfect for serving with cheese.

1 ▲ Lightly grease a baking sheet. Mix the semolina, white bread flour and salt together in a large bowl and make a well in the centre.

2 In a jug, cream the yeast with half the water, then stir in the remainder. Add the creamed yeast to the centre of the semolina mixture with the olive oil and gradually incorporate the semolina and flour to form a firm dough.

3 Turn out the dough on to a lightly floured surface and knead for 8–10 minutes until smooth and elastic. Place in a lightly oiled bowl, cover with lightly oiled clear film and leave to rise, in a warm place, for 1–1½ hours, or until doubled in bulk.

4 ▲ Turn out on to a floured surface and knock back. Knead, then shape into a fat roll about 20 in (50 cm) long. Form into an "S" shape.

5 Transfer to the baking sheet, cover with oiled clear film and leave to rise, in a warm place, for 30–45 minutes, or until doubled in size.

6 Meanwhile, preheat the oven to 220°C/425°F/Gas 7. Brush the top of the scroll with water and sprinkle with sesame seeds. Bake for 10 minutes. Spray the inside of the oven with water twice during this time. Reduce the oven temperature to 200°C/400°F/Gas 6 and bake for a further 25–30 minutes, or until golden. Cool on a wire rack.

~ VARIATION ~

Although sesame seeds are the traditional topping on this delectable Italian bread, poppy seeds, or even crystals of sea salt, could be used instead.

Pane Toscano

This bread from Tuscany is made without salt and probably originates from the days when salt was heavily taxed. To compensate for the lack of salt, this bread is usually served with salty foods, such as anchovies and olives.

MAKES 1 LOAF

1¼ lb (500 g) unbleached white bread flour
12 fl oz (350 ml) boiling water
½ oz (15 g) fresh yeast
4 tablespoons (60 ml) lukewarm water

6 ▲ Fold the sides of the round into the centre and seal. Place seam side up on the baking sheet. Cover with oiled clear film and leave to rise, in a warm place, for 30–45 minutes, or until doubled in size.

7 ▲ Flatten the loaf to about half its risen height and flip over. Cover with a large upturned bowl and leave to rise, in a warm place, for 30 minutes.

8 Meanwhile, preheat the oven to 220°C/425°F/Gas 7. Slash the top of the loaf, using a sharp knife, if wished. Bake for 30–35 minutes, or until golden. Cool on a wire rack.

2 Lightly flour a baking sheet. Cream the yeast with the lukewarm water. Stir into the starter.

3 Gradually add the remaining flour and mix to form a dough. Turn out on to a floured surface and knead for 5–8 minutes until smooth and elastic.

4 Place in a lightly oiled bowl, cover with lightly oiled clear film and leave to rise, in a warm place, for 1–1½ hours, or until doubled in bulk.

5 Turn out the dough on to a lightly floured surface, knock back, and shape into a round.

1 ▲ First make the starter. Sift 6 oz (175 g) of the flour into a large bowl. Pour over the boiling water, leave for a couple of minutes, then mix well. Cover the bowl with a damp dish towel and leave for 10 hours.

Tuscan Schiacciata

MAKES 1 LOAF

12 oz (350 g) unbleached white bread flour
½ teaspoon (2.5 ml) salt
½ oz (15 g) fresh yeast
7 fl oz (200 ml) lukewarm water
4 tablespoons (60 ml) extra virgin olive oil
FOR THE TOPPING
2 tablespoons (30 ml) extra virgin olive oil, for brushing
2 tablespoons (30 ml) fresh rosemary leaves
coarse sea salt, for sprinkling

This Tuscan version of Italian pizza-style flat bread can be rolled to varying thicknesses to give either a crisp or soft, bread-like finish.

1 Oil a baking sheet. Sift the flour and salt into a bowl and make a well in the centre. Cream the yeast with half the water. Add to the flour with the remaining water and olive oil and mix to a soft dough. Turn out on to a floured surface and knead for 10 minutes until smooth and elastic.

2 Place in a lightly oiled bowl, cover with lightly oiled clear film and leave to rise, in a warm place, for about 1 hour, or until doubled in bulk.

3 ▲ Knock back the dough, turn out on to a lightly floured surface and knead gently. Roll to a 12 × 8 in (30 × 20 cm) rectangle and place on the prepared baking sheet. Brush with some of the olive oil for the topping and cover with lightly oiled clear film.

4 ▲ Leave to rise, in a warm place, for about 20 minutes, then brush with the remaining oil, prick all over with a fork and sprinkle with rosemary and sea salt. Leave to rise again in a warm place for 15 minutes.

5 Preheat the oven to 200°C/400°F/ Gas 6. Bake for 30 minutes, or until light golden. Cool slightly on a wire rack. Serve warm.

Moroccan Holiday Bread

The addition of maize meal and a cornucopia of seeds gives this superb loaf an interesting flavour and texture.

2 ▲ Cream the yeast with a little of the water in a jug. Stir in the remainder of the water and the milk. Pour into the centre of the flour and mix to a fairly soft dough.

1 Lightly grease a baking sheet. Sift the flours and salt into a large bowl.

3 Turn out the dough on to a lightly floured surface and knead for about 5 minutes until smooth and elastic.

4 Place in a lightly oiled bowl, cover with lightly oiled clear film and leave to rise, in a warm place, for about 1 hour, or until doubled in bulk.

> ### ~ VARIATION ~
> For a plainer loaf, incorporate all the seeds in the dough in step 5 and leave the top of the loaf seedless.

MAKES 1 LOAF
10 oz (275 g) white bread flour
2 oz (50 g) maize meal
1 teaspoon (5 ml) salt
¾ oz (20 g) fresh yeast
4 fl oz (120 ml) lukewarm water
4 fl oz (120 ml) lukewarm milk
1 tablespoon (15 ml) pumpkin seeds
1 tablespoon (15 ml) sesame seeds
2 tablespoons (30 ml) sunflower seeds

5 ▲ Turn out the dough on to a lightly floured surface and knock back. Gently knead the pumpkin and sesame seeds into the dough. Shape into a round ball and flatten slightly.

6 Place on the prepared baking sheet and cover with lightly oiled clear film. Leave to rise, in a warm place, for about 45 minutes, or until doubled in bulk.

7 ▲ Meanwhile, preheat the oven to 200°C/400°F/Gas 6. Brush the top of the loaf with water and sprinkle with the sunflower seeds. Bake the loaf for 30–35 minutes, or until it is golden and sounds hollow when tapped. Transfer the loaf to a wire rack to cool.

Greek Christopsomo

MAKES 1 LOAF

½ oz (15 g) fresh yeast
scant ¼ pint (140 ml) lukewarm milk
1 lb (450 g) unbleached white bread flour
2 eggs
3 oz (75 g) caster sugar
½ teaspoon (2.5 ml) salt
3 oz (75 g) butter, softened
grated rind of ½ orange
1 teaspoon (5 ml) ground cinnamon
¼ teaspoon (1.5 ml) ground cloves
pinch of crushed aniseed
8 walnut halves
beaten egg white, for glazing

A Byzantine cross flavoured with aniseed tops this Greek Christmas bread, which is also decorated with walnuts for good fortune. The fluffy, light, butter-enriched bread contains orange rind, cinnamon and cloves – all the lovely warm tastes associated with Christmas.

1 ▲ Grease a large baking sheet. In a bowl, mix the yeast with the milk until the yeast is dissolved, then stir in 4 oz (115 g) of the flour to make a thin batter. Cover with oiled clear film and leave to "sponge" in a warm place for 30 minutes.

2 Beat the eggs and sugar until light and fluffy. Beat into the yeast mixture. Gradually mix in the remaining flour and salt. Beat in the butter and knead to a soft but not sticky dough. Knead on a floured surface for 8–10 minutes until smooth and elastic. Place in an oiled bowl, cover with oiled clear film and leave to rise, in a warm place, for 1½ hours, or until doubled in bulk.

3 Turn out on to a floured surface and gently knock back. Cut off 2 oz (50 g) of dough; cover and set aside. Gently knead the orange rind, cinnamon and cloves into the large piece of dough and shape into a round loaf. Place on the baking sheet.

4 Knead the aniseed into the remaining dough. Cut in half and shape each piece into a 12 in (30 cm) rope. Cut through each rope at either end by one-third of its length. Place the two ropes in a cross on top of the loaf, then curl each cut end into a circle, in opposite directions.

5 ▲ Place a walnut half inside each circle. Cover the loaf with clear film and leave to rise for 45 minutes, or until doubled in size. Preheat the oven to 190°C/375°F/Gas 5. Brush the bread with the egg white and bake for 40–45 minutes, or until golden. Cool on a wire rack.

Greek Tsoureki

Topped with brightly coloured eggs, this plaited bread is an important part of the Greek Easter celebrations.

MAKES 1 LOAF

FOR THE EGGS

3 eggs

¼ teaspoon (1.5 ml) bright red food colouring paste

1 tablespoon (15 ml) white wine vinegar

1 teaspoon (5 ml) water

1 teaspoon (5 ml) olive oil

FOR THE DOUGH

1 lb (450 g) unbleached white bread flour

½ teaspoon (2.5 ml) salt

1 teaspoon (5 ml) ground allspice

½ teaspoon (2.5 ml) ground cinnamon

½ teaspoon (2.5 ml) caraway seeds

¾ oz (20 g) fresh yeast

6 fl oz (175 ml) lukewarm milk

2 oz (50 g) butter

1½ oz (40 g) caster sugar

2 eggs

FOR THE GLAZE

1 egg yolk

1 teaspoon (5 ml) clear honey

1 teaspoon (5 ml) water

FOR THE DECORATION

2 oz (50 g) split almonds, slivered

1 Grease a baking sheet. Place the eggs in a pan of water and bring to the boil. Boil gently for 10 minutes. Meanwhile, mix the red food colouring, vinegar and water in a shallow bowl. Remove the eggs from the boiling water, place on a wire rack for a few seconds to dry then roll in the colouring mixture. Return to the rack to cool and dry.

2 When cold, drizzle the olive oil on to absorbent kitchen paper, lift up each egg in turn and rub all over with the oiled paper.

3 To make the dough, sift the flour, salt, allspice and cinnamon into a large bowl. Stir in the caraway seeds.

4 In a jug, mix the yeast with the milk. In a bowl, cream the butter and sugar together, then beat in the eggs. Add the creamed mixture to the flour with the yeast mixture and gradually mix to a dough. Turn out the dough on to a lightly floured surface and knead until smooth and elastic.

5 Place in a lightly oiled bowl, cover with lightly oiled clear film and leave to rise, in a warm place, for about 2 hours, or until doubled in bulk.

6 Knock back the dough and knead for 2–3 minutes. Return to the bowl, re-cover and leave to rise again, in a warm place, for about 1 hour, or until doubled in bulk.

7 Knock back and turn out on to a lightly floured surface. Divide the dough into 3 equal pieces and roll each into a 15–20 in (38–50 cm) long rope. Plait these together from the centre to the ends.

8 Place on the prepared baking sheet and push the dyed eggs into the loaf. Cover and leave to rise, in a warm place, for about 1 hour.

9 Preheat the oven to 190°C/375°F/Gas 5. Mix the egg yolk, honey and water for the glaze, and brush over the loaf. Sprinkle with almonds. Bake for 40–45 minutes, or until golden and sounding hollow when tapped. Cool on a wire rack.

Greek Olive Bread

MAKES 2 LOAVES

1½ lb (675 g) unbleached white bread flour, plus extra for dusting
2 teaspoons (10 ml) salt
1 oz (25 g) fresh yeast
12 fl oz (350 ml) lukewarm water
5 tablespoons (75 ml) olive oil
6 oz (175 g) pitted black olives, roughly chopped
1 red onion, finely chopped
2 tablespoons (30 ml) chopped fresh coriander or mint

~ VARIATION ~

Make one large loaf and bake
for 15 minutes longer.

The flavours of the Mediterranean simply ooze from this decorative bread, speckled with black olives, red onions and herbs.

5 ▲ Roll out the large piece of dough to a round. Sprinkle with the olives, onion and herbs, then bring up the sides of the circle and gently knead together. Cut the dough in half and shape each piece into a plump oval loaf, about 8 in (20 cm) long. Place on the baking sheets.

6 Divide the reserved dough into 4 equal pieces and roll each to a long strand 24 in (60 cm) long. Twist together and cut in half. Brush the centre of each loaf with water and place two pieces of twisted dough on top of each, tucking the ends underneath the loaves.

7 Cover with lightly oiled clear film and leave to rise, in a warm place, for about 45 minutes, or until the loaves are plump and nearly doubled in size.

8 Preheat the oven to 220°C/425°F/ Gas 7. Dust the loaves with flour and bake for 35–40 minutes, or until golden and sounding hollow when tapped. Cool on a wire rack.

1 Lightly grease 2 baking sheets. Sift the flour and salt together into a large bowl and make a well in the centre.

2 ▲ In a jug, blend the yeast with half of the water. Add to the centre of the flour with the remaining water and the olive oil; mix to a soft dough.

3 Turn out the dough on to a lightly floured surface and knead for 8–10 minutes until smooth. Place in a lightly oiled bowl, cover with lightly oiled clear film and leave to rise, in a warm place, for 1 hour, or until doubled in bulk.

4 Turn out on to a lightly floured surface and knock back. Cut off a quarter of the dough, cover with lightly oiled clear film and set aside.

Turkish Pitta Bread

These Turkish breads are a firm favourite in both the eastern Mediterranean and the Middle East, and have crossed to England and the USA. This versatile soft, flat bread forms a pocket as it cooks, which is perfect for filling with vegetables, salads or meats.

MAKES 6 PITTA BREADS

8 oz (225 g) unbleached white bread flour
1 teaspoon (5 ml) salt
½ oz (15 g) fresh yeast
scant ¼ pint (150 ml) lukewarm water
2 teaspoons (10 ml) extra virgin olive oil

> ### ~ VARIATION ~
> Replace half the white bread flour with wholemeal bread flour.

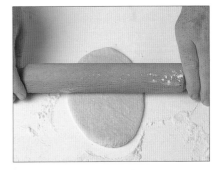

5 ▲ Roll out each ball of dough to an oval ¼ in (5 mm) thick and 6 in (15 cm) long. Place on a floured dish towel and cover with oiled clear film. Leave to rise at room temperature for about 20–30 minutes. Meanwhile, preheat the oven to 230°C/450°F/ Gas 8. Place 3 baking sheets in the oven to heat.

6 Place two pitta breads on each baking sheet and bake for 4–6 minutes, or until puffed up; they do not need to brown. If preferred, cook in batches. It is important that the oven has reached the recommended temperature before the breads are baked, to ensure that they puff up.

1 Sift the flour and salt together into a bowl. Mix the yeast with the water until dissolved, then stir in the olive oil and pour into a large bowl.

2 Gradually beat the flour into the yeast mixture, then knead the mixture to make a soft dough.

3 Turn out on to a floured surface and knead for 5 minutes until smooth and elastic. Place in a clean bowl, cover with oiled clear film and leave to rise, in a warm place, for 1 hour, or until doubled in bulk.

4 ▲ Knock back the dough. On a floured surface, divide it into 6 pieces and shape into balls. Cover with oiled clear film; leave for 5 minutes.

7 Transfer the pittas to a wire rack to cool until warm, then cover with a dish towel to keep them soft.

Polish Poppy Seed Roll

MAKES 1 LOAF

12 oz (350 g) unbleached white bread flour
½ teaspoon (2.5 ml) salt
1 oz (25 g) caster sugar
¾ oz (20 g) fresh yeast
4 fl oz (120 ml) lukewarm milk
1 egg, lightly beaten
2 oz (50 g) butter, melted
1 tablespoon (15 ml) toasted flaked almonds

FOR THE FILLING

4 oz (115 g) poppy seeds
2 oz (50 g) mixed chopped peel
2 oz (50 g) butter
3 oz (75 g) caster sugar
3 oz (75 g) raisins
2 oz (50 g) ground almonds
½ teaspoon (2.5 ml) cinnamon

FOR THE ICING

4 oz (115 g) icing sugar
1 tablespoon (15 ml) lemon juice
2–3 teaspoons (10–15 ml) water

A favourite sweet yeast bread in both Poland and Hungary, this has an unusual filling of poppy seeds, almonds, raisins and citrus peel spiralling through the dough.

1 Grease a baking sheet. Sift the flour and salt into a bowl. Stir in the sugar. Cream the yeast with the milk. Add to the flour with the egg and melted butter and mix to a dough.

2 Turn out on to a floured surface and knead for 8–10 minutes until smooth and elastic. Place in an oiled bowl, cover with oiled clear film and leave to rise, in a warm place, for 1–1½ hours, or until doubled in size.

3 Pour boiling water over the poppy seeds for the filling, then leave to cool. Drain in a fine sieve. Finely chop the peel. Melt the butter in a pan, add the poppy seeds and cook, stirring, for 1–2 minutes. Remove from the heat and stir in the sugar, raisins, ground almonds, peel and cinnamon. Set aside to cool.

4 Turn the dough out on to a lightly floured surface, knock back and knead lightly. Roll out into a rectangle 14 × 10 in (35 × 25 cm). Spread the filling to within ¾ in (2 cm) of the edges.

5 ▲ Roll up the dough, starting from one long edge, like a Swiss roll, tucking in the edges to seal. Place seam side down on the baking sheet. Cover with oiled clear film and leave to rise, in a warm place, for 30 minutes, or until doubled in size.

6 Preheat the oven to 190°C/ 375°F/ Gas 5. Bake for 30 minutes, or until golden brown. Transfer to a wire rack to cool until just warm.

7 ▲ Mix the icing sugar, lemon juice and sufficient water together in a small saucepan to make an icing stiff enough to coat the back of a spoon. Heat gently, stirring, until warm. Drizzle the icing over the loaf and sprinkle the flaked almonds over the top. Leave to cool completely, then serve sliced.

Polish Rye Bread

This rye bread is made with half white flour which gives it a lighter, more open texture than a traditional rye loaf. Served thinly sliced, it is the perfect accompaniment for cold meats and fish.

MAKES 1 LOAF

8 oz (225 g) rye flour
8 oz (225 g) unbleached white bread flour
2 teaspoons (10 ml) caraway seeds
2 teaspoons (10 ml) salt
¾ oz (20 g) fresh yeast
scant ¼ pint (140 ml) lukewarm milk
1 teaspoon (5 ml) clear honey
scant ¼ pint (150 ml) lukewarm water
wholemeal flour, for dusting

1 ▲ Grease a baking sheet. Mix the flours, caraway seeds and salt in a bowl and make a well in the centre.

2 In a bowl or measuring jug, cream the yeast with the milk and honey. Pour into the centre of the flour, add the water and gradually incorporate the surrounding flour and caraway mixture until a dough forms.

3 Turn out the dough on to a floured surface and knead for 8–10 minutes until smooth, elastic and firm. Place in an oiled bowl, cover with oiled clear film and leave to rise, in a warm place, for about 3 hours, or until doubled in bulk.

4 ▲ Turn out the dough on to a lightly floured surface and knock back. Shape into an oval loaf and place on the prepared baking sheet.

5 Dust with wholemeal flour, cover with oiled clear film and leave to rise, in a warm place, for 1–1½ hours, or until doubled in size. Preheat the oven to 220°C/425°F/Gas 7.

6 ▲ Using a sharp knife, slash the loaf with two long cuts about 1 in (2.5 cm) apart. Bake for 30–35 minutes, or until the loaf sounds hollow when tapped on the base. Transfer to a wire rack to cool.

Hungarian Split Farmhouse Loaf

Makes 1 loaf

1 lb (450 g) unbleached white bread flour
2 teaspoons (10 ml) salt
½ teaspoon (2.5 ml) fennel seeds, crushed
1 tablespoon (15 ml) caster sugar
¾ oz (20 g) fresh yeast
9 fl oz (275 ml) lukewarm water
1 oz (25 g) butter, melted
1 egg white
2 teaspoons (10 ml) fennel seeds, for sprinkling

A golden, fennel-seed-encrusted loaf with a moist white crumb. It is equally delicious made into rolls – just reduce the baking time to 15–20 minutes.

1 Lightly grease a baking sheet. Sift the white bread flour and salt together into a large bowl and stir in the crushed fennel seeds and caster sugar. Make a well in the centre.

2 ▲ Cream the yeast with a little water, stir in the rest, then pour into the flour. Stir in enough flour to make a runny batter. Sprinkle more of the flour on top, cover and leave in a warm place for 30 minutes, until the "sponge" starts to bubble and rise.

3 ▲ Add the melted butter and gradually mix in with the remaining flour to form a dough. Turn out on to a floured surface and knead for 8–10 minutes until smooth and elastic. Place in an oiled bowl, cover with oiled clear film and leave to rise, in a warm place, for 45–60 minutes, or until doubled in bulk.

4 ▲ Turn out on to a floured surface and knock back. Shape into an oval and place on the baking sheet. Cover with oiled clear film and leave to rise, in a warm place, for 30–40 minutes, or until doubled in size.

5 Meanwhile, preheat the oven to 220°C/425°F/Gas 7. Mix the egg white with a pinch of salt and brush over the loaf. Sprinkle with fennel seeds and then, using a sharp knife, slash along its length. Bake for 20 minutes, then reduce the oven temperature to 180°C/350°F/Gas 4 and bake for 10 minutes more, or until sounding hollow when tapped. Transfer to a wire rack to cool.

Russian Potato Bread

In Russia, potatoes are often used to replace some of the flour in bread recipes. They endow the bread with excellent keeping qualities.

MAKES 1 LOAF

8 oz (225 g) potatoes, peeled and diced
¼ oz (10 g) easy-blend dried yeast
12 oz (350 g) unbleached white bread flour
4 oz (115 g) wholemeal bread flour, plus extra for sprinkling
½ teaspoon (2.5 ml) caraway seeds, crushed
2 teaspoons (10 ml) salt
1 oz (25 g) butter

1 ▲ Lightly grease a baking sheet. Add the potatoes to a saucepan of boiling water and cook until tender. Drain and reserve ¼ pint (150 ml) of the cooking water. Mash and sieve the potatoes and leave to cool.

2 Mix the yeast, bread flours, caraway seeds and salt together in a large bowl. Add the butter and rub in. Mix the reserved potato water and sieved potatoes together. Gradually work this mixture into the flour mixture to form a soft dough.

3 Turn out on to a floured surface and knead for 8–10 minutes until smooth and elastic. Place in an oiled bowl, cover with oiled clear film and leave to rise, in a warm place, for 1 hour, or until doubled in bulk.

4 ▲ Turn out on to a lightly floured surface, knock back and knead gently. Shape into a plump oval loaf, about 7 in (18 cm) long. Place on the prepared baking sheet and sprinkle with a little wholemeal bread flour.

5 Cover the dough with lightly oiled clear film and leave to rise, in a warm place, for 30 minutes, or until doubled in size. Meanwhile, preheat the oven to 200°C/400°F/Gas 6.

6 ▲ Using a sharp knife, slash the top with 3–4 diagonal cuts to make a criss-cross effect. Bake for 30–35 minutes, or until golden and sounding hollow when tapped on the base. Transfer to a wire rack to cool.

~ VARIATION ~
To make a cheese-flavoured potato bread, omit the caraway seeds and knead 4 oz (115 g) grated Cheddar, Red Leicester or crumbled Stilton into the dough before shaping.

Jewish Challah

Makes 1 loaf

1¼ lb (500 g) unbleached white bread flour

2 teaspoons (10 ml) salt

¾ oz (20 g) fresh yeast

7 fl oz (200 ml) lukewarm water

2 tablespoons (30 ml) caster sugar

2 eggs

3 oz (75 g) butter or margarine, melted

For the glaze

1 egg yolk

1 tablespoon (15 ml) water

2 teaspoons (10 ml) poppy seeds, for sprinkling

~ COOK'S TIP ~

If wished, divide the dough in half and make two small challah, keeping the plaits quite simple. Reduce the baking time by about 10 minutes.

Challah is an egg-rich, light-textured bread baked for the Jewish Sabbath and to celebrate religious holidays. It is usually plaited with 3 or 4 strands of dough, but 8 strands or more may be used to create especially festive loaves.

1 ▲ Lightly grease a baking sheet. Sift the flour and salt together into a large bowl and make a well in the centre. Mix the yeast with the water and sugar, add to the centre of the flour with the eggs and melted butter or margarine and gradually mix in the surrounding flour to form a soft dough.

2 Turn out on to a floured surface and knead for 10 minutes until smooth and elastic. Place in an oiled bowl, cover with oiled clear film and leave to rise, in a warm place, for 1 hour, or until doubled in bulk.

3 Knock back, re-cover and leave to rise again in a warm place for about 1 hour. Knock back, turn out on to a floured surface and knead gently. Divide into quarters. Roll each piece into a rope 18 in (45 cm) long. Line up next to each other. Pinch the ends together at one end.

4 ▲ Starting from the right, lift the first rope over the second and the third rope over the fourth. Take the fourth rope and place it between the first and second ropes. Repeat, continuing until plaited.

5 Tuck the ends under and place the loaf on the baking sheet. Cover with oiled clear film and leave to rise in a warm place, for about 30–45 minutes, or until doubled in size. Meanwhile, preheat the oven to 200°C/400°F/ Gas 6. Beat together the egg yolk and water for the glaze.

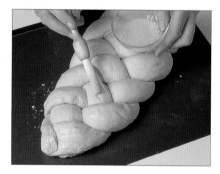

6 ▲ Brush the egg glaze gently over the loaf. Sprinkle evenly with the poppy seeds and bake for 35–40 minutes, or until the challah is a deep golden brown. Transfer to a wire rack and leave to cool.

American Pumpkin and Walnut Bread

Pumpkin, nutmeg and walnuts combine to make a moist, tangy and slightly sweet bread with an indescribably good flavour. Serve partnered with meats or cheese, or simply lightly buttered.

1 Grease and base line a loaf tin 8½ x 4½ in (21 x 12 cm). Preheat the oven to 180°C/350°F/Gas 4.

2 ▲ Place the pumpkin in a saucepan, add water to cover by about 2 in (5 cm), then bring to the boil. Cover, lower the heat and simmer for 20 minutes, or until the pumpkin is very tender. Drain, then purée in a food processor or blender. Leave to cool.

3 ▲ Place 10 oz (275 g) of the purée in a large bowl. Add the sugar, nutmeg, melted butter and eggs to the purée and mix together. Sift the flour, baking powder and salt into a large bowl and make a well in the centre.

4 Add the pumpkin mixture to the centre of the flour and stir until smooth. Mix in the walnuts.

MAKES 1 LOAF

1¼ lb (500 g) pumpkin, peeled, seeded and cut into chunks
3 oz (75 g) caster sugar
1 teaspoon (5 ml) grated nutmeg
2 oz (50 g) butter, melted
3 eggs, lightly beaten
12 oz (350 g) unbleached white bread flour
2 teaspoons (10 ml) baking powder
½ teaspoon (2.5 ml) salt
3 oz (75 g) walnuts, chopped

~ COOK'S TIP ~
Use any leftover pumpkin purée in soup.

5 Transfer to the prepared tin and bake for 1 hour, or until golden and starting to shrink from the sides of the tin. Cool on a wire rack.

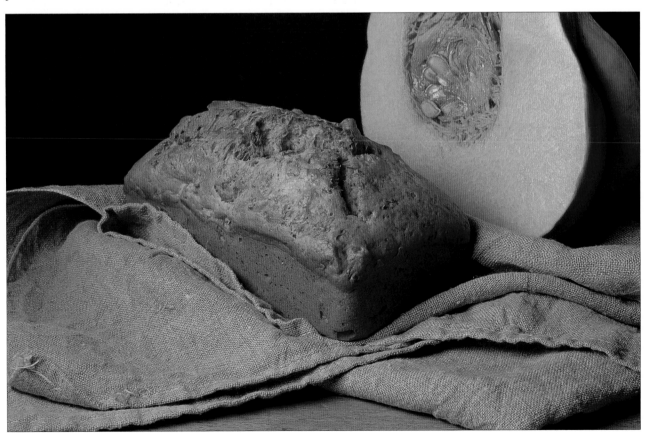

San Francisco Sourdough Bread

Makes 2 loaves

For the starter

2 oz (50 g) wholemeal flour

pinch of ground cumin

1 tablespoon (15 ml) milk

1–2 tablespoons (15–30 ml) water

1st refreshment

2 tablespoons (30 ml) water

4 oz (115 g) wholemeal flour

2nd refreshment

4 tablespoons (60 ml) water

4 oz (115 g) white bread flour

For the bread

1st refreshment

5 tablespoons (75 ml) very warm water

3 oz (75 g) unbleached plain flour

2nd refreshment

6 fl oz (175 ml) lukewarm water

7–8 oz (200–225 g) unbleached
    plain flour

For the sourdough

9 fl oz (275 ml) warm water

1¼ lb (500 g) unbleached white
    bread flour

1 tablespoon (15 ml) salt

ice cubes, for baking

In San Francisco this bread is leavened using a flour and water paste, which is left to ferment with the aid of airborne yeast. The finished loaves have a moist crumb and crispy crust, and will keep for several days.

1 ▲ Sift the flour and cumin for the starter into a bowl. Add the milk and sufficient water to make a firm but moist dough. Knead for 6–8 minutes to form a firm dough. Return to the bowl, cover with a damp dish towel and leave at 24–26°C/75–80°F for about 2 days. When it is ready the starter will appear moist and wrinkled and will have a crust.

2 Pull off the crust and discard. Scoop out the moist centre (about the size of a hazelnut), which will be aerated and sweet smelling, and place in a clean bowl. Mix in the water for the 1st refreshment. Add the wholemeal flour and mix to a dough.

3 Cover with clear film and return to a warm place for 1–2 days. Discard the crust and gradually mix in the water for the 2nd refreshment to the starter, which by now will have a slightly sharper smell. Gradually mix in the white flour, cover and leave in a warm place for 8–10 hours.

4 ▲ For the bread, mix the sourdough starter with the water for the 1st refreshment. Mix in the flour to form a firm dough. Knead for 6–8 minutes until firm. Cover with a damp dish towel and leave in a warm place for 8–12 hours, until doubled in bulk.

5 Gradually mix in the water for the 2nd refreshment, then mix in enough flour to form a soft, smooth elastic dough. Re-cover and leave in a warm place for 8–12 hours. Gradually stir in the water for the sourdough, then work in the flour and salt. This will take 10–15 minutes. Turn out on to a floured surface and knead until smooth and very elastic. Place in an oiled bowl, cover with oiled clear film and leave to rise, in a warm place, for 8–12 hours.

6 Divide the dough in half and shape into 2 round loaves by folding the sides over to the centre and sealing.

7 ▲ Place seam side up in flour-dusted *couronnes*, bowls or baskets lined with flour-dusted dish towels. Re-cover and leave to rise in a warm place for 4 hours.

8 Preheat the oven to 220°C/425°F/Gas 7. Place an empty roasting tin in the bottom of the oven. Dust 2 baking sheets with flour. Turn out the loaves seam side down on the prepared baking sheets. Using a sharp knife, cut a criss-cross pattern by slashing the top of the loaves 4–5 times in each direction.

9 Place the baking sheets in the oven and immediately drop the ice cubes into the hot roasting tin to create steam. Bake the bread for 25 minutes, then reduce the oven temperature to 200°C/400°F/Gas 6 and bake for a further 15–20 minutes, or until sounding hollow when tapped on the base. Transfer to wire racks to cool.

> **~ COOK'S TIP ~**
>
> If you make sourdough bread regularly, keep a small amount of the starter in the fridge. It will keep for several days. Use for the 2nd refreshment.

Boston Brown Bread

MAKES 1 OR 2 LOAVES

3½ oz (90 g) cornmeal
3½ oz (90 g) unbleached plain white flour or wholemeal flour
3½ oz (90 g) rye flour
½ teaspoon (2.5 ml) salt
1 teaspoon (5 ml) bicarbonate of soda
3½ oz (90 g) seedless raisins
4 fl oz (120 ml) milk
4 fl oz (120 ml) water
4 fl oz (120 ml) molasses or black treacle

~ COOK'S TIP ~

If you do not have any of the containers listed below, use one or two heatproof bowls.

Rich, moist and dark, this bread is flavoured with molasses and can include raisins. In Boston it is often served with savoury baked beans.

4 ▲ Fill the jug or tins with the dough; they should be about two-thirds full. Cover with foil or greased greaseproof paper and tie securely.

5 Bring water to a depth of 2 in (5 cm) to the boil in a deep, heavy-based saucepan large enough to accommodate the jug or tins. Place a trivet in the pan, stand the jug or tins on top, cover the pan and steam for 1½ hours, adding more boiling water to maintain the required level as necessary.

6 Cool the loaves for a few minutes in the jugs or tins, then turn them on their sides and the loaves should slip out. Serve warm, as a teabread or with savoury dishes.

1 Line the base of one 2 pint (1.2 litre) cylindrical metal or glass container, such as a heatproof glass coffee jug, with greased greaseproof paper. Alternatively, remove the lids from two 1 lb (450 g) coffee tins, wash and dry the tins, then line with greased greaseproof paper.

2 Mix together the cornmeal, plain or wholemeal flour, rye flour, salt, bicarbonate of soda and raisins in a large bowl. Warm the milk and water in a small saucepan and stir in the molasses or black treacle.

3 ▲ Add the molasses mixture to the dry ingredients and mix together using a spoon until it just forms a moist dough. Do not overmix.

American Bagels

Bagels are eaten in many countries, especially where there is a Jewish community, and are very popular in the USA. They can be made from white, wholemeal or rye flour and finished with a variety of toppings, including caraway, poppy seeds, sesame seeds and onion.

MAKES 10 BAGELS

12 oz (350 g) unbleached white bread flour
2 teaspoons (10 ml) salt
¼ oz (6 g) easy-blend dried yeast
1 teaspoon (10 ml) malt extract
7½ fl oz (210 ml) lukewarm water
FOR POACHING
4 pints (2.5 litres) water
1 tablespoon (15 ml) malt extract
FOR THE TOPPING
1 egg white
2 teaspoons (10 ml) cold water
2 tablespoons (30 ml) poppy, sesame or caraway seeds

1 ▲ Grease 2 baking sheets. Sift the flour and salt together into a large bowl. Stir in the dried yeast. Make a well in the centre. Mix the malt extract and water, add to the centre of the flour and mix to a dough. Knead on a floured surface until elastic.

2 Place in a lightly oiled bowl, cover with lightly oiled clear film and leave to rise, in a warm place, for about 1 hour, or until doubled in bulk.

3 Turn out on to a floured surface and knock back. Knead for 1 minute, then divide into 10 equal pieces. Shape into balls, cover with clear film and leave to rest for 5 minutes.

4 ▲ Gently flatten each ball and make a hole through the centre with your thumb. Enlarge the hole slightly by turning your thumb around. Place on a floured tray; re-cover and leave in a warm place, for 10–20 minutes, or until they begin to rise.

5 Preheat the oven to 220°C/425°F/ Gas 7. Place the water and malt extract for poaching in a large pan, bring to the boil, then reduce to a simmer. Place the bagels in the water a few at a time and poach for about 1 minute. They will sink and then rise again when first added to the pan. Using a fish slice or draining spoon, turn over and cook for 30 seconds. Remove and drain on a dish towel. Repeat with the remaining bagels.

6 ▲ Place five bagels on each prepared baking sheet, spacing them well apart. Beat the egg white with the water for the topping, brush the mixture over the top of each bagel and sprinkle with poppy, sesame or caraway seeds. Bake for 20–25 minutes, or until golden brown. Transfer to a wire rack to cool.

American Monkey Bread

MAKES 1 LOAF

¼ oz (10 g) sachet easy-blend dried yeast
1 lb (450 g) unbleached white bread flour
½ teaspoon (2.5 ml) salt
1 tablespoon (15 ml) caster sugar
4 fl oz (120 ml) lukewarm milk
4 fl oz (120 ml) lukewarm water
1 egg, lightly beaten
FOR THE COATING
3 oz (75 g) sultanas
3 tablespoons (45 ml) rum or brandy
4 oz (115 g) walnuts, finely chopped
2 teaspoons (10 ml) ground cinnamon
4 oz (115 g) soft light brown sugar
2 oz (50 g) butter, melted

This American favourite is also called bubble bread – because of the "bubbles" of dough. The pieces of dough are tossed in a heavenly coating of butter, nuts, cinnamon and rum-soaked fruit.

1 Grease a 9 in (23 cm) spring-form ring cake tin. Mix the yeast, flour, salt and caster sugar in a large bowl and make a well in the centre.

2 Add the milk, water and egg to the centre of the flour and mix together to a soft dough. Turn out on to a floured surface and knead for about 10 minutes until smooth and elastic. Place in an oiled bowl, cover with oiled clear film and leave to rise, in a warm place, for 45–60 minutes, or until doubled in bulk.

3 ▲ Place the sultanas in a pan, pour over the rum or brandy and heat for 1–2 minutes, or until warm. Do not overheat. Remove from the heat and set aside. Mix the walnuts, cinnamon and sugar in a bowl.

4 ▲ Turn out the dough on to a lightly floured surface and knead gently. Divide into 30 equal pieces and shape into small balls. Dip the balls, one at a time into the melted butter, then roll them in the walnut mixture. Place half in the prepared tin, spaced slightly apart. Sprinkle over all the soaked sultanas.

5 ▲ Top with the remaining dough balls, dipping and coating as before. Sprinkle over any remaining walnut mixture and melted butter. Cover with lightly oiled clear film or slide the tin into a lightly oiled large polythene bag and leave to rise, in a warm place, for about 45 minutes, or until the dough reaches the top of the tin.

6 Meanwhile, preheat the oven to 190°C/375°F/Gas 5. Bake for 35–40 minutes, or until well risen and golden. Cool on a wire rack.

New England Fantans

These fantail rolls look stylish and are so versatile that they are equally suitable for a simple snack, or a gourmet dinner party!

1 Grease a muffin sheet with 9 3 in (7.5 cm) cups or foil cases. Mix the yeast with the buttermilk and sugar and leave to stand for 15 minutes.

2 ▲ In a pan, heat the milk with 1½ oz (40 g) of the butter until the butter has melted. Cool until lukewarm.

3 Sift the flour and salt into a bowl. Add the yeast mixture, milk mixture and egg and mix to a soft dough. Turn out on to a floured surface and knead for 5–8 minutes until smooth and elastic. Place in an oiled bowl, cover with oiled clear film and leave to rise, in a warm place, for 1 hour, until doubled in size.

4 ▲ Turn out on to a lightly floured surface, knock back and knead until smooth and elastic. Roll into an oblong measuring 18 x 12 in (45 x 30 cm) and about ¼ in (5 mm) thick. Melt the remaining butter, brush over the dough and cut it lengthways into 5 equal strips. Stack on top of each other and cut across into 9 equal 2 in (5 cm) strips.

5 ▲ Pinch one side of each layered strip together, then place pinched side down into a muffin cup or foil case. Cover with oiled clear film and leave to rise, in a warm place, for 30–40 minutes, or until the fantans have almost doubled in size. Preheat the oven to 200°C/400°F/Gas 6. Bake for 20 minutes, or until golden. Cool on a wire rack.

MAKES 9 ROLLS

½ oz (15 g) fresh yeast
5 tablespoons (75 ml) buttermilk, at room temperature
2 teaspoons (10 ml) caster sugar
5 tablespoons (75 ml) milk
2½ oz (65 g) butter
13 oz (375 g) unbleached white bread flour
1 teaspoon (5 ml) salt
1 egg, lightly beaten

~ VARIATION ~

Add 1 teaspoon (5 ml) ground cinnamon to the remaining butter in step 4 before brushing over the dough strips. Sprinkle the rolls with a little icing sugar as soon as they come out of the oven.

Mexican "Bread of the Dead"

MAKES 1 LOAF

3 star anise
6 tablespoons (90 ml) cold water
1½ lb (675 g) unbleached white bread flour
1 teaspoon (5 ml) salt
4 oz (115 g) caster sugar
1 oz (25 g) fresh yeast
6 fl oz (175 ml) lukewarm water
3 eggs
4 tablespoons (60 ml) orange liqueur
4 oz (115 g) butter, melted
grated rind of 1 orange
icing sugar, for dusting

~ VARIATION ~
Ice the bread with 2 oz (60 g) icing sugar mixed with a little orange liqueur.

A celebratory loaf made for All Souls' Day. Even though the name of this bread suggests otherwise, it is actually a very happy day when both Mexicans and Spanish people pay their respects to the souls of their dead. Traditionally, the bread is decorated with a dough skull, bones and tears.

1 ▲ Grease a 10½ in (27 cm) fluted round cake tin. Place the star anise in a saucepan with the water. Bring to the boil and boil for 3–4 minutes, until the liquid has reduced to 3 tablespoons (45 ml) Discard the star anise and leave the liquid to cool.

2 Sift the flour and salt together into a large bowl. Stir in the sugar and make a well in the centre.

3 In a jug, dissolve the yeast in the lukewarm water. Pour into the centre of the flour and mix in a little flour, using your fingers, until a smooth, thick batter forms. Sprinkle over a little of the remaining flour, cover with clear film and leave the batter in a warm place for 30 minutes, or until the mixture starts to bubble.

4 Beat the eggs, the reserved liquid flavoured with star anise, orange liqueur and melted butter together. Gradually incorporate into the flour mixture to form a smooth dough.

5 ▲ Turn out the dough on to a lightly floured surface and gently knead in the orange rind. Knead for 5–6 minutes until smooth and elastic. Shape into a 10½ in (27 cm) round and place in the prepared tin. Cover with lightly oiled clear film and leave to rise, in a warm place, for 2–3 hours, or until almost at the top of the tin and doubled in bulk.

6 Meanwhile, preheat the oven to 190°C/375°F/Gas 5. Bake the loaf for 45–50 minutes, or until golden. Turn out on to a wire rack to cool. Dust with icing sugar to serve.

Iranian Barbari

These small Iranian flat breads can be made in a variety of sizes. For a change, make two large breads and break off pieces to scoop up dips.

1 Lightly dust 2 baking sheets with flour. Sift the flour and salt into a bowl and make a well in the centre.

2 ▲ Mix the yeast with the water. Pour into the centre of the flour, sprinkle a little flour over and leave in a warm place for 15 minutes. Mix to a dough, then turn out on to a lightly floured surface and knead for 8–10 minutes until smooth and elastic.

3 Place in a lightly oiled bowl, cover with oiled clear film and leave to rise for 45–60 minutes, or until doubled.

4 ▲ Knock back the dough and turn out on to a floured surface. Divide into 6 equal pieces and roll each one out to about 4 x 2 in (10 x 5 cm) and about ½ in (1 cm) thick. Space well apart on the baking sheets, and make four slashes in the tops.

MAKES 6 BARBARI

8 oz (225 g) unbleached white bread flour
1 teaspoon (5 ml) salt
½ oz (15 g) fresh yeast
scant ¼ pint (140 ml) lukewarm water
oil, for brushing

> **~ VARIATION ~**
> Sprinkle with sesame or caraway seeds before baking.

5 Cover the breads with lightly oiled clear film and leave to rise, in a warm place, for 20 minutes. Meanwhile, preheat the oven to 200°C/400°F/ Gas 6. Brush the breads with oil and bake for 12–15 minutes, or until pale golden. Serve warm.

Syrian Onion Bread

MAKES 8 BREADS

1 lb (450 g) unbleached white bread flour
1 teaspoon (5 ml) salt
¾ oz (20 g) fresh yeast
9 fl oz (275 ml) lukewarm water
FOR THE TOPPING
4 tablespoons (60 ml) finely chopped onion
1 teaspoon (5 ml) ground cumin
2 teaspoons (10 ml) ground coriander
2 teaspoons (10 ml) chopped fresh mint
2 tablespoons (30 ml) olive oil

The basic Arab breads of the Levant and Gulf have traditionally been made with a finely ground wholemeal flour similar to chapati flour, but now they are being made with white flour as well. This Syrian version has a tasty, aromatic onion and coriander topping.

~ COOK'S TIP ~

If you haven't any fresh mint to hand, then add 1 tablespoon (15 ml) dried mint. Use the freeze-dried variety if you can as it has much more flavour.

1 ▲ Lightly flour 2 baking sheets. Sift the flour and salt together into a large bowl and make a well in the centre. Cream the yeast with a little of the water, then mix in the remainder.

2 Add the yeast mixture to the centre of the flour and mix to a firm dough. Turn out on to a lightly floured surface and knead for 8–10 minutes until smooth and elastic.

3 Place in a lightly oiled bowl, cover with lightly oiled clear film and leave to rise, in a warm place, for about 1 hour, or until doubled in size.

4 ▲ Knock back the dough and turn out on to a floured surface. Divide into 8 equal pieces and roll into 5–6 in (13–15 cm) rounds. Make them slightly concave. Prick all over and space well apart on the baking sheets. Cover with oiled clear film and leave to rise for 15–20 minutes.

5 ▲ Meanwhile, preheat the oven to 200°C/400°F/Gas 6. Mix the chopped onion, ground cumin, ground coriander and chopped mint in a bowl. Brush the breads with the olive oil for the topping, sprinkle with the spicy onion mixture and bake for 15–20 minutes. Serve warm.

Indian Tandoori Rotis

There are numerous varieties of breads in India, most of them unleavened. This one, as its name suggests, would normally be baked in a tandoor – a clay oven which is heated with charcoal or wood. The oven becomes extremely hot, cooking the bread in minutes.

MAKES 6 ROTIS

12 oz (350 g) *atta* or fine wholemeal flour
1 teaspoon (5 ml) salt
8 fl oz (250 ml) water
2–3 tablespoons (30–45 ml) melted ghee or butter, for brushing

~ COOK'S TIP ~

The rotis are ready when light brown bubbles appear on the surface.

1 ▲ Sift the flour and salt into a large bowl. Add the water and mix to a soft dough. Knead on a floured surface for 3–4 minutes until smooth. Place in an oiled bowl, cover with oiled clear film; leave to rest for 1 hour.

2 ▲ Turn out on to a floured surface. Divide the dough into 6 pieces and shape each piece into a ball. Press out into a larger round with your hand, cover with oiled clear film and leave to rest for 10 minutes.

3 Preheat the oven to 230°C/ 450°F/ Gas 8. Place 3 baking sheets in the oven. Roll the rotis into 6 in (15 cm) rounds, place on the baking sheets and bake for 8–10 minutes. Brush with ghee or butter and serve warm.

Indian Naan

MAKES 3 NAAN

8 oz (225 g) unbleached white bread flour
½ teaspoon (2.5 ml) salt
½ oz (15 g) fresh yeast
4 tablespoons (60 ml) lukewarm milk
1 tablespoon (15 ml) vegetable oil
2 tablespoons (30 ml) natural yogurt
1 egg
2–3 tablespoons (30–45 ml) melted ghee or butter, for brushing

From the Caucasus through the Punjab region of northwest India and beyond, all serve these leavened breads. Traditionally cooked in a very hot clay oven known as a tandoor, naan are usually eaten with dry meat or vegetable dishes, such as tandoori.

1 ▲ Sift the flour and salt together into a large bowl. In a smaller bowl, cream the yeast with the milk. Set aside for 15 minutes.

2 ▲ Mix the yeast mixture, oil, yogurt and egg into the flour.

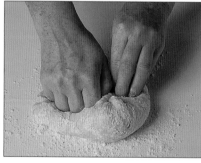

3 ▲ Mix to a soft dough and turn out on to a lightly floured surface. Knead for about 10 minutes until smooth and elastic. Place in a lightly oiled bowl, cover with lightly oiled clear film and leave to rise, in a warm place, for 45 minutes, or until doubled in bulk.

4 Preheat the oven to at least 230°C/450°F/Gas 8. Place 3 heavy baking sheets in the oven to heat.

5 Turn the dough out on to a floured surface and knock back. Divide into 3 and shape into balls.

6 ▲ Cover two of the balls of dough with oiled clear film and roll out the third into a teardrop shape about 10 in (25 cm) long, 5 in (13 cm) wide and with a thickness of about ¼–⅓ in (5–8 mm).

7 Preheat the grill to its highest setting. Meanwhile, place the naan on the hot baking sheets and bake for 3–4 minutes, or until puffed up.

8 Remove the naan from the oven and place under the hot grill for a few seconds, or until the top of the naan browns slightly. Wrap the cooked naan in a dish towel to keep warm while rolling out and cooking the remaining naan. Brush with melted ghee or butter and serve warm.

~ VARIATIONS ~

You can flavour naan in numerous different ways:

• To make spicy naan, add 1 teaspoon (5 ml) each ground coriander and ground cumin to the flour in step 1. If you would like the naan to be extra fiery, add ½–1 teaspoon (2.5–5 ml) hot chilli powder.

• To make cardamom-flavoured naan, lightly crush the seeds from 4–5 green cardamom pods and add to the flour in step 1.

• To make poppy seed naan, brush the rolled-out naan with a little ghee and sprinkle with poppy seeds. Press lightly to make sure that they stick.

• To make peppered naan, brush the rolled-out naan with a little ghee and dust generously with coarsely ground black pepper.

• To make onion-flavoured naan, add 4 oz (114 g) finely chopped onion to the dough in step 2. You may need to reduce the amount of egg if the onion is very moist to prevent making the dough too soft.

• To make wholemeal naan, substitute wholemeal bread flour for the white flour.

~ COOK'S TIP ~

To help the dough to puff up and brown, place the baking sheets in an oven preheated to the maximum temperature for at least 10 minutes before baking.

INDEX